Jews in Christian America

STUDIES IN JEWISH HISTORY   JEHUDA REINHARZ, General Editor

Jews in
Christian America

The Pursuit of Religious Equality

NAOMI W. COHEN

New York   Oxford
OXFORD UNIVERSITY PRESS
1992

Oxford University Press

Oxford New York Toronto
Delhi Bombay Calcutta Madras Karachi
Kuala Lumpur Singapore Hong Kong Tokyo
Nairobi Dar es Salaam Cape Town
Melbourne Auckland

and associated companies in
Berlin Ibadan

Published by Oxford University Press, Inc.,
200 Madison Avenue, New York, New York 10016

Oxford is a registered trademark of Oxford University Press

Library of Congress Cataloging-in-Publication Data
Cohen, Naomi Wiener
Jews in Christian America : the pursuit of religious equality / Naomi W. Cohen.
p. cm.—(Studies in Jewish history)
Includes bibliographical references and index.
ISBN 0-19-506537-9
1. Jews—United States—Politics and government.
2. Religion and state—United States.
3. Jews—Legal status, laws, etc.—United States
4. United States—Constitutional history.
5. United States—Ethnic relations.
I. Title II. Series.
E184.J5C619 1992
322'.1'089924073—dc20 91-35839

1 3 5 7 9 8 6 4 2

Printed in the United States of America
on acid-free paper

To the memory of my parents

Preface

American Jewish sensitivity to matters of church and state is a subject that has long engaged me. In other books and articles I have dealt with only a few of its aspects. My research for this full-length study has further convinced me of its importance. The concern of Jews for over two centuries with the constitutional guarantees of religious freedom is a key to understanding their pursuit of equality in American society.

The book makes no claim to all-inclusiveness. Written within a historical rather than legal context, its focus is on Jewish opposition to government sanction of Christian beliefs and symbols. It examines neither the subject of government aid to religious schools nor the interaction between Jewish law and American law, both of which merit separate studies. Nor does the book pursue the topic intensively beyond the mid-1960s. By then Christianity had lost its place as the public religion of the nation, and most of the major issues that had troubled American Jews since the nineteenth century had been resolved.

The book is divided into two parts. The first deals chronologically with the responses of American Jews to church–state issues from colonial times through World War II. The second is organized topically around issues resulting in cases that reached the Supreme Court within a short span of fifteen years (1948–63). These chapters are based primarily on archival material which, for the most part, has remained unexplored by historians. The actual choice of cases—aside from those generally recognized as landmark decisions—was made on the basis of contemporary Jewish perceptions and priorities. To provide some historical background relating to the second part, I have included a short overview of the postwar era.

The labors of a historian are often lessened by the contributions of others. In my case, several institutions were of particular assistance. The American Jewish Committee, American Jewish Congress, and Anti-Defamation League gave me full access to their files. Grants from the American Jewish Archives and the George N. Shuster Fund of Hunter College helped defray the costs of research. The history department of the Graduate Center of the City University of New York provided me with research assistants who ably helped with the legwork. The Jewish Publication Society graciously permitted me to reproduce, with modifications, material that originally appeared in my book *Encounter with Emancipation*. I am very grateful to all concerned.

It is also a pleasure to mention those individuals who generously provided me with specific materials or shared their expertise on a given subject: Abraham Ascher, Jerold S. Auerbach, Jerome A. Chanes, Richard T. Foltin, Jonathan Frankel, Stanley J. Friedman, Gail Gans, Robert T. Handy, Nathan M. Kaganoff, Dean M. Kelley, Ruth Limmer, Henry D. Michelman, Leo Pfeffer, Samuel Rabinove, Shlomith Yahalom. Nor does it minimize my appreciation of their aid when I express my special thanks to Marc D. Stern and Robert M. Seltzer for their unfailing encouragement and help since the inception of this study. Finally, I am fortunate to have had the able assistance of Nancy Lane and her associates at Oxford University Press.

I am indebted, as always, to my children for their sustained emotional support.

New York   N.W.C.
November 1991

Contents

Jews in Christian America

Introduction

Neither ghettoized nor recognized officially as a discrete corporate group, Jews in the United States had no reason to fight for emancipation. Unlike the Jewish experience in other Western lands, their absorption as individual citizens into the body politic was a nonissue. But citizenship stopped short of full equality. In a society whose culture was steeped in Christianity, and where the idea and practices of a Christian state still resonated, Jews were the quintessential outsiders. Even the path to legal equality, a less ambitious goal than social integration, was cluttered with obstacles of a religious nature. The guarantees of federal and state constitutions notwithstanding, Jews encountered laws and public usages that reflected the domination of Christianity, specifically Protestantism.

The story of colonial American Jews is one of piecemeal accretion of freedoms, from the rights of settlement and trade to the right of free worship. Jewish liberties expanded significantly with the adoption of the state and federal constitutions, yet barriers to full equality persisted. Christian oaths for state officeholders, Christian practices and symbols in schools and other public places, and requirements for the observance of the Christian Sabbath were the most common inequities. Such usages, sanctioned by fundamental or statutory law and, especially in the early nineteenth century, by the doctrine that Christianity was part of the common law, were loudly defended by many Christians. Calling themselves a God-fearing people who recognized the need of religious values in public life, they argued that since they constituted the vast majority of the American people, they could rightfully impose Protestant religious forms upon the entire nation. For such Christians, as observers noted, Christianity was the national public religion.[1]

From the earliest days of the Republic, American Jews overwhelmingly objected to religious trappings that compromised their civil status or that relegated them to the rank of second-class citizens. Paramount in their ongoing efforts at full integration within society was *equality under law,* a law that demanded neither repudiation of Jewish identity nor acceptance of Christian forms as preconditions to the enjoyment of rights. Legal equality differed qualitatively from toleration or even liberty of conscience. It meant not only the right to hold office but the right to do business on Sundays and the right of Jewish children to feel at home in a public classroom, one where Christian prayers and teachings had no place. In short, Jewish equality depended primarily on the removal of legally recognized Christianity, in whatever degree or form, from public life.

They had earned equality, nineteenth-century American Jews maintained, by virtue of their exemplary civil behavior, their patriotism, and their military service to the nation; they deserved it because their religion, the trunk from which Christianity sprang, was as respectable as the daughter faith. Jews had fulfilled their side of the contract with the nation, the reasoning implied, and in return they were entitled to equal treatment, a condition that accorded with the true spirit of the Founding Fathers and the principles of the Enlightenment. Intoxicated by the dream of full equality, most American Jews displayed a readiness to offer more—they would willingly renounce the traditional Jewish concept of *galut,* or exile. To be sure, only classical Reform consciously and deliberately repudiated the wish for a restoration to a Jewish homeland. But most American Jews, including supporters of Zionism and the state of Israel, have lived by the same philosophy. They believed that the ultimate attainment of equality would prove that "America was different," perhaps even the new promised land.

Theoretically there was another path to Jewish equality. If Jewish laws and customs received the same legal recognition accorded to Christian usages, the two religions, and their adherents, would be on an equal plane. For example, since the law recognized the sanctity of Sunday, it could similarly provide for the sanctity of the Jewish Sabbath. On rare occasions antebellum Jews argued along those lines—as in the cases of those who contested orders to appear in court on Saturdays—but the very small number of Jews always made it an impractical option in a society where majorities ruled. Not until the twentieth century did Jews develop any theories of pluralism or defend the encouragement of diverse religious beliefs by a benevolent government. Like their Christian neighbors they opted for a homogeneous nation, one shaped by the tenets of Americanism but, according to the Jewish version, without its Christian component. Equality within that kind of society was attainable only if religious distinctions remained strictly private concerns that elicited equal disregard from the state.

Within the Jewish community the determination to rid American law and institutions of their Christian flavor drew a powerful emotional and psychological response. In the historical memory of each wave of Jewish immigration to the United States—Sephardic, German, Russian—a Christian state represented legal disabilities, economic and cultural deprivation, and physical torment. Since Jews also believed that hatred of Jews throughout the ages was nurtured by Christian religious teachings, the elimination of Christian influence from public policy was essential for basic Jewish security as well as equality. Early American Jews who condemned any Christian usage, however trivial, were wont to raise the specter of a malevolent Christian state; Rabbi Isaac Leeser wrote before the Civil War that compulsory observance of Sunday was no different in kind from mandatory church attendance or involuntary baptism.[2] Later generations had no reason to fear a legally recognized Christian state, but the rooted memories, reinforced by vestigial symbols of the regnant faith, endured.

Government recognition of usages that were perceived as reminders of Christian control have always touched a raw nerve in American Jews irrespective of their levels of acculturation or sophistication. Charles Silberman recently wrote that his generation knew the United States as a white, Christian society, "a society . . . in which the . . . prayers we recited in school, the New Testament lessons that were read to us, the Christian hymns and carols we sang (who were the 'they,' we wondered, in 'They nailed Him to the cross'), the crèches on public property—drove home to us that we were, indeed, 'guests,' or 'strangers,' in someone else's country."[3] Accordingly, Silberman's generation, like their medieval rabbinic ancestors, labored to build "fences around the law," devices for shoring up the non-Christian character of American law. Jewish defense organizations, for example, agitated after World War II for the removal of Christian prayers from the public schools. When that was accomplished they fought on, resisting any kind of prayer—vocal or silent, mandatory or voluntary—that presaged, however remotely, the possibility that Christian teachings might find their way back into the classroom. Their underlying assumption remained constant: public religion in the United States could never be truly neutral, for it always connoted an advantage to Christianity.

Jews invoked accepted American principles on which to build their case against legally sanctioned Christian practices. From the establishment of the Republic, Jewish spokesmen set themselves up as guardians of the "authentic" American tradition, often urging conformity with the "spirit" of the national, religion-blind Constitution. Their task was facilitated by Reform Judaism, which in the nineteenth century postulated the identity of Jewish and American principles. Traditional Jewish reverence for law, or *halakha,* shifted, as Jerold Auerbach has persuasively argued, to the fundamental law of the United States.[4] Some observers commented that rabbis who publicly debated issues of church and state in the twentieth century sounded more like constitutional analysts than religious teachers. Often, their indictments of Christians who defended religious customs implied that they, the Jews, were the better Americans.

Until 1940, when the Supreme Court applied the restraints of the religion clauses of the First Amendment to state behavior, minorities relied on state laws and courts for the protection of their rights. Jews who contested a Christian form or usage generally invoked *freedom* of religion, a doctrine common to all state constitutions. They argued that Christian usages, which amounted to government discrimination against non-Christians, violated religious freedom as guaranteed by the fundamental law of the states. From the very beginning, however, Jews really meant *equality* of religion. Sunday laws, for example, neither forced Jews to observe Sunday nor compelled them to abandon their own Sabbath. Rather, the laws were obnoxious not merely for the economic hardships foisted upon Sabbatarians but because they relegated the Jewish Sabbath and its observers to an inferior status.

After World War II Jewish efforts centered on the establishment clause of the First Amendment. Their broad interpretation of religious freedom under the state constitutions gave way to an even broader interpretation of establishment, which now bound states as well as the federal government. Taking their cue from Justice Hugo Black's decision in the New Jersey bus case of 1947,[5] Jews argued that any mark of favor to Christian or for that matter to any religious forms violated the First Amendment. In the story of Jewish litigation, the establishment clause far outweighed the free exercise clause in importance. Only after the major court victories in the 1960s on religion in the schools did Jews feel sufficiently secure to defend the legitimacy of distinctive Jewish religious practices under the guarantee of free exercise.

Both before and after the nationalization of the Bill of Rights, and on both state and federal issues, Jews were outspoken and at times pugnacious defenders of church–state separation. A doctrine which since the Revolution commanded at least lip service from all Americans, separation was perceived by the non-Christian minority as the key to equality. Jews of all generations went on record on its behalf, and they appropriated the heroes of separationism—Roger Williams, Thomas Jefferson, James Madison—for their own. Over time Jewish spokesmen construed the principle ever more loosely. To be sure they were never purists; they supported practices like tax exemptions for churches and government provision for chaplains. Their readiness to accept Sunday laws, albeit with proper exemptions, also contradicted the logic of separationism. But the vast majority consistently preferred a solid *wall* of separation, dotted perhaps with a few necessary "leaks" and "cracks,"[6] to a "movable curtain."[7]

The religiouslike fervor with which Jews embraced separation is all the more striking precisely because the doctrine itself is not endemic to rabbinic Judaism. Although religion and politics were traditionally separate orbits, each with discrete roles and functionaries, politics, like any worldly activity, was judged by religious yardsticks. So, too, were public policies and institutions. A modern example: the Lubavitcher rebbe, who supported nonsectarian prayer in American public schools despite the fact that he maintained day schools for his followers, was affirming an age-old tradition in which any limits to the play of religious values within society were unnatural and improper.

Once having seized on separation as a means for attaining equality, Jews came to see other benefits in the idea that the religious condition of any group was of no public concern. They noted early on, as had Christians before them, that separation permitted the autonomous development of religion. Without government interference in matters of dogma or church organization, a religious system enjoyed opportunities for freer growth and flexibility. Furthermore, if the government ignored religious distinctions, the nonbelievers or those unaffiliated with synagogues were under less pressure to abandon Judaism formally. In the absence of favors to Christians, the danger of conversion receded. Finally, separation promised to strengthen the security of Judaism as well as of Jews. Were Christianity not shown official preference, then Judaism could claim equal respectability. At all times, Jewish responses to matters of church and state were sensitive to the need for ensuring equal status for Judaism as well as for Jews.

Other Americans have shared the conviction that fixed lines separate government from religion, but separation has meant more to Jews. In Peter Medding's words: "To be Jewish in America means, among other things, not to be Christian. . . . For [Jews]—but not for others—the separation of church and state constitutes and defines their individual and group status in American society, because to breach separation is to Christianize America, relegating Jews to second-class citizenship."[8]

The separation of church and state in America was hardly an accomplished fact by 1800 or even 1900. Since ideas of a Christian nation or Christian commonwealth lingered with varying degree of intensity until, in Robert Handy's words, the "second disestablishment" (1920–40),[9] and since residues spawned by those ideas are still present, the struggle for separation has been open-ended. Over time the minority's tactics against a Christian public religion changed, testimony to both developments in American law and the evolution of an acculturated and mature Jewish community.

Until the middle of the twentieth century Jews preferred to avoid litigation on church–state affairs. Nor did they effectively use the ballot to register their views; the injection of a Jewish point of view into elections was in itself, many argued, a breach of proper separation between religion and politics. Rather, their drive for religious equality concentrated primarily on arousing "enlightened" public opinion against the perceived disabilities, a task borne first by pamphleteers and Anglo-Jewish periodicals. To supplement their ongoing crusade, Jewish spokesmen and defense organizations drew up petitions and memorials on critical issues, formulated resolutions, called mass meetings, lobbied with government officials, and appeared before legislative committees. Although nineteenth-century Jews worked alone, avoiding active alliances with other minorities, they often sought to coopt prominent Christians for championing their cause before the American public. At all times Jews equated their demands with true Americanism; the inequities they suffered called for remediation primarily because they betrayed American principles rather than Jewish rights.

After World War II, when secular defense agencies spearheaded Jewish efforts on behalf of religious equality, pressures on legislatures continued but litigation and the submission of *amicus curiae* briefs assumed overriding importance. Legal experts rather than rabbis now led the community in the area of church and state. In another radical switch in tactics, Jews actively sought the cooperation of non-Jewish groups, secular and religious, to lend support to their separationist stance. They also embarked on sustained projects for monitoring and molding Christian public opinion. Nor were Jews inhibited as they had been about the use of the vote. Without apologies for "parochial" interests that breached the wall of separation, Jews have reacted strongly at the polls against modern Christianizers, and their strict separationist stance has become a commonplace in American politics. More assertive than their predecessors, they no longer buried specific group needs under an all-purpose American blanket. Arguments were still braced by appeals to broad American principles, but legal briefs spoke on behalf of Jewish and other minorities.

While tactics changed, certain features of the Jewish quest for equality remained constant in both the nineteenth and twentieth centuries. First, Jews of all stripes—immigrant or acculturated, Reform or Orthodox, aggressive or timid—weighed their activities against existing or anticipated popular opinion. Recognizing the vulnerability of a very small minority, non-Christian to boot, they never ceased to ponder whether a public stand on matters of church and state would in any way prompt an adverse reaction toward Jewish security or comfort. Was it wise to risk public notice, let alone criticism, during the years of the Know-Nothing movement, or Henry Ford's anti-Semitic campaign, or Joe McCarthy's witch-hunt? Indeed, in large measure, Jewish activity or inactivity on separationism is the inverse of the ebbs and flows of popular religious prejudice and American hypernationalism. Keeping a constant finger on the pulse of the American community, Jewish agencies and spokesmen rarely initiated areas of activity or propagated concepts that had not already been broached by respectable Christians.

A second "constant": the Jewish stand on a church–state issue depended on other communal priorities. If organizations had to cope with immediate and critical problems like persecution of European Jews, threats to restrict immigration, Israel's need of American aid, fewer resources were available for ongoing issues like separation. Moreover, how prudent was it to risk any Christian displeasure when every vote for the more urgent needs was required? Separationism was also weighed alongside less urgent matters. A desire to foster interreligious understanding in the post–World War II era, for example, tempered Jewish activity that might have alienated Protestants or Catholics. Needless to say, the first "constant," namely, perceptions of American opinion, influenced the juggling of priorities.

Jews often differed on how to interpret public opinion and how to rank communal priorities. Those differences explained a third "constant": never did the Jewish community behave as a monolith on church–state issues. All Jews agreed with the bald principle that church and state should be kept separate, but at no time did they speak as one on the optimal degree of separation or the proper tactics to employ. Differences arose between rabbis and laymen, Orthodox and non-Orthodox, outlying communities and metropolitan centers; bickering and rivalry divided one defense agency from another. Even within the same religious subgroup, whether Reform, Orthodox, or Conservative, opinions varied. True to the American pattern of congregationalism, the Jewish base was the largely autonomous individual synagogue. Umbrella organizations, whether of a religious or secular nature, were powerless to exact strict conformity. Disunity produced weaknesses and duplication of efforts. Nevertheless, despite opposition within the ranks, the strict separationists usually succeeded in projecting the image to the larger society of a unitary stand on church–state issues.

Subtler than the constants was Jewish concern lest strict separationism adversely affect religion in general and Judaism in particular. Indeed, for the better part of the nineteenth century prominent American Jewish spokesmen favored a neutral-to-all-religions over a divorced-from-religion government. They realized that Judaism or any religion required a congenial atmosphere in which to flourish. Rabbis, like their Christian counterparts, despised atheists and "nothingarians"; they also deplored the menace of secularism. In the 1880s the *American Hebrew* cautioned against a classroom devoid of religious values or purposely oblivious to the common tenets of Western religions. An "agnostic" school, it said, was worse than any form of religious fanaticism.[10] The Jewish periodical pinpointed an issue which stirred intense debate after World War II: if the logic of strict separationism dictated that moral instruction grounded in religion had no place in public education, then the doctrine itself was highly questionable. Implicitly the *American Hebrew* was seeking a clearly defined boundary between separationism and a secular—or, worse still, a secularist—state.

Concerned Jews, notably after the *Engel* decision of 1962, posed other questions that bore upon Judaism specifically. What was Jewish about Jewish separationism? How salutary was it for American Judaism as a living creed if all religious usages, even those that took note of Jewish sensibilities—a Sunday law that exempted Sabbatarians, nonsectarian prayer in the classroom, the display of a Hanukkah menorah alongside a

Christmas tree—were expunged from the public arena? After all, could those largely inoffensive practices tip the scale of equality? Finally, was separationism at bottom a foolproof means to equality? A religion-blind government notwithstanding, weren't Jews eternally the outsiders in a Christian culture? The internal debate continued, but the separationist stance of Jewish defense agencies has barely changed since 1965.

The pursuit of equality by way of separationism is a distinctive feature of the American Jewish experience. To be sure, like generations of diaspora Jews before them, American Jews were always accommodationist (in the broad sense of adjusting to, and accepting, existing laws and social forms), law-abiding, and fearful of arousing public disfavor. They argued within the conventional legal framework, and the very points they raised derived from interpretations of American principles. Often referring to the Jewish commitment to religious education and the Jewish experience with religious prejudice, church–state briefs ignored Jewish law and rabbinic tradition. But, unlike their European forebears or contemporaries, America's Jews went beyond accommodationism. While they labored for integration on American terms, they contributed, as David Biale suggested, to changes in America's definition of itself.[11] Biale does not refer to separationism, but in fact it stands out as a case in point. The Jews built on an American principle but ventured to shape that principle to suit their own needs. Thus, at the same time that they were accommodating to a tenet of Americanism, they were actively redefining the rules of the American game. Their agitation for legal equality, like the activities of other religious minorities, helped to expand the liberties of all Americans and worked to transform the United States from a Protestant nation into one that acknowledged the needs of different religions.

PART I

PART I

1

From Toleration to Freedom

A Heritage Transplanted

Until the French Revolution the identity and status of European Jews remained fixed within a medieval context. The workings of a society where religion mixed freely with the secular and where the primacy of the group eclipsed the individual still underlay both Christian and Jewish perceptions of the Jews. Those notions were part of the cultural baggage of the Jews who landed in the British colonies before 1776. To the Jews, a pre-Enlightenment people, the concepts of the individual's right to freedom of religion and the separation of church and state were at direct variance with their personal experience.

The normative existence of the premodern Jew was determined by religious tradition, both Christian and Jewish. The first, harking back to classical church teachings that mandated the continued existence of Judaism and its adherents—albeit in a subordinate status—perpetuated the separation of Jews from Christians. In its this-worldly or legal form it made the Jews into aliens or strangers who lived in a discrete community, or *kahal,* often recognized by a charter of incorporation, on the fringe of Christian society. The second, Jewish religious tradition, governed the details of daily living within the communities. That governance had the force of civil law, for Christian rulers usually upheld the authority and discipline of the *kahal* over its members.[1] From the majority and minority faiths, then, the premodern Jew experienced the intrusion of religion into secular affairs.

That intrusion was not entirely unwelcome. It enabled the communities to behave as autonomous units in many areas of internal concern—religion, education, philanthropy, economic regulation, civil litigation. Despite abuses of power on the part of communal leaders, an autonomous, tradition-bound *kahal* provided psychological sustenance to its members, sheltered their existence, and nurtured collective Jewish survival. It is no wonder that, when faced later with the reality of Jewish emancipation, some Jewish leaders feared that the attendant abolition of the legal community was too high a price to pay.[2]

Theories on the dissociation of the church from secular affairs presaged

11

radical changes in both Christian and Jewish organized society. They also advanced the course of Jewish emancipation, for if the state discarded religious criteria for citizenship, the naturalization of Jews could proceed automatically. Yet the idea of a neutral or secular society, even without the additional feature of Jewish emancipation, was confined in the seventeenth and eighteenth centuries to a very small number of writers and thinkers. Within Jewish circles it was even less pronounced. Only when the abolition of corporate existence and admission into the polity became real possibilities or were in fact achieved did Jews consider the nature of the state, its relation to its citizens, and its nexus with the established Christian churches.[3]

There was one early exception. Benedict Spinoza, a Dutch Jew of the seventeenth century, formulated a philosophy that, in the words of one writer, "is the first statement in history of . . . democratic liberalism." Spinoza wrote of the dangers of sectarian struggles injected into politics, and he defended the doctrine of religious freedom as a requisite of civil peace and prosperity. Nevertheless, he rejected the idea of separation of government and religion, since it impinged upon the sovereignty of the state. He proposed rather a national religion, a rational and ethical religion, which the state would translate into positive law.[4]

Although Spinozist thought attracted both Christians and Jews, it is unlikely that the philosopher's theories were familiar to the Jewish settlers in America. Not a highly cultured group, they probably knew his name if at all as the radical agitator whose heresies had resulted in his excommunication by the Jewish elders of Amsterdam. Nor is there any evidence that the pre-Revolution Jews were familiar with the ideas of John Locke or other theorists on individual rights or religious toleration. Their introduction to the principles of freedom of religion and separation of church and state came from their experience in colonial America. Jewish input into those principles cannot be discerned until the ideas of Moses Mendelssohn were brought over by nineteenth-century Jewish immigrants.

Just as foreign as a secular state was the concept of a secularist or atheist Jew. Formal renunciation of religion or belief in a god, especially in an age when religious identification mattered, was alien to the early Jewish settlers. Reinforced by close ties with European and Caribbean Jews, their faith remained at least nominally Orthodox, and they were more likely than non-Jewish colonists to be affiliated with a place of worship. To be sure, in the open society of the New World religious laxity and intermarriage took a serious toll among Jews from the very outset, but those losses resulted less from theological conviction than from the natural process of a minority's acculturation within a receptive environment.[5]

Premodern Christians as well as Jews affirmed the primacy of the Jewish collectivity above its individual members. Within a society of coordinate estates and corporate groups, the Jewish community *as a whole* enjoyed certain rights or bore certain responsibilities. The *kahal* or specially designated functionaries mediated between the ruler and his Jewish subjects, as in the case of collection of taxes. Individuals like the "Court Jews" of the Age of Absolutism might be granted special favors, but even they never escaped the group label. The word "Jew" was less likely to connote an individual than a stereotypical figure upon whom Christian society foisted its images of the entire religious out-group.

The group determined the identity of its members. An individual was born a Jew and was subject to the community's authority and discipline as well as protection; his only way out was by conversion. The concept of collective responsibility, or communal wariness lest an individual endanger the well-being of the *kahal,* reinforced the group mind-set of the premodern Jew. The early Jews of New Amsterdam, like their Sephardic brethren in Holland and Venice, referred to themselves as members of a *nation*— Hebrew, Jewish, or Portuguese.[6] The tension between individual identity and group belonging that would incessantly bedevil postemancipation Jewry was as yet unborn.

Political centralization in the eighteenth century rapidly made an anomaly of corporate groups. In the modern nation-state a powerful central government operated directly upon its individual subjects. "The new order," as Jacob Katz wrote, "could not possibly suffer in its midst autonomous Jewish communities with their singular rights and restrictions." Emancipation of the Jews, or their admission *as individuals* into the body politic, was essential at least as much for the emerging centralized state as for the Jews.[7]

Whether of Sephardic or Ashkenazic origin, Jews in colonial America affirmed the centrality of the community in Jewish secular and religious affairs. Never did they plan on jettisoning the all-inclusive, ethnoreligious *kahal.* Indeed, each of the five colonial Jewish settlements (New York, Newport, Philadelphia, Charleston, Savannah) sought to recreate the familiar European community within an American context. Jacob Rader Marcus explained: "Jews could not and did not achieve corporate status under English rule in the colonies, but that did not prevent them from establishing . . . a de facto parish or *Gemeinde* or kehillah system . . . in every colonial American Jewish settlement. It was simply assumed that every Jew in a town and its environs belonged to the 'community.' " The fact that the internal operations of the *kahal* starkly contradicted the principles of individual freedom of conscience and separation of church and state was hardly a consideration. Abstract concepts unfamiliar to the new immigrants were easily eclipsed by the social and religious benefits that a tightly organized community provided.[8] It is reasonable to conjecture that even if the colonies had chartered separate communities legally empowered to tax and regulate the everyday affairs of their members, the early Jews would have raised little objection.

Without civil sanction, the authority of the American *kahal* hardly approximated that of its European model. Whereas the London Jewish community, among other things, supervised and taxed business activities, monitored ethical behavior, and censored publications, the colonial congregations wielded only the power that the denial of religious privileges carried. Even the dreaded ban of excommunication was drastically vitiated in an open society where acculturation was rapid and where the government freely tolerated defectors. Jews who violated the Sabbath or dietary rules were threatened, but since the *kahal* depended more on individual members than in Europe, threats could prove counterproductive. Twice before the Revolution the New York congregation, Shearith Israel, attempted to tax out-of-town Jews for the benefit of the *kahal,* and it also levied a tax on kosher meat for export. But those were only residual vestiges of a system which in its full strength could not be transplanted in America.

The power of the *kahal* rested at bottom on the commitment of its members to Judaism as an all-encompassing way of life and the continuance of Old World habits. The *kahal* itself, lacking trained rabbis, teachers, and educational materials, did little, however, to promote more than a passive faith. Nevertheless, although religious practice was largely one of custom and rote, most colonial Jews continued to accept the authority of traditional Judaism. If the revitalization of Judaism was not their fundamental purpose, neither was the abandonment of their age-old religion. A long history of disabilities may have inured them to a less-than-equal status within Christian society, but it had also reinforced Jewish antipathy toward the faith of erstwhile oppressors. Mass conversion to some brand of Christianity was, like secularism or atheism, never an option.[9]

Although Jews still clung to the *kahal* and to their traditional religion, history alone would foster their receptivity to the theory of separationism. Throughout the Christian era oppression at the hands of religiously inspired rulers was a commonplace, and European Jews had ample cause to believe that Christian religious teachings underlay Jew-hatred. Many of the early Sephardic immigrants or their families had personally experienced the terror of the Inquisition. One Duarte Lopez, for example, a Portuguese Christian of Jewish origins, left his homeland for America in the wake of an inquisitorial trial of New Christians. In Newport he reverted to Judaism, and as Aaron Lopez became the well-known Jewish merchant prince of pre-Revolutionary America. Fear of the Holy Office, which had crossed the Atlantic into the empires of Spain and Portugal, affected entire settlements as well. The Jews of Recife, Brazil, uprooted themselves and sought other havens when the Portuguese reconquered the seaport from the Dutch in 1654. Some of those exiles subsequently reached New Amsterdam, the first significant Jewish outpost on the continent.[10]

A deep-seated fear of a militant Christian state accompanied the Jewish immigrants to the New World. A very small minority of colonial Jews—

fewer than two thousand in 1776—searched for a haven, another outpost in the diaspora, in which they would be tolerated. Unlike other religious groups that sought their fulfillment in America, Jews did not plan a new social and political experiment in which religion played a pivotal part. Their city on the hill was the real Jerusalem, still an integral component of their theology and their identity as a people. Unconcerned with the vitality or nurture of Judaism, their modest religious aims touched only themselves. Hoping for toleration, they neither conceived of competition with other religious sects nor did they plan on missionizing.[11] From the beginning, Judaism was a private affair that engaged only its adherents, a posture that fed the yet dormant sense that the best society was the one least involved with affairs of conscience.

The idea of a Christian state accompanied the exploration and colonization of continental America. The letters patent to Sir Humphrey Gilbert and Sir Walter Raleigh granted the right to "finde out . . . such remote, heathen and barbarous lands . . . not actually possessed of any Christian Prince, nor inhabited by Christian People." Here, Christianity connoted a higher civilization, and non-Christians and their lands were fair game for the superior, Christian, Europeans. The first royal charter for the Virginia Company included the propagation of Christianity as one of its purposes, to bring, as it said, the "Infidels and Savages, living in those Parts, to human Civility." The equation of Christianity with civility and civilization remained fixed; federal court decisions almost four hundred years later, most markedly in cases involving Indian claims, still testified to that usage.[12]

The charters that followed for the original thirteen colonies also employed a Christian vocabulary and often included the promotion of Christianity as a primary aim. The compact colonies (Plymouth, Rhode Island, Connecticut, New Hampshire), which began with agreements drawn up by the original settlers, were no less concerned with religion. The Fundamental Orders of 1639, the social compact that established the first government of Connecticut, committed the inhabitants "to mayntayne and presearve the liberty and purity of the gospell of our Lord Jesus which we now professe, as also the disciplyne of the Churches, which . . . is now practised amongst us."[13]

In all colonies statutory law reinforced the Christian character of society. Civil law prohibited blasphemy and public worship on the part of minorities; it also mandated church attendance, Sunday observance, and financial support of the colony's established church and its schools. Political rights—citizenship, voting, officeholding, service as jurors and witnesses—were usually limited, if not to church members then at least to those who took oaths of allegiance formulated in Christological terms. Since rights of trade often depended on legal citizenship, religious control penetrated the economic sphere. Christianity formally governed well nigh all aspects of life; an early law of Rhode Island recognized only *Christian* marriages, and a Virginia law, a throwback to medieval tradition, stipulated that non-Christians could not hold white Christian servants. Some early colonists frowned particularly on religious dissent, which they regarded as anti-Christian, an "abomination," and tantamount to sedition.[14]

Nor did formal toleration acts necessarily advance Jewish equality. That of Maryland of 1649 recognized the religious rights of most Christians but went on to state that anyone who denied "our Saviour Jesus Christ to bee the sonne of God, or shall deny the holy Trinity" could lose his property or be put to death. Ten years later, a Jew, Jacob Lumbrozo, was convicted under the law. The first Jew to be haled before an English or American court for blasphemy, he probably escaped death by formal conversion to Christianity.[15]

Fortunately for the Jews, not all the disabling laws were carried out. Some were quietly overlooked or undone by royal intervention; some lapsed as the initial religious zeal of a colony waned. If the issue was raised, as in the case of the disputed New York election of 1737 when the defeated candidate for the colonial assembly charged that the votes of Jews, who legally did not qualify for suffrage, had helped elect his opponent, the disability could be reaffirmed. At times Jews benefited, at least in theory, when colonies broadened the rights of other religious minorities. The minorities specifically concerned (e.g., Anglicans in Puritan Massachusetts or Catholics in Anglican New York) were no more enamored of the Jews or more committed to the universalistic principle of religious equality than the majority, but changed legal formulas provided loopholes even for non-Christians.[16]

Stamping the non-Christian as less than equal, the disabilities suffered by colonial Jews reflected the transplanted European heritage more than any active anti-Jewish animus. Most colonists probably never encountered Jews; they knew not the real but the mythical or stereotypical Jew. Only a few weeks after the first group landed in New Amsterdam—hardly enough time to have formed any opinion of the newcomers—Governor Peter Stuyvesant wrote a damning letter about them to the Dutch West India Company. Employing images familiar throughout Christendom, he referred to the arrival of the "deceitful race," the "hateful enemies and blasphemers of the name of Christ," with "their customary usury and deceitful trading with the Christians." In early Massachusetts Bay, the seeming contradiction between the Puritans' veneration for the Old Testament, Hebrew, and the ancient Israelites, on the one hand, and their receptivity to contemporary Jews only as objects of conversionary efforts, on the other, is reconcilable when set against the canvas of the mythical Jew. The Puritans, the new children of Israel, had inherited the Bible, which they incorporated into their legal system, precisely because the original children and their descendants had erroneously rejected Jesus and the "new dispensation."[17]

Those thinkers who deviated from the traditional Christian norms scored only limited success in raising the status of the Jew. William Penn, for example, permitted freedom of worship to all in his Quaker colony who believed in God; believers were not to be molested or required to attend or support any church. Nevertheless, the same legal code reserved freemanship, suffrage, and officeholding to Christians. Penn, too, was apparently steeped in the lore about the mythical Jew; he shared the Puritans' respect for Hebraism as well as their desire to convert the errant people who were guilty of deicide.[18]

John Locke, better known in the colonies for his ideas on civil government, contributed to religious toleration by his work on the Fundamental Constitutions of Carolina, the proposed framework for that proprietary colony. Although the Constitutions stipulated an established Anglican church, a provision which Locke said he opposed, the document promised protection of the religious practices of prospective freemen. Jews, unlike Catholics and atheists, were specifically included (admittedly with an eye to their conversion). Locke failed to delimit clearly the boundaries between church and state, but the liberal spirit of the document broke new ground in seventeenth-century thought. Nevertheless, the Constitutions attracted few Jews to South Carolina. Those in the colony fared well until a steady process of erosion of Jewish civil rights began in the first decade of the eighteenth century.[19]

The most radical deviant from the church–state consensus of the period was Roger Williams. Hailed later by American Jews and other champions of separationism for his enlightened views, Williams, in fact, predicated his principles of freedom of conscience and separation of church and state on theological grounds. Since, for example, no church could prove that it alone held the keys to the kingdom, it could not require conformity. Furthermore, the protection of the church from the corrupting influences of the secular world, rather than the dangers to society at the hands of aggressive churches, mandated separationism. Religion also underlay Williams's view of the Jews—his belief that Christianity was superior to all other religions, his hope for the conversion of the Jews, his denunciation of anti-Jewish oppression as un-Christian. Williams may not have known Jews in England or even the few who arrived at Newport before his death. In his writings the Jew stands with the "Turke" and the "Pagan" as the stereotypical alien outside the pale of Christendom. Nevertheless, when urging their readmission into England, Williams apparently contemplated some change in the status of contemporary Jews. On that occasion he noted a different wall of separation, one to be torn down rather than erected: "I humbly conceive it to be the *Duty* of the *Civil Magistrate* to break down that superstitious *wall* of *separation* (as to Civil things) between us Gentiles and the Jews." Whether he would have supported political rights for Jews, at a time when such rights were denied in England, remains unknown.[20]

Despite Williams's principles and the liberal charter of 1663 which he secured from the crown, Jews did not flock to Rhode Island. No evidence exists of a Jewish settlement prior to 1677, and even that lasted only a few years. Nor did Rhode Island live up to the logical implications of freedom of worship or separation of church and state. A law of 1665 providing freemanship to all those with adequate means and "of civill conversation" probably excluded Jews, since "civill conversation" translated to acceptable Christian conduct. Some twenty years later a Jewish petition for freemanship was explicitly rejected; Jews could expect only "as good protection here as any stranger, being not of our nation." Cotton Mather may have described Newport as "the common receptacle of the convicts of Jerusalem and the outcasts of the land," but the idea of a Christian state in Rhode Island held fast.[21]

Jews preferred to avoid closed religious societies like Massachusetts Bay, but they were accustomed to disabilities and unequal status just because they were not Christians. Even if the principles of Locke and Williams had gained currency among Jews, those ideas doubtless appeared chimerical, unworkable, or perhaps dangerous. Jewish history had taught the need to accommodate to given situations (barring those that called for serious infractions of Jewish law) in order to survive most comfortably, and the settlers in America were hardly more daring than their medieval ancestors. Different from those religious minorities that came to the New World imbued with the aim of substituting disestablishment for the dominant European church pattern, Jews had no such agenda. For one thing, disestablishment alone fell short of the needs of the non-Christian. The term "Protestant" in America encompassed numerous churches, but a variety of sects could jointly uphold the religious character of society as vigorously as one dominant church. Indeed, disabilities based on Christianity existed in Pennsylvania and Rhode Island no less than in colonies like New York and South Carolina that had an established church. True religious equality, calling for the extirpation even of a recognized "common-denominator" Christianity, was a radical concept, as alien to the colonial Jewish mind as it was to the host colonies.[22]

On the scale of Jewish priorities the rights to settle in a colony and earn a living were primary. In New Amsterdam, for example, Jews labored step by step to secure the right of settlement and then legal permission to trade, own property, open retail shops, and engage in crafts. The right of public worship as well as political rights were distinctly secondary. Pragmatically, the need for a cemetery was crucial, but restrictions on public worship did not preclude the practice of Judaism. Nor were political rights deemed essential for Jewish survival, and the goal of political equality, like that of religious equality, was still in the distant future. To be sure, Jews took advantage of colonial indifference that often permitted them to vote, and occasionally Jews held certain local appointed offices, but where they were rebuffed by law, they meekly retreated. When Rhode Island denied

Aaron Lopez's naturalization petition, in direct violation of England's Naturalization Act of 1740, the merchant turned to Massachusetts, where he achieved his objective. In 1776 Francis Salvador, a Jewish member of South Carolina's provincial congress, registered no objection to the denial of suffrage to non-Protestants in the first state constitution.[23]

Passivity with respect to political rights was in keeping with age-old habits. Enjoying greater toleration in the colonies than in most European countries, Jews may also have feared that political demands, as opposed to the slow accretion of economic privileges, might generate a backlash and result in the rescission of rights already theirs. The existence of a strong *kahal,* a Jewish world within the world, served to vitiate the emotional impact of restrictions and inferior status. In the background there also loomed the threat of excommunication, adopted in 1648 by the Sephardic Jewish leaders in London, on anyone who voted in an election or took sides on a political question. Not only the dread of incurring popular hostility, but the correlation by traditionalist Jews of political activism with religious apathy and backsliding, accounted for such strictures. As Isaac Leeser, the first American rabbi of national prominence, said two centuries later: "We can do without voting at elections; we can live without holding offices; but we are nothing without religion, we die without our faith."[24]

The priorities of colonial Jews jibed with those of England. Imperial mercantilist policies during the century after the Restoration aimed at augmenting the country's wealth and international power, and colonies were essential to service the needs of the mother country. To attract settlers to the New World, in 1740 Parliament passed the Naturalization Act. It provided that foreigners who had resided in the colonies for seven years were eligible for naturalization, and it specifically exempted Jews from the Christian form of the required oath of allegiance. Exemption was a far cry from the denial of a Christian state or the admission that rights belonged to all human beings, but on paper the act was a dramatic step well ahead of its time. It made colonial Jews equal to other foreign immigrants and, with respect to colonial life, it implied that they were equal to the English colonist in matters of suffrage and officeholding. As it turned out, however, the colonies refused to broaden the exercise of political rights, and at best the act merely confirmed economic rights that most Jewish colonists on the mainland already possessed.[25]

If the colonies balked at accepting the Jews as political equals, they did permit them freedom of conscience and basic economic rights. Like England, but for their own purposes, they too needed manpower. The overwhelming concentration of Jews in mercantile pursuits made them a signal economic asset; and, few in number, eagerly accommodationist, and not averse to mixing socially with Christians, the real (as opposed to mythical) Jews aroused little fear. In the eighteenth century, when the religious zeal of the first settlers had abated and the number of "unchurched" Americans rose, fewer scruples blocked the qualified acceptance of non-Christians. The rise of new sects during the Great Awakening further compounded the religious heterogeneity of the colonies, and it became virtually futile to insist upon religious uniformity. The Great Awakening and the Enlightenment, each in its separate way, also sowed new ideas in pre-Revolutionary America about church establishment and about the individual's right to religious freedom.[26]

The various forces that explained colonial toleration worked to reshape the European mind-set of both Christian and Jewish settlers. In a society that had escaped the castelike stratification of feudalism, those forces gradually but steadily shifted the focus from the group to the individual. The emphasis on the worth and importance of the individual rose, and the primacy of the group receded. Colonial Jewry never suffered enforced ghettoization, restrictions on the part of entrenched guilds, or an anti-Jewish civil bureaucracy. By the time Americans wrote their state and federal constitutions, the European model had grown more remote.

Revolution and Constitutions

The concept of a Christian state, particularly with respect to church establishments and the political rights of non-Christians, was radically modified during the Revolutionary era. To be sure, neither disestablishment in the sense of total separation nor full equality for non-Christians was effected. Often the confrontations between the old and the new ideas resulted in contradictions and ambivalences on issues of religious freedom and the role of civil government in religious affairs. Some earlier traditions lived on, bequeathing a significant legacy to fundamental and statutory law.

The call for disestablishment arose in part from the Revolution itself. Although the Declaration of Independence ignored the subject, the privileged Anglican church, which held sway in many colonies, was another symbol of the king's despotism. Theoretically, one established church could be replaced by another; a recent study suggests that it was the English establishment but not the principle of establishment itself that irked most Americans. On the other hand, the momentum of Revolutionary thought—what historians have called the "shock of revolution," or the "contagion of liberty," which linked the struggles for civil and religious liberty—underlay popular challenges to establishment.[27]

Some religious groups took an active role on behalf of disestablishment. The Great Awakening had splintered the existing religious order and had invigorated the currents of nonconformist thought. Dissenting religions at odds with any particular established church increasingly questioned civil support of religion on *religious* grounds. In Virginia, after the war, Baptists and Presbyterians followed by other groups argued for separation in terms reminiscent of Roger Williams. The Presbytery of Hanover directed several oft-cited memorials to the state legislature that forcefully asserted the distinct orbits of religion and the state. Dissenters did not necessarily support Jewish rights, but a few petitions did. One, probably also from Presbyterians, opposed public financial support of religion. It said that "to compel Jews by law to support the Christian religion . . . is an arbitrary & impolitic usurpation which Christians ought to be ashamed of."[28]

A more powerful challenge to the idea of a Christian state was the Enlightenment. Those who subscribed to the doctrines of the Age of Reason usually questioned the authority of church establishment if not of Christianity itself. To be sure, inconsistencies abounded and there were Deists who favored established churches, but the popularity of rationalism, individual rights, and natural law—the very ideological concepts on which Americans justified their break from England—boded ill for the perpetuation of church dominance in a republic. Like the dissenters, the "enlightened" did not repudiate the beneficial influence of Christianity upon worldly and even state matters, but the Christian state they now envisaged operated without the sanction of civil law. Two streams, then—one pietistic, seeking to protect religion from society, and the other rationalistic, seeking to protect society from religion—served to broaden freedom of worship and to warn against state alliances with religion. Later Jews paid more attention to the shared target of the two streams than to their separate origins, and they enshrined Jefferson and Madison alongside Roger Williams in their pantheon.[29]

For American as well as European Jewry the Enlightenment set the ideological framework for legal emancipation and integration within the nation-state. The tenets of individualism and universalism, which blazoned from the Declaration of Independence and the French Declaration of the Rights of Man, promised the acceptance of Jews as human beings without religious or national qualifications. That the men of the Enlightenment, Voltaire and his circle, exhibited a strong Jew-hatred from which later secular anti-Semitism sprouted, mattered little at that time. Of more immediate significance, the heretofore legal distinctions between Christian and non-Christian had been dealt a severe blow.

Like other colonists, Jews were caught up in the new intellectual ferment. Although there is virtually no evidence of a Jewish reaction to the Declaration of Independence itself, the promise of equal rights and church disestablishment was doubtless a major consideration in directing Jews to the rebel side. They may not have understood the philosophical basis of Jeffersonian thought, and the stark drama of the change from marginal existence to full incorporation into the state may have escaped them, but doubtless the promise of equal rights was easily grasped. Dr. Benjamin Rush, a noted Quaker liberal, put it correctly: "The Jews chose for the most part to be Whigs, even though they had no particular grievances against the British."[30] To be sure, not every Jew behaved according to the logic of Jefferson's teaching. Some were Tories; they either missed the significance of the new ideology or reasoned that the same ends might be served in the long run by loyalty to England. In those cases Jews abided by conservative tradition or chose sides for economic reasons. Contradictions emerged within the Christian community as well, and in some instances Jews *as a group* were suspected of disloyalty—a throwback to the age-old "Jew as alien" theme—even by Whigs, who subscribed to the new intellectual currents.

For Jews as for other non-English ethnic groups, the Revolution worked to hasten the process of acculturation and social integration. In the decade that followed the Stamp Act of 1765 Jews joined fellow Whigs, not as Jews but as aggrieved colonists, in nonimportation agreements and boycotts of England. During the war years Jews, like other patriots, served in the rebel cause. That experience raised Jewish status as Americans while simultaneously heightening their expectations and self-assuredness. Propelled to a level of political involvement never before exhibited, Jews began to exchange their customary political passivity for an activism that would come to characterize the American Jewish community. At the end of the war they pointed to their service on behalf of the patriot cause to further validate their claim to full equality.

An experience of Moses Michael Hays, a prominent merchant of Newport, illustrates the new mood among Jews. A patriot who had signed a statement of loyalty to the government, Hays refused to sign a second loyalty oath demanded by the Rhode Island legislature. He explained, among other reasons, that "I am an Israelite and am not allowed the liberty of a vote or voice in common with the rest of the voters. . . . I ask . . . the rights and priviledges [*sic*] due other free citizens." Resentful that Rhode Island denied him the franchise, Hays never doubted that he was entitled to all the rights that citizenship bestowed. A far cry indeed from the first Jews of New Amsterdam, whose humble petitions for specific rights—submitted with all "due" or "submissive reverence"—were admissions that any gesture of equal treatment to Jews was a favor and not a right![31]

The theme of Jewish loyalty, and particularly of military service, became more pronounced in petitions for equality after the Revolution, but it, too, had older roots. In 1655 leaders of the Amsterdam Jewish community, requesting the Dutch West India Company to permit the settlement of the first Jewish arrivals in New Amsterdam, had emphasized the loyalty to Holland that the prospective settlers had shown in Recife when the Dutch were at war with the Portuguese. Indeed, the idea that military service in some instances carried the reward of citizenship went back to ancient times. American Jews reworked that premodern concept to fit the new situation; a political baptism of blood, as it were, was their passport to equality within the state. Throughout the nineteenth century Jews persistently focused on their service in American wars—from the Revolution to the Spanish-American War—to defend their civil rights and to counter popular anti-Semitism.[32]

Pursuant to a recommendation by the Continental Congress in 1775, eleven of the thirteen original states drew up constitutions before 1787. (Connecticut and Rhode Island chose to function under their colonial charters, and not until 1818 and 1842, respectively, were Jews accorded political equality in those states.)[33] Here, then, was the first opportunity to disavow the legal constraints of a Christian state and to translate the ideological principles underlying the Revolution into fundamental law.

Jewish equality depended on how the first constitutions fixed the place of religion in fundamental law. From that perspective the results were mixed. Massachusetts and New Hampshire (in its second constitution) liberally acknowledged freedom of worship, but both mandated public support of Protestant institutions and limited officeholding to Protestants. New Jersey, North Carolina, and Georgia also affirmed the right of religious freedom but stated that only Protestants could hold office. Pennsylvania's constitution held out a broader promise, at least to all believers. Its declaration of rights affirmed the "natural and unalienable" right of free worship, adding: "nor can any man, who acknowledges the being of a God, be justly deprived or abridged of any civil right as a citizen, on account of his religious sentiments or particular mode of religious worship." Nevertheless, the constitution required a religious oath of officeholders affirming belief in God, divine reward and punishment, and the divine inspiration of both the Old and New Testaments. Apparently the framers thought that the restrictive clauses were mild, because in deference to Benjamin Franklin, who opposed all religious restrictions, they added that "no further or other religious test shall ever hereafter be required."

Pennsylvania's neighbor, Delaware, also specified a religious oath, which in this case included a belief in the Trinity. South Carolina and Maryland prescribed other restrictions. The former limited the franchise and officeholding to Protestants, and in its second constitution (1778) extended only "toleration" to all "who acknowledge that there is one God, and a future state of reward and punishment, and that God is publicly to be worshipped." Maryland, in addition to excluding non-Christians from holding office, explicitly offered religious liberty solely to Christians. Both southern states, and Georgia as well, permitted multiple religious establishments, where not one but several churches could theoretically receive government support on a nonpreferential basis.[34]

In sum, Christianity or its teachings were mentioned in one form or another in all of the nine state constitutions here discussed. Only Christians or Protestants enjoyed full political rights; others were still unequal. In four states the constitutions allowed assessments for Christian (Maryland and Georgia) or Protestant (Massachusetts and New Hampshire) churches. Several states barred ministers of all denominations from various state offices, but those restrictions derived more from opposition to the Anglican church than from an antireligious animus. The Christian-state model had been modified, but despite the use of phrases like natural or unalienable rights, it had hardly been discarded. Even some who supported rights for Jews did so on religious grounds. Christian generosity, they said, might attract Jews to the dominant faith. Generally, however, where critics spoke out against religious qualifications of political rights, their voices failed to sway the majority.[35]

Of those nine states, Jewish communities existed only in Pennsylvania, South Carolina, and Georgia. Contemporary accounts indicate that awareness of colonial Jews played little part in the actual writing of constitutions. In no state was the subject of rights for American Jews addressed directly. Since the focal point was the protection of Christianity, non-Christians generically, rather than the few Jews among them, represented threats to the religious order. In Pennsylvania, for example, the oath initially considered for officeholding required merely belief in one God. Public protest arose, however, against a provision that would permit "Jews or Turks" and "other enemies of Christ" to achieve wealth and political power and thereby threaten the safety of Christians and the state. One impassioned defender of a Christian state wrote: "An Episcopal church, a Presbyterian meeting house, a Roman Catholic church, a mosque, a synagogue or heathen temple, have now in Pennsylvania all equal privileges!" Demands for increased religious qualifications continued after the test oath was adopted, and then, too, Jews were linked with Turks and other perceived deviants whose enjoyment of political rights made a mockery of the dominant religion.[36]

The picture brightened in New York, the home of the largest Jewish settlement. The state did not ignore religion—indeed, the state convention called for a day of fasting and prayer to implore "divine assistance" in the establishment of a government—but a consensus obtained from the very outset on the need to guarantee religious liberty and disestablishment. Although anti-Catholic prejudice was blatant, the Jews could not have fared better. Under Article 38, which revealed the influence of Enlightenment thought as well as the framers' studied purpose of distancing America from European traditions, Jews were incorporated into the polity as full and equal citizens. That famous milestone in the history of American Jewry read:

> WHEREAS we are required by the benevolent principles of rational liberty ... to guard against the spiritual oppression and intolerance, wherewith the bigotry and ambition of weak and wicked priests and princes, have scourged mankind: This Convention doth further, in the name and by the

authority of the good people of this State, ORDAIN, DETERMINE and DECLARE, that the free exercise and enjoyment [the original draft said "toleration"] of religious profession and worship, without discrimination or preference, shall forever hereafter be allowed within this State to all mankind.[37]

For the few Jews in Virginia (there was no organized community until 1789) the first constitution was a disappointment. By retaining colonial requirements for voting, it excluded Jews from equal political rights. Nevertheless, Jews and other minorities reaped substantial benefits in the long run from Virginia's pioneering efforts on behalf of religious liberty and separationism. In no other state during the years between independence and the writing of the federal Constitution was there so comprehensive a discussion or so illustrious a series of documents on the subject.[38]

Virginia's bill of rights, a model for the first eight amendments to the federal Constitution, eloquently addressed the subject of religious liberty. Thanks to James Madison, the word "toleration" with its unpleasant connotations was purposely removed. The article on religion said in part: "That religion, or the duty which we owe to our Creator, and the manner of discharging it, can be directed only by reason and conviction, not by force or violence; and therefore all men are equally entitled to the free exercise of religion, according to the dictates of conscience." Thomas Jefferson drafted a bill on religious freedom to provide supportive legislation, but the measure along with the issue of disestablishment dragged on, generating considerable legislative and popular debate. In 1784, when the legislature considered a measure for state support of "teachers of the Christian religion," Madison successfully countered on behalf of separationism with his famous "Memorial and Remonstrance." Finally, in 1786 an Act Establishing Religious Freedom, written by Jefferson and called one of the great charters of human liberty, nailed down the victory. Both the statute and the "Memorial" fused the two principles of freedom of conscience and separationism; without either, their authors believed, true religious liberty could not prevail.[39]

The accounts of Madison's and Jefferson's activities indicate that they and their supporters considered the rights of the Jew insofar as they derived from precepts of natural, universal law. As was the case in Pennsylvania, references were to the mythical Jew rather than to the few Jewish families in the state or those who served the Revolutionary cause. On the 1784 bill of assessment, for example, one Virginian wrote that the fundamental issue in the legislature was whether "Turks, Jews and Infidels were to contribute to the support of a Religion whose Truth they did not acknowledge." With respect to the act of 1786, an attempt to insert a reference to the divinity of Jesus Christ in the preamble was defeated by Jefferson's followers. They intended, Jefferson wrote, "to comprehend within the mantle of [the act's] protection the Jew and the Gentile, the Christian and Mahometan, the Hindu and Infidel of every denomination." Opponents of the measure also resorted to the same image; "Jew" signified neither neighbor nor acquaintance but, like Turk, Mohammedam, atheist, or Deist, a genus distinct from the familiar Christian American.[40]

The Virginia experience shows how the lines between the Christian-state idea and a secular definition of religious liberty were still very blurred. The same bill of rights that spoke of "reason" and "conviction" underlying man's beliefs also stressed the need of "Christian forbearance, love, and charity" for civil behavior. Madison, too, employed religious terms in defense of church–state separation. In the "Memorial and Remonstrance," he said that state support of Christian teachings would sap the vitality of Christianity and make it less attractive to potential converts. (If such arguments weighed little for him personally, he probably thought that they could persuade Christian-staters to recognize the advantages inherent in voluntarism.) George Washington was inconsistent as well. Although he stated in his famous letter to the Jews of Newport that the day of narrow toleration had passed, that all men possessed "liberty of conscience and immunities of citizenship," he supported the assessment bill of 1784. True, he asked that Jews and other non-Christians be exempted, but exemptions by definition mandated civil inquiry into religion and admitted tacitly to different grades of citizenship.[41]

Despite such inconsistencies, eighteenth-century Jews could well appreciate the Virginia documents. The very use of the words "all men" or "every man" furthered the Jewish quest for full equality. Madison's "Memorial" taught a small minority—and indeed it became the crux of later American Jewish defense—that support of Christianity or, for that matter, support of religion in general was no less threatening than the establishment of one particular church. One section of the "Memorial and Remonstrance" appeared particularly apposite to the Jewish experience:

> [The assessment bill] degrades from the equal rank of citizens all those whose opinions in religion do not bend to those of the legislative authority. Distant as it may be, in its present form, from the inquisition, it differs only in degree. The one is the *first* step, the other the *last*, in *the career of intolerance.*

In those last words Madison warned of the danger of the entering wedge, another doctrine that later Jews repeatedly affirmed.

The statute of 1786 was a resounding victory for Jews eager for equality before the law. It provided that "no man shall be compelled to . . . support any religious worship . . . whatsoever; nor shall . . . suffer on account of his religious opinions or belief; but that all men shall be free to profess . . . their opinions in matters of religion, and that the same shall in no wise diminish, enlarge, or affect their civil capacities." The act included the unusual provision that any attempt to repeal or narrow its operation would constitute "an infringement of natural right." Thus, the statute ranked with fundamental or "higher" law. And, as if to confirm its intent, one Isaiah Isaacs, in 1788, became the first Jew ever elected in Richmond to a municipal office.[42]

Jews did not participate in the bodies that drafted the state constitutions, but they were keenly aware of developments that bore upon their rights. New York's *kahal,* Shearith Israel, wrote a letter to Governor Clinton emphasizing Jewish support of the Revolutionary cause. It added: "We now look forward, with Pleasure to the happy days we expect to enjoy under a Constitution, Wisely framed to preserve the inestimable Blessing of Civil, and Religious Liberty."[43]

Philadelphia's Jews were less sanguine. Having obtained copies of the constitutions of all the states, they saw that they had fared less well than their fellow Jews in New York. The injustice of Pennsylvania's religious oath for officeholders led the board of the Philadelphia *kahal* to appeal for relief when the wartime emergency had passed. In 1784 they petitioned the state's Council of Censors, a body empowered to review infractions of the constitution, maintaining that the test oath contradicted the provision for religious liberty in the state's bill of rights. In addition to the now familiar argument that Jews had acquitted themselves so well in the continental army, the petition warned that prospective immigrants from Europe might choose to bypass Pennsylvania in favor of a state like New York where Jews enjoyed full equality. It also pointed to Judaism and Jewish collective behavior as proofs that Jews merited equality: "In the religious books of the Jews . . . there are no such doctrines or principles established, as are inconsistent with the safety and happiness of the people of Pennsylvania"; "as a nation or a religious society, [Jews] stand unimpeached of any matter whatsoever, against the safety and happiness of the people." Although some Christians endorsed the petition, the Council of Censors took no action. Jonas Phillips appealed again on behalf of the Philadelphia *kahal,* this time to the Constitutional Convention of 1787, but not until 1790 was the disability finally removed.[44]

The words of the Jewish petitioners indicated how the older definition, that Jews were a nation, was changing; now, Jews were also calling themselves a religious society. Nevertheless, they were unprepared to relinquish their identity as a discrete people. Nor did they conceive of separating the defense of one Jew from the defense of the Jewish group and Judaism, and this would hold true for the defense activities of succeeding American Jews. The petition of 1784, like some of the state documents discussed previously, bore traces of the contradictions between the old and new mindsets. It denied that Jews were eager to hold office (a retention of former habits), but it requested "the rights of a free citizen" (a new focus on the

individual rather than the group). Blurring the lines still further, the intended beneficiary of the rights of a free citizen (singular) was the entire
Jewish religious society (plural).

Phillips's petition of 1787 also deserves clarification. The Philadelphian
asked the Constitutional Convention to "alter" Pennsylvania's test oath,
which, he pointed out, contradicted the sense of the state's bill of rights.
The oath read: "I do believe in one God, the Creator and Governor of
the universe, the rewarder of the good and the punisher of the wicked.
And I do acknowledge the Scriptures of the Old and New Testament to
be given by divine inspiration." To place all religions on an "Equal footing," Phillips wanted the excision of the reference to the New Testament.
He may have envisioned a uniform federal oath replacing that of the states,
for he added that "I solicit this favour . . . for the benefit of all the Israelites
through the 13 united states of America." Phillips did not argue on lofty
ideological grounds for the universal rights of man. He challenged neither
the rectitude of a religious oath per se nor its violation of church–state
separation. His was a narrow, pragmatic petition concerned solely with
the issue of Jewish equality, which, he said, was earned because of Jewish
loyalty to the Revolution. His approach set the tone for American Jewish
defense, and not for another hundred years was it exchanged for one that
pressed in universalistic terms for the rights of nonbelievers as well as
believers.[45]

By the end of the century a few of the original states in addition to
Pennsylvania liberalized their constitutions on matters of religious requirements. Influenced by the federal Constitution, the terms of the new constitutions of South Carolina (1790), Delaware (1792), and Georgia (1798)
permitted Jews to hold office. Vermont, the fourteenth state, abolished
religious disabilities in 1793. In the first half of the nineteenth century,
advances followed in other states, and only in North Carolina and New
Hampshire did political equality elude the Jews until after the Civil War.[46]

No matter how progressive the individual constitutions, the breadth of
religious freedom depended from the outset on statutory law enacted by
the states. State laws often lagged behind the sweeping pronouncements
in the constitutions on the sanctity of liberty of conscience, a fact best
explained by fundamental, popular assumptions on the subject of religion
in society. In the first place, Americans believed that—whether written
into the constitutions or not—theirs was a Christian if not a Protestant
nation. Furthermore, all good citizens agreed that the state was obligated
to encourage religion, the base on which civic virtue and successful republican government rested. Freedom of religion hardly translated to freedom from religion or into equal encouragement of non-Christians or non-
Protestants.

Quite naturally, then, the civil agendas of the new states included religious issues. Where no established churches existed, legislatures generally abstained from preferential treatment of particular sects. But uninhibited by considerations of a "wall of separation," states proceeded to enact features of Protestant or Christian teachings into law. For non-Christians such laws, mandating the observance of Sunday or requiring Christian religious oaths of witnesses and jurors, operated to the disadvantage of Jews. In other cases old restrictions, like Virginia's law limiting the right to officiate at marriages to Christian ministers or Maryland's law prohibiting a black from testifying against white *Christians,* remained on the books.[47]

Laws adopted for the purpose of encouraging organized religion could also interfere with the rights of religious groups. A New York statute of 1784, for example, provided for incorporation of religious societies. Although it denied any interference with the governance of those societies, it said that anyone who attended an incorporated congregation for a year was legally a member of the group. As one historian noted, the law served to weaken the discipline of New York City's *kahal.* If Shearith Israel used the ban of excommunication against a transgressor, the latter could well appeal to the secular authorities under that law for the reinstitution of his synagogal rights. In this case the law broadened the religious freedom of one individual but simultaneously weakened the liberty of the group seeking the free exercise of its traditional religious customs.[48]

Early American Jews did not challenge the abstract right of the states to oversee religion. A long way from the strict interpretation of church–state separation, they shared the common belief that religious morality underlay proper governance. What they wanted—the recognition that Judaism merited the respect accorded to Christianity as a source of civic virtue—had been articulated in the Philadelphia petition of 1784. What they objected to was the idea of a Christian state, a concept that branded other faiths and their adherents as inferior. Nineteenth-century Jews used the rhetoric of separationism to contest the remnants of the Christian-state legacy, but until the last decades of the century most preferred a neutral-to-all-religions government to a divorced-from-religion state.

With respect to the religious disabilities, rights, and regulations established by their constitutions and laws, the states answered only to themselves. The Constitution and the Bill of Rights did not alter the fact that, except in connection with federal officeholding, religion remained exclusively within their province. Jonas Phillips's request in 1787 that the national government override a state restriction confirmed the traditional Jewish disposition to seek the support of *central* authorities, but it rang hollow in the antebellum republic. The consensus of Americans on the matter was affirmed in the 1845 case of *Permoli* v. *Municipality,* where the Supreme Court disavowed any federal jurisdiction over the protection of religious liberties: "This is left to the State constitutions and laws; nor is there any inhibition imposed by the Constitution of the United States in this respect on the States."[49] Until 1940 attainment of full religious equality depended primarily on state legislative repeal of objectionable statutes and on state court decisions that found such laws invalid under state constitutions.

The Federal Constitution

The Continental Congress, which governed the United States until the adoption of the Constitution, affirmed the inviolability of freedom of conscience. Although it stood aloof from religious matters within the states, it manifested a positive interest in religion. Its records, as Anson Phelps Stokes wrote, were replete with references to "God," "Jesus Christ," "the Christian Religion," and the "Free Protestant Colonies," and its legislation spoke of matters like Sunday observance, public worship, thanksgiving, and Christian education. Congress meant Protestantism or at best Christianity when it referred to religion, but the literal terms of the famous Northwest Ordinance of 1787 were broader. It stated: "No person, demeaning himself in a peaceable and orderly manner, shall ever be molested on account of his mode of worship"; and religion, like morality and knowledge, was "necessary to good government and the happiness of mankind." Although the Christian-state idea was stripped of legal sanction, two assumptions—first, that religion was the foundation of political morality, and second, that religion deserved civil encouragement—stood firm.[50]

At the Constitutional Convention of 1787 religion was hardly an area over which the framers would waste powder and shot to insist on federal jurisdiction. The consensus that religious matters belonged to the states went unchallenged and readily explains the "religion-free" debates. On August 30, when much of its substantive work was over, the convention considered a motion by Charles Pinckney of South Carolina to outlaw religious tests for federal offices. Roger Sherman of Connecticut, the only delegate to address the subject, thought that the liberal mood of the age made the resolution superfluous. Although Pinckney's motion was passed without any further debate, the convention's act did not signify unanimity on the intrinsic merit of a test oath. Indeed, at least two delegates who approved the resolution also approved the test oaths of their respective states. Neither one construed the action of the framers to have toppled Christianity from its favored position as the American faith.[51]

Article VI section 3 of the Constitution included the clause in question: "no religious test shall ever be required as a qualification to any office or public trust under the United States." William Miller wrote that this indicated that the nation "was electing to be nonreligious in its civic life." Nonreligious, however, did not mean antireligious. During the "pamphlet war" that accompanied ratification, supporters made clear their belief that the clause did not substitute secularism for the established religious order. Some claimed that it was a logical extension of religious liberty or that the qualities of men's characters rather than their religion should determine their eligibility for office. Most important, religious test or not, there was little likelihood that Americans would ignore the question of religion and choose officeholders who thought differently from themselves.[52]

Both James Madison and Edmund Randolph of Virginia, who had served at the convention, defended the clause largely because it legitimated religious pluralism. A multiplicity of sects, like a multiplicity of secular interest groups, which Madison defended in *The Federalist,* would guard against tyranny by any one faction. Randolph upheld the clause in similar fashion at his state's ratifying convention. In approval of the clause he added: "It puts all sects on the same footing." Neither man envisioned a threat to Christianity in general.[53]

Religion did not figure prominently in the debates over ratification, but it added to criticisms of the proposed constitution. Some Anti-Federalists thought that there was insufficient protection for religious freedom; others feared that the very clause outlawing religious tests indicated that Congress claimed the right to regulate religion. For the most part, opponents attacked the clause with the familiar bogeys of "atheists," "Jews," "Turks," "infidels," "Papists," and "pagans." One pamphlet warned that the pope could become president, and a New York writer commented that a Jewish president, as commander-in-chief, might order the rebuilding of Jerusalem! A delegate to North Carolina's ratifying convention added that the clause was "an invitation for Jews and pagans of every kind to come among us" and that the immigration of those people from the Old World "might endanger the character of the United States."[54]

The heart of the opposition centered on the perceived threat to the endurance of the republic. The absence of a religious test symbolized a turning away from the acknowledgment of Christianity as the foundation of public and political morality. Critics charged that the framers had seen fit neither to recognize or encourage Christianity nor to substitute an equally secure foundation. Without that base, many believed, the new government was doomed. One anonymous New Englander linked the need for a government supported by religion with that for Protestant officeholders; civil government required the assistance of religion, and only a Protestant "is fit to be a ruler of protestants [sic]."[55]

Anti-Federalists succeeded in forcing the adoption of a bill of rights, one that would secure the right of conscience against federal action. Madison feared that defining the limits of congressional power over religion, as opposed to leaving the matter vague, might actually constrict religious liberty. Nevertheless, he spearheaded the passage of the first ten amendments through Congress. The First Amendment addressed the subject of religion in two clauses: "Congress shall make no law respecting an establishment of religion, or prohibiting the free exercise thereof." Along with Article VI, it served notice that the new federal government was blind to religion, at least in the sense that it neither recognized nor ranked the different faiths.[56]

The meaning of the First Amendment—the intent of the framers, the distinction between "free exercise" and "establishment," the definition of establishment—has been subjected to ongoing analysis on the part of contemporary courts and scholars.[57] Construed narrowly, it underscored federal detachment from an area that all acknowledged belonged to the states. (When Madison proposed to add "that no State shall violate the equal rights of conscience," his suggestion was summarily dismissed by the Senate.) Yet to attempt any broader interpretation for an era when lines between church and state were fluid immediately invites controversy. The same Congress that adopted the Bill of Rights seemingly contradicted the ban on meddling in religious affairs when it called for a day of prayer and thanksgiving, reenacted the Northwest Ordinance, and appointed chaplains for the army and both House and Senate. The overriding reality, however, was that Christianity meshed with everyday secular life in the seamless fabric of eighteenth-century American culture. "Customs like days of prayer and thanksgiving appeared not so much matters of religion as part of the common coin of civilized living," Thomas Curry wrote. "A contemporary would in many instances have been hard put to define where Protestantism ended and secular life began."[58]

American Jews enthusiastically hailed the new Constitution. "Jew and Gentile are as one," Rebecca Samuel, a young Jewish matron of Virginia, reported in 1791 to her parents in Germany. The barriers to full equality imposed by the states still remained, but in the eyes of the federal government Jews were equal citizens. (Jews barred by states from officeholding could, at the same time, fill federal posts. Thomas Jefferson appointed Reuben Etting as marshal of Maryland twenty-five years before that state removed its officeholding disability.)[59] Once established, the new government was hardly likely to regress on the issue of religious equality; it could, however, serve as a model to prod or inspire the less liberal states. The American way, so long as the Constitution survived, was officially one that rejected a legally recognized Christian state.

From a historical perspective, Jewish equality under the Constitution appeared anticlimactic. The drama of emancipation, which in Europe divided critics and defenders of the old order, never played in America. Unlike France, where citizenship for Jews followed years of discussion and debate, American public attention to the subject of Jewish rights was minimal. Nor did Americans ever imply that Jews were expected to pay a price for full citizenship—that is, to reform their religion, economic distribution, or manners.[60] The reasons for the differences in the United States have been alluded to: the small numbers of Jews in the country, the work force required for a new society, the absence of a feudal heritage, the plurality of religious sects, new ideologies, and the consignment of jurisdiction over religion to the state governments. Together, and with scarcely any input from the Jews, they assured the inevitable achievement of American Jewish emancipation.

Jews quickly assimilated the vocabulary of the Revolutionary era and internalized its application. The synagogues had been drawn into American life, if only by the special services they held on patriotic occasions, and now the quest for equality reverberated within the world of the *kahal*. New York's Jews talked of a bill of rights for their synagogue; in Philadelphia, Savannah, and the new community in Richmond, the synagogues enlarged the rights of their members by placing limitations on the heretofore all-powerful governing board. Less radical than the first state constitutions, which reduced the executive to a shadow of the colonial governor, the principle was analogous. Since all Jewish congregations in the aftermath of the Revolution were led by war veterans and Whigs, the changes in the synagogues' by-laws were not surprising. As has been suggested, democratization of the synagogues may also have been calculated to prove how ready Jews were to accommodate to American values.[61]

The very words of Shearith Israel's constitution of 1790 showed the influence of the new liberalism. Probably the work of Solomon Simson, an ardent Whig and an official of the *kahal,* the document included several paragraphs that drew readily from Enlightenment thought. The opening section mentioned a "compact" and "covenant" entered into for the preservation and enjoyment of religious rights. The preamble to the constitution's bill of rights echoed John Locke more explicitly:

> Whereas in free states all power originates and is derived from the people, who always retain every right necessary for their well being individually, and, for the better ascertaining those rights with more precision and explicitly, frequently [form] a declaration or bill of those rights. In like manner the individuals of every society in such state are entitled to and retain their several rights, which ought to be preserved inviolate.[62]

Jewish liberalism stopped short of theology. To be sure, the influence of deism had penetrated the Jewish settlements. Laxity in observance increased as a result of the war and so did the number of the "unsynagogued." Responding realistically to these changes, synagogues revised standards of observance for members. But since new immigrants brought more traditional views with them, the synagogues remained traditionalist.[63]

It was only a matter of a few decades, however, before the exclusive *kahal* of the major coastal cities collapsed. New immigrants established synagogues more in tune with their particular customs; Jews headed west and left the geographical orbit of the first settlements. The strength and the all-encompassing nature of the early *kahal* also dissipated. The Revolutionary era and its ideology had made the country more accepting of minorities and hastened their acculturation. Fast becoming Americanized within a receptive environment, Jews delighted in their legal rights. The concern with individual rights and the inroads of religious liberalism worked in tandem to erode the strength of the group-based *kahal*. Jews grew increasingly independent of a religious community, especially one that also governed their social and cultural life. They still sought Jewish associations and they never repudiated their group ties, but by the early 1800s they were substituting secular organizations to perform functions originally belonging to the *kahal*. In effect, they increasingly applied the maxim of separation between secular and religious to their own affairs.[64]

The *kahal* presented an inadequate defense of its power in the changed surroundings: a static faith; a vapid culture; an absence of religious leaders. ("There is no rabbi in all of America to excommunicate anyone," Rebecca Samuel noted happily.)[65] In little more than a century, the once vibrant, multifunctional American community of the colonial era was rapidly contracting and becoming almost solely a place of worship.

In the long run the erosion of the powerful community affected the posture of American Jews on matters of church and state. Since the focus on individual rights had undercut the primacy of the group mind-set, and with it the foundations of the *kahal,* the latter no longer could serve as the safe harbor that blunted the emotional impact of state-imposed disabilities. Bereft of that support, Jews grew more conscious of the residue of disabilities that remained. Compared with what they had gained, those matters were minimal, but they appeared more glaring once the Jews faced the Christian world without the buffer of the *kahal*. The weaker the community, the more intense was the Jewish passion to erase all legal evidence of a Christian state and to enter the larger American society. And the more victories the Jews chalked up in their quest for full equality, the weaker still did the Jewish community grow.

In this ongoing cycle not only were most Jews prepared to sacrifice communal strength, but they were propelled to ever broader interpretations of the idea of separation. Perhaps they reasoned that the total divorce of Christianity from government would provide a more valuable substitute for the security that they had formerly derived from their own community. Within the Jewish group, as was the case with other collective bodies, a serious tension developed between the group and the individual. The Constitution focused on the rights of the individual, and when a group labored to remove the disabilities on its members, its victories redounded to the benefit of the individual members and not to the group. Thus, a successful campaign could prove counterproductive for the group, since the "individualist consequences" augured ill for cohesiveness and collective vision.[66]

Nevertheless, the quest for religious equality, the primary focus ever since Jonas Phillips requested an "Equal footing" for all religions, was never totally divorced from the Jewish collectivity. In the first place, the group was essential for the individual's full enjoyment of religious liberty; it was the group, with rights to incorporate congregations, conduct public services, and purchase burial grounds, that permitted the Jew to practice his faith as tradition dictated. Second, although most Jews may have put greater emphasis on individual rights, they could not easily shake off their collective identity, at least so long as the outside society identified them primarily as members of a non-Christian people. Third, whereas early American constitutions and law distinguished among citizens on grounds of religion but ignored nationality and ethnicity, most Jews (including radical Reformers of the nineteenth century) could not bury peoplehood as a dimension of Judaism. Jewish ethnic interests, as opposed to strictly cultic interests, had to be subsumed under the rubric of religion, and those interests were collective. On the scale of American Jewish priorities, equality for the group and for Judaism accompanied the emphasis on equal rights for the individual Jew.

Bolstered by the rights guaranteed by the federal and state governments, American Jews soon advanced a new and broader interpretation of religious liberty. They spoke of freedom of religion when they attacked the residual disabilities of the Christian state, but what they really meant was *equality* of religion. Technically, those disabilities did not invade liberty of conscience, but Jews preferred to invoke that principle just because its inviolability was universally recognized. A student of religious liberty in America, who was also a spokesman for the Jewish community formulated a definition of religious freedom to which the group subscribed: "I use the term 'religious liberty' in its American connotation to include not merely constitutional safeguards protecting liberty of conscience . . . but also the constitutional restraints against . . . all attempted discriminations." Legal disabilities, nineteenth-century Jews explained, were penalties incurred just because they followed the wrong faith, and as such were abridgments of their religious freedom.[67]

Concomitantly, Jews latched on with greater enthusiasm to the ideas of the Enlightenment to justify their arguments against Christian trappings in law. The successors to the Revolutionary generation projected a conscious ideological motive into the patriotism of their ancestors, a sentiment which more accurately bespoke their own beliefs. Physician and communal activist Jacob De La Motta, speaking at the consecration of a synagogue in Savannah in 1820, impassionedly interpreted the thoughts of Georgia's colonial Jews: "They panted for Liberty and an enjoyment of equal rights, that 'nature and nature's God' intended they should partake." A rigid acceptance of Enlightenment principles led on occasion to extremist statements. One mid-century Jew went so far as to call the first sentence of the

Declaration of Independence an "unchristian principle." He said that since Jefferson's reasoning translated into the desired separation of church and state, its opposite, namely, Christian teachings, was the implied but obvious enemy.[68]

The record of the first presidents on issues of religion bore out Jewish confidence in the new government. Washington's letter to the Newport congregation affirmed the "inherent natural rights" to "liberty of conscience and immunities of citizenship." The next three presidents, in correspondence with individual Jews, also endorsed freedom of religion and equality for Jews. Jefferson and Madison were the champions of separation. The former, who refused to issue religious proclamations on the grounds that the president as well as Congress was restricted by the First Amendment, wrote the oft-cited letter to the Baptists invoking a "wall of separation" between church and state. Jefferson's successor abided by the ideas he had put forth in the "Memorial and Remonstrance"; he vetoed a ten-dollar gift in land provided by Congress for a Baptist church, and he carefully directed his proclamations for days of prayer only to groups so disposed to mark those occasions religiously. During the terms of those presidents Jews were tapped for federal office—the most notable appointment that of Mordecai Manuel Noah as consul to Tunis in 1813—and even the military, traditionally the bastion of conservative classes, was open to Jews. (A Jew graduated in the first class of West Point.)[69]

Particularly gratifying to adversaries of the Christian-state idea was the treaty of 1797 between the United States and Tripoli. One clause stated that "the government of the United States of America is not in any sense founded on the Christian religion." The fact that the words did not appear in the Arabic original in no way minimized their significance. The American Senate without objection ratified the treaty with the fraudulent gloss, testifying to the universal consensus on a religion-blind Constitution.[70] Some may have seen in the treaty another proof that Americans had discarded the idea of a Christian nation, but that assumption proved to be premature.

2

Separationism Takes Root

A Voluntary Christian Commonwealth

The dramatic resurgence of evangelical Christianity in the first half of the nineteenth century asserted anew the central role of religion in American social and political life. Protestant churches, committed to individual and social regeneration, led a multifaceted crusade to fashion a thoroughly Christian (Protestant) America. On the premise that religious faith was indispensable to the maintenance of American freedom, they worked to arrest the trends of religious apathy, return the unchurched to the fold, and undo the pernicious doctrines of deism and humanistic philosophy. Employing techniques designed to win over the masses—missions, revival meetings, circuit preaching, Sunday schools—they unleashed a rising clamor for a Christian state. The acceptance of denominationalism, or the legitimacy of sectarian theological differences, enabled them to construct a network of Bible, tract, missionary, and educational societies; those, transcending church lines, mobilized resources and reaped advantages that accrued to strong, unified endeavors. Since churches aimed for the salvation of the nation, they spearheaded reform mo ements that attacked immorality and vice (as they interpreted them), and they grappled with social issues ranging from temperance to education. The result of their labors, if not a godly America, was a de facto establishment of Protestantism and a fusion of Protestantism with American civilization.[1]

The new climate of opinion, spawned by the second Great Awakening, was more of a rude awakening for American Jews. On several levels they found themselves out of step. Just as soon as they had fully appropriated the Jeffersonian teachings on religious freedom, those same Enlightenment principles were being brushed aside or repudiated by religious activists. While Jews remained frozen in an eighteenth-century philosophy that questioned the legitimacy of a religious state, America moved on to a nineteenth-century romantic mood that held Christianity to be the progenitor of individual rights and social values. Furthermore, Protestant activism demonstrated that the battle against a Christian state and for church–state separation had entered a new phase. No longer were there merely vestigial remains of the colonial heritage to expunge from the law codes;

now, more frequent resort to Christian usages and imagery augured a stronger alliance between Christianity and the government. Jews keenly felt the potential menace of a militant Protestantism. Even if rescission of rights was a remote possibility, further advances in the quest for equality could be stymied.

To be sure, the proclaimed watchword of the Protestant activists was voluntarism. Just as individuals would voluntarily embrace the true faith, so would a society of those regenerated individuals behave, without coercion, according to the revealed word of God. Religious leaders enthusiastically hailed liberty of conscience and separation of church and state. Some pointed out the positive results of disestablishment and religious freedom: they permitted interdenominational cooperation and, more important, they generated self-reliance and self-reinvigoration of those churches that hoped to survive in the "free market" of religion. Accommodating to the Revolutionary settlement of formal disestablishment, church spokesmen maintained that persuasion rather than legal sanctions would bring about the desired result of a believing citizenry bound by a passionate commitment to the guidance of Protestant tenets.[2]

Affirmations of voluntarism projected the image of a situation more open than the one which actually obtained. In the first place, the religious causes of the first half of the nineteenth century fed upon fixed customs and laws bequeathed by the early settlers on subjects like Sunday observance, blasphemy, and religious instruction in the schools. Americans were historically and in fact a homogeneous Protestant people; the task of the churches was to breathe new life into Christian roots already embedded, to create not a Christian nation but a more religious Christian nation. Second, the lines between voluntarism and coercion easily blurred. How could reforms be implemented without the help of legislation; how could there be Sunday laws without laws? Other reform causes in which religious leaders were prominently involved—temperance and prohibition, school curriculums and textbooks—also depended for their success on legislative responses to popular petitions and political lobbying. Moreover, even without the sanction of law, the "unconverted" were subjected to strong peer pressure where religion rode high. The same pressures operated on legislators and judges when they framed laws or rendered court opinions. And, if church leaders injected religion into politics—as in their support of the Antimasonic party of the 1820s and 1830s and in Ezra Stiles Ely's call (1827) for a Christian party and the election of dedicated Protestants only—they also transcended the limits of pure voluntarism.[3]

Concerned Jews found scant comfort in the byword of voluntarism. A Christian state, however established, raised the dreaded specters of legal disabilities and alien status. Hadn't the cries for a Christian state withheld rights from European Jews in the post-Napoleonic settlement of 1815? American Jews may have agreed with the goal of the Christian-staters, "a free, literate, industrious, honest, law-abiding, religious population," but if Christian values and Christian behavior were the foundations of such a society, non-Christians, the adherents of an allegedly inferior faith, would be hard put to win full acceptance. Smarting under the insults to them and their religion, some Jews longingly recalled the freer spirit of the Revolutionary era. The *Occident,* the first long-lived Jewish periodical, mused unhappily about the waning of liberalism in the country, and it warned that "the fruit of our revolutionary toil" could well be taken away. It commented in 1853 that if the issue were brought up then rather than in 1787, a "large vote" would be registered in opposition to honoring the universal rights that belonged equally to Jews.[4]

The place of the Jew in society claimed no special priority on the Christian agenda. To be sure, if Jews were singled out instead of Christians for public honor, zealots sputtered angrily about the choice of an infidel or Christ-killer and the disregard of Christianity's rightful position as America's recognized religion.[5] But since the vision of a regenerated Christian society held out the promise of divine redemption for all, the small Jewish community (some three thousand) could not be totally ignored. Organized missions to the Jews appeared for the first time on the American scene after the war of 1812, goading the Jews to face up to the aggressive purveyors of a revitalized Christianity.[6]

Jews resented the missionaries' contemptuous and abusive portrayal of Judaism as a dead religion and its followers as stiff-necked and morally backward. Often the only source of information about the Jew, missionaries who canvassed outlying districts kept alive anti-Jewish stereotypes, and their rhetoric readily translated to this-worldly situations. Jews very likely feared the inroads of missionaries within their community—after all, a wave of conversions had swept over western European Jews during the prolonged struggle for emancipation. Of greater import, however, was the challenge that the mission societies, perceived as the vanguard of a Christian state, posed to the vision of equality. For those reasons the American Society for Meliorating the Condition of the Jews (ASMCJ), a group incorporated in 1820 and supported by a veritable galaxy of American dignitaries, became their primary target.

Israel Vindicated, a response to the ASMCJ which was probably written by a Christian freethinker and financed by Jews, laid out the problem: the ASMCJ assumed the superiority of Christians and Christianity over Jews and Judaism, thereby implying that non-Christians were "immoral," "uncultivated," and "undeserving of the rights of citizens." Since the society had obtained a public charter, the legislature that granted the charter tacitly sanctioned the society's objective. Mission societies underwritten by law, the author warned, could effectively consign Jews to second-class citizenship. *Israel Vindicated* as well as other Jewish responses charged that conversionary activities flouted the spirit of the Constitution and sought to enthrone Christianity as the established religion. Linking the operations of the ASMCJ to an establishment of religion, these opponents of the missionaries began what would become the traditional broad construction of the establishment clause by American Jews. Simultaneously, they rested their case on American rather than Jewish reasons: the destruction of the American religious balance would result in serious religious strife.[7] Separation of church and state was good Americanism and religious establishment was un-American. By defending the former and resisting the latter Jews were the better Americans.

Isaac Leeser, rabbi of the prestigious Sephardic synagogue of Philadelphia, joined the antimissionary ranks in the 1830s with a series of letters to the *Philadelphia Gazette*. His main purpose was to contest the stigma foisted on Judaism by the missionaries, but he also expatiated on the theme of equality, which he defined as the antithesis of a Christian state. Jews had earned equality, and here Leeser repeated what earlier spokesmen had said, because of military and other contributions to the nation. Since they were innocent of atheism or similar practices "injurious to society at large," their right to full liberty of conscience—not as "tolerated aliens" but as equal citizens—could not be abridged. Leeser insisted that even if rights were written into law, the spirit of legal equality could well be undermined by those who sought to degrade both Jews and Judaism and who disseminated anti-Jewish prejudice.[8]

The rabbi kept his eyes trained on conversionist activity when he commenced publication of the *Occident* in 1843. There and in the two other major pre–Civil War journals (*Asmonean* and *Israelite*) missionaries singly or in societies were repeatedly attacked. The social reform movements in which Christian clergy engaged, such as temperance and abolition, also became suspect.

Most proponents of a voluntary Christian commonwealth refrained from contesting the rights already enjoyed by non-Christians under the federal and state constitutions. The constitutions of new states and revised constitutions of the old even showed some liberalization on the matter of religious freedom. To be sure, in North Carolina, where a test oath barred Jews from officeholding, it is likely that the religious spirit of the day hardened the opposition to the oath's removal. On the other hand, some longstanding laws that ignored or slighted Jews—for example, the right of Christians to incorporate religious societies in Washington, D.C., the inadmissibility of testimony in Maryland courts by slaves or Indians against white Christians—were changed in response to Jewish demands.[9]

In Maryland, the pervasive religious mood of the day colored the debates over the "Jew Bill," which would eliminate the Christian oath that barred Jews from office. Hezekiah Niles, editor of the Baltimore-based *Niles' Weekly Register* and a supporter of Jewish rights, depicted the issue in the context of church–state separation: "Those who profess to follow his [Christ's] leading by uniting the affairs of religion with those of state, do all they can to pretend to establish for him a kingdom here PROVIDED THEY THEMSELVES MAY GOVERN IT and persecute those who do not come up to their standards of POLITICAL RELIGION."[10] But the debates involved more than separationism. Those who favored amendment of the test oath were forced to counter the notion that equality for Jews menaced Christianity or a Christian state.

The debates on the Jew Bill marked the first time that Jewish rights were widely discussed in America. From Roger Williams to the federal and state constitutional settlements, Jews were mentioned only in connection with other non-Christian "deviants" in the broader context of universal religious freedom. The case of 1809 in North Carolina, where Jacob Henry's right to retain his seat in the legislature was challenged on constitutional grounds, was resolved in Henry's favor as an exception to the rule without becoming a group issue.[11] In Maryland, however, the subject of Jews as a group, contemporary rather than mythical, drew the legislature's attention. Had a visible Jewish community existed in 1776 when the state adopted a constitution that mandated a belief in Christianity for officeholding, Jews— like Quakers, Dunkers, and Mennonites—might well have been exempted. But not until a small group became active in the economic life of Baltimore after the War of 1812 did the issue assume importance.

The long battle to abolish the restriction on officeholding began in 1797 with a petition from a Baltimore merchant, Solomon Etting. His theme was the familiar one of equality; he asked that Jews be placed on the same footing as other citizens of Maryland. Jews raised the same point twenty years later, citing their military service on behalf of the nation and the rights they enjoyed under the federal Constitution. They opposed a version of the bill that would have removed all religious tests; like Jonas Phillips in 1787 they asked merely for an exemption for themselves. Not only did that stance seem more likely to receive the necessary votes, but by distancing themselves from secularists and atheists, they affirmed Jewish commitment to the principle that republican government rested on religious values. Jews wanted religious equality but not necessarily equality without religion.

Sustained attention by the legislature to the Jew Bill began in earnest in 1818, and by then, the climate of religious opinion inevitably reacted upon the question of Jewish rights. The religious hysteria fomented by Protestant journals and bigoted legislators, warning that equality would cause a massive influx of Jews as well as the establishment of Judaism as the state religion, contributed to the delay of the bill's passage. In 1823 an opponent of the Jew Bill made the issue the subject of an election campaign. Running on a "Christian Ticket," he called the Jew Bill "an attempt . . . to bring into popular contempt, the Christian religion."[12]

Besides applying pressure behind the scenes, Maryland's Jews could do nothing but rely on Christian defenders within the legislature. Christian supporters defended the Jews, their religion and contributions to the nation, and the principle of religious equality. Sensitive to the religious mood of the day, they weighed the issue against Christian interests. Thomas Kennedy, the foremost champion of the measure, argued that good Christians, following the moral precepts of their faith, should abandon the un-Christian doctrine of persecution and recognize that force would not convert the Jews. Henry Brackenridge raised the direct question of whether political equality for Jews was incompatible with the respect due to Christianity. His answer, that state support both impugned the strength of Christianity and actually weakened the church, echoed the arguments of the ardent religious voluntarists. William Worthington disputed the notion that rights for Jews would undermine Christianity; didn't Christianity still flourish in states that had abolished religious oaths? None of those states, however, disavowed the superiority of Christianity.[13]

In the public debate generated by the Jew Bill, some Republican papers sneered at religious bigotry, which impeded equality. Jews, too, addressed the religious issue. Pitching their defense of Jewish equality to Christian religious activists, they endeavored to counter charges that Jews were nonbelievers or that they were bent on converting Christians. They and their faith were unjustly maligned, the authors of a memorial to the Maryland legislature insisted. Jews pressed for equal rights and, at the same time, for an equal status for their religion. They and the Christian-staters would have agreed at least that both goals were inextricably linked.[14]

The Jew Bill was finally enacted in 1826. Religious tests remained, but Jews were permitted to take office if they swore to a belief in a future state of rewards and punishments. With this law, incorporated into the constitution of 1851, Maryland became the only state whose constitution specifically mentioned Jews. Over one hundred years later American Jews would again challenge Maryland's test oath. Then, however, their organizations urged the repeal of all forms of religious preconditions.[15]

Protestant activism before the Civil War taught American Jews that the provisions of the state and federal constitutions had not expunged the Christian-state idea. Since public opinion under religious pressure could and did retain old disabilities, Jews felt the inadequacy of formal rights written into political codes. What they increasingly desired was popular acceptance of a broad interpretation of the constitutional spirit—an affirmation of the immutable principle of Jewish equality. The evangelical ferment put Judaism very much on the line, and since most Jews still found the alternatives of conversion and atheism distasteful, they struggled for the same respect and status for their religion as that enjoyed by the majority faith.

The sporadic responses of early-nineteenth-century Jews to aspects of Protestant activism were too new to reflect or fix a uniform defense pattern. Nevertheless, certain features endured. The use of periodicals to fight Jewish battles, a sensitivity to the currents of public opinion, the cooptation of Christian champions—all tactics of a rational accommodationist nature— became hallmarks of nineteenth-century American Jewish defense. Substantive arguments, like the mention of military service and the qualities of Judaism, persisted as well. Most significant was the appeal to the "spirit of the Constitution." Along such lines the Jews, setting themselves up as the true defenders of Americanism, justified their cases for equality and for the separation of church and state.

The German Jewish Immigrants

The immigration of Jews from central Europe,[16] which began to assume significant proportions in the 1830s, swelled the American Jewish population to 50,000 in 1850 and 150,000 in 1860. In many ways the German experience ran parallel to trends already under way in Jewish life. But just because their struggle in Europe for full emancipation was blocked by obstacles never encountered by early American Jews, the Germans (or Ashkenazim) proved from the outset the more fervent and doctrinaire exponents of religious liberty and a religiously neutral state.

Early-nineteenth-century events had sharpened German Jewish sensitivity to the menace of a Christian state. Emancipation in German provinces that followed the conquests of the French revolutionary armies was but short-lived. The restoration of the status quo ante by the Congress of Vienna in 1815 heralded the rescission of Jewish rights, the imposition of severe economic disabilities, and the outbreak of anti-Jewish riots. Legitimacy, the byword of the post-Napoleonic settlement, marched in tandem with a reaction against the Enlightenment and the flowering of Romanticism. The new zeitgeist resounded with calls for a Christian state, where the unity of government, people, and religion would prevail. Under the twin-headed assault of political reaction and religious conservatism, Jewish rights, a relic of a now despised interlude, were tossed aside and Jews again were reduced to outsiders. Conversion to Christianity, as it had always been, was an option for frustrated European Jews, and now, when the new emphasis on a Christian state coincided with the Jewish urge for emancipation, many did succumb. Thus, at the same time that it paralyzed the progress of freedom for the Jew, the Christian-state idea menaced the very survival of Judaism.[17]

Political regression notwithstanding, Jews refused to relinquish their dreams of emancipation and equal rights. Ardent devotees of the Enlightenment's precepts, most supported the liberal cause in the revolutions of

1830 and 1848. (Where Jews had been only passive bystanders in 1789, they became active participants in 1848.) The failure of liberalism in Germany weighed heavily in directing immigration before 1860 to America. There it was only natural for German Jews to line up with their American coreligionists in defense of Jeffersonian teachings and in opposition to the crusade for a Christian commonwealth. Scarred by the recent trauma of rescission, the Germans injected an urgency into in the newly emerging defense brief of American Jews.[18]

The European experience also nourished a Jewish commitment to separation. If a Christian state meant disabilities, a government divorced from religion seemed to offer the most secure base for Jewish civic equality. Furthermore, separation freed Jews from restraints set by their own religious leaders. The same forces that had paved the way for emancipation— political absolutism, capitalism, enlightenment, and secular education— had slowly eroded the power of the rabbis over this-wordly affairs. In that process most Jews readily turned their backs on their former way of life and were prepared to limit the sphere of Jewish religious authority strictly to matters of faith. Their horizons broadened, Jews asserted their independence of the once-powerful community in order to expand their economic and social opportunities. By repudiating communal jurisdiction over secular affairs, they could prove their readiness for full acceptance by their countrymen. And since Jews advocated the confinement of religious influence in the larger society, how could they do less within their own communities?[19]

Before they left Europe, many German Jews had been exposed to philosophical debates on freedom of religion and separation of church and state. One of their own, the scholar and philosopher Moses Mendelssohn, explored these themes in *Jerusalem,* a book published in 1783. The design of the treatise, to set forth the inviolate right of free thought and to demonstrate that Judaism was a religion of reason, reflected the author's deep concern for Jewish emancipation. From his interpretation of the individual's rights and duties in the state of nature and of the social contract, Mendelssohn outlined the discrete evolution and roles of secular and religious societies. Although he opposed purist separation, he discussed essential differences that kept the two spheres distinct. The state dealt with actions, religion with convictions: "The state gives orders and coerces, religion teaches and persuades." On no valid grounds could religion lay claim to the right of coercion, and coercion by the state on matters of thought was also limited. Moreover, the state could not interfere in church affairs. In a similar vein Mendelssohn opposed the use of coercion by the Jewish community, specifically the ban of excommunication. Going beyond the theory of John Locke, which he knew, Mendelssohn included atheists as beneficiaries of tolerance. Neither the state nor the church, he wrote, had the right to reward or punish any particular religion. Since the fusion of church and state in both the Jewish and Christian tradition violated reason, he advocated that it be terminated.[20]

Mendelssohn's views, which were apparently influenced by America's War of Independence, were transported in turn to America by the philosopher's followers. Since his teachings drew from Enlightenment soil, they hardened both Jewish devotion to rationalist principles and Jewish opposition to a Christian state. As one mid-century American Jew put it: "Christianism and all *isms,* which deny the right of free inquiry and demand the unconditional surrender of reason to creeds and dogma, are the antipodes of religious liberty."[21]

The German Jewish immigrants spread out into almost all the states and territories of continental America. Less attached than colonial Jews to the European-style community, many were prepared to forgo the wherewithal to live a traditional religious life as well as the support of established communal institutions in order to participate in the burgeoning economy that accompanied the nation's westward expansion. Since they arrived at a time when the American *kahal* was on its way out, the immigrants hardly thought of resurrecting the older communal model even as a temporary shelter. To be sure, they founded scores of new synagogues, purchased cemeteries, and organized schools, but as one enthusiastic immigrant wrote: "Everybody can choose freely whether or in which synagogue he wants to be enrolled."[22] Ties of peoplehood also weakened, particularly as Jews readily identified with and participated in the sociocultural milieu of the German Christians with whom they had immigrated. Perforce, the synagogues, the centers of their new settlements, were more religious than ethnic in spirit and content. An infrastructure of secular Jewish organizations divorced from the synagogues soon followed, and the separation between the sacred and the temporal in the American Jewish world was sealed.

The immigrant pattern of religious organization, by accepting the conventional American practices of voluntary affiliation and congregational autonomy, was eminently fitting in the new country. The fact that Jews of this wave of immigration thought of themselves primarily as members of a religion rather than a people dovetailed neatly with America's refusal to recognize the legitimacy of separate ethnic enclaves. For our purposes the character of the German institutions takes on an added importance insofar as it contributed to the posture of American Jew on matters of church and state. As Jews increasingly identified as Americans "of the Jewish persuasion," and as they whittled down the power of an all-encompassing synagogue—the one institution that could serve as a buffer between them and the state—they were entrusting their security to society's respect of religious freedom. Therefore, the protection of that principle, which to them held out the surest guarantee of Jewish rights and full equality in their adopted homeland, was a primary commitment. What the earlier Jews had come to by circumstance became a more deliberate, purposeful mission in the minds of the Germans. They labored to nurture religious freedom, guard it against infringements, and broaden its construction. And the Germans believed those ends would best be served by a religiously neutral state. Rabbi Isaac Mayer Wise, the editor of the *Israelite,* reported almost monthly in his influential journal on various aspects of church–state questions. Nothing was more "disgusting," he asserted, than the combination of religion and politics. In his view, "separation was the only way to establish a republic, and liberty . . . is safe only as long as Church and State remain separate."[23]

The German Jews may have redefined the meaning of Jew and Judaism, and those definitions may have weakened the cohesion of the group, but they never repudiated the Jewish collectivity. Nor did a formal willingness to renounce Jewish peoplehood effectively dull the responsibilities that the individual was encouraged to assume on the group's behalf. A proper Jew, the German Jewish leaders preached, took pride in his Judaism, responded to the collective needs of other Jews, and was ever mindful that he and his actions reflected upon an entire community. Nevertheless, as was the case with their Sephardic predecessors, the focus on individual freedoms heightened the tension between the individual Jew and the group. The more secure the individual grew, the less he needed the support of the group, and as communal ties weakened, the collective vision receded correspondingly.

Many Jewish immigrants also distanced themselves from religion, at least in the form of European Orthodoxy. The trend had begun in Europe where a hunger for civil rights and social acceptance impelled them to discard religious and cultural habits which they saw as obstacles to their goals. No counterimperative greeted them in the United States. At a time when religious zeal in Christian America rode high, the picture of American Judaism was dull and unattractive. Jews experienced no major "awakenings" or revivals (Jews were too sober and intelligent, the *Israelite* explained), and a static and uncreative Orthodoxy remained formally in place. Religious apathy and neglect were pervasive: "A youth would rather not be recognized as a Jew, and never thinks of visiting a synagogue," a founder of the B'nai B'rith order commented.[24] Since the established Jews, who were themselves defecting from the synagogue, showed little inclination to absorb the Germans, the latter felt few constraints with respect to beliefs or practices. In this setting Reform Judaism, largely a product of German ideas that were disseminated by German Jewish immigrant rabbis, took root before the Civil War.

The new Judaism in no way resembled the various creeds that emerged after America's second Great Awakening. Emotionally charged individual conversions were the hallmarks of the Christian experience, cold reason characterized the Jewish; the first reflected the stamp of Romanticism, the second the imprint of the Age of Reason. In the spirit of Mendelssohn, Reformers taught that reason was the tool for ascertaining religious truths and that universalism transcended parochial national creeds. Judaism, a religion of reason, transmitted a universal message. Unencumbered by outmoded ritual minutiae and ethnic trappings, modern Jews were the "priest people," whose mission was to spread the ethical teachings of the Bible to the rest of the world. Those essential beliefs were written into American Reform's official creed, the Pittsburgh Platform of 1885. Reform's theology strengthened American Jewish attachment to Enlightenment thought and gave that philosophy the stamp of religious legitimacy.[25]

According to Reformers, the debt that both Judaism and Americanism owed to the Enlightenment forged an ideological link between the two. Some rabbis suggested more than a common matrix. Samuel Hirsch, for example, stated that American freedom rested on the universal truths of Judaism, and Wise similarly wrote that liberty, "our [Jewish] birthright," was embraced by the United States. Reduce the Constitution and American laws to their primary elements, Wise's *Israelite* said, and you will find each in the laws of Moses. By emphasizing the similarities between Judaism and Americanism, Reform posited a debt that the United States owed to the Jewish tradition.[26] Christians vastly outnumbered Jews, but the nation was "Jewish" in its commitment to universal freedoms. Like the Protestant crusaders, Reformers too made religion, in this case Judaism, coterminous with America. Perhaps it was no accident that the formative years of Reform Judaism coincided with the heyday of American manifest destiny. Both, their separate adherents maintained, were fulfilling a mission aimed at expanding the area of freedom. In effect American Reformers constructed a symbiotic nexus: America drew from Judaism and Judaism, they said, was destined to reach its highest fulfillment in America. Following that design, Reformers rejected the concept of *galut* (exile) and substituted a faith in America for the traditional hope of a return to a Jewish homeland.[27]

Reform theology infused Jewish opposition to a Christian state with greater determination. The idea of a Christian state contradicted the belief in a Jewish mission to disseminate universal truths and, indeed, its basic assumption that Judaism was the font of ethical and moral wisdom. Reformers wore their religious faith with pride. Hardly would they leave unchallenged the notion in pre–Civil War America of the superiority of Protestantism over other religions.

Separation of church and state, the antidote to a Christian nation, served Reform's partisan purposes as well. It permitted the free development of their movement—the right to emend tradition and question

Orthodox authority, and the right to establish anti-Orthodox congregations—without the worry that government, as it often did in Europe, would
support the traditionalists. Religious equality resting on separation also
bore out Reform's denial that Jews in America were in exile. Moreover,
Reformers aimed to stem defection from the ranks of Judaism without
jeopardizing Jewish integration into the larger society. On their part they
facilitated acculturation and integration by defining Judaism solely in religious terms, but only if the United States met them halfway, by recognizing the equality of the minority faith, could they hope to realize their
aims.[28] It is not surprising, then, that Reform organizations pioneered in
the ongoing Jewish resistance to any union of church and state.

Theory and Tactics of Jewish Defense

In antebellum America, Jewish spokesmen reacted with suspicion to every
manifestation of Christianity in the public arena. Missionaries, official proclamations that employed Christian images, Sunday laws, and religion in
the classroom took on an importance as symbols of Jewish inequality that
transcended the specific situation. Since Jews reasoned that all were integral
components of a Christian state, the success of any one, limited as it might
be, hastened the fulfillment of the overall Protestant design. "Once open
the door to the most innocent admission of any especial prerogative," the
Occident warned, "and it will not be long before more and more concessions
will be asked, and at length demanded and exacted . . . by the power which
the majority has to pass laws."[29] Each issue became a significant entering
wedge in the contest for a religiously neutral state; it had to be fought as
if the war depended on the outcome of the single battle.

Between 1840 and 1860, as the German Jews rapidly acculturated,
Anglo-Jewish periodicals became the standard vehicle of communal defense. The most prominent journals of that period were the *Occident* (Philadelphia), the *Asmonean* (New York), and the *Israelite* (Cincinnati). The
primary artery of communication within the expanding community, they
purposely assumed the role of group defender.[30]

Hard as they tried, however, their efforts to quash the notion that
the United States was a Christian nation was at best an uphill fight. So
accustomed were Americans to calling the country Christian, the *Occident*
confessed in 1855, that it was impossible to eradicate the idea. To the
journal's chagrin, "most Jews" also admitted that it was a Christian
nation. One of those was the prominent Mordecai Manuel Noah, journalist, politician, and communal activist. Noah agreed that Christianity
was part of the law of the land, and he personally took the words "you
are a good Christian" as a compliment. He may have used the word
"Christian" interchangeably with "moral" and "civilized," but his support

of Protestant Bible societies and Sunday laws indicated a readiness to accept Christian sectarian usages to which Jews would have to accommodate. Unlike the journals, which stood squarely behind a government neutral to religion, Noah would have sacrificed principle in the hope of easing the acceptance of Jews into the larger society.[31]

Sensitivity to principle accounted for Jewish outrage over gubernatorial proclamations in the 1840s and 1850s that called, in Christian terms, for a religious day of Thanksgiving. To concerned individuals, the common practice designated Jews as a class apart, whose religion, or rather lack of Christian faith, denied them the right to celebrate with the rest of the nation. Since Jews had marked Thanksgiving in synagogues since the eighteenth century, regression under the new religious temper was all the more distressing. As Leeser bitterly commented on behalf of Pennsylvania's Jews:

> We contend that we are a part of the commonwealth; as much citizens as all others; equal in the eyes of the law, being so by the spirit *and* letter of the constitution. We contribute by our taxes and military service to the protection of the State, and hence there can exist no reason *why we should be forgotten* whenever the people of the commonwealth are called on for any service. We ask for no exemptions of the burdens because we are Jews; we recognise not in the Christians the prerogative to support and defend the republic; nor do we recognise in them the right of appropriating to themselves the whole protection of the laws, all the offices, all the immunities of freemen, much less the rights of being alone regarded as religious and God-fearing men.

The *Israelite*'s editor, Isaac Wise, echoed Leeser's sentiments. The *Israelite,* like the *Occident,* reviewed the annual holiday proclamations. When the editors took offense, they alerted the offender, who frequently apologized; at other times Jews boycotted the holiday.

A Thanksgiving episode in South Carolina revealed that Jewish sensitivity was sometimes matched by determined Christian purposes. In 1844 Governor James Hammond called on South Carolinians to observe Thanksgiving with special prayers to "God their Creator, and his Son Jesus Christ." When presented with a protest from one hundred irate Jews, Hammond defended his use of Christological imagery: "I have always thought it a settled matter that I lived in a Christian land . . . [among] a Christian people." The omission of a reference to Jesus would have offended Christians and contradicted customary usage. For their part, the protesters were displaying the "same scorn for Jesus Christ which instigated their ancestors to crucify him." Hammond pointedly asserted the constitutionality of his proclamation, which in no way penalized any who refused to observe the holiday. Indeed, he confirmed the Jewish fear that law alone was inadequate to protect their desired equality: "Whatever . . . the language of . . . [the] Constitution, I know that the civilization of the age is derived from

Christianity, that the institutions of this country are instinct with the same spirit, and that it pervades the laws of the State as it does the manners and I trust the hearts of our people." The governor's Jewish critics could respond only that the Constitution knew of neither Judaism nor Christianity and that the protection of minority rights was as important to a democracy as majority rule.[32]

The ongoing battle against a Christian state forced the Jewish periodicals to discuss the principles that supported their interpretation of religious freedom and equality. Time and again they reiterated beliefs which they shared in common: the essence of Americanism as distilled by the Founding Fathers stood in direct opposition to the idea of a Christian state; Jewish security required church–state separation; a single breach of separation was often an entering wedge that menaced the entire constitutional balance; a wronged Jewish minority had to assert its claims and look for redress, primarily by enlightening public opinion.

The journals never seriously considered the idea of nonpreferential aid to religion as a feasible alternative to government neutrality toward all religions. On one occasion the *Asmonean* suggested that Jewish children receive instruction in their faith through the public schools. And the *Occident* once argued that consistency demanded the same recognition of the Jewish Sabbath that was accorded the Christian Sunday. But for such isolated exceptions there was an instinctive awareness that equal accommodation of Judaism in an overwhelmingly homogeneous Protestant nation was totally unreal.[33]

As the journals grappled with current issues, omissions and contradictions came to light. For example, none of them entertained purist separationism. They employed the rhetoric of total divorce between church and state, but all three were happy to accept state aid to religious charitable institutions and to settle for exemptions for Jews in matters like religious oaths and Sunday laws. Another serious problem left unresolved was the need to reconcile antisecularism, on which they all agreed, with opposition to a Christian state. The *Occident,* in particular, endorsed the idea that the United States was a religious nation and that Americans were a religious people. Not only would rejection of a religious nation link Jews with the abhorrent classes of secularists and atheists, but a secularist society would have destroyed Rabbi Leeser's vision of a setting in which a vibrant Judaism could flourish. But how could a small minority uphold the virtues of a religious society if that society ignored all faiths but Christianity? In an era before the acceptance of religious pluralism, most Americans saw only two antithetical poles: Christianity and irreligion.

Nor did the *Occident* present a clear case on how Jews should defend themselves against religious crusades. It encouraged Jews to participate in the political process, but it cautioned its readers to maintain a low political profile and to avoid the appearance of a bloc vote. Leeser also advised

Jews against the lure of officeholding. On principle the disabilities that remained in North Carolina and New Hampshire called for eradication, but political ambition, he believed, fostered religious apathy. Leeser said that Jews should neither oppose the will of the majority nor form a separate political party. But whether and how they should seek out non-Jewish allies, approach public officials, use the ballot to express Jewish interests, or mount public "agitation" were topics that evoked contradictory responses. Thus, if Jews purposely avoided political visibility as Jews, they were left only with "enlightened public opinion," a weapon whose efficacy was at best questionable.

Leeser's message of political neutrality was echoed by the *Israelite,* but editor Wise arrived at the same stand by a different route. He shared neither Leeser's timidity nor his fear that political entanglement bred religious apathy. In the case of the Reformer, the logic of church–state separation was the determinant. Just as Jews criticized the injection of Christianity into American politics, so were they obliged to keep Jewish interests out of the political arena. For Jewish voters to act otherwise, or for rabbis to air their views on political issues when they criticized the Christian clergy for so doing, was both unprincipled and unpatriotic. The third periodical, the *Asmonean,* which was edited by a layman, Robert Lyon, argued differently. It commented freely and candidly on political issues, and it favored sustained involvement by Jews in politics. Undeterred by threats that such activity would generate anti-Semitism, it reasoned that full political equality could be achieved only in response to the political pressure of a united and organized Jewry.[34]

Officially American Jewish spokesman adopted the strictures on political neutrality almost unanimously. Over the years, neutrality generated self-imposed rules, for example, no Jewish political clubs, no "Jewish" vote, no support of Jewish candidates just because they were Jewish. Political neutrality, however, was unnatural for the individual Jew and unreal in the American system of contending factions. Since rigid neutrality ignored the immediate interests of the Jewish group—nativist movements, rights for foreign Jews, threats to the separation of church and state—it was often honored in the breach.[35] The wonder is that the very idea, which bifurcated the Jewish world into American-or-public and Jewish-or-private orbits, could take root and last well into the twentieth century. Not until American Jews admitted openly that their collective interests were as legitimate as those of other groups could aspects of the Christian-state idea be effectively countered in the political arena.

Nativism before the Civil War focused its attack on Catholics and on the hordes of newly arrived Irish and German immigrants. An offshoot of the Protestant crusade, it proved, as Robert Handy wrote, that "the earnest professions of concern for freedom made by the evangelicals could sound rather hollow." It proved, too, that the theme of a Christian commonwealth was a euphemism for Protestantism, and that the vision of a homogeneous religious people, in its extremist form, openly repudiated religious equality. Although Jews were not specifically targeted, the popularity of the American, or Know-Nothing, party boded ill for them also. The nativists proposed restrictions on foreigners as well as disabilities on Catholics; the Know-Nothing platform of 1855 affirmed that Christianity was "an element of our political system."[36]

The response of the Jewish community was divided. Arguing on grounds of constitutional principle and Jewish self-interest, the three major journals as well as individual Jews spoke out publicly against the nativists. But the Know-Nothings mustered a surprising degree of Jewish support. Historical memories of Catholic oppression embittered many; the church represented the Jewish badge, the excesses of the Crusaders, and the Inquisition. Isaac Wise himself once wrote that "Catholicism is no religion but a misfortune to mankind." Other Jews may have imbibed anticlericalism in Europe or have hoped that identification with the regnant Protestants would secure their own positions. Jews also differed on whether they, as Jews, should take an open political stand on the nativist issue. The *Asmonean* actively campaigned against the Know-Nothing party from 1854 through the presidential election of 1856; Wise and Leeser refused to advise their readers to unite against the "religious fanatics." Both argued that Jews would fare equally ill under Protestant or Catholic domination and that the wiser course was to steer clear of Protestant–Catholic strife.[37]

Although it may have been logical for the two religious minorities, Jewish and Catholic, to unite against the incursions of a dominant Protestantism, the Jews were as yet unprepared to seek out formal alliances with any non-Jewish group, least of all with the Catholics. Indeed, their deeply embedded animosity against Catholics and Catholicism rose significantly at the end of the same decade in the wake of the famous Mortara affair.[38]

The failure of American Jews to secure the government's intercession in the Mortara case hastened the establishment of the Board of Delegates of American Israelites (BDAI). The first nonrabbinical attempt at permanent unity, the board was founded by a small number of congregations to serve the internal needs of the community and to defend the rights of American and foreign Jews. As an independent agency (1859–78) the BDAI failed to unite the Jewish community. Synagogues jealous of their autonomy and divisiveness between the Orthodox and Reform prevented its development into a powerful national body. Institutionalized defense also troubled some Jews. The very idea of a protective agency might seemingly contradict Jewish protestations of political neutrality or Jewish faith in the United States. Isaac Wise, whose disaffection stemmed from a fear that Orthodox congregations would use the agency to block Reform, rationalized that the "constitution and the spirit of liberty" were adequate guardians. Temple Emanu-El of New York (Reform) even suggested that the existence of a board could evoke the charge that Jews had created a state within the state.[39]

From its inception the board kept close watch on Jewish disabilities of a religious nature, such as Sunday laws, North Carolina's test oath, and the chaplaincy issue in the Civil War. During its first twenty years it neither put a distinctive mark on American Jewish defense nor, for that matter, dislodged the Anglo-Jewish periodicals from their self-assumed position as the primary defenders of Jewish rights. Ultimately, in 1878 the BDAI was absorbed by Reform's Union of American Hebrew Congregations.[40]

Jews could well have used a stronger national agency in their campaign again America's treaty with Switzerland.[41] A commercial treaty negotiated by the two countries in 1850 explicitly stated that "Christians alone are entitled to the enjoyment of privileges guaranteed by the present Article in the Swiss Cantons." Under the Swiss constitution, only Christians were guaranteed religious freedom; moreover, the cantons had the right, which some put to use, of refusing entry and commercial privileges to foreign Jews. Since Switzerland's federal government was powerless to countermand cantonal regulations, the United States could ignore the anti-Jewish regulations or forget about a treaty. To the chagrin of American Jews, their government chose the first option and accepted the discriminatory draft treaty.

Jews focused not on the few who might be affected by the actual provision but on the principles involved. The episode seemingly belied their faith in the spirit of the national government, which, as they were fond of affirming, defended religious equality more zealously than the states. Fundamental law as well as spirit had been flouted; as one Jew argued to Secretary of State Daniel Webster, the recognition of distinctions among religions was tantamount to a prohibition of free exercise of religion and hence a violation of the First Amendment. Furthermore, the government's consent to a treaty that distinguished between Christians and Jews meant that the United States, like the prejudiced country itself, thought of them first as Jews rather than as equal American citizens. Since the treaty implied that the country recognized a "dominant or superior religion," it was but a further example of the success of the Christian-state idea.

A campaign against ratification was launched by Sigismund Waterman, a New York physician prominent in communal affairs, and abetted by the *Asmonean*. Strong letters of protest to influential political leaders, and a memorial to the Senate from "Importers, Merchants, and others" of New York City, denounced the "bartering away" of Jewish equality.[42] As a result, the treaty, with the objectionable clause removed, was returned to Switzerland. In 1855, however, the government formally ratified a revised treaty. This version deleted references to exclusively Christian privileges, but it provided that rights of domicile and commerce obtained only where they did not conflict with cantonal law. Semantics aside, the government still accepted discrimination against Jews.

The passage of the treaty apparently went unnoticed by most Jews, but protests sparked anew when the canton of Neuchâtel expelled an American Jewish merchant. In 1857, at meetings in various cities of the East, Midwest, and South, Jews, sometimes joined by Christians, loudly denounced the treaty. We were betrayed, some lamented, perhaps, as Leeser explained, because the government did not think us important enough. Amid the drives for petitions and for delegations to the president, the journals worked incessantly to sustain effective opposition. The *Asmonean* boldly counseled the Jews to shed inhibitions about using their numbers, wealth, and commercial position to proper advantage. The *Israelite* pushed vigorously for loud and concerted public agitation against a treaty that violated the Constitution and to which only "slaves and cowards" would submit. As in 1851, the protesters focused on the abridgment of Jewish equality in violation of the spirit if not the letter of the Constitution. Some critics charged that by permitting Switzerland to screen American citizens on grounds of religion, the federal government was acceding to a test oath expressly forbidden by Article VI of the Constitution. The logic of the protest demanded that the treaty be abrogated or at least its objectionable clause nullified.

Most Jews refrained from making the issue a partisan one. Timidity and a reluctance to inject Jewish interests into politics restrained the others. They preferred to describe the matter as American and nonsectarian. Jewish leaders also faulted their coreligionists for ignoring events immediately preceding ratification. Leeser, a traditionalist, blamed the Reformers for lulling the community into false security when Jewish rights, even in America, were in danger. "We are in *Galuth,*" he wrote despairingly. "We have our theoretical rights, but practically they are dependent on the will of those who have numbers on their side; and if we make all the noise in the world, and brag aloud after our heart's content, *we are yet strangers* in stranger lands."

In October 1857 a national convention—a first in American Jewish defense—was called to discuss the treaty. A breakdown in communication and severe internal bickering prevented the emergence of any body that could really be called representative of American Jewry, but the truncated assembly, consisting of Jews from only four states, drew up a memorial to be presented to the president. It said in part:

> This government disclaiming all religious distinction as to the political rights of its citizens at home cannot consistently recognize such distinction

abroad. . . . The treaty in question has clearly failed in that object . . .
declaring us unworthy to participate in the rights of our fellow citizens,
on account of our professing the Israelitish religion.[43]

Buchanan responded graciously and advised the minister to Switzerland,
Theodore S. Fay, to work for the removal of the discriminatory clause.
Accordingly, Fay, who independently supported the Jewish demands,
wrote a lengthy note to the Swiss government in opposition to Jewish
disabilities.

Although Minister Fay confidently expected the removal of restrictions,
American Jews were only partially comforted. Their primary goal—to wrest
an admission from their own government that it would not sanction discrimination against American citizens—had been sidetracked. To their
further dismay, in 1860 the government entered into a treaty with China
which, while establishing the right of all American citizens to residential
and commercial privileges, singled out the Christian religion for protection.
In its first report the BDAI noted almost wistfully that equal protection
for Jews had "up to this time, been very feebly recognized by the treaty-
making power." Six years later the board announced that the Swiss
restrictions had been lifted, but the humiliation at the hands of the government continued to rankle. Half a century after Waterman's initial protest, one young Jewish lawyer, who wrote a historical account of the Swiss
affair, concluded: "It was demonstrated to us that while we were American
citizens, our citizenship was distinctly qualified—we were and we are
American-Jewish citizens, at least as far as our international rights were
and are concerned."

Common Law and Sunday Legislation

Local ordinances and state laws that embodied a religious purpose often
reached the courts for final resolution. Although Jewish spokesmen were
highly sensitive to breaches of the wall of separation, some were reluctant
to become involved in legal cases. Leeser of the *Occident* stated that court
cases should be avoided; both time-consuming and costly, they subjected
the plaintiff to public criticism. Besides, judges were of the popular majority and subject to the same weaknesses and pressures that affected
legislators. It was more than likely that judges would uphold what was
unjust and unconstitutional and would perpetuate sectarian privileges. A
minority, therefore, did better to keep a watchful eye on the lawmakers
than to rely for its security upon the judiciary.[44]

Since judges frequently affirmed that Christianity was part of the common law of the land, they raised yet another obstacle to Jewish faith in
the courts. The common law doctrine, which was invoked to validate,

among other things, restrictions on non-Christian witnesses or jurors and laws against blasphemy and the desecration of the Christian Sabbath, rested on English usage. American civil libertarians contested it; Jefferson called it "a conspiracy . . . between Church and State." Nevertheless, the doctrine lived on, underwritten in numerous judicial decisions. All societies, those courts explained, required religious foundations for preserving social morality and the public good. Christianity, the religion of the settlers of the country, provided just that foundation and "cement" for American institutions. Recognized by the people, legislatures, and courts, the common law doctrine brought stability, well-being, and liberty. Contrarily, to deny it would result in "barren soil upon which no flower ever bloomed." One state court summarized the doctrine as a fundamental fact of American life: "We are a Christian people . . . imbued with the sentiments and principles of Christianity; and we cannot be imbued with them, and yet prevent them from . . . influencing . . . all our social institutions, customs, and relations."

On one essential point the judges qualified the British meaning. As one state judge said in 1824, "not Christianity with an established Church, and tithes and spiritual courts, but Christianity with liberty of conscience to all men." Indeed, the government could not shape opinions or beliefs, and non-Christians had the right to organize their own churches and worship as they pleased. Nor did the maxim breach the wall of separation, because no religious establishment, but rather the voluntary preferences of the people, was involved. Holding fast on the one hand to the common law doctrine and on the other to the ideas of no establishment and liberty of conscience, the judges were proclaiming that Christianity, or a general Protestantism (which was in fact the reality of American society), was sanctioned by law.[45]

The result fell short of religious equality for non-Protestants and particularly for non-Christians. If Christianity was part of the common law, unobstructed by the content and spirit of the federal and state constitutions, all other faiths were automatically relegated to an inferior position. Their status and rights were determined in effect by Christian bounty. The antithesis of religious equality, the common law maxim haunted American Jews into the twentieth century.

Prominent defenders of the doctrine openly denied the equality of religious. When validating a prohibition on blasphemy, Chancellor James Kent of New York stated flatly that other religions did not deserve similar protection: "We are a christian people, and the morality of the country is deeply engrafted upon christianity and not upon the doctrines or worship of [non-Christian] imposters." In a famous Sunday law case of 1861, the Appellate Court of New York reiterated Kent's views. It said that Christianity was part of the common law of the state, entitling that religion and its precepts to respect and protection "as the acknowledged religion of the people."[46]

Kent's contemporary, Justice Joseph Story of the Supreme Court, also affirmed that Christianity was part of the common law. In his famous *Commentaries on the Constitution,* Story explicitly disavowed the separation of church and state. He wrote that in a Christian country the right of the government to interfere in matters of religion would hardly be contested by those who believed that religion and morality were intimately linked with the well-being of the state. The justice agreed that freedom of conscience and worship was inviolate, but the authors of the First Amendment never intended to level all religions. "The real object of the amendment was, not to countenance, much less to advance Mahometanism, or Judaism, or infidelity, by prostrating Christianity; but to exclude all rivalry among Christian sects, and to prevent any national ecclesiastical establishment, which should give to an hierarchy the exclusive patronage of the national government."[47]

In an early case that reached the Supreme Court Story defended nonpreferential aid by government to churches. Some years later, in the case of one Stephen Girard, whose bequest for a school in Philadelphia carried the stipulation that no clergyman be allowed to enter the premises, the justice affirmed that Christianity was part of the common law of Pennsylvania. Although he found that Girard's will did not run afoul of that law, he intimated that his decision would have been different had the bequest been "for the establishment of a school or college, for the propagation of Judaism, or Deism, or any other form of infidelity . . . in a Christian country." The Supreme Court had not officially recognized Christianity as the law of the land, but Story's opinion, often cited by defenders of the common law maxim, well suited the antebellum clamor for a Christian commonwealth.[48]

The theory of Christianity's superiority under the common law doctrine did not engage Jews until it was applied to specific cases. One type of Jewish disability concerned their status as witnesses. The renowned jurist and champion of common law, Sir Edward Coke, had ruled in the early seventeenth century that "Jews are perpetual enemies" who, like other infidels, were unworthy of belief and without the capacity to sue or testify in an English court. Although those disabilities were discarded upon the readmission of Jews into England during the Cromwellian era, traces of barriers against Jewish witnesses, usually in the form of Christian oaths, lingered on in the British colonies and the United States. In colonial New York, for example, the assembly ruled in 1737 that evidence presented by a Jew was inadmissible, and religious competency of witnesses remained an issue until specifically repudiated by the revised state constitution of 1846. Even then, judges in various ways upheld the common law belief that only a Christian was a competent or credible witness. In Georgia, the question of whether lack of faith in Jesus permitted the exclusion of testimony offered by a Jew arose as late as 1871.[49] A survey of state and federal cases at the end of the century disclosed that the issue involved more than Christian versus non-Christian or believer versus atheist; courts also inquired as to whether witnesses believed in a future state of divine rewards and punishments.[50]

A curious case involving the oath to be taken by Jews arose in New York. There, the special form of swearing in a Jewish witness—on the Hebrew Bible and his head covered—was challenged by the prisoner's counsel. Garbled testimony from one Jew had suggested that some Jews employed a more stringent form, "with a skein of silk about the arm, and other ceremonies." The counsel's request for that stricter form was overruled, but in this as in other cases the basic requirement for a special Jewish oath remained unquestioned. Some thought that the form of the oath became an issue especially in cases where attorneys sought to discredit a Jewish witness's testimony.[51]

Laws on Sunday observance, also sanctioned by common law, were of far greater concern. The Sunday laws of the British colonists—some mandating church attendance, forbidding travel, curbing labor and trade, and limiting recreation—set the tradition for the new republic. Vermont's constitution even recognized Sunday in its declaration of rights, advising every Christian denomination "to observe the Sabbath or Lord's day." Christian reformers of the antebellum years crusaded vigorously for renewed dedication to the Calvinist form of Sabbath observance and for the aid of local and state law. Many looked upon Sunday as the keystone in the master plan for a Christian commonwealth; nonobservance, it was said, would render Christianity impotent. Their efforts were well received by state courts. Some judges called Sunday laws, which aimed at securing an undisturbed day of worship, aids to the enjoyment of the rights of conscience. Other decisions that validated the regulations on the grounds of common law or "historical" evidence often revealed the popular desire for a culturally homogeneous society. Thus, a court in Missouri reasoned that the state constitution was written by and intended for Christians of a common background and not for "strangers collected from all quarters of the globe, each with a religion of his own, bound by no previous social ties, nor sympathizing in any common reminiscences of the past."[52]

In the 1820s religious crusaders undertook a vigorous campaign to compel the federal government to ban the transportation of mail on Sundays. Success would have meant that the commitment of the federal government to the principle of separation, heretofore stronger than that of the states, was not unshakable. The efforts of the campaigners released a flurry of petitions to Congress, but congressional committees decided against the petitioners. Jews loudly applauded the committee reports of Senator Richard Johnson, later a congressman. His ardent plea on behalf of broad separation contained specific references to the Jews. He demanded not religious toleration but religious rights, rights which could not be taken away from any group by the government. He stated that the Jews, whose consciences were as sacred under the Constitution as those of Christians, were entitled to the equal protection of the laws, and their equality was flouted by Sunday laws. The Sunday law crusade simmered on, but not until the 1880s was a widespread effort for federal regulation renewed.[53]

Adverse effects of the laws, both in principle and in operation, on Jews and nonbelievers failed to restrain the Sunday crusaders. As early as 1788, when the New York Assembly debated a law that forbade travel, labor, and forms of recreation on Sunday, Assemblyman Egbert Benson spoke up for the minority. He said that the measure, in violation of the New York constitution, was tantamount to taxing a Jew who observed the Sabbath "one sixth part of his time." Benson, who stressed the idea of religious equality, thought that exemptions were insufficient to protect Jewish rights. The supporters of the bill maintained, however, that it did not compel non-Christians to worship on Sunday and that the state constitution only intended to guarantee freedom of conscience. "The day which the Christian Church has in all ages observed, and doth still observe, . . . is the day which is the will of Christ we should observe as our Christian Sabbath."[54]

Explained as a natural outgrowth of Christian behavior, Sunday laws belied protestations of voluntarism. Where other religiously supported reform movements gave Jews the option to remain aloof, laws permitted few choices. The religious base of the laws also flouted a broad interpretation of separation. Even if Sabbatarians were exempted from the restrictions—a less than satisfactory solution for those who preferred to avoid a group identity setting them apart from other Americans—the very act of exemption overstepped separation. In addition, Sunday laws were punitive since they deprived observant Jews, most of whom were merchants and shopkeepers, of two days of work. Exemptions did not completely mitigate the economic hardships; some lost out where Sunday generally became a slow business day, and others, sensitive to the opinion of their neighbors, agreed to keep closed on Sunday. These points were raised constantly by the Anglo-Jewish press, but the supporters of Sunday laws brushed aside such arguments. "Inconveniences" suffered by Jews and other Sabbatarians could hardly challenge the legitimacy of the laws themselves.[55]

Leading Jewish spokesmen understood that Sunday laws were an integral component of the Christian-state idea, of the same cloth as religiously worded Thanksgiving proclamations and religion in the public schools. Mordecai Noah argued that Jews would behave similarly in a Jewish state, and Robert Lyon of the *Asmonean* reasoned that violators of the Jewish Sabbath forfeited their right to exemptions, but Jews like Leeser and Wise found Sunday laws particularly odious because they abridged Jewish equality. Indeed, Judaism was under attack, just as Jews were. Not only might Jews be enticed for economic reasons and concern about public opinion to desecrate the Jewish Sabbath, but the very recognition of the Christian day, without the equivalent of "Saturday" laws, proclaimed that Judaism and its practices were less than equal. Leeser echoed Benson of New York when he insisted on unqualified equality: "Why claim that [a Christian] conscience should be more guarded than ours? . . . Who protects our faith and its practices?"[56]

Leeser called Sunday laws "an infringement on natural right," a violation of religious liberty, and an entering wedge by the Christian-staters—logically akin to forced baptism—working to tighten the coercive yoke of Protestantism. Isaac Wise ranted: "We are slaves if we stand this outrage [Sunday laws], if we thus allow priest-ridden demagogues to deprive us of our rights." The Jewish journals closely monitored developments in various states, reprinting statements in favor of separationism by Christian individuals or newspapers, and both the *Occident* and the *Israelite* counseled Jewish resistance. Rhetoric notwithstanding, the rabbis cautiously limited resistance to constitutional means, such as petitions, elections, and public enlightenment. Moreover, despite the serious talk of separation and equality, Jewish leaders compromised principle and realistically settled for exemptions.[57]

In 1859 an anti–Sunday law petition joined Jews of New York City with Seventh-Day Baptists, Germans, and Yankees. Purposely emphasizing the range of views regarding the observance of Sunday, the petitioners argued against the efforts of the New York Sabbath Committee to obtain strict enforcement of the various Sunday laws, which had fallen into disuse. The petitioners injected a new note of ethnic and religious pluralism in their demand for religious equality: "This is not . . . a Jewish nation, nor a Greek; it is not Christian nor Mahomedan. Its broad banner bears a welcome to men of every clime, and of every faith, and its blood-cemented foundations have engraved upon them, in ineffaceable characters, the character and bond of *perfect religious freedom and equality* FOR ALL, WITHOUT DISCRIMINATION OR PREFERENCE." A state committee which reviewed the arguments of both sides agreed, however, with the Sunday protagonists. Its report emphatically rejected the pluralistic argument. Since the masses of the people as well as the courts regarded Christianity as the "prevailing" religion, the principles and practices of the Christian society had to be enforced. Religious liberty notwithstanding, the "smallest portion of the community" could not ask the majority to abandon the enforcement of Sunday laws. A New York statute of 1860 held fast to the recognition of Christianity and a Christian Sabbath. It was argued that exemptions for observant Jews and other Sabbatarians adequately shielded their rights.[58]

As the movement for the strict observance of Sunday gained strength, increasing numbers of Sabbatarians who violated the laws were haled before city magistrates and state courts. An early, albeit incomplete compilation of court cases involving Jews listed nineteen cases for the period of 1793 to 1860. Nine concerned Sunday laws, eight where Jews were indicted for breaking the law and one where the court considered the validity of an award of arbitration made by Jews on a Sunday. (The last afforded the spectacle of a Sabbath-observing Jew who sued other Jews on the basis of a Christian statute.) Four of the nineteen recorded cases dealt with the obverse of the Sunday coin, claims of Sabbath-observing Jews that they be exempted from appearance in court or court orders served on Saturday. It is unlikely that Jews were goaded by the Sunday laws into a drive to establish the legal equality of their own Sabbath. The few who made that attempt generally failed, and it became clear early on that equality with respect to Sunday laws could be achieved only with their repeal.[59]

In the two decades before the Civil War, Sunday laws were a burning issue for the vigilant *Occident*. From correspondents in various states Leeser obtained copies of judicial opinions and newspaper articles on the cases. The material usually served as a point of departure for the editor to illustrate the menace of the Christian-state idea and the yet fragile nature of religious equality. He fretted over breaches of the wall of separation, but since the repeal of Sunday laws appeared unattainable, he welcomed exemptions for Jews. At the same time he pleaded with his readers not to bow to the logic of the laws or public opinion by desecrating the Jewish Sabbath. On both levels—modification of the laws and Jewish traditional Sabbath observance—his was often a losing battle.[60]

An early case which received extensive coverage by the *Occident* involved a Charleston Jew, Solomon Benjamin, who violated a municipal ordinance by selling a pair of gloves on Sunday. His defense rested on the guarantee of "free exercise and enjoyment of religious profession and worship, without discrimination or preference" in the state constitution. Also claiming that he was enjoined by the Decalogue to work six days a week, Benjamin maintained that a law limiting a Jew's labor to five days impinged upon his religion.[61] The city magistrate found for Benjamin, but a unanimous state court overturned the decision.

Jews were more put out by the court's reasoning than by the verdict itself. According to Judge John O'Neale, Christianity was not only part of the common law of South Carolina but it was the source and standard of all morality. The very right of religious freedom derived from Christian mercy and love. In no way did the Sunday law abridge religious freedom, for Jews were not compelled to desecrate their Sabbath or to worship on Sunday. (The claim that divine commandment required six days of work was summarily dismissed.) Nor did the law show a preference for any religion; the constitution recognized citizens, not Christians and Jews, and the law was a police regulation which applied to all citizens. The Jews abstained from business on Saturday because of their religious teachings and not the secular law, but if Jews wanted the benefits of American life, of which religious freedom was one, they had to abide by the community's decision to observe a different day of rest.

Readers of O'Neale's decision in the *Occident* protested, vehemently denouncing the judge's condescension to Jews—the implication that religious freedom was theirs not by right but as a gift from Christianity, and the studied omission of Judaism as the source of morality. One irate Jew wrote: "I call upon Judge O'Neal [*sic*] to point out one moral precept in the Christian's New Testament, which is not found in the Bible of the Jew. Take from the Christian *our* moral law, *our* standard of morals, and he will, indeed, be enveloped in thick darkness." The judge later disclaimed any intention of snubbing the Old Testament, but by then the community was aroused. The decision confirmed Isaac Leeser's fears about reliance on courts, which, he charged, often followed personal bias and public opinion at the expense of what was right.[62]

Barely had the flurry over the O'Neale decision subsided when the *Occident,* in a series of articles entitled "Political Inequality," apprised its readers of a Sunday case in Pennsylvania. The defendant in *Specht* v. *Commonwealth* was a Seventh-Day Baptist, but the issues and arguments paralleled those of the Jewish cases. Although the two religious minorities did not actively cooperate, they shared an awareness of each other's activities with respect to Sunday laws. The decision in *Specht,* where a farmer was charged with laboring on Sunday in violation of a 1794 statute, also linked Jews specifically with Christian Sabbatarians.

Judge Thomas Bell of the state's supreme court upheld Specht's conviction. The Sunday law was a civil or police regulation, enacted for the well-being of the community; because the majority were Christians the legislature had selected Sunday as the day of rest. Inconveniences resulting for Jews and other Sabbatarians proved neither the law's unconstitutionality nor a conferral of a superior status on Sunday observers. Freedom of belief remained inviolate; dissenters were not forced to adopt the beliefs of the majority or to desecrate their own day of rest. One of Bell's colleagues on the bench justified the Sunday law precisely because it guarded the Christian Sabbath in a Christian state from "profanation." In an opinion which, ironically, resembled Leeser's argument that the purpose and language of the law were religious, he questioned the right of the legislature to call for cessation of labor purely on secular grounds.[63]

Specht, like the *Benjamin* case, underscored a predicament of the Sunday law opponents. Even if a decision denounced legislation of a religious nature, the simultaneous legitimation of such laws on grounds of police power made them no less objectionable. And when police power joined with a Christian rationale, as in both cases, the combination was unbeatable. In light of the courts' reliance on police power, itself a fluid category, American Jews were forced to broaden their attack on Sunday laws. Uncomfortable as it was for an accommodationist minority to challenge the principle of legislative power, they had to grapple with the issue of Sunday as a *civil* day of rest. They could argue, as did one petition of Richmond's Jews, that a police regulation of Sunday observance was inappropriate, different from laws on homicide and incest where infractions blatantly subverted society. They could also insist, the way Leeser did, that the use of police power was but a subterfuge for hiding religious motives, that the ostensible protection of the poor laborer was in reality a victory for the Protestant churches. Both ways, however, weakened a defense predicated solely on lofty principles of fundamental law. In the courts the use of police power to validate Sunday observance steadily increased. According to one study, 25 percent of Sunday decisions between 1817 and 1887 offered a Christian rationale, a percentage which dropped to less than 10 between 1888 and 1920.[64]

Pennsylvania's law allowed for no exemptions, but even in Ohio, where exemptions were permitted, Jews appeared in litigation. Shortly before the *Benjamin* decision, one Jacob Rice of Cincinnati was fined for trading under an ordinance that forbade common labor on Sunday. Since the ordinance specifically exempted Sabbath observers, the matter rested on the definition of the word "common." Rice's Christian attorneys ventured further, claiming that a law which set limits on Sunday activity violated religious convictions. Their reasoning seemed to presage a challenge to the very idea of Sunday laws, but the attorneys hastily retreated. They did not seek to weaken the existing legislation, they explained; they sought only to ensure Christian respect for the rights of others. Rice's conviction was overturned, but the Sunday law, albeit with a broader exemption, stood. The *Occident* applauded the decision, since exemption, admittedly a far cry from religious equality, could not be taken for granted. A second Ohio case (1858), however, more narrowly construed the exemption provision. The fine imposed on a Jewish ice-dealer was upheld by the court on the grounds that he did not "conscientiously" observe the Jewish Sabbath. At this Leeser exploded: "We require not ordinary law-judges to vindicate our religion." Just as it was not a republican government's business to enforce Sunday laws, so it was "no one's business . . . whether we Israelites keep Sabbath or not."[65]

At the same time Leeser was somewhat mollified by the outcome of the *Newman* case in California, the only one before the Civil War where a court ruled a Sunday law unconstitutional on grounds of religious liberty. The decision overturned the conviction of a Jewish peddler of Sacramento for selling clothes on Sunday. Newman's defense was argued by a Jew and former judge, Solomon Heydenfeldt, who contended that Sunday laws were religious institutions that gave preference to one sect. Chief Justice David Terry, who wrote for the court, agreed. He elaborated on the meaning of religious liberty, insisting that in the larger sense it meant "a complete separation between Church and State, and a perfect equality without distinction between all religious sects." The recognition of one form of Sabbath in a community of various religious denominations constituted a breach of that equality and a preference for one faith. Even as a civil regulation the law would be invalid, Terry added, for the legislature could not enforce compulsory abstinence from labor.

The assault on both foundations of Sunday laws, Christianity and police power, was marred by the dissenting opinion of Justice Stephen Field. The latter argued at length on the civil nature of the enactment and on the powerlessness of the courts to pass upon the wisdom of such legislation. He denied the religious character of the statute; at most it inflicted only inconveniences on non-Christians. That Field's rather than Terry's opinion more accurately reflected the public mood was proved three years later when California's highest court reversed the *Newman* decision. He was not surprised, Leeser said, for the second decision was in keeping with other constitutional violations that aimed to make Christianity "the religion of the law." He for one would continue his repeated attacks, at least "while the liberty of complaining . . . has not been taken from us" by those "who claim all right in the Christian state which they fancy to be theirs."[66]

3

The Christian Agenda

War and a Christian Amendment

At the outbreak of the Civil War geography dictated loyalty: Jews, like their countrymen, fought for the Union or the Confederacy in the field and on the home front. During the war years, however, a wave of Judaeophobia swept both the North and South. An upsurge in religious passion accompanying the national crisis reinforced the age-old negative stereotypes of the Jews—Christ killers, accursed and stiff-necked people, unscrupulous money changers, aliens, and traitors. Harassment and vilification culminated in General Grant's notorious Order No. 11, which in December 1862 expelled Jews "as a class" from the military department of Tennessee. A rare example of official discrimination aimed openly and exclusively against Jews, the order was readily accepted by Americans. The explanation, as a bitter Isaac Leeser found, lay in naked Christian prejudice: "The parties threatened with such ill-usage were not Christians, not even negroes, nothing but Jews! . . . and those, every one knows, are enemies of Christ and his apostles."[1]

Although Lincoln quickly revoked the order, his administration was guilty of other slights against the Jews. One stemmed from an executive order which, studded with references to Christian servicemen and "a Christian people," called for Sunday observance in the armed forces. To concerned Jews it represented a breach of separation and, since no provision was made for the Jewish soldiers and their Sabbath, a violation of religious equality. Another threat to equality was Congress's failure to provide for Jewish chaplains. A conscious omission, it was challenged by Representative Clement Vallandigham on the floor of the House as a breach of the establishment clause of the First Amendment. "This is not a 'Christian *Government,*' " he said, "nor a Government which has any connection with any one form of religion in preference to any other form." A spirited public exchange ensued. While some Protestant groups shuddered at the thought of blasphemers as chaplains, the Board of Delegates of American Israelites (BDAI) contended that the act established a religious test for a federal office and thereby violated both Article VI of the Constitution and the First Amendment. Only after the board intervened with Congress and the president was the chaplaincy law revised.[2]

Religious passions kindled during the war years fired visions of apocalypse and millennium. Both Northerners and Southerners put God center stage and read the wartime struggles in religious terms. Some devout northern Protestants explained that God was wreaking his vengeance upon a nation whose Constitution ignored his succor and indeed his very existence. Their solution: to engraft Christianity upon the Constitution. To be sure, regrets at the omission of references to the Almighty had been voiced at the first ratifying conventions and were revived periodically by individual crusaders. But only when the nation faced its most serious ordeal did the sentiment assume significant proportions.[3]

Shortly after Lincoln's election, Senator Charles Sumner introduced a memorial from a Reformed Presbyterian synod in Pennsylvania that called for a constitutional amendment acknowledging the authority of Christ and the recognition of the paramount obligations of a divine law. Two years later representatives of eleven Protestant sects met in Xenia, Ohio, and launched what ultimately became a national movement to secure a religious amendment. Precisely because the Constitution ignored God, one position paper explained, a calamity had befallen the nation. In January 1864 the movement, under the name of National Association to Secure the Religious Amendment to the Constitution, formulated a petition to Congress. The sponsors asked that the preamble to the Constitution begin with the words: "We, the people of the United States, humbly acknowledging Almighty God as the source of all authority and power in civil government, the Lord Jesus Christ as the Ruler among the nations, his revealed will as the supreme law of the land, in order to constitute a Christian government. . . . " Endorsing appropriate changes in the body of the Constitution to conform to the revised preamble, they made short shrift of equality for non-Christians. At the same time, however, since they upheld liberty of conscience, they denied that they sought a union between church and state.[4]

Lincoln adroitly withheld his support, and so did Congress. A second and almost identical memorial from the Presbytery of Cincinnati railed further against an "atheistical" Constitution and for a Christian nation. But despite the seeming groundswell of enthusiasm, Congress buried the petitions. Senator Lyman Trumbull reported in March 1865 that the Senate Judiciary Committee had not technically voted against the recognition of God in the Constitution but merely asked to be discharged from consideration of memorials both for and against the proposal. The committee thought a religious amendment was unnecessary and injudicious, "at this time, at any rate." Besides, they said, the Constitution already recognized the existence of God; it was assumed in the clause that required oaths of officials and in the religion clauses of the First Amendment.[5]

The initial rebuff failed to deter the petitioners. From 1863 to 1869—

the first phase of the movement—the crusaders for a religious amendment held regional meetings and annual conventions. From the outset the cause attracted a good number of respected laymen and clergymen, decent men who could not be read off as extremists. Concomitantly, the crusaders launched an effective public relations drive through pulpits, periodicals, public meetings, and their own long-lived journal, the *Christian Statesman*. For a few years the theme of divine punishment for a godless Constitution persisted, but the war's end led the organization to amend its rhetoric and expand its horizons. By 1866 it had broadened its purpose to include religious amendments in state constitutions.[6]

A call for a national convention in 1869 revealed a further expansion of aims. It cited those reprehensible views "which are now struggling for a baneful ascendancy in State and national politics: such as, That civil government is only a social compact; That it exists only for secular and material, not for moral ends; That Sabbath laws are unconstitutional; and that the Bible must be excluded from our Public Schools." Only a constitutional amendment affirming that the United States was a Christian nation whose fundamental law was Christian law could remedy the deplorable state of affairs.[7] By carving out multiple and open-ended objectives, the crusaders for a religious amendment stood to augment their popular following at the same time that they ensured the movement's survival.

Although the actual chances for a religious amendment were very slim, the attempt reflected in extremist form the defensive posture of Protestantism in the last third of the nineteenth century. Sober Americans of many stripes wondered if and how a homogeneous Protestant America could withstand the challenges of rapid secularization, a by-product of urbanization and industrialization, and of the massive influx of non-Protestant immigrants. Those challenges, or "perils" in popular parlance,[8] drove many to the side of organizations that worked actively at maintaining the Protestant character and institutions of the country. The amendment movement was the most radical, but the premises of two simultaneous campaigns, for Sunday observance and for religion in the public schools, were identical. In one fashion or another all three strove for the preservation of a Christian nation.

The years that later historians called the critical period in American religion constituted a critical period for postbellum American Jewry. Frightened by the major threats to church–state separation, Jews also felt the grip of a pervasive social anti-Semitism. In their view both developments rested on a common base: a militant and aggressive Christianity. Responses, however, varied. Whereas timidity in the face of prejudice caused many to keep a low profile, others were led to a stricter separationist line on behalf of religious equality.

Concerned Jewish leaders carefully monitored the efforts to Christianize the Constitution. Still the principal defenders of Jewish rights, the Anglo-Jewish periodicals sensed the urgency of the Christian crusade, which was both all-encompassing and avowedly political. Isaac Leeser, who was among the most outspoken from the beginning, offered his readers an incisive analysis of how the war had generated religious passion as well as *"rishuth"* (the Hebrew word for wickedness, used by German Jews for anti-Semitism). A people understandably depressed by the war sought comfort and readily turned to legislators for solutions. The advocates of an amendment capitalized on that sentiment, and building on the political successes of the antebellum reform crusades—temperance, Sunday laws, abolition—they fed their "lust for dominion" by preparing to Christianize the law of the land. The rabbi warned of the movement's seriousness, for now a union of several Protestant groups, always a danger signal to a non-Christian minority, had been effected. It was not inconceivable, therefore, that the amendment crusade—an "intended inquisition"—would rally a popular majority. Even if rights were not rescinded, a Protestant alliance could well twist the law against Jews. Yet, despite the horrible consequences, the *Occident* had little to suggest by way of Jewish response other than "silent, yet energetic action through the ballot, and by pen and speech to rebuke the sacriligious [*sic*] attack [on] the Constitution."[9]

Leeser's alarmist opinions frightened some Jews who doubtless believed that attacks on the amendment scheme might arouse further anti-Jewish animosity or afford free publicity to an undeserving movement. Since Jews were the "chief parties," as Leeser called them, in the opposition, the more timid souls preferred to keep silent unless non-Jewish supporters stepped forward and dispelled the notion of a "Jewish issue." The young BDAI took a wait-and-see attitude. The *Jewish Messenger,* a new periodical in New York, disputed the premises of the amendment group and soberly noted how it was linked to various components of the Christian-state idea. Simultaneously, however, the paper assured its readers that they had no real cause for alarm, and it apologized for any seemingly bellicose tone![10]

Isaac Wise of the *Israelite* ridiculed the first manifestations of the Christian movement. (In later years he pinpointed it as the immediate cause of the wave of social anti-Semitism which erupted full-blown in the fourth quarter of the century.) Nevertheless, recalling the agitation of the Know-Nothings and the temperance and abolition crusades, he warned the Jewish community to be on alert. Within a year Wise abandoned ridicule, calling the movement a "revolution" to destroy the basic tenet of religious liberty. In a series of lengthy editorials on church and state, he advanced many arguments, from the theological to the practical, on the unacceptability of the amendment. As the Jews were wont to do, he equated the Jewish with the national interest. The issue was an American one rather than one of Judaism against Christianity, and Jews, the defenders of American principles, took a position not as Jews but as lovers of liberty and justice. Since enlightened Americans also opposed the movement, Wise optimistically believed that the Christianizers would be "killed" at the ballot box.[11]

The second memorial to Congress from the amendment group (1864), followed by a widely publicized convention, heightened Jewish apprehensiveness. A flurry of activity ensued. Isaac Leeser hastened to New York and as presiding officer of the BDAI called a meeting of the executive committee. All agreed that the board's inaction could no longer be justified; agitation might lend importance to the Protestant plan, but silence on the part of the Jews would endow it with greater determination. The board resolved, therefore, to present a counterstatement to Congress. Leeser also conferred with a self-constituted committee of prominent New York Jews on the amendment; they appointed a delegation to proceed to Washington, "to take such measures as may be necessary to defeat the object of the Petition."[12] (The fact that the New York group preferred to function independently reflected the fragile unity represented by the BDAI.)

The BDAI's memorial, drafted by Leeser, charged that the amendment sponsors would deprive the Jews of their inalienable rights and the equal status intended for them by the Founding Fathers. In apologetic tones the memorialists invoked once again the military services of the Jews to the land as well as their incomparable virtue. Sumner presented the board's petition to the Senate, and both he and Trumbull assured the Jews that the proposed amendment had little chance of success in committee. They promised that if the question came before the Senate, the BDAI would be afforded an opportunity to testify. Still apprehensive, the board gloomily concluded that the "zealots and fanatics" would persist in their efforts for the evangelization of the country and for a union of church and state.[13]

The cause of the Christianizers made rapid strides in the scandal-ridden decade of the 1870s. Adopting the name of National Reform Association (NRA), the crusaders drew up a constitution which, in addition to calling for a Christian amendment, pledged itself to promote needed reforms regarding "the Sabbath, the institution of the family, the religious element in Education, the Oath, and Public Morality as affected by the liquor traffic and other kindred evils." In this, its second phase, the society embraced multiple goals which enabled it to attract the various reform elements who constituted the "Moral Majority" of the post–Civil War era. Under the presidency of William Strong, who was appointed to the Supreme Court in 1870, the society's prestige soared, and other prominent figures added their names to the roster of officers. Nevertheless, the NRA failed to secure a hearing of a Christian amendment on the floor of Congress. The House Judiciary Committee reported in 1874 that an amendment ran counter to the intent of the Founding Fathers—who, the committee pointed out, were Christian—and thus did not merit consideration.[14]

Jewish concern continued unabated. Leaders believed that the NRA's success in any area, even without an amendment, would both undermine Jewish equality and prove an entering wedge for furthering the overall Christian design. The Jewish press and the BDAI criticized the appointment of Strong to the Supreme Court and urged the Senate to withhold its consent. In 1872, when the agitation of the NRA crested, the irrepressible Wise asked for Strong's impeachment. Rabbis, despite their self-imposed code of political neutrality, publicly denounced the amendment movement. Wise, who charged that the "fanatics" intended not the union of church and state but—even worse—the subjugation of the state to the church, actively campaigned against an NRA sympathizer in 1876.[15]

Wise's colleague Dr. Max Lilienthal sounded a different note. He invoked the "contract" between America and its Jews, whereby the country was required to maintain church–state separation, the prerequisite for liberty, equality, and intergroup harmony. Jews for their part had lived up to the bargain by totally effacing their Jewishness with an American identity: "Hence, we have given up all ideas of ever returning to Palestine. . . . Hence, we have given up our sectarian schools, and send our children to the free schools."[16] The negative implication was clear: if America disavowed separationism and became like other nations, the transference of Jewish religious allegiance would have been in vain.

Jewish concern failed to trigger concerted communal action. Rabbis in Pittsburgh, joined by a few Christian ministers, attempted to cement a union of opponents to the amendment, but their efforts were barely recognized outside their city. In 1874, unlike its behavior nine years earlier, the BDAI presented no countermemorial to Congress to offset that of the NRA. It still relied on the sympathy of Senators Sumner and Trumbull and the promise that Jews would obtain a hearing should the amendment proposal reach that stage.[17]

Anti-Semitic signals from the NRA accounted at least in part for Jewish wariness. At the NRA's national convention of 1873, for example, speaker after speaker lashed out against the enemies of the movement. One minister attacked those who impeded America's progress as a Christian civilization by opposing Sunday laws, Bible reading in the classroom, and legislation to enforce Christian morality. A second speaker was more explicit: "The enemies of our movement naturally draw into their ranks all infidels, Jews, Jesuits, and all opposers of Him who is Lord over all, our Lord Jesus Christ." A third participant observed that there was a "confederacy of the Jesuit and Jew, infidel and atheist, in their attacks upon the Bible in our schools." Disparate elements without a common cause, they nevertheless had "stricken hands like Herod and Pontius Pilate in the common work of crucifying Christ." A year later, the NRA was horrified at the appointment of Felix Adler to a visiting professorship of Hebrew and Oriental literature at Cornell University. The naming of a Jew clearly imperiled Christian interests. Within a short time representatives of the society also admitted openly that a Christian Constitution "would disenfranchise every logically consistent infidel."[18]

Jewish inaction was somewhat offset by the appearance of a welcome ally, Francis E. Abbott. Abbott, a Unitarian turned self-proclaimed anti-Christian, actively worked with other freethinkers on behalf of the Free Religious Association. A firm believer in separationism, he reported in his newspaper, the *Index,* on disabilities suffered by Jews that were grounded in religion. One of his numerous liberal projects was a petition campaign in 1872 against the Christian amendment. The petition amassed some thirty thousand names, and, forwarded to a sympathetic Senator Sumner, it helped to undercut the NRA. Ever disinclined to agitate without assurance of non-Jewish sympathy, appreciative Jews hailed Abbott's efforts. Some influential rabbis and laymen supported his local Liberty Leagues as well as the establishment of the National Liberty League (1876). The direct opposite of the NRA, the League pressed for a "religious freedom amendment" that would put an end to Sunday laws and religious instruction in the schools.[19]

Jewish identification with Abbott, albeit short-lived, departed from earlier Jewish criticisms of agnostics and atheists. It revealed, first, that Jews themselves were succumbing to new intellectual currents, and, second, they could not afford to spurn any support in the crucial struggle against a Christian amendment. The friendships that were forged in that common effort inevitably led some Jews to the camp of the secularists.

How much influence the NRA exerted on moderate Protestants is impossible to gauge. At the very least, it doubtless confirmed the popular belief that the United States was a Christian nation whose freedoms rested on Christian precepts. In 1888 the *New York Tribune* candidly articulated that view. It fully appreciated the value and virtues of "our Hebrew fellow-citizens," the paper said, but

> they should recognize . . . that the Republic which offers a refuge and the broadest religious freedom to all men, expresses, in so doing, the highest teaching of Christ—the brotherhood of humanity. If it had not done so they (the Hebrews) would have had no foothold here. The United States . . . is Christian in its foundation, its structure and its development, and none . . . who have taken refuge here have more reason to thank God for its Christian spirit than the Hebrews.[20]

The drive for a Christian amendment subsided until the 1890s, but under the encouragement of the NRA pressures escalated for stricter Sunday observance and for religious instruction in the public schools.

Sunday Laws

As a recent study noted, the theocratic ideas of the NRA permeated the post–Civil War Sunday movement. Its supporters looked upon Sunday legislation not only as a means of inculcating public religion but as a symbolic recognition of Jesus Christ as the nation's ruler.[21] To be sure, moderate Protestants who rejected the notions of a theocracy and a religious amendment also upheld the imperative of Sunday laws. The oft-cited Philip Schaff, eminent church historian and theologian whose views on liberty of conscience were unimpeachable, believed that Christianity played a pivotal role in shaping the religious freedoms of the Constitution. He agreed that the church and the state moved in separate orbits, but they met on moral issues, and therefore absolute separation was impossible. Schaff preferred a "friendly separation," a system under which both church and state preserved Sunday laws and religion in the schools. The only alternative that he and other prominent Protestants saw was an "infidel" separation, which rested on hatred of religion and wrought havoc with morality. The polarity thus constructed better suited an earlier homogeneous community when religious meant Christian and when all agreed that church and government served identical ends. The reality was fast changing, but on the simplistic dualities of Christian–infidel, religious–atheist, majority–minority, the defenders of American Protestantism still rested their case. Religious minorities had to yield to the Protestant majority, for a minority that challenged the Protestant design risked the stigma of heathen or godless.[22]

From the minority's point of view it made little difference if support of Sunday laws or religion in the schools came from a Schaff or an NRA member. The success of those causes, irrespective of their supporters, presaged a larger danger, the entrenchment of other public Christian usages. As Rabbi Max Samfield of Memphis argued, if Sunday laws, grounded as they were in religion, were validated by law, religious instruction in the public schools and a religious amendment to the Constitution would be equally legitimate.[23]

With the cooperation of both national and local societies, in 1879 the NRA began the drive for a national Sunday law to reverse the currents of religious laxity. Its larger purpose was to retain an America uncorrupted by secularism and unyielding to the influences of non-Protestant immigrants. Agitating now on both state and federal levels, Sunday law advocates encountered serious obstacles, for the same social currents that had increased nonobservance in the first place escalated opposition to the Sunday crusade. A highly politicized issue, the Sunday question heightened the visibility of the Jews, principally as violators or potential violators of the laws.[24]

Unlike the amendment issue, the subject of Sunday laws failed to muster Jewish unity. Aside from a mild recommendation for exempting Sabbath observers, the Board of Delegates kept silent. Among the Anglo-Jewish journals, which carefully monitored the subject, opinions differed. The *Jewish Messenger* upheld Sunday laws as police regulations which ensured the necessary day of rest for all. It favored moderate Sunday laws, permitting opportunities to those who desired to rest and those who preferred to use Sundays for recreation. That Sunday was a Christian institution was irrelevant; Sunday laws did not make the United States a Christian nation. The statutes, with proper exemptions for Sabbatarians, were hardly too onerous for the minority, who, out of respect for the religious sensibilities of their neighbors, were obliged not to add to the secularization of Sunday. Far worse than the laws were two kinds of Jews: those who violated their own Sabbath yet claimed exemption from the laws, and those whose attacks on the laws cast doubts on Jews as law-abiding citizens.[25]

The *Messenger*'s views were of little comfort to concerned separationists or to observant Jews forced to eke out a subsistence living in five days. In keeping with its approach to all public issues of a controversial nature, the accommodationist journal refused to challenge the majority's acceptance of Sunday laws. Its Jewish traditionalist posture doubtless fed the *Messenger*'s forceful denunciation of Jews who violated their own Sabbath as well as its aversion to a secular nation wherein a vibrant Judaism could hardly flourish.

Isaac Wise's *American Israelite* (the paper's name was changed in 1874) entertained no defense of legalized Sunday observance. "All Sunday laws, together with the penalties attached to them," one editorial stated flatly, "are unjust, despotic, and damnable." In an unending stream of arguments, Wise appealed primarily to principle: Sunday laws were religious in nature and intent, they were a salient component of the Christian-state idea, they nurtured the movement for a Christian amendment, and, alien to the American republican spirit, they aimed at a union of church and state. Not only did the actual laws defy logic and consistency, but, since neither morality nor true Christianity could be advanced by legislation, they were utterly pointless. Jews in particular had cause to distrust the Sunday law movement, for some agitators readily resorted to anti-Semitic slurs. His readers would do well, Wise advised, to respond actively, petitioning legislators and cooperating with other Sabbatarians.[26]

Just as the *American Israelite* differed from the *Jewish Messenger*, so did differences exist within the Reform camp itself. At a public meeting on Sunday laws, Rabbi Samuel Sale of Baltimore advocated not the abolition of the laws but modifications to permit recreation and amusements. Lawyer Simon Wolf of Washington agreed that Puritanical laws were unsuitable to the spirit of the age, but, stressing principle, he interpreted all Sunday legislation to be an encroachment on individual liberties. By the turn of the century, when the new immigrant presence intensified the focus on Sunday observance, Reform opinion ran the gamut from those who desired total repudiation of religious legislation to those who preferred to soft-pedal the issue in light of the new urban problems.[27]

Despite his ideological rhetoric, Rabbi Wise realistically acknowledged that Jews could attain no more than exemptions. In 1876, at the annual meeting of Reform's Union of American Hebrew Congregations, he introduced a resolution which called for petitions to state legislatures asking for exemptions of Sabbath-observing Jews. When specific attempts for exemptions were made in Pennsylvania, he counseled Jews to repudiate the opponents at the polls. The Reform leader's forceful and defiant tone, and his consideration of Sunday laws as part of a larger Christian design, may have distanced him from the timid, accommodationist *Jewish Messenger,* but at bottom both worked for the same objective—exemptions.[28]

The two papers were joined by a third influential journal in 1879, when a group of Conservative Jews founded the *American Hebrew* of New York. The new weekly was centrist with respect to Sunday laws as it was in religion. On one occasion it sounded like the *Israelite:* "But even if we did not keep the Sabbath . . . we claim that the law has no right 'to select the day that shall be the day of rest.'" For the most part, however, it limited its rhetoric to demands for fair exemptions and even-handed enforcement. Legislation without exemptions, the journal elaborated, especially for the poorer classes, surpassed even the cruelties of the missionaries. How honest were July Fourth orations on religious liberty, and how meaningful was the First Amendment, if Sabbath observers were arrested for Sunday labor?[29] Where the *Israelite* fought the theory of all Sunday laws, the *Hebrew* implied that proper exemptions fulfilled the requirements of religious liberty and equality. Neither was yet prepared to agitate for the growing number of Jews who violated their own Sabbath but on grounds of principle objected to the observance of the Christian Sunday.

Although it is tempting to correlate Jewish reactions with religious orientation, it would be inaccurate to conclude from the sampling of the journals that Reform Jews were consistently "hard" separationists, the Orthodox "soft" separationists, and the Conservatives somewhere between. The timidity of the *Messenger* did not necessarily follow from the traditionalist posture of its founder, S. M. Isaacs; Isaac Leeser had been a traditionalist too. Indeed, Wise the Reformer rather than Isaacs had inherited Leeser's mantle and his belief that justification of Sunday laws as police regulations was an outright subterfuge. Two other factors doubtless accounted for the different approaches: personality—Wise the noisy and ubiquitous crusader—and politics—the *Messenger* was Republican, the *Israelite* was Democratic, the editorial board of the *Hebrew* was mixed. It is probably most accurate to conclude that the nexus forged by Reform between Judaism and Americanism made its spokesmen especially sensitive to matters of church and state. Generally more affluent and acculturated than the traditionalists, and better unified, Reformers shaped the response of the community on all significant church–state issues for fifty years after the Civil War.

In anticipation of the centennial in 1876 commemorating American independence, the BDAI advised Jews to contribute to the occasion "by concurrent and distinctive action." B'nai B'rith suggested a work of art underwritten by the Jewish community, and it commissioned sculptor Moses Ezekiel to execute the project. Some Jews were opposed. Why they and not any other religious group? To suggest, even unintentionally, that Jews owed a special debt of gratitude to the government for the freedoms they enjoyed, when equality was theirs by right, showed an undignified lack of self-respect. Despite the opposition, Ezekiel's statue, named *Religious Liberty*, was contributed by B'nai B'rith to the centennial exposition in Philadelphia.[30]

Agitation over Christianity as the public religion marred Jewish enjoyment of the celebration. In the spring of 1876 the legislature of Pennsylvania, the host state of the exposition, overwhelmingly rejected a proposal to exempt Sabbatarians from Sunday laws. In the shadow of the NRA's crusade, many Jews also resented Bishop Matthew Simpson's opening prayer at the centennial exposition, in which the United States was called a Christian nation. The *Messenger* attempted to defuse opposition; fearful lest Jews be distanced from the rest of the citizenry, especially in the centennial year, the journal admitted that except in the crucial area of law it was not incorrect to refer to America as a Christian country. At the other extreme, the *American Israelite* termed Simpson's statement a "falsehood" and bitterly criticized the use of the exposition for "sectarian advertisement."[31]

More upsetting was the decision of civil authorities to keep the exposition closed on Sundays. Again the leading Jewish journals reacted in characteristic fashion. The *Jewish Messenger* suggested a compromise: forbid the operation of machinery and sale of liquor but permit a limited number of exhibits for the benefit of workers, not exclusively Sabbatarians, who had no other day of leisure. The *American Israelite* fumed over the disregard of constitutional liberties and noted bitingly how comfortable the regulation would be for visitors from despotic lands. Wise suggested that in accordance with the principle of religious equality the fair should also be closed on Fridays and Saturdays. Reform Rabbi David Einhorn, prominent civil libertarian and ally of Isaac Wise on that subject, addressed the fair's closing in a centennial sermon. How free was America, he asked, if bigotry forbade "to citizens who earn their livings honestly by the sweat of their countenances, every recreation on Sunday, even the sight of the world exposition."

Einhorn's sermon went on to discuss the social problems of the nation, and he also pointed to a grave inequity that troubled Jews in particular: "While the Declaration of Independence knows of no religion and does not even mention the word 'Christian' a single time . . . there has for years resounded in your midst with ever greater intensity the ominous cry: 'The United States is a Christian country.'" Hence, America, "Where is your equality?"[32]

In the last two decades of the century, no uniform trend with respect to Sunday laws developed. The statutes were liberalized in some states and toughened in others. The pattern of enforcement also varied, not only from state to state but within a single state. State and federal[33] courts generally upheld Sunday laws, but they too emitted contradictory signals. Although some judges invoked religious reasons, most found the laws to be a proper exercise of state police powers. Judicial refusal to countenance religious legislation may have gratified the Jewish minority, but, as discussed earlier, the police power rationale weakened their case. Accommodationist Jews could not very well challenge the authority of elected lawmakers to provide for the well-being of society, particularly when a guaranteed day of rest for the American worker was at stake. Their repeated argument that the laws under any guise were religious in intent rang hollow, and pragmatically the best chances for relief lay in securing immunity for Sabbatarians.[34]

Over twenty states provided for exemptions, but some were narrowly limited to servile labor, as opposed to business or shopkeeping, or to occupations that caused no public disturbance. Efforts to broaden exemptions usually encountered vigorous opposition from Sunday law defenders. Among other reasons, they argued that the majority's choice of Sunday had to be honored uniformly. One Sunday law supporter stated: "We want but *one* Sabbath in this country. We don't want any Judaizing here." Nonconformists not only violated the mood of the day, but they enticed Christians to desecrate the Christian Sabbath. Besides, exemptions for Sabbatarians provided them with a distinct economic advantage over their competitors. Clearly, those who most blatantly resisted a Christian Sunday were the Jews.[35]

Admittedly, exemptions alone did not erase all hardships. Enforcement generally threw the burden of proof upon the Jew, who had to prove to the satisfaction of the charging officer or court that he was in fact a conscientious Sabbath observer. Furthermore, under the requirement that exempted activities cause no public disturbance, exemptions were dependent on who was disturbed. In New York, for example, a Sabbath-observing Jew who operated a sewing machine in his own house on Sundays was charged with willful disturbance by a Methodist church next door. According to one city newspaper, the case revealed a glaring inequity: "Suppose, for instance, a Christian coppersmith or boiler maker has his shop near a Jewish synagogue, can he be compelled to stop work during the hours of service in the synagogue on Saturdays?" Had the Jew lived elsewhere, his activity might have gone unchallenged. Such seemingly trivial episodes revealed countless variations in the Sunday law structure as well as different levels of intergroup tension.[36]

Shortly after the Civil War, two cases in the South considered the Jewish position under Sunday laws. A court in Alabama, a state without exemptions, ruled that an owner of a dry-goods store, a Sabbath-observing Jew, could not be excused from Sunday closing regulations. Basing its decision on the state's police powers, the court explained that "acts must . . . be . . . *in fact* religious, in order that an immunity from legislative prohibition may be claimed." In Louisiana the court weighed the constitutionality of a Shreveport ordinance that exempted those who closed their stores on Saturdays. The judges noted the large number of Jewish merchants in Shreveport, but they found the exemption invalid. A law that gave a special privilege to Jews alone violated the constitutional guarantees of equality for Jews and gentiles.[37]

In northern cities, where the Jewish population far exceeded that of Mobile and Shreveport, broad exemptions were hard sought. *Commonwealth* v. *Has,* a test case in Massachusetts that excited Jews in various parts of the country, failed to secure a broad interpretation of exemptions. The court upheld the right of Sabbath observers to labor or do business on Sunday, but it said that doing business did not permit them to keep open their stores and thus encourage others to violate the Sunday law. Nor did the court pay serious attention to Has's argument that the Sunday laws operated to subordinate one religion to another. Although the judge consistently referred to Sunday as the "Lord's day," he insisted that Sunday laws were civil rather than religious enactments. A Jew had to conform, not because his religion was subordinate but because he was required to submit to the rules of the community.

The usually timid *Jewish Messenger* denounced the decision, calling it an affirmation of a "State religion." The furious *American Israelite* lashed out against the hypocrisy of Massachusetts, which on the one hand avowed Christian love for "Negroes, Chinese, Fiji Islanders, or Hottentots" but on the other denied Jews the rights of man. It suggested that Jews along with liberals petition the state legislature repeatedly until public opinion compelled an amendment. The journal's Washington correspondent advised a different remedy: a concerted campaign by Boston's Jews to make all conform to the letter of the law—not even concerts, traveling, or unnecessary walking on Sunday. "Make the odious law odious to all." All protests, however, were futile. Ten years later the same court, citing the *Has* decision, ruled that immunity did not even extend to a Jewish ritual slaughterer who opened his butcher shop on Sundays to supply meat only to other Sabbath-observing Jews.[38]

Tighter enforcement and narrower interpretation of exemptions also troubled Sunday law opponents in New York. In the largest center of American Jews, acceptable exemptions for Sabbatarians had existed until 1882. That year, however, a new penal code provided: "It is a sufficient defense to a prosecution for servile labor on the first day of the week, that the defendant uniformly keeps another day of the week as holy time. . . . " Narrower than the earlier law, it specified "servile labor" and not work, and it restricted immunity to defense only *after* an offender had been charged.[39]

Upon the promulgation of the code, New York City police promised a crackdown on Jewish merchants who did business on Sundays. The police commissioner of Brooklyn said that "you cannot allow a Jew to sell goods which a Gentile may not sell." Shopkeepers pondered the warnings, but many decided to risk a violation rather than lose one day's income. Sunday, they said, was the only free day for workers and hence the busiest day for the stores. True to their word, the police, whose anti-Jewish prejudice contributed to their zeal, swooped down on the violators. "There are a great many of this shrewd people . . . who are expected to play double," they announced. To prevent "deception" on the part of Jews, the police quietly made a count of those businesses that were shut on Saturday. Within a week, a group of thirteen East Side merchants obtained temporary injunctions to halt police harassment that forced them to close on Sundays. Twelve were Jews, and eleven of these, joined shortly by five others, kept closed on Saturdays.

At the trial in the Superior Court, one of the attorneys for the Jews agreed that there should be a legal day of rest, but that Jews had the right to choose their day. For those who chose to observe Saturday, doing business on Sunday was "a work of necessity" (the typical exception made by Sunday laws to what was proscribed). Justice William Arnoux ruled otherwise. The exempting clause in the code referred only to servile labor and correctly so, for a Jew who opened his store on Sunday was presenting non-Jews with the temptation to violate the law. Moreover, the clause did not protect even the Jewish laborer from arrest but only provided him with a defense to his prosecution. Citing the Shreveport case, Arnoux added that broad exemptions gave Jews an unfair advantage.[40]

New York Jews as well as the Board of Delegates charged that the law was unconstitutional. Submitting its own proposal to the legislature, the board called repeatedly but unsuccessfully for broad exemptions. Christian journals disagreed, and the influential *Independent* candidly suggested that if the Jews did not like it, they were free to leave. The offensive law lasted well into the twentieth century, compelling the Jews, as one observer said, "to labor surreptitiously on Sunday."[41]

As if to compound the injury with insult, the New York Court of Appeals in 1893 defined the "Christian Sabbath" as a civil institution whose desecration the state was empowered to prevent. The police power rationale notwithstanding, the Christian aura around Sunday legislation still lingered.[42]

The Public Schools

When the American public (or common) schools took root in the second third of the nineteenth century, the churches relinquished their traditional control over education. Nevertheless, since clergymen figured prominently in the establishment of the new system, and since a common religious core acceptable to most Protestants was retained, the public schools were hardly religion-free. Horace Mann, in his oft-cited report on education in Massachusetts, pioneered for nonsectarian schools, but nonsectarian in his day, as David Tyack wrote, "meant that the Protestant churches agreed to suspend their denominational quarrels within the public schoolhouse." Nor did the circle of the "nonsectarian fellowship" intend to include Jews or Catholics.[43]

In a Protestant-controlled society the schools easily became appendages of the dominant faith. The vast majority of Americans expected if not demanded readings from the Protestant Bible elucidated by moral Christian teachers and supplemented with proper textbooks, prayers, and holiday exercises. Only one state, Massachusetts, required Bible reading by law; in most of the others it was freely accepted as a fact of school life. Religion in the schools had a patriotic rationale as well, one that went back to the Founding Fathers. Dr. Benjamin Rush of an earlier generation had written that teaching the principles of Christianity was a sure way to implant the principles of republicanism, and ninteenth-century educators agreed. They entrusted to the schools the responsibility of inculcating the virtues necessary for republican survival, and by their definition moral virtue was grounded in Christianity. Through a school system that entwined Americanism and Protestantism for native-born and immigrant children, evangelical Protestantism, as Lawrence Cremin succinctly observed, defined the prevailing "American *paideia*."[44]

The Protestant majority stoutly resisted any encroachment on their turf, and objections by Catholics or Jews to denominational trappings in the schools easily triggered the wrath of zealots and nativists. Frequently they justified their reluctance to accommodate the others on the grounds of numbers and homogeneity. In the earliest recorded state case on the constitutionality of Bible reading in the schools, *Donahoe* v. *Richards* (1854),

Catholics in Maine brought suit when a school expelled a Catholic girl for refusing to participate in readings from the King James Bible. Her lawyers argued that the requirement, a preference for Protestants over Catholics, constituted a religious test that operated to exclude an entire class of citizens from the enjoyment of public education. The court, however, held that use of the Bible as a textbook *in reading* was constitutional. Not employed to impart theological doctrines, it neither infringed upon liberty of conscience nor did it show a preference for any sect. How much more preferential were Sunday laws favoring Christians over Jews, the judge said, and yet they too had been upheld by the courts.[45]

Non-Protestants had limited options: to enroll their children in the free schools despite the discriminatory features (an insult to taxpaying minorities and an intimidation of their children), to erect a private school system of their own (an impossible task for impoverished immigrants), or to carry the fight against the religious features of the schools into the political arena (an invitation to nativist harassment). Catholics and Jews could be found in each category, but the former took the lead in politicizing grievances against the Protestant-flavored classroom. Agitation abated somewhat only after 1884 when the Catholic church required a parochial school education for its children.[46]

The antebellum Jewish press also criticized the public schools for their Christian content, but they differed on remedies. Leeser's *Occident,* which frequently warned of the dangerous influences on Jewish children, grudgingly conceded that not *all* Bible reading or very general prayers were improper. Lyon's *Asmonean* urged that the Bible be kept out of the classroom, and so did Wise's *Israelite.* According to Wise, since all religions enjoyed equal rights, the problem centered on which version of the Bible was read. He suggested Bible reading without comment and in the original, the Hebrew Old Testament and the Greek New Testament! For a short time the journals endorsed the alternative solution of separate Jewish day schools.[47]

From the outset, however, most Jewish children were probably enrolled in the public schools. Certainly there were enough to warrant Leeser's early plea: excuse the Jewish child at prayer time and forbid teachers to speak disrespectfully of Jews and their faith. In New York, Jews in one district joined Catholics and Universalists in 1843 to protest religious instruction under school auspices. The specific Jewish complaint addressed the sectarian and offensive nature of certain textbooks, but it was highhandedly dismissed by a committee of the Board of Education: if Jews, upon entering a Christian country, encountered institutions at odds with their own views, they could hardly expect changes merely for their convenience. As a gratuitous insult to the upstart immigrants, the committee added, albeit erroneously, that the public schools had long antedated the presence of the Jews. At the same time the Board of Education affirmed that the Bible was not sectarian and its reading did not conflict with state law.[48]

Despite such rebuffs, Jews swallowed their pride and refrained from noisy protests. They were meeker than the Catholics, largely because of their very small numbers (fifty thousand in 1850), the autonomy of the individual synagogue, and a habitual reluctance to call attention to themselves. The fury that the Catholics provoked with assaults on the public schools augured even worse for a weaker minority, non-Christian to boot, that challenged Protestant rule. Why get involved in a Protestant–Catholic battle, or why allow American anti-Catholicism to rub off on them? Nor did a long-term alliance with their traditional oppressors, the Catholics, appear attractive. After all, Jews reasoned, Catholics did not favor the elimination of Christianity from the classroom but would merely have substituted a religious atmosphere congenial to themselves.

After mid-century, when Jewish day schools rapidly declined and the move to public schools was fully under way, Jews formulated an ideological justification for their choice, one that would also serve the later immigrants from eastern Europe. Isidor Busch, a Viennese journalist who became a St. Louis businessman, was an early and fervent exponent of the value of public schooling for Jews. Launching his crusade in 1851, Busch insisted that the public school was vital for Americanization and social integration. He warned that self-imposed separation through Jewish schools would not only fail to eliminate anti-Jewish prejudice but would exacerbate it. What better means do our children have of overcoming intolerance, he asked, than by early mingling with their gentile peers? Moreover, how could Jews effectively oppose the teaching of Christianity in the schools if their children were not enrolled? Busch, who was prepared to sacrifice traditional Jewish education for the benefits of public schools, confidently expected the struggle against Christian usages to win out. Reform leaders shared his views, and in 1855 the Reform-dominated rabbinical conference in Cleveland registered its formal opposition to Jewish day schools.[49]

From the 1850s on, the love affair between American Jews and the public schools blossomed. Not conversion, as Heine had said, but public education would be the passport to civilization or, in American Jewish terms, to rapid acculturation, equality and opportunity, achievement through merit, and the dissipation of prejudice. After the Civil War, Jewish loyalty to the public schools, their Christian practices notwithstanding, hardened into a veritable creed. "Bible or no Bible," Rabbi Max Lilienthal of Cincinnati said in 1870, "our children will visit the public schools." That message took root. Twenty years later Rabbi Edward Calisch addressed his rabbinical colleagues on the greatness of America's public schools: the expounders of republicanism, the equalizers of citizens, they were the "strength and glory" of the nation. American Jews would not build parochial schools, he promised. Despite the insult and injustice to which their children were subject, Jewish parents would stake their future on the yet imperfect public school "because they love learning and they love law, and they believe that the public school system of America is the embodiment of them both."[50]

The Jewish position on the schools differed in spirit from that on Sunday laws. To be sure, both issues represented the strength of the Christian-state idea and the less-than-equal status of the Jews. Just as Jews had seen the ties between the Sunday law and the Christian amendment movements, so did they note the link between the amendment and religion in the classroom. But the fight against Sunday laws never rested on the hope of capturing the benefits of Sunday for all citizens. The day itself had no intrinsic value, and with or without laws Sunday observance still set off Christians from Jews. Ridding the schools of Christianity, however, prom-ised a distinctive advantage. Jews would become full partners in the public school system, where their legendary love for learning could be fully in-dulged. Nonsectarian schools, which adumbrated true equality for the chil-dren and for the nation that those children would construct, might even breach the wall of social anti-Semitism. Mid-century Jews, like other Amer-icans, supported the ideal of a homogeneous nation; a commitment to the philosophy of pluralism was still in the future. In Jewish eyes the public school, where Americanism would ultimately be the only creed, was the great homogenizer.

After the Civil War, a defensive Protestantism, abetted by startling rev-elations of political and economic corruption, resolved to preserve the inculcation of Christian moral principles through the public schools. Not only the NRA, but professional educators and clergymen added their jus-tification of compulsory classroom prayers, hymns, and Bible readings. Some believed that only by religion in education could God's covenant with American be guaranteed. Much emotional rhetoric attended the calls for Christian usages, particularly Bible reading, and the issue was rapidly politicized. Again, as in the Sunday crusade, the perceived opponents—Catholics, Jews, secularists—were held less than moral and less than pa-triotic. With isolated exceptions, the courts followed suit and validated the practice of Bible reading.[51]

Jews who attended public schools after the war vividly recalled the Christian ambience of the classroom. "I remember very well ... how out of place I felt," Rabbi Henry Berkowitz said of his school years in Pitts-burgh, when he was required to join in singing hymns, reading the Bible, and reciting the Lord's Prayer. Those exercises, along with anti-Jewish passages from readers, geographies, and history textbooks, "brought the blush of confusion and shame to our cheeks." Louis Marshall testified to the contempt and hatred conveyed on Good Friday in a Syracuse school by the teacher's reading an account of the crucifixion, and to the resulting "scurrilous remarks" and "physical violence" suffered by Jewish children at the hands of their classmates. In Philadelphia, according to Nina Morais, secular subjects were also linked by teachers to Christianity. Pitied if not worse for being a Jew, the Jewish child was commonly ostracized by his classmates. His absence from school on Jewish holidays was a punishable offense, and the school arbitrarily set examinations for those days.[52] If only for the emotional effect on the children, the eradication of Christian features from the schools became an urgent priority.

Trying for a rapprochement between Protestants and Catholics on the school issue, the Board of Education of Cincinnati resolved in 1869 to prohibit all religious instruction, including Bible reading, from the public schools. The stormy debates sparked by the ban reflected a culturally and religiously diverse population. The ensuing court case was, as Robert Michaelsen pointed out, the first to hear a full articulation of the "civil" view, or that which affirmed that since the state was secular, even a minimal religious core in the schools was out of place.[53]

No single Jewish position on the issue prevailed; the two Jews on the Board of Education divided. But the two prominent Reform rabbis of the city, Isaac Wise and Max Lilienthal, lined up with Catholics, liberal Protestants, and freethinkers on the side of the board and against the mainstream Protestants. Lilienthal took the lead, and from 1869 on he hammered away at sectarianism in the schools. He denounced the fanaticism of both Protestants and Catholics: Catholics, he explained, disapproved of what they called "atheistical" schools and wanted only state support of their own schools. To avoid the perils of interreligious conflict, he pleaded for a common Americanism transcending the faith of all denominations. At a rabbinical conference in 1870, and again at the first annual meeting of the UAHC in 1874, Lilienthal secured the passage of a resolution equating Americanism with nonreligious education: "We love and revere this country as our home and fatherland . . . and therefore consider it our paramount duty . . . to favor by all means the system of free, unsectarian education, leaving religious instruction to the care of the different denominations."[54]

Wise seconded these views in the *American Israelite*. Just as Lilienthal endorsed "unsectarian" education, Wise now called for secular schools. In an oft-cited editorial he wrote: "We are opposed to Bible reading in the schools. We want secular schools and nothing else. . . . Having no religion, [the state] cannot impose any religious instruction on the citizen." The rabbi had moved significantly from his earlier view on reading the Bible in its original to one more in keeping with strict separationism. To be sure, as spokesmen for a minority that preferred to keep a low profile, Wise and Lilienthal had not broken new ground on the school question. Doubtless the popular debate encouraged them to speak out, for the form in which the rabbis couched their arguments, particularly the use of the terms unsectarian and secular, closely resembled that of their Protestant allies.[55]

The meaning of nonsectarian schools and the rights of non-Protestants were discussed when the Cincinnati case *Minor* v. *Board of Education* was heard by the Superior Court in 1870. Attorneys for the board emphasized, among other things, the duty of the schools to heed the views of the minorities whom they also serviced. Counsel for the plaintiffs, however, warned Jews against challenging school practices on the grounds of religious liberty. He wondered how those ungrateful parvenus who had built "elegant warehouses," "palatial homes," and "costly and magnificent temples" could deny that they enjoyed full religious liberty. The same attorney claimed that the Jews had consented to Bible reading. Hadn't they closed their own schools and enrolled their children in the public schools when the practice was still required?

The court found for the plaintiffs, but the lone dissenter, Judge Alphonso Taft, eloquently supported non-Protestant schools and a society in which non-Protestants enjoyed the same rights as the majority. His opinion, a vindication of the Jewish separationists, vigorously denied that only Protestantism and Protestants were protected by the constitutional guarantees of religious freedom. "Between all forms of religious belief the State knows no difference." Taft rejected the argument that Jews had willingly accepted Christian practices in the schools, a phenomenon which he likened to their "conversion" or reconciliation to the New Testament. Jews never intended to waive their rights of religious liberty, Taft insisted. Their presence in the public schools testified only to their recognition of the superior resources of the common schools.[56]

The Board of Education appealed to the state's highest court, and there the ban on Bible reading as well as Taft's dissenting views were upheld. Judge John Welch's opinion denied that Ohio's constitution required the teaching of religion; nor did it mean Christianity where it stated that religion was essential to good government. To say that Christianity was part of the common law was equally inaccurate. Religion *was* essential for both the individual and the government, but good government was an outgrowth of religion and not the legal defender of any one faith. In the free competition of ideas among religions, government stood aloof. The only impartial solution for the schools, the court concluded, was to abstain from any religious teaching. Hailed by the champions of religion-free schools, the decision proved to be ahead of its time, for the city reintroduced Bible reading some twenty years later.[57]

Isaac Wise and the *American Israelite,* continuing to denounce Bible reading in the schools, hewed to the line of the decision and proudly noted how the Midwest was in advance of the East. Other Reform rabbis agitated independently in their communities toward that same goal. However, Jewish definitions of a proper nonsectarian school varied. The Reform *Jewish*

Times, for example, called for the exclusion of the Bible, but when the editor visited a school in New York City he seemed satisfied with the principal's explanation that the biblical selections were from the Old Testament. The more traditionalist *Jewish Messenger* took a sharply different stand. Although it consistently opposed blatant sectarianism and the inculcation of religious dogma, it saw nothing wrong with daily Bible readings or nonsectarian hymns. Indeed, it had disapproved of the original action taken by Cincinnati's board of education. Favoring a broad common religion in the classroom, the paper suggested the use of a common manual that distilled the ethical precepts of all religions. Meantime, it advised Jews to "reverence" the public schools, the agent of patriotism and progress, and to bear the inequities of the Protestant trappings without agitation. In this, as in other matters, the *Messenger* ranked accommodationism first.[58]

The Conservative *American Hebrew,* more than its two rivals, worried about a newer problem, the schools' responsibility to inculcate morals, which the antebellum periodicals had not probed. Much as it deplored sectarianism in the classroom, the alternative of public schools identified with agnosticism was worse. The journal kept abreast of attempts to teach morals divorced from religion, a task which it finally concluded was well-nigh impossible. For its part, the *Hebrew* believed that the schools should find some means of teaching three basic tenets common to all religions: "1. The existence of God, 2. The responsibility of man to his Maker, 3. The immortality of the soul." Debating a subject that would continue to plague educators and religious groups throughout the following century, the journal for a time also toyed with the idea of having civil authorities enforce attendance at the religious school of one's choice.[59]

The Cincinnati case was a landmark in the story of American Jews and church–state separation. A victory for the Reform separationists, it broadened the base of their quest for religious equality. Now Jews supplemented references to the Founding Fathers and the Enlightenment's teachings with talk of a secular state, where government moved in an orbit totally divorced from religion. In a secular state, as Judge Welch had put it, "legal Christianity is a solecism, a contradiction in terms," and legal equality for non-Christians flowed naturally from a secular government. Unlike earlier Jews who had rejected secularism out of hand, these separationists increasingly fixed on that same doctrine to emphasize the impropriety of religion in law and in publicly funded institutions. Wise's editorial of 1869 sounded the first blast, and in succeeding decades the words "secular" and "secularism" appeared more frequently in the pages of the his newspaper: "The Jew must and does labor for a secular state and secular free schools as the necessary safeguards for the inalienable human rights." Used initially in connection with the public school, the affirmation of a secular state was added to the arguments against Sunday laws and acknowledgment of the

United States as a Christian nation. In one piece Wise wrote of "the absolute necessity of state secularization to the perpetuation of the republic."[60]

As the school debate raged on in the 1870s, Jewish objections to a Christian-flavored classroom and in favor of a secular state echoed sentiments heard in different quarters—not only from members of the Liberal League but also from some Christian educators and members of the clergy.[61] To be sure, liberal Protestants who defended secular schools did not mean a positive commitment to irreligion or atheism. Rather, they were stating that a Protestant core, however generalized, was sectarian and unacceptable. The common ground in the schools that they now sought lay somewhere between nondenominational Protestantism and nonreligious teaching.[62]

Jewish strict separationists disputed any middle way. To them, nonsectarian schools meant those totally devoid of religion. Reform Rabbi Bernhard Felsenthal said that if complete separation of church and state was "atheistical," as critics charged, then "may our constitutions and state institutions remain 'atheistical' just as our manufactories, our banks, and our commerce are." The teaching of morality had a place in the schools, but he argued that it could be achieved without religion. Max Lilienthal also divorced morality from conventional religion. Schools were "godful" rather than godless, he said, if they made the American creed their religion.[63] Of all the Reformers, Lilienthal came closest to a *religious* rationalization of an American secular state. Advising that Jews as well as Christians check their religious baggage at the school's door, but yet unable to defend morality devoid of a religious base, he found in Americanism a surrogate religion acceptable to all.

Jewish proponents of secular schools or a secular state were hardly secularists as the term is generally understood; the spokesmen here cited were all religious men. Yet their assumption that a believer could simultaneously advocate a secular state was incomprehensible to most Christians. The sober *Philadelphia American* puzzled over why "Hebrews" were attracted to secularism, an ideology completely at odds with the Old Testament, and it concluded that Jews sought thereby to secure their civil rights. The newspaper reasoned correctly. Not their religion but rather their experience in Christian lands had led Jews to the idea of states separated from and oblivious to religion. In eighteenth-century Europe, Jews sided with secular humanists and against closed Christian states in order to attain their emancipation. For the Jewish community as a whole, however, the alliance stopped there. Jews shared neither the secularist repudiation of all religions nor the secularist expectation of the eventual erosion of Jewish religious identity. But even a halfway alliance with secularists exacted a price. In some American circles it was sufficient to raise suspicions about the respectability of Jews and Judaism. That taint lasted into the second half of the twentieth century, for many Americans consistently denied that a secular state could properly provide for the moral education of the youth. Furthermore, as Jews themselves were forced to acknowledge, secularism failed to provide a foolproof solution to the problem of the non-Christian's place in society. A secular state could not obliterate the Christian component of American culture, and, as one essayist noted, "The secular society in the lands that used to be Christendom . . . is more neutral against Judaism than against Christianity."[64]

Not all Jews were happy with the secularist image they projected, but the voice of the strict separationists echoed more loudly. In 1881 a committee of the Washington Hebrew Congregation considered religion in the schools. Objecting to a school board ruling that made Good Friday and Easter Monday excusable absences, the committee protested the recognition of religious holidays as well as the practices of reading the Bible and singing sectarian hymns. The state and the school were secular, not Christian, Jewish, or infidel, and all hymns or Bible readings were improper. Like Lilienthal, the committee desired a classroom where the only religion was Americanism. They recognized "only one text-book—the Constitution of the United States; only one law—the law of equality of all; only one doctrine—the United States must and shall be kept free and intact from sectarian interferences." In its call for secular schools the committee injected a new note in the pattern of Jewish defense. It insisted that it spoke not as Jews but as representatives of all good Americans who valued the public schools.[65] The universalist pitch differed sharply from earlier statements where Jews had pleaded as Jews for Jewish rights, and it presaged the approach that Jews would adopt in the twentieth century.

Under the influence of the separationist rabbis, American Jews went on record in opposition to religion in the schools. Reformers had taken the first step at the Cleveland rabbinical conference of 1870, and they repeatedly reiterated that stand through their organizations. Not only did they express a point of view that later Orthodox and Conservative Jews endorsed, but their resistance to publicly sanctioned religious practices firmly fixed the image of the separationist Jew in the American mind.

The Issues Converge

Although America at the end of the century was rapidly becoming a religiously pluralistic society, Protestant hopes for the ultimate triumph of Christianity remained high. Religious spokesmen repeated time and again that the United States was a Christian nation in law and institutions. They exhorted loyal Protestants to resist all who challenged that axiom; indeed, the opponents of Protestant schools or the Protestant Sunday were enemies of the nation. Congregationalist minister Josiah Strong warned of the perils to society menaced by "Romanism and Secularism." According to Strong, secularists included many Christians, agnostics, and "all Jews."[66]

Protestant optimism was doubtless reinforced by the spurt of federal attention to religious issues. Senator Henry Blair of New Hampshire launched the trend in 1888 with proposals for a national Sunday law as well as a constitutional amendment requiring public schools to educate "in virtue, morality, and the principles of the Christian religion." In 1889 the senator, who hoped "that instead of selecting a final toleration of so-called religions, the American people will . . . gradually expel from our geographical boundaries every religion except the Christian," introduced a second Sunday bill. His were not the only proposals. Between 1888 and 1896 over two dozen bills that bore upon the causes dear to militant Protestants were introduced into Congress. Most related in one fashion or another to the Sunday question, and four dealt with a religious amendment. Even if congressional interest was prompted by crass political considerations, the very acknowledgment that the voters desired federal action testified to the considerable strength of the Christian-staters. When in 1892 the Supreme Court said in the *Holy Trinity* case that the United States was a Christian nation, the decision spurred on the efforts of the crusaders.[67]

To concerned Jews it might have appeared as if the dire conditions predicted earlier by the Leesers and the Wises had materialized. Each of the three dreaded movements—a Christian amendment, Sunday laws, religion in the schools—had come to a head within a federal context. That they all claimed attention at the same time seemed to prove conclusively that each was nurtured by the others and that each was an integral component of a larger Christian design. The success of any of the three in Congress presaged not only increased disabilities for the non-Christian but, more important, unimpeded progress on both the state and federal levels for the Christian-state idea. Serious congressional attention to each cause also threatened Jewish beliefs that the federal government, limited by the religion-free Constitution and the First Amendment, was a firm guarantor of religious equality.

The new developments failed, however, to provoke mass Jewish protests or unified attempts at counterlobbying. Measured against earlier episodes, the poor response was surprising. In the 1850s leaders of a community that numbered only 100,000 had noisily agitated against the discriminatory Swiss treaty; in the 1860s, spokesmen for 150,000 Jews had lobbied with senators against the NRA's early efforts for an amendment. Now, an ever-growing Jewish population, over 450,000 by 1890, faced multiple challenges that threatened their broad definition of church–state separation and perhaps their very equality with Christians. Yet, aside from sporadic rabbinical prodding, the community appeared becalmed.

Any one of a number of reasons may have accounted for Jewish inertia. First, the recent immigrants from eastern Europe, although significantly augmenting the size of the community after 1880, were unfamiliar with the problem of church–state relations and doubtless ignorant of the new developments. Other Jews may have failed to grasp the qualitative difference implicit in the proposed congressional legislation and may have regarded the national Sunday and education bills merely as more of the same. The religious amendment, too, was familiar; a cause pushed by cranks and bigots, it had failed before. Still others may have acknowledged the importance of the religious proposals but have abdicated responsibility to their established watchdog committee, the Board of Delegates.

The board at this time, like other communal defenders, was beset with numerous problems that vied for attention. Anti-Semitism in Bismarckian Germany and czarist Russia, and in the 1890s the Dreyfus Affair in France, turned the situation of European Jews into a foremost priority. Jews arriving from eastern Europe in great numbers needed immediate material relief, and the forecast of an irreversible trend in this mass emigration demanded that American Jews defuse the campaigns of immigration restrictionists. The spread of racial anti-Semitism from Europe to the United States also underscored the vulnerability of established American Jews. A reading of the two New York weeklies, *American Hebrew* and *Jewish Messenger,* for the years 1888–96 reveals that the rank and file knew at least something of the Christian religious campaigns; rabbis and lecturers had no need to instruct their popular audiences about the general problem. Yet the same journals sounded a new tone, one that expressed a greater concern for Jewish–Christian amity and a greater emphasis on Jewish responsibility for eruptions of prejudice. Heightened wariness, superimposed upon customary accommodationism, accounted for Jewish reluctance to challenge mainstream American opinion.

Credit for any sort of a coherent defense on church–state issues belongs to Reform Jews. Simon Wolf and Lewis Abraham of the Board of Delegates, now affiliated with Reform's Union of American Hebrew Congregations (UAHC), concentrated in 1888–89 on the national Sunday bills and lobbied against the feverish efforts of the Sabbath societies. Like Wilbur Crafts of the American Sabbath Union, who admitted that the purpose of the Sunday law was to advance the course of a "national Christianity," the board called it an entering wedge for the union of church and state that menaced all lovers of freedom. Although the board's efforts were supplemented by articles from the *American Israelite,* the absence of a coordinated public campaign exposed, as Abraham himself admitted, a pitifully inadequate Jewish defense.[68]

The Jews could well have used a strong defender at the hearings on Blair's first Sunday bill. Most witnesses either ignored the Jews or dismissed them along with atheists, deists, and Seventh-Day Christians. One advocate of the measure implied that the Jews did not merit any consideration; but a fraction of the population, they had not registered any opinion either for or against the bill with the committee. Dr. Wilbur Crafts, who orchestrated the testimony from the Sunday law societies, submitted pages from his book *The Sabbath for Man,* in which he had included suggestions for Jews. A prospective Jewish immigrant should understand, Crafts wrote, that his options were to work five days or not to immigrate at all. If he found when he arrived in the United States that he could not make a living, he could choose to live elsewhere. Did not his own "Mosaic law" compel strangers and non-Jews to rest on the Jewish Sabbath? But although American Sunday laws were far more liberal than Jewish law, Jews did not reciprocate that generosity. "No people have so persistently violated the Sabbath as Jews of the baser sort, who would sacrifice the interests of the nations which have most heartily befriended them." As "the stranger within the gates" of American Christian society, it behooved the Jews to accept the laws willingly and perhaps even change their own day of rest.[69]

Neither the Sunday bills nor the school amendment reached the floor of Congress, but agitation for the legal recognition of Christian forms continued. A seemingly trivial matter—the Sunday closing of the World's Fair scheduled for 1893 in Chicago—escalated under popular and political pressures into what one senator called a theological discussion. In the course of congressional debate, Senator Joseph Hawley of Connecticut expatiated at length on the United States as a Christian nation, and Senator Alfred Colquitt of Georgia piously dissociated himself from the likes of Voltaire and Robert Ingersoll. When one senator suggested that the fair be closed on Saturdays, since that was the Sabbath of Jesus, he was sneered at and overwhelmingly outvoted. Under such pressure an intimidated Congress qualified its appropriation to the fair with the stipulation about Sunday closing.[70]

Jewish spokesmen were concerned less about the fair than about the law, which the Board of Delegates described as an entering wedge for the Christian-state idea.[71] The matter came before the Central Conference of American Rabbis (CCAR), Reform's newly organized rabbinical arm, but the rabbis found themselves in a moral quandary. Could they as rabbis, legitimately concerned with Jewish Sabbath observance, oppose the Sunday closing, which so many religious Americans endorsed? Rabbi Edward Calisch, the sponsor of the resolution, protested his reverence of the country's institutions, among which was Christianity. But, he continued, when Christianity encroached upon a minority's liberties, or when Christianity claimed that it was responsible for the country's freedoms, it had to be stopped. "We have been on the defensive for centuries. It is time that we are on the offensive." Joseph Silverman of New York's Temple Emanu-El disagreed. The CCAR could protest the closing as Jews but not as religious leaders, who in the same breath urged a more meaningful observance of their own Sabbath. That, he thought, was sheer "chutzpa." Siding with Silverman, the rabbis adopted a resolution which ignored the fair but launched the CCAR's unremitting defense of religious equality through separation:

> Whereas, There is a growing tendency toward the introduction of religious legislation in many States of the Union, and even at the National Capital. Whereas, Such legislation is antagonistic to the principles of our country's Constitution, thereby endangering the stability of all American institutions; therefore, be it
> *Resolved,* That it is the sense of this Conference that we, as a body of American ministers, do emphatically protest against all religious legislation as subversive of religious liberty.[72]

Between 1894 and 1896 four proposals for a religious amendment to the Constitution were submitted to Congress. Isaac Wise may have said earlier that if all the names of God were written into the Constitution it still could not change the nonreligious nature of government, but the NRA tenaciously pushed its objective. At congressional hearings in 1894 the Board of Delegates protested what it called the establishment of a "Christocracy." The board's spokesmen focused on one central point: "the inalienable rights of American citizenship, from which body all members of our fold would be expelled if ecclesiastical bodies have supreme control of Civil Legislation." Several Reform rabbis devoted sermons to the dangers of an amendment, and the *American Israelite* advised Congress to stay clear of religious issues: "Mind your own business, gentlemen." The board feared a new round of heated religious debates in Congress, but the amendment was not reported out of committee.[73]

If Jews needed further evidence of the fate intended for them by the advocates of a Christian constitution, it came at a House committee hearing on yet another amendment proposal in 1896. To be sure, supporters led by the NRA insisted that religious freedom would remain inviolate, that in fact they desired neither a state religion nor a union of church and state. Nevertheless, when asked directly "What about the rights of Jews and Mohammedans?" one witness admitted that the amendment would deny federal officeholding to Jews. The pro-amendment people explained that the Jews, unlike the Christians, had not settled America. Hadn't the Supreme Court itself said that the United States was a Christian nation?

Lewis Abraham, who represented the Jews, presented neither a forceful nor convincing rebuttal. He claimed at the very outset that he spoke simply as an American citizen, and indeed his statement never mentioned Jews. Before the chairman cut short his remarks, Abraham raised only two general points: how the Founding Fathers broadly conceived of religious freedom, and how religious legislation generated persecution. His testimony failed to disabuse the amendment supporters of the notion that the Jews, precisely because they were non-Christians, could not be full Americans.[74]

The hearings of 1896 revealed serious differences among amendment supporters—and hence an advantage for the non-Christian minority—over which Christian usages, and which brand of Christianity, to adopt. The NRA supported not only an amendment but Blair's school proposal, a national Sunday law, "Christian Acknowledgments" in Thanksgiving proclamations, and Christian declarations in the platforms of political parties. The last demand, particularly in a presidential election year, contributed to the amendment's defeat. In the end the House committee concluded that congressional involvement in the determination of what were God's laws would inevitably lead to religious despotism. "It is not the . . . province of the Legislature to determine what religion is true and what is false. . . . Whatever may be the religious sentiments of citizens and however variant, they are alike entitled to protection from the Government."[75]

As a result of the debates on the fair and the 1896 hearings Reform Jews grew more sensitive to the specter of national religious legislation. The immediate threats of an amendment, a national Sunday law, and congressional sanction of religion in the schools had not materialized, but the strength of public opinion in defense of religious usages indicated that the dangers could well erupt again. The UAHC, which expected a resumption of activity by the NRA, considered plans on how to coordinate an alert of American Jews. The amendment agitation also propelled the Reform organization to the adoption of a harder separationist line. A resolution adopted in 1896 stressed not the major issues brought before Congress but rather the innocuous subject of religious references in executive proclamations. Even mere figures of speech, the UAHC now insisted, were guilty of "giving color to the oft repeated assertions that our Government recognizes a religion."[76] In reaction to the religious ferment of 1888–96, Reform's vision of a secular government had grown perceptibly more popular. Whether the popular mood would permit the public airing of such views in the new century was a different question.

The Christian challenges of the 1890s erupted against a background of a more virulent strain of racial anti-Semitism that was infecting America as well as Europe. Altogether, events of the decade spread gloom in some Jewish quarters. One newspaper columnist wrote: "At the beginning of the nineteenth century there were great hopes that the progress of human enlightenment in this country would be uninterrupted; but with its close that optimistic spirit no longer prevails."[77]

4

Separationism Is Moderated

After the turn of the century, the customary zeal of the strict separationists was slowly tempered. Graver challenges faced by the rapidly expanding and maturing Jewish community—the unremitting persecution of Russian Jewry under the czars, the plight of the new immigrants, the entrenchment of racial anti-Semitism at home—reordered priorities, consumed resources, and generated fear. American Jews lost their nineteenth-century optimism and worried more about "mah yomru ha-goyim" (what will the gentiles say) to Jewish attacks on a Christian-flavored public religion. At the same time Jewish spokesmen were forced to concede that church–state separation was no longer an adequate guarantee of Jewish security. The rights of a "people" or a "race," labels increasingly foisted on the Jewish community by Jews as well as by Christians, lay beyond the bounds of separation.

In the aftermath of World War I, the problems mushroomed. The Red Scare, the wide dissemination of the *Protocols of the Elders of Zion,* the fulminations of Henry Ford's *Dearborn Independent,* and the activities of a renascent Ku Klux Klan nurtured the popularity of a new anti-Christ, the "Bolshevik Jew," conspiring to overthrow Christian civilization. Hostility toward Jews—from discrimination in employment and universities to immigration restriction—rose to unprecedented heights.[1] The decade of the 1930s was worse. Hard-hit by the Great Depression, Jews witnessed the severe attrition of their educational institutions and other communal agencies. Abroad, the Nazi war against the Jews, along with British restrictions on Jewish immigration into Palestine, cried for heroic measures on behalf of the survival of European Jewry. At the same time, a rash of anti-Semitic organizations, many feeding on Nazi propaganda, sprang up in the United States. In their everyday lives Jews confronted economic and social discrimination, elections tainted by anti-Semitism, and street violence by Jew-baiting rowdies in eastern cities. Overwhelmed by the problems, many Jews chose silence over visibility.[2]

In that setting, questions of church–state relationships paled in significance. Where such issues surfaced, Jewish organizations responded cautiously or not at all. For example, in 1929, a lower court in Georgia

93

disqualified Jews from serving on juries, but the defense agencies did nothing. Moreover, although Jews opposed the anti-evolution laws of the 1920s, only forty years later did the American Jewish Congress challenge in the courts the ban on the teaching of evolution. With regard to prohibition, an achievement of Protestant and progressive forces that was hailed as "a striking victory for the advance of Christian civilization," Jews neither fought the passage of the Eighteenth Amendment nor agitated for its repeal. (Isaac Mayer Wise had denounced the crusaders for a dry America and linked them with the Christian-staters, but that argument failed to inspire his descendants.) And in 1931, when the Supreme Court stated for the second time that the United States was a Christian nation, Jews kept utterly silent.[3]

If anti-Semitism was the principal cause of a moderated separationism, developments within the Jewish community abetted the process. Reform leaders, who since post–Civil War days were the primary defenders of separation, now faced the competition of new religious organizations, Orthodox and Conservative, that questioned Reform's hegemony over the community and in several instances its insistence on a rigid division between church and state. Within Reform's own ranks dissent also increased. Some concerned rabbis, acknowledging their movement's loss of popularity and the need to revitalize Jewish usages, were willing to reassess the value of public religion. At the same time, serious Jews of all three wings, like their Christian contemporaries, were disturbed by the rampant inroads of secularization which menaced the survival of all religions.

For any one or a combination of such reasons Jewish separationism in some instances appeared irrelevant or even foolhardy. Accordingly, as the following discussion demonstrates, many Jews in the first decades of the new century proceeded to moderate their public stand on separation or to seek other ways[4] of finding security for a Jewish minority in a Christian society.

Peoplehood and Race

Between 1880 and 1915 over two million Jews from eastern Europe landed at the ports of New York, Philadelphia, and Baltimore. Many arrived impoverished, refugees from economic as well as physical persecution. The need for relief and employment, as well as amelioration of the squalid ghetto conditions in which they lived, taxed the energies and resources of the established Jewish community. Communal leaders also felt obliged to work for the benefit of east Europeans still trapped in Romania and Russia. In the spirit of the rabbinical injunction to ransom captives, they desperately sought ways to end the European oppression while simultaneously laboring to preserve America's traditional policy of unrestricted immigration.[5]

Few of the acculturated Jews genuinely welcomed the new arrivals. Different from the German Jews in customs, manners, and religious practices, they were perceived as a threat to Jewish security. The immigrants did not cause American anti-Semitism, but by their numbers, visibility, and "outlandish" ways they stoked the fires of bigots whose anti-Jewish tirades rarely distinguished between the old and new arrivals. Heightened anti-Semitism compounded Jewish timidity on matters like separation, but, at the same time, the east European presence emboldened established Jews to agitate politically on behalf of a growing and more visible constituency. Banker Jacob H. Schiff, for example, forthrightly reminded Theodore Roosevelt before the 1904 election that 100,000 Jewish votes on New York's Lower East Side might be swayed by presidential action on the rights of American Jews in Russia.[6]

The principle of separation did not figure in the intellectual baggage of the east Europeans. They desired liberty of conscience and limits to ecclesiastical power, but the American condition, where lines divided religion and public law, was alien to them. (In the Russian school system the study of religion, or "God's Law," as it was called, was obligatory.)[7] Once in the new country, the immigrants would absorb that knowledge from personal experiences with matters like Sunday laws and religion in the schools, from the Yiddish press, and from the tutelage of their predecessors.

To be sure, in common with the previous waves of Jewish immigrants, the new arrivals from czarist Russia had suffered persecution at the hands of a despotic government allied with the regnant church. After 1881 the Orthodox church cooperated in the government policy of instigated pogroms; Jews dreaded the approach of Easter week, the season when clergy frequently aroused the peasants against the Christ killers. And the charge of ritual murder brought against Mendel Beilis in 1913 Kiev echoed a medieval superstition. Despite its palpable presence, however, the church was viewed primarily as a functionary of the autocracy rather than as an independent menace.

Very much like the early Sephardim, a pre-emancipation people, the Russian Jews did not deliberate the desired relationship between the civil and religious powers.[8] The western European model of emancipation, allied with the liberal emphasis on individualism and individual rights, had bypassed them. Different from the Jews of central Europe, they could not boast of a Moses Mendelssohn or a Gabriel Riesser. Some *maskilim* (propagators of enlightenment) who touched in their writings on church–state separation derived that theme from their knowledge of western European conditions. Those who fought rabbinical control within local Jewish communities were acting out the idea of separationism, but what they may have appropriated through experience was not formulated into a general creed. Nor were western European liberalism and individual rights the primary focal points in wider Russian circles. As Jonathan Frankel has shown, collectivities rather than individuals were the key objects of both Russian and Russian-Jewish political attention.

East European Jews retained the premodern concept of a corporate ethnic identity that transcended religion. In keeping with the multiethnic society in which they lived, that concept was reinforced in the last quarter of the century by the Russification movement and racial anti-Semitism. Ideologues who preached Zionism or diaspora nationalism assumed the primacy of the ethnic group. Even Jewish Socialists compromised their adopted creed in order to meld Socialist with Jewish group interests. Unlike the Jews of western and central Europe who sought full integration within gentile society, the east Europeans spoke in a different idiom. For them Jewish survival meant primarily the survival of a culture and a people. Their objective was not the assimilation of the group into the larger society but its corporate and autonomous development within a restructured environment. The centrality of peoplehood, now decked out for the most part in secular garb, weakened the hold of traditional religion, and since Judaism denuded of its ethnic component was unthinkable, the possibility of a serious Reform movement in eastern Europe was precluded. The Russian Jews either held on to the Orthodoxy they knew or repudiated Judaism along with all religions out of principled anticlericalism. Thus, even before the masses of east Europeans set foot on American shores, basic philosophical differences set them off from the established American Jewish community.

Consciously or unconsciously the east Europeans perpetuated the primacy of the group in their American surroundings. Their pattern of settlement as well as their social and political behavior attested to an ineradicable sense of peoplehood. Jewish mutual aid societies and *landsmanshaftn* (fraternal societies), Socialist and Zionist organizations, and the short-lived New York Kehillah mirrored their perceptions of a corporate, secular distinctiveness. Encouraged by the Yiddish press, the younger immigrants eagerly participated in the political process; to the dismay of the German Jewish leadership, they formed Jewish political clubs and openly used the ballot on behalf of specifically Jewish interests.[9] Much of that behavior could not survive unaltered in a nation which frowned upon ethnic separatism and on Socialist and antireligious creeds. Nevertheless, the east Europeans stamped the dimension of peoplehood indelibly on the American Jewish community, and acculturated Jewish leaders were slowly influenced by the surge of a reinvigorated ethnicity. Some grew more sensitive to Jewish ethnic interests, and, in the case of American-born Louis Brandeis and Judah Magnes, argued seriously about the advantages of ethnic pluralism before that theory was fully developed.[10]

With rare exceptions, Reform Jews, the most zealous defenders of separation, closed ranks against public displays of Jewish ethnicity. Conscious that the east Europeans by sheer weight of numbers would inevitably control the destiny of the community, they attempted to instruct the immigrants in proper American behavior. Although the Reformers themselves never succeeded at total self-deethnicization, their group activities were kept within the confines of the community and were limited in the main to areas of religion, philanthropy, and social fellowship. The behavior of the new arrivals, who publicly paraded a peoplehood and a collective identity that encompassed secular ideologies and politics, contradicted Reform's very definitions of Judaism and Jewish survival, and, according to the apprehensive rabbis of the CCAR, belied Jewish readiness to assimilate within the body politic. Some Reform leaders charged that the fusion of Jewishness with secular actions violated the principle of church–state separation. Jewish nationalism and organized Zionism evoked a particularly hysterical response; among other things, they hinted at an *imperium in imperio* and hindered Jewish efforts at maintaining a firm wall between church and state. As one rabbi said: "If the Jewish communities in this country cannot go before the general community with clean hands on the very question of the separation of church and state, . . . I feel we will have great trouble in our insistence on this principle."[11]

Ironically, the government seemingly validated the east Europeans' emphasis on peoplehood by its practice of classifying the new Jewish arrivals from Russia as "Hebrews." The immigration laws of 1903 and 1907 called for tabulation by nationality and race, and "Hebrew," used to designated a discrete race or nationality, was substituted in the case of Jews for country of origin. To be sure, references to Jews as a race were common in popular and Jewish parlance; the word race was used to denote ethnic group or ties of peoplehood. However, when interest in racism sparked at the end of the century, the established American Jews grew apprehensive. They recognized the link between racist thought and the spread of a new kind of anti-Semitism in Europe and America. National and racial categories cast doubts on the assimilability of the Jew and, indeed, on his desirability as a citizen. Classification of "Hebrews" also enabled immigration restrictionists to focus on the staggering numbers of non-Christians who were pouring into the country and, out of anti-Semitic bias, agitate for the closing of American doors.[12]

The pervasive notions of a Jewish race or nationality, aired simultaneously by the government and the new immigrants, threatened the very design for communal security so assiduously cultivated by nineteenth-century Jews. For the sake of achieving equality the latter had accepted American conditions: proper Americanization and assimilation demanded disavowal of ethnic separatism; group distinctiveness was acceptable only within the churches. Accordingly, Jews had either renounced their ethnicity formally, as in the case of the Reformers, or had kept it concealed within the covers of their prayerbooks and the walls of the synagogues. In exchange, their rights as a religious group were fully protected by the religion clauses of the Constitution and the First Amendment. Blatant racist and ethnic identification, however, stripped Jews of that protection, exposed their vulnerability anew, and seriously weakened their quest for equality.

Since Jewish defenders who challenged the practice of immigrant classification were unable to invoke constitutional protection against racist acts, they attempted to shift the issue to one of religious discrimination. Simon Wolf and Julian Mack argued along such lines to the restrictionist Dillingham Commission in 1909, but they were no match for Senator Henry Cabot Lodge. The latter insisted that the classification of Jews was racial, and rightfully so, and in no way religious. Thus, he forestalled arguments on unconstitutional religious interference or discrimination by the government.[13] That same year, in a case involving a Russian immigrant who faced deportation, the American Jewish Committee (AJC) filed its first *amicus curiae* brief. In the manner of Wolf and Mack, the brief dismissed the argument that Jews were a race, and it held that the designation of an immigrant as a Hebrew, a religious category, violated the First Amendment. The specific case never reached the courts, and government classification of "Hebrew" immigrants lasted until the 1930s.[14]

Although increasingly aware that reliance on church–state separation inadequately met the reality of anti-Jewish discrimination, Jewish leaders refused to relinquish their time-honored and hitherto strongest weapon. In 1911 the AJC mounted a public campaign to force the Taft administration to abrogate a treaty of commerce with Russia.[15] Similar to the earlier episode of the treaty with Switzerland, the czarist government was discriminating against American Jewish passportholders, and worse still the United States was passively acquiescing to such behavior. That Russia targeted them as a discrete *people* mattered little to American Jews. Faulting America, the committee defined the issue as one of religious inequality and discrimination. As Louis Marshall stated in an address that launched the campaign, if Russia refused to honor the passports of Protestants or Catholics, America would regard that act as an insult not merely to a specific religion but to the country's honor. When an anti-abrogationist retorted that race rather than creed was the problem, the committee sidestepped the argument.

After World War I, native as well as foreign-born Jews deferred to popular usage and more readily accepted the designation of race. Like their fellow Christians, friends and foes alike, they called themselves a racial as well as religious group. Since anti-Semitism increasingly blurred the lines between religious and racial prejudice, Jews used the phrase "racial intolerance" interchangeably with religious discrimination. Indeed, precise classification was impossible. For example, did Protestant ministers who enlisted in the Klan or religious demagogues like Gerald Winrod and Charles Coughlin, who purveyed Nazi-made propaganda, exemplify racial or religious prejudice? Similarly, was a statement that coupled the image of "Jew as Bolshevik" with a complaint about Jewish resistance to Sunday laws a religious or racial charge?[16] Doubtless it mattered little to the bigots; the opposite of Jew, whether in religious or racial terms, was generally Christian. On the Jewish side, all disabilities and discrimination were perceived as components of one ugly anti-Semitic pattern. Inevitably, the fusion in Jewish minds between abuses of separation and other forms of prejudice left an enduring suspicion that antiseparationism was a handmaiden of anti-Semitism. In turn, the perception that the typical antiseparationist was also an anti-Semite served to convince the ethnic-minded immigrants of the necessity of separation.

Among the numerous agencies which arose to service the needs of the east European immigrants were the religious associations of Orthodox and Conservative Jews. Like their Reform prototypes, these congregational and rabbinical organizations were actively involved in current issues, but although all three movements were committed to the principle of church–state separation, priorities differed. The Orthodox concentrated primarily on the preservation of Jewish ritual; separation was less important in theory than for its connection, as in the case of Sunday laws, with Jewish Sabbath observance. On the eve of the Great Depression, the Conservative rabbis established a Social Justice Committee, which dealt with matters of church and state, but its major focus before World War II was on socioeconomic issues.[17] The more assertive the new groups became, the more numerous would become the opinions on church–state issues.

Two prominent agencies active in church–state matters also date from the early twentieth century. In 1906, the AJC, the first organization predicated on a noncongregational base to deal solely with the defense of foreign and American Jews, was founded. An elitist group that wielded great influence just because its members had achieved status in American society, the AJC soon eclipsed earlier defense committees in importance. By 1918 the CCAR's Committee on Church and State admitted that the AJC was more effective on matters of church and state; several years later (1925) the UAHC for similar reasons disbanded the Board of Delegates. The shift of leadership to a secular agency was telling; it revealed that in the wake of the east European immigration the Reform agencies could no longer claim that they spoke for the majority of Jews, and that secularization was blunting rabbinical influence within the Jewish community.

A second defense agency, the Anti-Defamation League (ADL), began in 1913. An arm of B'nai B'rith, it concentrated initially on popular anti-Semitism. Like the AJC, it became actively engaged in litigation on behalf of church–state separation after 1945. The two organizations shared a common bond: leadership and style were fixed by the established Jews of German origin. For their part the new immigrants shied away from the *yahudim* and and their elitist methods. Only after 1922, when the American Jewish Congress (Congress) was permanently established, did east European participation become significant in a major defense agency.[18]

Justice Brewer and the Jews

Before World War I, the theme of a Christian state had not yet burnt out. Even the burgeoning social gospel movement, a product of modern Protestantism, posited a Christian America and accepted the conventional barriers between Jews and Christians. The drive for a religious amendment had slowed down for a few years, but the NRA again pushed the familiar proposals between 1909 and 1910, now to the accompaniment of an emerging Christian party and aggressive talk of "Christian citizenship." And, testifying to the respectability of the Christian-state idea, Justice David Brewer reaffirmed that faith—the reasons that made America a Christian nation and the reasons why it would remain one—in a series of lectures published in 1905.[19]

Recognizing that the theme of a Christian nation abetted the spread of both anti-Semitism and anti-immigrant sentiment, Jewish spokesmen faced hard choices. A counterchallenge to the Christian-staters might backfire and evoke greater hatred of Jews; passive acceptance displayed a lack of self-respect and could be interpreted by Christian militants as Jewish acquiescence to their religious goals. It is against this background that the Jewish public responses to Brewer's book need to be read.

Concern began with Brewer's decision in *Church of the Holy Trinity* v. *United States* (1892). The case itself addressed the question of whether the prohibition of contract labor applied to the hiring of a minister. Speaking for the court, Brewer found for the church "because this is a religious people." (A priest and a rabbi, he added, would also be unaffected by the labor law.) To support his point he dredged up examples of religious allusions in official documents that dated back to Columbus's commission. Proceeding to equate religion with Christianity, he cited judicial decisions in which judges affirmed the connection between Christianity and the common law. Such official utterances along with numerous voluntary Christian societies proved that "this is a Christian nation." Although this was the first time the words were spelled out, the Court had implied as much before. In decisions which had mentioned "other Christian nations" or alluded to moral standards of a Christian country or people, the assumption was that the United States was one of the fraternity.[20]

The decision moved the Court beyond Story's opinion in the *Girard* case. Its tone also differed from later rulings in the Mormon cases where the Court had defined freedom of belief in sweeping terms and had approvingly cited Jefferson's "wall of separation." The Court's detachment from matters of conscience was understood; its role was to guard the barrier between belief and harmful social action that resulted from belief. The *Holy Trinity* case, however, replaced detachment with cordiality—cordiality to religion and specifically to one religion. Technically Brewer's discourse had no relevance to the immediate issue at hand, but it caused great rejoicing in some Christian circles. In 1905, the justice himself engaged in a curious bit of circular reasoning, and cited the ruling as further proof that America was a Christian state. He showed thereby how religious crusaders could use the case as a weighty precedent. Indeed, succeeding state and federal courts found numerous opportunities to refer to the decision. More than ninety years later, in the case of *Lynch* v. *Donnelly*, one Supreme Court justice still labored to bury the *Holy Trinity* opinion.[21]

Jews took little immediate public notice of the decision. Only one substantive reply, by Louis Marshall, was published, and that low-keyed piece appeared four years after the ruling.[22] The publication of the justice's lectures in 1905 under the title *The United States a Christian Nation* elicited many more comments, articles, and pamphlets. It also prompted Jews to venture into new territory, a public campaign to eliminate Bible reading in the public schools. Both types of reaction, the theoretical replies and the school campaign, revealed once again that Jewish opinion on matters of church–state separation and on defense strategy was never an unrelieved monolith.

Brewer developed his thesis in three lectures delivered at Haverford College in the fall of 1905. The first sketched the historical background: Christianity had been woven into the fabric of American history since the arrival of the first colonists. The colonial charters, early requirements for officeholding, Sunday laws, state court decisions on Christian common law—all reflected the special place of one religion, Christianity, within America. If Judaism was mentioned in those sources, Brewer said, it was only "by way of toleration of its special creed." Although there was no established religion, for indeed separation was the product of Christian views on the relationship of man to God, and although all Americans were not of that faith, Christianity had always been "a mighty factor in the life of the republic." The second lecture, an echo of evangelical fervor, put Christianity on a civic pedestal alongside patriotism. The "best of all religions," it deserved the same kind of respect accorded the American flag. Since it was Christianity that preserved morality, individual freedoms, and social welfare, loyal citizens had to understand and honor its ordinances and institutions. Only an America living according to the spirit of Christianity, Brewer explained in the third lecture, would reap the rewards of the nation's promise.

Many of these ideas were bound to alarm the Jewish minority. Pushed to their logical conclusion, the justice's beliefs made a shambles of the proposition that Jews and Judaism were equal to Christians and their faith. One could also infer that patriotism, linked with Christianity, was ever beyond the grasp of Jews, or that non-Christian immigrants, who threatened the fulfillment of the American promise, should be barred from entry. In racist terms the message could reinforce the belief that the Jew, the quintessential non-Christian, remained the unassimilable alien. Others had said such things before, but Brewer had the added authority conferred by a seat on the nation's highest court.

Blanket condemnations of the book came from rabbis across the country.[23] For a short time the two arms of the Reform movement, the CCAR and UAHC, planned a joint publication to prove "that from a constitutional standpoint this is not a Christian country." The idea was dropped after it evoked unfavorable comments from both secular and Christian periodicals. A snide warning appeared in *Harper's Weekly*. Even if we admit that from a constitutional viewpoint the United States is not a Christian nation, the journal asked, "will it pay the Jewish brethren to rub it in?" Since agitation by the Jewish minority might impel the vast Protestant majority to insist on Christianizing the Constitution, "the Hebrew brothers would find it just as profitable to lie low about the Constitution, and content themselves with the free enjoyment of their religious preferences, and the fair chances in trade." Others wondered at the ingratitude of the Jews, who in no other country were so cordially received. An angry Baptist minister in New York expostulated: "If you don't like conditions in ... our Christian country, then go back, you don't have to stay. But if you do stay, you stay as those who stay in Christian America."[24]

Individual answers to Brewer based on law also appeared between 1907 and 1910. Only one response, that by Isaac Hassler, undertook an all-out attack on the justice's statements. A native-born Philadelphian who was active in Jewish communal affairs, Hassler was a member of the bar and author of legal articles. His pamphlet, *A Reply to Justice Brewer's Lectures*,[25] began by deploring the aid and comfort given by the justice to the "aggressive religionism" of the time. The narrow and sectarian opinion from a Supreme Court justice proved that such views were not confined solely to the unenlightened classes. It cried for refutation, not because Jews feared the loss of religious liberty, but because it contradicted the unique position of the United States as the exemplar of true equality. To show how Brewer's ideas were un-American, Hassler proceeded with a detailed textual critique of the justice's major points.

Asserting that vestiges of the legal recognition of Christianity were but "relics of a barbarous age" which had no applicability to contemporary America, Hassler argued forcefully against Brewer's implication that Judaism was merely a tolerated creed: "We insist that equality is the principle, upon the platform of which there is neither tolerator nor tolerated." Numbers neither conferred a superior status on Christians, nor, since constitutions were framed to restrict the power of the majority, did they endow Christians with broader rights. Moreover, Brewer erred in contending that Christianity was bound up with citizenship or patriotism, for civic duties derived from the people's share in the national enterprise and not from religious principles.

Hassler's views closely corresponded with the case for equality that American Jewish leaders had been building since the Revolutionary era. While he echoed Leeser and Wise, who admittedly had not been challenged by the critical problems of the east European Jews and the simultaneous entrenchment of a virulent anti-Semitism, most other respondents surprisingly found little to condemn.[26] Americans were a religious people, and the customs, affiliation, and institutions of the majority were in fact Christian. (Albert Friedenberg also argued that despite Jefferson's denial, Christianity *was* part of the common law.) Besides, Brewer had used the term Christian loosely, in the sense of ethical or righteous, and he probably believed that Jews were as moral as Christians. (Max Kohler even faulted the Jews for *their* erroneous perceptions of the justice's views!) True, the United States was not Christian according to fundamental or statute law. Jews enjoyed equal rights; no special privileges were accorded to Christianity, and the danger of ties between church and state was receding. Sunday laws and prohibitions of blasphemy were only police regulations for upholding public order and decency, and even Bible-reading, if kept strictly nonsectarian, was inoffensive to non-Christians. Although the possibility of the enactment of religious laws was always a danger, the Jewish minority had little to fear from Brewer's interpretation of a Christian state.

However those respondents are labeled—timid, realistic, fearful of reinforcing anti-Jewish or anti-immigrant sentiment, secure in the protection of the state and federal constitutions—they studiedly ignored the spirit and tone of Brewer's lectures. None challenged the justice's link between Christianity and citizenship or his views on the "toleration" of Jews or the superiority of the Christian religion. By explaining away judicial opinions that affirmed the religious base of state legislation, they weakened the entire separationist structure, particularly Jewish opposition to Sunday law enforcement and to Christian usages in the public schools. Moreover, even a qualified acceptance of the Christian label—on the grounds that most Americans were Christian or that the original colonies were Christian—consigned Jews permanently to the status of deviant minority. To argue that the trend was increasingly against the acknowledgment of religion in law might have been accurate, but it was scant comfort in the first decade of the twentieth century, when Jews knew that Massachusetts had rejected a bill to secure the rights of Sabbath observers on Sunday, that Bible reading was upheld in Ohio despite the *Minor* case of 1872, and that Oklahoma considered the recognition of Jesus in its revised constitution.

The Jewish respondents, nevertheless, appeared willing to modify their broad defense of church–state separation, at least in deference to Brewer and his influence, and to bear the discomforts foisted upon non-Christians in a Christian America.[27]

On a deeper level, perhaps the respondents were hinting that the Jewish goal of integration as fully equal citizens of society was illusory. Hard as Jews might try and even succeed in the struggle for a religion-blind or secular state, the United States was and would remain a Christian nation by heritage, culture, and values. As long as Jews chose to identify as Jews, they were automatically set apart from Christian Americans. Jewish denials notwithstanding, America was—albeit in the most comfortable possible way—still exile. In 1910, however, as throughout their history, most American Jews were unprepared to entertain such misgivings consciously, let alone to articulate them publicly.

Justice Brewer's book prompted the CCAR to launch a national drive on behalf of nonreligious public schools. Concentrating only on one facet of the Christian-nation design, the move was strategically wise. Aside from the special commitment of American Jews to the public schools, which intensified as vast numbers of immigrant children were enrolled, it appeared that the Christian-staters had shifted their sights to the schools. "Putting religion into the constitution has given way to putting religion into the public schools," a Jewish newspaper commented. If, as Brewer said, Christianity had to be promoted because it was tied to the national welfare, then logic demanded Christian instruction in the schools. Hence, one rabbi maintained, a challenge to religion in the schools was essentially a challenge to the larger aims of the Christian-staters.[28]

Christian determination to hold on to the schools validated Jewish assumptions. Protestant crusaders fought vigorously for the retention of Bible reading in the schools, especially after the *Weiss* case in Wisconsin (1890). There the state's supreme court had ruled unanimously that Bible reading, even without comment, was sectarian instruction which impinged on the rights of conscience of Jews, Catholics, Unitarians, and Quakers. The right of objectors to be excused, the court said, was irrelevant; the usage itself destroyed the equality of the pupils.[29] A weighty precedent for later courts, the *Weiss* decision troubled many Protestants. The New York conference of Methodists, for example, called it "un-American and pagan, and . . . a menace to the perpetuity of our institutions." Although Bible reading remained an accepted practice in most classrooms throughout the country, such groups were determined to resist any countermovement. They labored to endow the practice with legal status, not only for its own sake but also for the ongoing defense of the Christian-state idea.[30]

Jewish concern mounted in direct relation to Christian efforts against secular schools. In 1904, President Joseph Krauskopf of the CCAR spoke out impassionedly against those "who trespass upon our citizenship rights" in their attempts to make the schools sectarian. "Have all the Christianity you wish, . . . enthrone it in your church, but keep it from public schools." At his urging the Reform rabbis appointed a special committee to prepare for a "vigorous campaign" should the need arise to combat sectarianism in public institutions.[31] Two years later, in the wake of Brewer's book and two school episodes, the CCAR would embark on that vigorous campaign.

In 1905, in connection with a bill for Washington, D.C., that mandated religious teaching in the schools, the battle between the Christian-staters and their opponents was joined. One Episcopalian minister argued the right of the majority to impose its will on the schools. Fusing religion with racism, he told a meeting of representatives of different faiths that foreigners should take the country as they found it: "This was an Anglo-Saxon nation, and therefore a Christian one." Simon Wolf, aided by Rabbis Abram Simon and Louis Stern, spoke to the Board of Education for the UAHC and the Jewish community. Emphasizing the need of separation for the harmony and tranquility of the republic, Wolf identified himself first as a citizen rather than a representative of the Jews. Nevertheless, in defense of the Jews specifically, he denied that opposition to religion in the schools stemmed from godlessness: "If there be any contributions which the Jews have made to the world, it is the Bible and the religions which are derived therefrom. They, of all people, cannot be suspected of hostility either to the Bible or to religion." Wolf's side won the Washington round, and since legislation for religious exercises in the schools of the District of Columbia would have meant a congressional act, Jews appreciated the victory.[32]

Reform leaders were further aroused by another incident in 1905, one involving a Brooklyn public school where the majority of the children were Jewish. At a Christmas assembly the principal, Fred Harding, made comments of the following sort: "I want you all to have the feeling of Christ within you"; "Christ loves all but the hypocrites and the hypocrites are those who do not believe in him." Irate parents petitioned for Harding's dismissal, and a legal case ensued. The counsel for the parents, retained by the Union of Orthodox Rabbis, broadened the question to one of religious practices and symbols in the public schools, which, he argued, led logically to Christianizing. Reform spokesmen considered the issue analogous to Bible reading and yet another manifestation of Christian determination to conquer the schools. Rabbi Tobias Schanfarber, who egged on the Brooklyn Jews, expostulated: "The Jew does not attend the public schools on tolerance. The Jew is not a citizen of this commonwealth on sufferance. . . . The time has come to sound in no uncertain notes that this is not a Christian country." The Harding case effectively joined a grassroots Orthodox move to a legalistic Reform approach, showing that the idea of a Christian state could, at least on an ad hoc basis, ally two groups that were usually at loggerheads.[33]

In response to the events of 1905 the newly created Committee on Church and State of the CCAR called for a campaign of education to "reconquer" public opinion in support of separation. The necessity to create "a healthy public opinion" on that issue, it stated, was underscored by Justice Brewer's book. The committee understood that a national campaign mounted by Jews was out of the ordinary and fraught with serious intergroup problems, but it defended an activist stance: "For once the Jew must turn a deaf ear to the confirmed optimist in his ranks who is ever crying out that all will be right in the end . . . for once, instead of waiting for untoward consequences, he must endeavor to direct public opinion."[34]

In this, the first major public relations campaign by American Jews, the Committee on Church and State produced a well-researched and widely distributed pamphlet entitled "Why the Bible Should Not Be Read in the Public Schools." As American Jews had always done, the pamphlet stressed equality, but this time Jews were not mentioned. Rather, the pamphlet rested its case on American and universalistic values. It argued that since Bible readings, in what were literally the "public's schools," were never impartial, they led inevitably to other religious and divisive practices. In turn, the growth of democracy, which rested on a nondiscriminatory and classless school system, was stymied.

The CCAR succeeded in firing the enthusiasm of many of its members; its campaign was accompanied by a rash of protests that erupted in various cities, on religious exercises in the schools.[35] Unchallenged publicly by any other Jewish position, its stand was understood by Christian America to be *the* Jewish point of view. Where Catholics had been in the forefront of the school fight in the nineteenth century, Jews now occupied that place. Christians saw a Jew different from his nineteenth-century predecessors, one who actively resisted the Christianizers and publicly demanded Jewish equality in universalistic and secularist terms.

On the surface the CCAR's campaign belied any moderating trend on church–state issues. But the resistance it encountered from members within the rabbinical organization revealed that contrary views had penetrated this stronghold of separationism. Some rabbis were fearful of arousing anti-Jewish sentiment. It was one thing to write in a Jewish periodical that Jews need not apologize for their existence but quite another to incite the eruption of anti-Jewish hostility, particularly within small communities outside the metropolitan areas.[36] Others worried about the school's task to inculcate moral and ethical values. To argue that the defense of separation transcended the need for moral instruction grounded in religion was an uncomfortable, if not untenable, position. "We must never lose sight of the fact," one member of the CCAR told his colleagues, "that it is a poor and negative and barren victory that we Jews enjoy in . . . keeping the Bible out of the public school." Moreover, how could they as religious leaders defend that stand to their Christian neighbors? The CCAR's pamphlet ignored the problem, but in closed sessions the rabbis reverted to it time and again.[37]

The debate between those who sought to extirpate Bible reading from the schools and those who emphasized the "tyranny of godlessness" belied any blanket correlation of Reform with purist separationism. It also exposed problems inherent in the separationist stance. Were the majority boxing themselves into a secularist corner and sacrificing Jewish religious interests in the process? Some called for the substitution of the "religion of Americanism" in public schools, but even if that could be defined and attained, could it, or for that matter any substitute, remove the stamp of Christianity from American education? When Rabbi Max Heller, one of the few Zionists in the CCAR, voiced such doubts and suggested that only in a Jewish state could Jews develop their religious individuality, his views were called cowardly. Rabbi Samuel Schulman answered with the classical Reform message: America offered the best chance for the development of Judaism. "Not political Zionism, but the eventual triumph of the principle of the separation of church and state in all countries, is what the Jew as a man and as one loyal to his faith, should seek to accomplish."[38]

The CCAR operated independently, forging no alliances with like-minded Protestant, Jewish Orthodox, or secularist groups. Nor did the campaign elicit Christian support. Whereas some Protestants responded angrily, the Catholics (despite opposition to use the King James Bible) distanced themselves. While the Jewish campaign was under way, James Cardinal Gibbons ranted against both Jews and godless schools: "There are so many cunning little schemes being always devised by Atheists, unbelievers and non-Christians to put God out of the public school that the authorities of this country and in every state should exclude Atheists and non-Christians from any office of authority."[39]

The CCAR's school campaign, a logical culmination of the Wise–Lilienthal approach in the *Minor* case, signaled a new phase in American Jewish responses to the Christian-state idea. The generation that launched the campaign knew that they were challenging the principle of a Christian state by an attack on one of its components, religion in the schools. Succeeding generations often fixed on that component and forgot the deeper principle. Earlier, a public school system divorced from religion had been both an end in itself and a means for combating the broader goal of a Christian state, but eventually it became merely an end, indeed the sole end. By mid-twentieth century any threat to their concept of the proper school—prayer, Bible reading, released time, religious holidays—had replaced Christian state as the code words that triggered Jewish alarm on church–state separation. Hence the seemingly disproportionate zeal with which many responded thereafter to issues of religion in the classroom.

The CCAR continued to run a strong campaign even after the stimulus of Brewer's book had faded, and in several states it succeeded in preventing the passage of Bible-reading laws. Its efforts, however, could not withstand the determination of its adversaries. "The truth is," the Committee on Church and State reported in 1916, "that in practically every city in the country the Bible is read, either with the sanction of the law or, when the law forbids, with the connivance or ignorance of the school authorities." The movement to protect Bible reading by law, the product of Protestants on the defensive, grew more popular during the period between the two world wars, doubtless in reaction to the popular mood of religious indifference. One prominent member of the CCAR spoke of an "epidemic of Bible Bills" that were introduced in the state legislatures. By 1941 twelve states and the District of Columbia required Bible reading, seven states permitted it, eleven prohibited it, and eighteen made it optional.[40]

Since most states forbade sectarian teachings, the decision of whether Bible reading fell into that category depended on judicial definitions of "sectarian." Mixed signals emanated from the courts, but most permitted the reading of the Bible or sections of it. Where the law was silent on the matter, or the practice went unchallenged, the decision rested with the local school authorities.[41]

Two cases illustrate the broad spectrum of judicial opinions. A Texas court's decision of 1908, relying on the tried definition that nonsectarian meant what was common to all Christian sects, stated that Bible reading, prayers, and other religious exercises in the school were neither sectarian nor in violation of constitutional rights. Nor did the majority need "to starve the moral and spiritual natures of the many" in deference to a few objectors. The judges warned particularly against the elimination of Bible reading and the Lord's Prayer from the schools of a Christian state where "Christianity is . . . interwoven with the web and woof of the State government."[42] Diametrically opposed, an Illinois court in 1910 banned Bible reading. It maintained that the public school, like the government, was a secular institution. It admitted that "this is a Christian State. No doubt this is a Protestant State." But the law knew no distinction among believers or between believer and nonbeliever. Nor could majoritarianism determine the parameters of religious liberty; indeed, majorities could take care of themselves.[43]

The wide array of judicial opinions persisted during the interwar period. Some libertarians grew restive, and in 1930 the American Civil Liberties Union (ACLU) looked for a test case on Bible reading to bring up to the Supreme Court. Since the organization wanted a "follower of religion" rather than a nonbeliever, the CCAR canvassed its members for any congregant who might be interested.[44] However, the highest tribunal would not pass on a Bible-reading case for another thirty years.

Sunday Law Exemptions

The CCAR's campaign against Bible reading bypassed the newly arrived immigrants, yet they were, albeit passively, very much involved. Religion in the public schools was basically offensive to the east Europeans, whose children crowded the classrooms in ever increasing numbers. Like the missionaries who rebounded in ghetto neighborhoods, Christian usages weakened confidence and pride in the Jewish heritage.

Sunday laws raised a more immediate problem for those barely able to earn a living in seven days. The immigrants who swelled the number of self-employed peddlers, small businessmen, and storekeepers—those not protected by exemptions excusing Sabbath observers engaged in "servile labor"—were especially hard-hit. Their work week was automatically reduced to five days. At a CCAR meeting Rabbi Jacob Voorsanger denied that a bare 3 percent of the population could, in five days, effectively compete in a setting where Saturday was a particularly important business day. Warning of the "ultimate pauperization" of the Jew, he understood full well why many felt constrained to work on the Sabbath.[45]

The Reform rabbis, interested in attracting the new arrivals to their camp, could not ignore immigrant impatience with the Sunday laws. Nor could they permit the east European to take matters into his own hands. Wildcat action threatened their principled response to the problem and their very control of the community. Jewish resistance to Sunday laws, especially if it involved payoffs to the police, could sully the group image that communal leaders sought to project. Conceivably resistance could boomerang and, if Jews were accused of spoiling the mood of the Christian day of rest, result in harsher laws and heightened Jew-hatred. It was reasonable to expect, therefore, that the immigrant presence would have invigorated the struggle against all Sunday legislation.[46]

Nevertheless, after the turn of the century Jewish leaders focused not on the removal of Sunday laws but rather on securing broad exemptions for observant Jews. In previous decades the operative goal had also been exemptions, but the attendant rhetoric often called for the repeal of all Sunday legislation. The death of Isaac Wise in 1900 coincided with the onset of a moderating trend; gone was the hyperbole of the fiery editor on Sunday "slavery" or the Christian-state design that underlay the laws. Solitary voices still ranted against the very concept of Sunday laws, but the general tone had softened. When Rabbi Samuel Schulman wrote a piece directed to the east Europeans, he sounded that new note. Insisting that the rights of a Sabbath-observing minority demanded proper exemption to the laws, he added that the efforts of Christians to "hallow" Sunday deserved equal respect and genuine sympathy. Schulman was concerned primarily about the desecration of the Jewish Sabbath, and in that spirit he could ill afford to sneer at Christian worries about the sanctity of Sunday.[47]

Schulman's views on the importance of a religious day of rest reflected a phase of soul-searching on the part of Reform. Plagued by ennui within their ranks and even random suggestions about a merger with Unitarianism, some Reform leaders acknowledged that their religion of reason, which minimized ritual and ceremonial, was incapable of ensuring a meaningful ongoing existence. As rabbis pondered the spiritual crisis, some thought that one of the ways to revitalize Reform lay in an emphasis on the Jewish Sabbath. Schulman told the CCAR that Reform, by its "ethicization of religion," could not escape responsibility for the erosion of Sabbath observance. He urged the rabbis to strengthen the Sabbath idea, both by encouraging Jews to keep their own Sabbath and by educating the American public on the right of the Jew to do so.[48]

The new emphasis on the need for religious rituals modified Reform's rigid posture on Sunday laws. True, the CCAR's Committee on Church and State still maintained that Sunday laws, like religion in the public schools, rested on the Christian-state idea, and in 1914 it recommended that the rabbis work for legislation, such as that in California, which would leave the choice of a weekly day of rest up to the individual. Nevertheless, the rabbis resolved only to cooperate "in safeguarding the rights of religious minorities in the matter of Sabbath observance." The resolution could be interpreted either broadly—blanket opposition to the recognition of Sunday for whatever reason—or narrowly—full exemptions for seventh-day observers. The latter seemed more likely, for when a Sunday bill with exemptions was introduced for Washington, the CCAR raised no objection.[49]

Reform's new approach tacitly acknowledged the stark reality: Sunday laws were well-nigh unassailable. Despite the advances of secularization, the volume of Sunday legislation between 1890 and 1911 rose dramatically. Of all the states and territories in 1909, only Nevada and Arizona had no such statutes; Idaho passed its first Sunday law in 1907. Pushed by clergymen and organizations like the American Sabbath Union, attempts also continued to gain congressional sanction of Sunday observance. Without any pretense at uniformity, laws varied from state to state on what acts during what hours and under what penalties were forbidden. Most states provided exemptions for those who observed Saturday as their religious day of rest, but here too provisions varied on the scope of permitted activities. Broad exemptions were still elusive; in three states with sizable Jewish populations—New York, Pennsylvania, and Massachusetts—conditions remained the same as they had been in the 1880s.

The vagaries of police enforcement further compounded the inconsistencies and variations. At times leniency alternated with severity within the tenure of the same municipal administration. Various factors—from payoffs by Jewish storekeepers to political infighting between the police department and the city administration—influenced police behavior.[50] The *American Hebrew* described how the Jews in one New York City neighborhood were reminded of their days in Russia when the police swooped down upon tradesmen on a Sunday and held many in jail overnight. According to the paper, an order had come from on high to clean up vice in the district, but only Sunday violators had been targeted. It was subsequently learned that most of those arrested were merchants who had not given Christmas presents to the patrolmen on the beat. Doubtless the mutual antipathy that existed between the Jewish merchant and the Irish Catholic policeman contributed to the woes of the Sunday law victims.[51]

The extremely high number of Jews arrested for violation of Sunday laws was also part of the reality. An account published in 1912 reported that "tens of thousands of arrests . . . were made in the large cities, especially in New York City, . . . where the cases never went higher than the first instance, because the poor man, if he was not discharged in the Police Court, had to pay his fine or be imprisoned." Where cases reached higher courts, the decisions generally upheld the legality of Sunday legislation. Like enforcement and like the laws themselves, the rulings varied, even within the same court. Most judges treated the statutes as products of the police power, but, as one Jewish observer noted, the "mysterious" term "police power" was invoked to cover a multitude of frequently illogical interpretations.[52]

To be sure, religious considerations had not entirely evaporated. In a Maryland case of 1894 the court admitted that Sunday laws fostered and encouraged the Christian religion. But, it continued, "in what professes to be a Christian land" there was all the more reason for the enforcement of such laws. Commenting on the case, one scholar observed that the decision probably represented "the general view of American legislators and courts" in the new century. A Missouri court was even more outspoken. Unconcerned with the rights of minorities, it stated in 1908 that Sunday laws were enacted to secure the full right of conscience of a Christian people who believed that the day was hallowed time. The evidence proves that religious habit if not motive still figured prominently in both the enactment and interpretation of the Sunday laws. If health alone was the reason for such laws, why were healthful recreational activities forbidden? Besides, if a day of rest for the worker was truly the sole goal of legislators and courts, they might have turned, as did the CCAR's Committee on Church and State, to California's solution.[53]

The impregnability of Sunday laws convinced Jews that it was futile to seek more than broad exemptions. In 1909 the UAHC, long the advocate of strict separation, appointed a committee to consider how best to prevent the enactment of Sunday laws which hurt Sabbatarians. By focusing on future legislation, the committee admitted that existing laws were beyond assault and signaled its expectation of further legislative activity. In addition to exemptions for the Sabbath observer, the committee asked merely that terms like "Lord's day" and "Sabbath"—which by their religious color influenced magistrates in a sectarian direction—be avoided. It also advised Jews how to conduct themselves in their efforts for exemptions: "Proper respectful agitation by means of discussion and papers . . . arguing along the lines of general human right and justice and criticizing the religion-colored decisions of the judges." At no point did the UAHC proclaim that all Sunday legislation was unconstitutional.[54]

Reality also sharpened the fears of ultra-accommodationist Jews. A crank threat that warned of a Kishinev-like pogrom if Jews pushed too hard for broader exemptions, or even an anti-Semitic tirade by a Kansas City judge who charged that Jews used their money to defy the laws of a Christian nation, was not overly serious, but when added to the ever-present worries about anti-Semitism and immigration restriction, each compounded the desire for a low profile. Reform Rabbi Maurice Harris of New York City, noting adverse public opinion as well as police assaults on Jews, advised that Jews tone down their demands about Sunday laws. When Mayor Seth Low permitted the relaxation of Sunday laws during one Passover season, Harris thought that the result—crowded, filthy streets in the Jewish sections, about which Christians complained—would stir up anti-Semitism. Offense to Christian sensibilities, something that nineteenth-century Jews had foresworn, appeared more serious than the hardships of Sunday laws.[55]

The *Jewish Messenger,* whose timid views had been outshouted fifty years earlier by Wise's *American Israelite,* now represented mainstream Jewish opinion. Not long before it ceased publication, the paper turned again to the Sunday law issue, a problem made more significant by the immigrant presence. One lengthy editorial called for concessions from both sides—the Christian to recognize the injustice of Sunday laws for Sabbatarians, and the Jew to be content with narrow exemptions: "Why ask for more? . . . It is natural to insist upon our rights, but it is not always advisable to pose as martyrs before our neighbors. . . . The Jew must be doubly prudent. If the strict Sabbath keeper has his burdens, he has his compensations as well." Until the eventual liberalization of Sunday laws, cautious Jews would do well to appreciate the reverence of Christians for their Sabbath and resist the secularization of Sunday.[56]

Broad exemptions for Sabbath observers were particularly important in New York, the state with the largest concentration of Jews. As discussed previously, the trouble began with the adoption of a more stringent penal code in 1882. Jewish storekeepers were forbidden to conduct business on Sundays even if they conscientiously observed their own Sabbath. Furthermore, courts throughout the state held to a narrow interpretation of the law; exemption for "servile labor" constituted a defense against prosecution but not against arrest.[57]

Bills for broader exemptions were introduced almost annually in Albany. Despite opposition from Protestant ministers, delegations of Jews or representatives of philanthropic, religious, and fraternal agencies often appeared at hearings of legislative committees. In this matter east Europeans, who agitated for equal rights as well as economic benefits, were highly visible. Unlike the Bible-reading campaign where the CCAR was conspicuously involved in local communities, the Reform rabbis stayed clear of the New York situation. The drive for an amendment was spearheaded by attorney Louis Marshall acting for the AJC and the New York Kehillah, and it was aided by the activities of the Orthodox-led Jewish Sabbath Alliance.

Marshall's proposed amendment addressed the two basic problems, exemption for the Orthodox Jewish storekeeper and freedom from prosecution for observant Jews who violated Sunday laws. Focused narrowly on observant Jews, it aroused opposition from both Jews who desired to work seven days and those who preferred to leave the choice of day of rest to the individual. Marshall, a conscientious Reform Jew, had no patience for the former, whom he faulted for contributing to the failure of an amendment. He explained that protection of religious scruples and the right to equal opportunity did not absolve Jews from the social requirement to keep one day of rest. The lawyer described the problem to a state legislative committee: either observant Jews violated their Sabbath or they suffered financial losses, which, he pointed out, were a serious economic waste for the state. Although Sunday laws did not literally run afoul of the religious freedom guarantees of New York's constitution, they did, he claimed, impinge on the "spirit" of those clauses. Marshall's persistent efforts on behalf of disadvantaged Sabbatarians failed, and the problem itself dragged on.[58]

After World War I, Jews noted that Christian zeal for Sunday laws had abated somewhat, but the long-sought broad exemptions to statutes on the books failed to materialize. Continuing the trend which had begun before the war, Jews kept to a moderate course. No one advocated the abolition of the laws, and two suggested solutions for New York even skirted the usual insistence on broad exemptions. One proposed the creation of geographical zones where local option would determine Sunday observance; another advocated the adoption of the five-day work week. The Synagogue Council of America (SCA), an umbrella agency of the major Reform, Conservative, and Orthodox organizations which was established in 1926, opted for the second. It explained that a five-day work week, whereby Saturday and Sunday would be consecutive days of rest, would free all workers from the need to labor on their respective Sabbaths. The SCA did not condemn the theory of Sunday legislation; rather, it wanted work-free Saturdays "in order that a great historic religion may be helped, without outward handicap, to exert its morally and spiritually educating influence upon those who profess it." Here, too, the SCA was not *against* Sunday laws but *for* the acceptance of Jewish religious behavior. But, aware that its goal was unattainable—at least until business and labor, for their own reasons, acceded—it simultaneously demanded exemptions in pending legislation. No overall solution was reached, and Jews could only hope for isolated laws and court decisions that remedied specific local grievances.[59]

As the attempts to amend New York's Sunday laws showed, Jews no longer talked about the menace of a Christian state or belabored the religious origin of the legislation. The official rationale of police power was now so firmly entrenched that to argue against a Sunday law per se would have put Jews in the unenviable position of less than loyal citizens. The irony lay in the fact that an increasingly secularized society still practiced religious discrimination. Refusals to entertain amendments that in no way undercut the alleged basis for the laws—that is, the physical well-being of the public—gave credence to the suspicion that in many quarters police power was still, as Isaac Leeser had said long before, but a subterfuge. Also ironic was the fact that secular Jews (Marshall and the AJC) had assumed a central role on a *religious* issue and that their tone was more moderate than that of nineteenth-century religious spokesmen.

As Jews qualified their negative stand on religious usages in the public arena, some sought advantages in situations where the government was benevolent toward, rather than removed from, religion. During World War I, no Jews charged the government with breaching the wall of separation by providing for chaplains, nor did they question efforts of the Jewish Welfare Board, an umbrella organization of the three religious movements and a few secular agencies, to secure furloughs for Jewish servicemen on religious holidays. After the war small favors for observant Jews were also requested: paid absences for municipal and federal employees on Jewish high holidays; state regulation of kosher food sales; and, during Prohibition, permission to use wine for ritual purposes. The attempt to plant Hanukkah alongside Christmas in the public schools, a position popular with many Jews, similarly reflected a compromise of separationist principles.[60]

The quest for government accommodation stemmed from the growing assertiveness of traditionalist groups within the community. In addition, as the newer immigrants gained experience in American political bargaining, elected officials in urban centers paid closer attention to the Jewish vote. On their part, Jews may also have reasoned that favors were a proper tradeoff where pure separation was unattainable. In any event, the self-imposed restrictions of nineteenth-century leaders on injecting religious interests into politics were largely discarded.

Those most troubled by the matter of government favors were the Reformers, the strongest exponents of separation and political neutrality. Bitterly critical of the Orthodox and Conservatives who supported Hanukkah celebrations, *kashruth* laws, or excused absences for religious holidays, they wondered how Jews, whose history was replete with suffering that resulted from church–state unions, could ever invoke state aid on religious matters. Those who sought state protection of religion were "putting a weapon in the hands of our enemies," the CCAR said. (In one instance where Orthodox Jews in Louisville, Kentucky, requested and obtained excused absences for their children on all Jewish holidays, Reformers lodged a protest with school authorities. Very likely the school superintendent was highly entertained by the spectacle of one Jewish group undermining another in order to cancel an official favor!) While the traditionalists disregarded such criticisms—what else, they doubtless asked, could be expected from those who sneered at *halakha*—Reformers were forced to acknowledge significant deviations within the community on matters of separation.[61]

Debates on Released Time

The CCAR retreated from strict separationism in the 1920s when it endorsed dismissed time in the schools. A seemingly small matter—consent to the shortening of one school day with the tacit understanding that children would receive religious instruction in church schools of their choice—took on a larger significance precisely because it emanated from an organization that for twenty years had railed publicly against any link between religion and the schools. The secular school was sacrosanct to the Reform rabbis, and, as discussed earlier, in its defense they had subsumed their fears of the Christian-state idea. Between the wars, however, that defense weakened. The lengthy debates on dismissed and released time revealed not only the differences of opinion within Jewish ranks but the strong competing pressures upon the non-Christian minority.

The roots of the matter lay in the desectarianization of the public schools, which church groups correlated with a rise in religious illiteracy and moral laxity. Unlike the Catholics and the Jews, who had relied on their own schools for religious training, the Protestants were hit hardest. Admitting the inadequacy of their Sunday schools, many fought for retention of Bible reading in the classroom and, at the same time, latched on to the released time idea. First broached in 1905, a program was introduced eight years later in Gary, Indiana, whereby pupils were released from secular studies during designated hours to attend religious classes. The idea spread to other cities, and its attractiveness was enhanced by the postwar revolution in morals. The Gary plan spawned various forms that differed in name and procedure: "released" time usually meant excusing the pupil during the school day; "dismissed" time meant shortening a school day by an hour or so. The number of school systems and children involved in the plans increased substantially between the wars, and by 1940, usually following local practice already in place, eight states had passed laws specifically permitting released or dismissed time. Protestants were the driving force behind the plans, which were most successful in towns and small cities. Catholic support came only later, and most Jews, if not opposed to all plans, preferred dismissed over released time.[62]

A few Jewish leaders commended the released time plan, and indeed Jewish children participated in the Gary program. One rabbi happily endorsed its interfaith nature—Protestants, Catholics, and Jews were cooperating in a common cause. The eminent Louis Marshall applauded the attempt to provide children with religious and moral training. Since the plan kept the training out of the classroom, he was satisfied that it observed the boundaries between church and state.[63] But released time sounded a warning to other Jews. The mere fact that school officials were involved, at the very least by keeping records of the participating pupils, violated pure separation. Besides, legal permission for the implementation of the plan was tantamount to state support of religion. A possible entering wedge, it could lead to renewed government involvement in religious matters. "If we allow ourselves to be permitted to give religious education," Rabbi Jacob Nieto of San Francisco said, "then we do tacitly admit the right of the Legislature subsequently to enforce."[64]

Such fears were not unfounded. Some supporters of released time maintained that freedom of religion was designed to protect, not destroy, religious beliefs and the right to acquire religious instruction.[65] That interpretation posited a religious nation; it hinted at the denial of equal favors to the nonreligious or secularists. It substituted an active role for government for the traditional one of noninterference in religious matters, and it indicated encouragement of, if not aid to, religion. Such eventualities, in a country where the vast majority were Protestants, threatened the equality of religious and nonreligious minorities. These fears brought Jewish critics of released time, even religious ones, to the side of a secularist state. From their perspective the program might start a domino reaction, breaking down their attacks on religion in the schools (like the campaign against Bible reading), which in turn would destroy their defenses against a Christian state.

For three years the CCAR debated the Gary program as well as similar plans that linked public school authority with private religious instruction. Pressures were mounting from both Jews and non-Jews on the Reform body to change its role as the obdurate *naysayer* on issues of religion and the schools. Were the CCAR to adhere to its negative and counterproductive course, the Committee on Church and State warned, it faced serious consequences: "[The CCAR] must add something to its No; or run the risk of seeing its unstatesmanlike attitude rebuked by a reversal of America's traditional policy of the separation of church and state." Once again the Reform group was impaled on the horns of dilemma—on one side, commitment to principle and a genuine fear that released time presaged worse abuses, on the other side, their responsibility as rabbis for the inculcation of religious values as well as the pressure of public opinion.

The debates exposed serious divisions among the Reformers. Although the majority agreed on the need to project a public image of cooperation, there was little consensus beyond that. One rabbi suggested a program of moral instruction in the classroom worked out with the Federal Council of Churches, a second proposed an interdenominational Bible reader, and a third pointed out the dangers for atheists and agnostics in any compromise. Three positions emerged on the specific issue of released time. On one side were the determined opponents who out of their personal experiences in the field offered proof of Protestant plans for a total takeover of the schools. Directly opposed stood those like Rabbi Samuel Schulman, who urged his colleagues to compromise. Americans were a religious people, Schulman emphasized, and if Jews claimed to be an integral part of that people, they were obligated to accommodate to popular sentiment. In the middle were those who believed that at least a partial compromise was necessary to avert graver dangers. They reluctantly advocated dismissed rather than released time, a position which both the CCAR and UAHC finally adopted. To put a brighter face on their retreat, some hailed the opportunity under dismissed time to strengthen Reform's educational outreach.

The Reformers had only approved a shorter school day; the resolution made no explicit mention of the expectation of religious instruction, and it ignored the administrative details that fell to the schools in the implementation of the program. Had the vote been not on dismissed time but on released time, where children were excused from school in the middle of the day and school involvement—attendance records, provision of escorts to religious classes, and so on—was blatantly underscored, the outcome might have been different.[66]

In 1925, while the CCAR was wrestling with the question, California's legislature considered a bill providing for the release during the school day of children whose parents requested that they receive instruction in a religious school. The bill enjoyed the backing of many Protestant churches and the Ku Klux Klan. A driving force against the measure was Louis I. Newman, a young Reform rabbi of San Francisco and an officer of the Western Association of Jewish Ministers. That organization denounced the bill, and Newman and others canvassed non-Jewish groups to join the opposition. The rabbi's testimony, along with a statement from the

Seventh-Day Adventists, persuaded the legislature's Committee on Education to table the proposal.

Newman positioned himself squarely as an uncompromising defender of church–state separation. His interpretation of religious freedom, he readily acknowledged, led logically to the support of a secularist state; any other position would only result in more dangerous laws. To avoid the evils of religious faith by compulsion, and to preserve the rights of agnostics and atheists, released time had to be rejected. The rabbi agreed with his Christian counterparts on the problem of moral laxity and the need of weekday religious instruction, but to ask assistance of legislatures—which he proudly asserted was not done by Jews—was a confession of the churches' weaknesses.

When the state assembly called the bill out of committee, Newman and a Unitarian minister arranged an emergency meeting at which civic and religious leaders adopted a set of resolutions in opposition to released time. The following morning, copies of the resolutions along with Newman's brief entitled "The Sectarian Invasion of Our Public Schools" were distributed to the assembly. A long and stormy debate followed. Supporters set the measure in the context of defending American youth against the nefarious influences of jazz, criminality, and evolution. Opponents injected charges of religious bigotry and un-Americanism; one called the bill an attempt to deny elective office to Jews or Catholics. Finally, by a close vote the assembly rejected the released time proposal.[67]

Vigorous opposition had greeted an attempt in 1917 to introduce released time in New York City. Riots erupted at public hearings, and the proposal was abandoned until after the war. Most Jews of New York opposed the plan, but in this case pressures for accommodationism won out over separationism. The issue came before the legislature in 1940, and by then the dramatic rise in anti-Semitism at home and abroad had so exacerbated the fears of American Jews that agitation along the San Francisco lines was hardly likely. The brutalities of the totalitarian states and the outbreak of war also convinced many Americans that religious instruction was necessary to preserve the democratic way of life. Those sentiments effectively muzzled loud Jewish protests. Furthermore, since Catholic leaders had abandoned their earlier opposition to released time and were joining Protestants on released time in ever-increasing numbers, Jewish intransigence would have underscored an isolation from the mainstream churches and would have set back the course of the nascent interfaith movement. New York at that time had a Jewish governor, and New York City's Jews possessed educational resources that made released time superfluous for them, but the Jews fell into line. When Governor Herbert Lehman signed the bill, he denied that constitutional principles had been violated. Doubtless the bill's provision of excused absences for religious holidays also helped to win over the community.[68]

At a public hearing on the operational plans for the program, Jewish religious and lay organizations proposed the alternative of dismissed time, but theirs was an empty gesture. Simultaneously, the Board of Jewish Ministers and the Jewish Education Committee surrendered by promising full Jewish cooperation in any implementation of released time. One Jewish educator explained that his organization had given way because experience with released time had not substantiated earlier fears and because interfaith cooperation promised the protection of religious minorities. Above all, Jews could not risk alienating their neighbors or creating a serious Jewish–Christian problem. Doubtless his response was conditioned by the accusation from Protestants and Catholics that Jews were obstructing the religious education of Christian children.[69] Jewish laymen and lay agencies, also calling for a decision in the interests of intergroup harmony, forcefully denounced opposition to the plan as a "tragic blunder." Thus, for the sake of Christian goodwill, the strict separationists yielded. When released time went into effect in 1941, Jewish participants in the program were very few.[70] Strict separationists had lost the legal round, but the released time plan of New York City more than any other single factor sharpened Jewish sensitivity to the problems of religion and the public schools.

During the 1920s the released time plan was adopted locally in communities outside New York City, and its constitutionality was tested twice. In 1925 a court struck down the program in Mount Vernon, ruling that religious instruction during school hours violated the statutory requirement on public school attendance. It stated that religious instruction, which could not be substituted for instruction in the public school, belonged to parents and churches off school property and after school hours. The court also held that in many districts, where only one church was near a particular school, released time worked to favor that particular denomination. Two years later, in the case of *Lewis* v. *Graves,* the state's Court of Appeals decided differently. Justice Cuthbert Pound found nothing about the program in White Plains that violated the state constitution or statutes. Since no public money, other than slight use of teachers' time, was allocated for the program, released time did not constitute a form of state aid to denominational schools. Writing for a unanimous court that included two respected Jewish judges, Benjamin Cardozo and Irving Lehman, Pound stated: "Neither the Constitution nor the law discriminates against religion."[71] Since the released time issue reached the judiciary only in New York, its constitutional status across the country on the eve of World War II was as yet uncertain.

Contemporaries have noted how World War II sparked greater interest in religion among Americans, specifically with respect to the religious roots of democracy. According to that reasoning, a healthy democracy, in contradistinction to totalitarianism, was sustained by religion, which in turn endowed it with divine sanction. The preservation of the American democratic way of life depended, therefore, on the proper recognition and acceptance of religious principles.

Jewish spokesmen watched the renewal of interest in religion with mixed feelings. Rabbis welcomed the opportunity to reassert the centrality of the faith within the Jewish community—to emphasize the role of religion in the prosecution of the war and in the blueprints for peace. They also saw a chance to teach the essential compatibility of Judaism with democracy, or, in other words, to equate Jewish with American values and to explain the war against the Axis as a religious as well as democratic crusade. At the same time, however, they recognized how the focus on religion presaged a major reevaluation of the relationships between religion and the state, perhaps even threatening traditional separation. In particular, the religious upsurge invigorated the forces that sought to connect the public schools with religious instruction.[72]

Leading Christian educators who posited the menace of irreligion to a healthy democratic state considered several ways of tying religion to the school system. One was to extend the system of released time, which, since the late 1930s, had been adopted by more and more communities. During the war its attractiveness increased still further as concerned citizens, frightened by the rise in juvenile delinquency, demanded that religious principles be invoked in building character. Since church schools lacked the authority to command attendance, it seemed that only involvement by the public schools could successfully supply the youth with proper training.[73]

Some professionals suggested more sweeping changes in the public schools. F. Ernest Johnson of Teachers College argued that only an education with a positive religious component could supply the needed synthesis between the spiritual and temporal so vital for a healthy society. Walter Bower of the University of Chicago similarly emphasized the need of religious education to serve as a unifying principle in a diversified society, and he formulated a detailed program to incorporate religion into the school curriculum. Such men believed that separation of church and state did not preclude cooperation between the two; nor did supporters of "functional religion," advocating nonsectarian religious instruction, see any violation of separation. Rather, as Dean Luther Weigle of Yale maintained, the schools *without* religion were sectarian because they had been surrendered to the "sectarianism of atheism and irreligion."[74]

All schemes bearing on religion in the schools raised Jewish apprehensiveness. Religion, as one rabbi explained, came with a label, and the differences between the Jewish and Christian way of life and faith were irreconcilable. Good intentions notwithstanding, instruction in religion that involved methods of teaching and curriculum content augured the inevitable intrusion of the majority faith into the classroom.[75] Majoritarianism again reared its head, and coercion of a minority by a revival of nondenomi-national Christianity in the schools appeared quite possible.

Under these new pressures, compounded by a steady rise in wartime prejudice, the Jewish community appeared hopelessly divided on issues of religion in the schools. In 1944, at the urging of the CCAR, the SCA arranged a conference on Jewish views of religion in the schools. Its purpose was to explore the possibilities of defining a Jewish consensus and of for-mulating a program of Jewish action. For the first time rabbinical and lay representatives of the major national agencies—religious, defense, edu-cational—met for joint deliberations.[76] The very makeup of the conference reflected the amorphous power structure within the Jewish community. Not only was leadership divided between religious and lay groups whose activities often overlapped, but the professionals, the educators involved in implementing the Jewish component in programs like released time, also shaped policy by the very technical services they rendered.

The subject before the conference, religion and the schools, turned primarily into a discussion of released time. In his opening remarks, Rabbi Israel Goldstein, president of the SCA and Conservative leader of New York's prestigious B'nai Jeshurun, focused exclusively on that matter, call-ing it important, controversial, and delicate: "It is delicate for us just because being the smallest of the three religious groups, we have the most at stake in the separation of church and state, and on the other hand it might be embarrassing that the impression created is that of all the religious groups, we alone resist the program . . . for religious instruction." In the discussion that ensued, participants generally lined up against released time. Of all the religious groups and defense agencies the ADL and UAHC were most outspokenly opposed to the plan and its attendant abuses.[77]

The keynote speaker, Dr. Israel Chipkin of the American Association of Jewish Education, went beyond customary platitudes. Sharply critical of a Jewish stand of unqualified rejection, he said that opposition to re-leased time caused a greater evil, namely, a serious rift with Christians. By touting the principle of separation, Jews left their Christian opponents with the impression that they, the Jews, considered themselves the better Americans. Particularly since they offered no viable alternatives for re-leased time, Christians also concluded that Jews were far less concerned with the need for religious education. Resentful and disapproving, the Christians in turn accused the Jews of impeding the moral training of children and thereby contributing to religious illiteracy and juvenile delin-quency. To underscore his point Chipkin cited editorials in the Jewish press urging Jewish participation in released time programs if only for reasons of public relations.

Chipkin outlined the graver dangers inherent in plans to introduce functional or nonsectarian religion into the school curriculum. He explained that educators like Bower were attempting to stem what they perceived to be the excesses of liberalism. Maintaining that individual liberty, the heart of classical liberalism, should be tempered by "corporateness" and social responsibility, they reasoned that religious education would fill the essential need of unifying a diversified society. Chipkin recalled Jewish unpreparedness to the onset of released time programs, and he challenged his audience to come up with positive responses to these more fundamental threats. Advising pedagogical rather than legalistic arguments, and pleading for a cooperative attitude, Chipkin urged Jewish participation in the committees that would implement the courses in nonsectarian religion. Only a Jewish presence in the planning stages would prove a commitment to religious education and would, at the same time, remind the Christians to respect Jewish sensitivities as they worked out the actual courses.

Chipkin's address disclosed the wide gap that separated the professional educators from the strict separationists. On released time the former said that they were opposed in principle to anything other than dismissed time, but for pragmatic reasons they were prepared to follow the American majority.[78] On other plans for tying religion to the public schools, they preferred a positive attitude—a willingness to listen to ideas and a readiness to cooperate—over the conventional negative stance that rested solely on legalisms.

The most extreme comments in an overwhelmingly separationist-minded assembly came from Reform Rabbi Ahron Opher. He warned of the threat of secularization to Jewish children, and expressing his sympathy with those Christians who refused to equate freedom *of* religion with freedom *from* religion, the rabbi announced his readiness to bend the rules of separation. Opher also agreed with the argument of majoritarianism; a small minority, he said, had no right to set itself up as ultimate interpreters of democracy. His implicit suggestion that the design of the strict separationists was skewed, that Jewish security depended more on the education of the children than on purist legalisms, may have shocked the audience. But, like Chipkin's discussion of the conservative theory of "corporateness," which clashed with the liberal foundations of the Jewish quest for equality, it failed to trigger a full-scale debate on principles.

In the end, no dramatic breakthrough occurred. Although they tacitly admitted that in certain communities public relations compelled Jewish acquiescence to some form of religious education, the organizations did not amend their formal opposition to released time and to similar plans. They agreed to monitor the movement for sectarian education and—their one constructive resolution—to present the alternative plan of dismissed time more aggressively to the public. Overall Jewish unity was still elusive, but with the promise to keep interagency consultation alive, the first step had been taken toward the establishment of a permanent body on matters of church and state.

PART II

Overview: 1945–1965

In accounts of the postwar Jewish community, the period 1945–65 has been called the "golden age" of American Jewry. Never before had Jews as a group appeared so well integrated in the larger society. Opinion polls registered a sharp decline in anti-Semitic sentiment, and barriers in higher education, the professions, and business management slowly crumbled. Geographical mobility accompanied economic well-being; Jews, now predominantly native born, joined the exodus from the urban metropolises. They settled in the suburbs, built new synagogues, and launched programs of Jewish studies at colleges and universities. Like their Christian neighbors, they felt the currents of religious renewal in the late 1940s and 1950s, and synagogue affiliation in the three branches of Judaism rose significantly. Politically, Jewish identification with the causes of civil rights and social welfare, testifying to the viability of the liberal consensus, was eminently respectable as Congress and the courts outlawed discrimination and broadened the dimensions of a welfare state. And, by 1965, key objectives of church–state separationists had become part of American law.[1]

American Jewish defense took a dramatic turn in the years immediately following World War II. Instead of focusing exclusively on immediate threats to Jewish rights, the big three—the American Jewish Committee (AJC), American Jewish Congress (Congress), and Anti-Defamation League (ADL)—moved from conventional reactive operations to ongoing programs of positive social action. Disparate stimuli accounted for the change: the assertiveness of a generation imbued with the confidence of native-born Americans and pride in the state of Israel; the lessons of Nazism and the Holocaust, which underscored the urgency of shoring up Jewish security; and the New Deal's legacy of an activist government where experts planned for the extension of economic and social democracy. Since anti-Semitism showed a decline after the war,[2] the defense agencies were free to channel more of their resources into social rather than strictly Jewish issues.

Unlike their nineteenth-century predecessors who sought equality for Jews within a fixed American framework, the Jewish agencies now formulated ideas of an improved America, one that was constantly evolving, where Jews could most comfortably survive.[3] The new leaders—lawyers and social workers, usually of east European backgrounds—predicated optimum survival on a democratic welfare state. Their thrust was egalitarian, their political outlook generally liberal or socialist. Seeking to erase social as well as legal discrimination, they aimed for a pluralist state in which all religious and ethnic minorities enjoyed basic rights, opportunity, and public respect. Toward that end the agencies labored to nurture a sense of social responsibility among their constituents. Jewish well-being, they reasoned, depended on the stability of democratic institutions and on the condition of other minorities. It was affected as much by a McCarthy witch-hunt that trampled on civil liberties, or by discriminatory employment practices against blacks, as by naked anti-Semitism. Accordingly, the agencies embarked on new ventures—civil rights for blacks, interreligious and interethnic projects, mass educational campaigns against bigotry, and the like—enterprises that often put them in the vanguard of open-ended social experimentation.

At times the expanded agencies appeared more reformist than Jewish. To be sure, a Jewish rationale for social action could easily be found, particularly in the prophetic books of the Bible. Jeremiah's admonition to the exiles in Babylonia was always relevant: "Seek the welfare of the city to which I have exiled you and pray to the Lord in its behalf; for in its prosperity you shall prosper." But specifically Jewish motivations were usually ignored. A social action program, predicated on universalist rather than Jewish values, fired the consciousness of Jewish believers and non-believers alike. For many it became a convenient surrogate for Judaism, eclipsing the synagogue and religious observance.

Dr. Alexander Pekelis of the Congress drew up guidelines for the agency's newly organized Commission on Law and Social Action in 1945. Aptly entitled "Full Equality in a Free Society," it elaborated on the desired course of action for the achievement of a democratic, pluralistic state. Pekelis insisted also on an expanded interest in the furtherance of cultural and spiritual values within the Jewish community, but that component never equalled the agency's commitment to social action. Although Pekelis wrote for the Congress, his basic philosophy was adopted by the AJC and ADL.[4] Indeed, style and tactics more than abstract principle divided the postwar Jewish organizations. Their work was frequently repetitive, but jealous of their separate turfs, they defended pluralism *within* the Jewish community. Their activities, reflecting multiple areas of social concern, testified to the ongoing importance of the private sector within a welfare state.

Although the subject of church–state relations was familiar to the expanded defense agencies, it, too, took on new features. In the spirit of their social action programs, Jews were no longer content to be bystanders in situations which they perceived as discriminatory. Less timid than their predecessors, they actively worked for separation through courts as well as legislatures. Resort to litigation, heretofore avoided by Jewish organizations, became a standard defense technique. Often their participation in litigation was influential in securing broader interpretations of the separationist principle. Since the agencies now purposely searched for like-minded Christian allies, a separationist stand linked them more closely with Protestant groups of the "liberal establishment."[5]

The big three maintained separate legal departments that drafted model bills and *amicus curiae* briefs; occasionally they cooperated in the preparation of joint briefs. Based in New York City, each agency consulted its national constituency before arriving at policy decisions. The AJC and Congress, both membership organizations, deliberated with local chapters, the ADL with its regional councils. Overall the Congress, strictest on the principle of separation, took the lead in filing briefs and initiating litigation. Its legal talents and skills, developed under the tutelage of Leo Pfeffer, soon made it one of the three national organizations—along with the American Civil Liberties Union (ACLU) and Protestants and Other Americans United—that dominated separationist activity.[6] The agency's reputation soared in direct relation to its numerous undertakings in the area of church–state relations, and Pfeffer and the Congress became household words among supporters and opponents alike.

For five years the big three worked together on matters of church and state through the Joint Advisory Committee (JAC), a small body established in 1947 by National Community Relations Advisory Council (NCRAC) and the Synagogue Council of America (SCA). Joint enterprise, however, failed to quash interorganizational rivalry and jealousy. The AJC and ADL resented the Congress's growing fame and its influence over the JAC and local community councils. They also feared what to them was rashness—the eagerness of the Congress to hold forth publicly on sensitive issues and its uncompromising defense of strict separation with seemingly insufficient regard to intergroup relations. (Joseph M. Proskauer, outspoken president of the AJC, once said that the function of his agency's representatives to NCRAC was to exercise "a moderating influence." The anti-Congress implication was clear.)[7]

In 1951 NCRAC commissioned Professor Robert MacIver to suggest how a division of labor among the agencies could avoid costly duplication. MacIver's report acknowledged the superior performance of the Congress on legal matters but, since neither the AJC nor the ADL was prepared to yield any jurisdiction, stopped short of recommending exclusive authority to their competitor. A year later the AJC and ADL withdrew from the JAC and stayed away until the mid–1960s.[8] Usually, however, they pursued separate but largely parallel activities.

The agencies recognized that litigation was hardly the sole weapon for preserving strict separation. All acknowledged that Jews as well as non-Jews needed to know about the reasons that underlay Jewish separationism. Accordingly, they plunged into an endless stream of fact-finding surveys, conferences, workshops, and position papers geared to Jewish and Christian consumption. Education of Jews was aimed usually at forging a sorely needed consensus among the widespread local communities. Education of non-Jews was equally critical. Success in reaching those who molded Christian opinion promised to mitigate the pervasive and hostile perception of Jewish intransigence. Out of a new understanding, perhaps Christians would also endorse the minority's need of strict separation.

Just as the agencies expanded their efforts, so did they broaden their objectives. A century after Isaac Leeser and the *Occident,* Jewish spokesmen were no longer content with a government neutral to all religions. Rather, they roundly defended the concept of a secular government. They were not purists; even the strictest separationists among them never contemplated banning practices like hospital and military chaplaincies. Nevertheless, in the postwar era they fought for more than exemptions from Sunday laws or permission to be excused from religious exercises in the public schools. The usages with or without exemptions, most claimed, were unconstitutional by their very nature.

The changed focus questioned the intrinsic value of a neutral government. Neutrality, some argued, could lead to a watered-down nondenominational religion which no self-respecting religious group would endorse.[9] More important, the American experience taught that government neutrality was itself unfixed, a policy determined at bottom by the wishes of the majority. For example, a "neutral" religious practice in schools could be defined one way in the Protestant Bible Belt and yet another way in predominantly Catholic neighborhoods of the large metropolises. In either case the Jew remained the outsider. The supposition that religious symbols and ceremonies were inoffensive so long as they presented no "entering wedge"[10] could lead to equally fluid guidelines, for entering wedge was itself open to conflicting interpretations.

The changed focus also resulted in part from a secularist strand within the defense agencies. Unlike their predecessors, the professionals who formulated policies for the expanded agencies brought a new element to Jewish separationism. Rooted in the east European immigrant experience, many had imbibed a secularist indoctrination or secularist leanings. They spoke for a religious community, but, as one longtime defense worker wrote, their actions in opposition to public religion reflected their own indifference if not hostility to religion itself.[11] Whereas Isaac Mayer Wise and the Central Conference of American Rabbis, despite calls for a secular state and secular schools, could identify with the religious motivation of their Christian counterparts, the new policymakers often had little sympathy for any faith.

To be sure, NCRAC's alliance with the SCA, a religious body, worked to keep blatant secularism in check, and public pronouncements scrupulously distanced Jews as a community from secularism. Nonetheless, the proclivities of the professionals hardened the Jewish stand on separation and lent credence to the secularist image of American Jewry. That image, troublesome to many Jews, evoked sharp criticism from outspoken Christian defenders of public religion. Since many did not distinguish between "secular" and "secularist," they often accused Jewish separationists, even believers, of atheism.[12] The equation of separationism with godlessness placed Jewish separationists on the defensive throughout the postwar era, and they failed to convince most Americans that rigid opposition to public religion did not necessarily preclude devotion to religion.

Only once in the postwar era were the agencies forced to counter a direct attempt at the establishment of a Christian state. As in the last third of the nineteenth century, the challenge—spearheaded by the Christian Amendment Movement, an organization that closely resembled the earlier National Reform Association—took the form of a Christian amendment to the Constitution. Each year the Christian Amendment Movement renewed its efforts for congressional passage of the amendment, and in 1953 its standard-bearer was Senator Ralph Flanders of Vermont. Predicating the drive on the need to combat immorality and communism, his pro-amendment constituents received the support of self-styled Christian "patriots."[13]

Liberal Protestant spokesmen condemned the proposal. The *Christian Century* said that "for sheer mischief-making possibilities, [it is] hard to surpass." Providing for recognition of the "authority and law of Jesus Christ" in the Constitution, the bill simultaneously disclaimed any intention of establishing one particular church or of abridging the right of religious freedom. Its supporters also insisted that the amendment in no way violated the principles of civil equality or separation. Nor, they said, was it anti-Semitic.[14]

The Jewish agencies thought otherwise. The New York Board of Rabbis forthrightly condemned Flanders's bill, calling it a violation of religious freedom. The defense agencies, which initially wondered whether to take the measure seriously, responded quickly when hearings were scheduled before a Senate subcommittee in May 1954 (only a few months before Jews marked the tercentenary of their settlement in America). In written or oral testimony all argued along customary lines: the amendment contradicted American principles and precedents, and it would seriously divide the nation. While the ADL preferred to emphasize the "American" rather than the special Jewish interest in the issue, the SCA and NCRAC determined to testify *as Jews* and squarely injected the matter of Jewish equality. "It is now proposed," their statement read, "that . . . five million Jews . . . be reduced to a status of second-class citizens." Even if the amendment did not lead to religious tests for civil rights or to instruction in Christianity in the public schools, the very inclusion of a Christian clause insulted the faith of every believing Jew.

Amendment supporters updated the efforts of the nineteenth-century Christian-staters. Jews figured in Christian testimony more prominently than they had before, and charges reminiscent of the notorious *Protocols of the Elders of Zion*—of how Jews infiltrated and corrupted all areas of American life in order to subvert Christianity and control the nation— were aired.[15] Flanders's bill failed to pass the committee. The abortive measure, however, served to justify Jewish commitment to the eradication of public religion. Precisely because the amendment's supporters defended the vestiges of a Protestant America, those practices appeared more threatening.[16]

The Jewish agenda on church–state matters focused primarily on the vestiges: religion in the schools, public displays of Christian symbols, and Sunday laws. Now, in some Christian circles the religious sentiments underlying those practices were often cast in secular terms. Just as Sunday laws claimed legitimacy on nonreligious grounds, so did other issues. A nativity scene was called a symbol of democracy and goodwill; Bible reading was explained as merely a way of teaching morality. Why then, proponents asked, should Jews be opposed?[17] But the substitution of secular explanations—"moral" or "American" for Christian—made the practices no more palatable for American Jews. In a sense, "Christian secularists" carried on the work of the nineteenth-century religious crusaders. The transmutation of Protestant usages into symbols of an American civil religion could well achieve the goal of a redefined but nonetheless Christian state.

Some Americans may not have understood the vehemence of the Jewish response to those church–state issues,[18] but even in postwar America the memory of disabilities at the hands of Christian majorities could not easily be shrugged off. Furthermore, Jews detected tinges of Christianity that still adhered to the defense of public religion. In the battle over religion in the public schools, some Christian spokesmen pointedly advised Americans of their duty to withstand assaults on Christianity. Others called for "moral and spiritual values" or the "teaching about religion" in the classrooms, using these terms as euphemisms for Christianity. The crusading zeal of the nineteenth-century Christianizers had long been spent, but such occasional reminders confirmed for Jews the wisdom of their stand.

At the same time, the sentiments of the Christian majority, and not merely of a few extremists, limited how much the separationists could hope to excise from public religion. For example, since Christian Americans dug in their heels on the issue of Christmas celebrations in the public schools, the Jewish agencies were forced to compromise. Implicit in the holiday issue were fundamental questions that surfaced in postwar debates on church and state: Did the nature of American pluralism raise a minority's religious or antireligious sensibilities to equal status with those of the majority? Was the obliteration of Christian usages, where compliance was voluntary, a legitimate component of the Jewish pursuit of equality?

The specters of public hostility and intergroup tensions had effectively tempered Jewish responses to matters of church and state ever since the nineteenth century. But in the 1950s, the decade of consensus, when Americans saw themselves pitted against the menace of atheistic communism, pressure for conformity was compounded. Other variables widened the dimensions of the public relations factor. One concerned the newly created state of Israel. Not only might aid to Israel suffer if Jews alienated Americans and their lawmakers, but a Jewish state in which organized religion wielded vast political power appeared to contradict American Jewish professions of loyalty to separation. Another concern stemmed from the new public face of American Catholics. Catholics at mid-century no longer opposed the vestiges of Protestantism in society, and in a dramatic reversal of their nineteenth-century stand became the ardent, even aggressive, defenders of Sunday laws and religion in the schools. Jewish resistance to a Protestant-flavored public religion could count on neither Catholic assistance nor neutrality. For a small non-Christian minority to dispute both Protestant and Catholic opinion seemed downright foolhardy.[19] Furthermore, the same defense agencies that dealt with church and state also maintained interreligious departments. How could the agencies knowingly undercut the Christian position on the one hand and affirm their commitment to intergroup harmony on the other? A striking example of the need to balance communal priorities arose with Vatican Council II. Here, efforts to obtain modifications of classical Catholic teachings on anti-Semitism dictated a policy of prudence, if not appeasement, on other issues.

Concentration on the vestiges of a Christian state drew Jewish organizations into major court cases and fixed their presence permanently in litigation. Jewish defense broke no new ground on the theory of separation. The approach was pragmatic, the concern the elimination of government-supported practices that in any way operated to make the Jew an outsider, or somehow less than equal, in American society. Jewish public statements and briefs now stressed the threat of "divisiveness" that religious usages posed to schools and society, and under that rubric the open-ended pursuit of equality was also subsumed.

During the two decades after the war the defense agencies labored primarily to shore up restraints on government under the establishment clause. They reasoned that the establishment clause, broadly interpreted, was the shortest route to both religious freedom and religious equality. Leo Pfeffer, the guiding spirit of Jewish litigation, often said that the establishment and the free exercise clauses were two sides of the same coin, expressing the unitary principle that freedom required separation. Like earlier defenders of Jewish rights, the agencies invoked the Founding Fathers to justify their defense of strict separation. After 1948 they adopted Justice Hugo Black's broad interpretation of "establishment" in *Everson* and *McCollum* as their frame of reference.[20] Using those standards, they judged whether public practices violated the separationist principle.

Jews never expected direct assaults on the principle of separation, but they fervently resisted attempts at reducing its potency. In a statement to a Senate Subcommittee on Constitutional Rights, the agencies of NCRAC and the SCA explained in 1955: "The principle of separation is so deeply ingrained in our tradition and so universally recognized . . . that any frontal attack upon it would be futile and self-defeating. . . . The danger to separation of church and state . . . lies in watering down, evasion, circumvention and compromise, while lip service is paid to the principle itself."[21]

The principal battles over public religion were fought before the courts between 1945 and 1965. On the matter of greatest concern to the Jews, the public school, separationists scored their greatest victories. The early rulings in which the Supreme Court broadly defined establishment were followed by decisions that outlawed released time classes on public school premises as well as prayer and Bible reading in the classroom. Spawning various interpretations of the religious clauses of the First Amendment, the cases goaded religious spokesmen as well as courts and scholars into wrestling with definitions of separation and guidelines for appropriate state behavior.

5

Tests of Released Time

Weighing the Facts

As the nation moved with scant respite from a hot war into a cold war, religious educators trained their sights increasingly on the public school. Many concluded that a pervasive godlessness infected the schools; it contributed to the spiritual void that was exposed by America's ongoing battle against totalitarianism, and it dangerously undercut the defense of democratic life. The charge was not a new one in American history. In 1845 a religious group in New Jersey had warned that the "race of irreligious and infidel youth, such as may be expected to issue from public schools, deteriorating more and more with the revolving years, will not be fit to sustain our free institutions."[1] One hundred years later identical sentiments prompted the search for ways that reasserted the religious function of the schools. So intense was the postwar campaign that some Jews feared for the survival of the nonreligious public school. One prominent Reform rabbi explained that "this was something much bigger than even a Jewish issue; it was the issue as to whether the American public school was to retain its essential character."[2] Such Jews had clearly forgotten that the first public schools had been charged with the responsibility of inculcating moral and religious values. In the rabbi's mind the goal of a religion-free school, for which Wise and Lilienthal had fought, had become the historical reality.

In November 1946 NCRAC and the SCA convened a second conference on religious instruction and the public schools. Delegates from the major national religious, educational, and defense organizations, and from local Jewish community relations councils, met for two days in full and tightly structured sessions. They were better prepared than the conferees of 1944; less reluctant to reach a conclusion, their very tone exuded greater authority. Technically, their decisions did not bind the agencies they represented, but any statement that they formulated, reflecting the considered judgment of foremost rabbis and lay experts, was bound to influence communal behavior.

Despite the broader title, the conference, like that of 1944, concentrated almost exclusively on released time. Most delegates shared the belief that the challenge ran deeper than a minor link between schools and churches. A portent of an inevitable flood of religious practices in the classroom, released time presented them with a limited choice: either secular schools or Protestant schools. Since they saw no viable middle ground, even God-fearing Jews would opt for the former. When the conferees, fully armed with data gleaned from government, educational, and their own private surveys, debated the operations of the released time program, they confronted certain bald facts:

1. Released time, in effect in forty-six states, was thriving.[3] A few communities had discontinued the program for lack of public interest, but they were the exceptions.

2. Both Protestants and Catholics warmly supported the plan. (As one rabbi put it, released time had become the "Messiah of religious instruction.")[4] Desirous of religious education stamped with the authority of the school system, they usually rejected the alternative of dismissed time. Most Christian supporters did not believe that released time overstepped the line between church and state, and their concern about separation noticeably lessened when the programs were established. In some districts the original promise to keep the religious classes out of school buildings was casually ignored.[5]

3. The issue of released time divided Jewish communities. Some Jews, usually the right-wing Orthodox, defended the merit of the program while opponents frequently disagreed on a proper response. Overall, Jewish participation was conspicuously limited, either because of opposition or because of inadequate facilities.

4. Opposition often evoked public antagonism. Jews were accused of antireligious sentiments, and since some districts required Jewish participation before a released time program was implemented,[6] opposition was construed as rank obstructionism. Nonparticipation also caused difficulties for Jewish students. Where no Jewish facilities existed, some joined Christian classes; others elected to stay away—and were made to feel different from their classmates.

5. Since state legislatures and courts in New York and Illinois (*Latimer* v. *Board of Education,* 394 Ill. 228, 1946) had validated the program, opposition on grounds of strict separation isolated Jews from the larger community. Their only potential allies, mainly ultraliberal Protestants, atheists, and left-wingers, were an unsavory bunch to middle America.

Summing up the facts, the delegates admitted to a serious dilemma. By floundering as well as by opposing released time, Jews faced a public relations problem of major proportions. To some degree, at least, the issue appeared as a conflict between Christian and Jew, a situation that American Jews consistently sought to avoid. If, however, Jews knuckled under to public pressure, they might be risking further incursions by Christianity into the schools and increasing the vulnerability of their children. Indeed, speakers reported a heightened Protestant assertiveness and even scattered attempts at proselytization that accompanied local programs. Rabbi Max Kapustin of Danville, Virginia (where no Jewish facilities for released time classes existed), for example, told how Jewish children were actively induced to participate in Christian classes. The teachers would approach them with comments like "Why don't you want to listen to these pretty Bible stories? We just talked today about King David; you know he was a Jew." That, according to the rabbi, was sufficient to make Christian children wonder at Jewish nonattendance and to make Jewish children succumb.

Seven Jewish communities had been invited to relate their experiences with released time, but no two accounts were identical. The methods used by the initiators of released time programs varied from city to city; so did the degree of involvement on the part of the schools, the impact on the Jewish children, and the degree of interreligious friction that was generated. Geographical location as well as local history and customs largely determined the operations of the program in a particular city. (In Danville, for example, the Baptists, who in the eighteenth century had been flogged publicly for their nonconformist views on separation, joined the Jews in opposition to released time.) The Jewish response was usually a product of the local setting as well as the size and resources of the Jewish community. In all communities Jews displayed a wide range of reactions from determined resistance to willing cooperation. Testimony to the normative autonomy of the individual Jewish congregation, the seven stories revealed the insurmountable obstacles to the definition of any single point of view for the entire group.

Like the communal accounts, the speeches by the representatives of the national and local agencies reflected several points of view. Most agreed on the threat of released time to church–state separation, but they divided on how to resolve the tension between principle and public relations. Three broad positions were defined. On one side stood the Congress. Its director, David Petegorsky, urged that Jews forthrightly condemn this blatant example of sectarianism. To wait for the released time system to collapse of itself was unwise, because the principle of its legitimacy would live on. Dismissed time was also wrong, but if circumstance compelled the local communities to accept some form of school-sanctioned religious instruction, it was the better choice. In either case Jews should make their position known, boycott any program, and carefully monitor the plans in operation for any extensions or abuses. Insisting that the courageous defense of a democratic principle actually improved the Jewish image, Petegorsky urged communal leaders not be cowed into silent acquiescence by the fear of public relations. The Congress's position failed to elicit general approval. Even the CCAR, the rabbinical group which had opposed released time long before the others recognized it as an issue, held back. Not only had the rabbis already endorsed dismissed time, but they had never agreed to boycott the released time programs.

Diametrically opposed to the Congress stood the Orthodox, the most active in encouraging Jewish participation in the released time programs and in servicing classes for Jewish children. Although they would not have initiated the released time idea, they were content to utilize it to their advantage. Several Orthodox delegates affirmed their loyalty to the doctrine of separation, but, they asserted, they did not consider released time a breach of principle. One Orthodox lawyer who took the nonpreferentialist approach to the relation of the state to religion maintained that the First Amendment "did not declare the Government of the United States to be irreligious, or that the people of the United States must . . . refrain from the exercise of religion of one kind or another, privately or even publicly." Just as Americans, a religious people, worried about godlessness in society, so should Jews consider religious education by whatever means a foremost priority.

Support of the Orthodox position came from Jewish educators and from a Jewish member of an interfaith body, the Greater New York Coordinating Committee on Released Time. On nonreligious grounds they advised Jewish acceptance and implementation of released time. The educators claimed that the dangers that had been feared, such as discrimination among the schoolchildren or the erosion of the afternoon Hebrew school, had for the most part not materialized. Released time was proving a valuable asset to Jewish education, reaching those children who otherwise remained unexposed or supplementing the classes of those who attended Hebrew or Sunday schools. In many cases it served as a conduit for enrolling children in Hebrew schools. Although the educators had originally yielded to the program under Christian pressure, released time "has been a growing conviction with us," Dr. Alexander Dushkin of the Jewish Education Committee stated.

Between the Congress and the Orthodox were the advocates of a compromise position. Like most compromises, it could attract the largest number and most easily generate a climate of unity precisely because it lacked the fervor of either extreme. The clearest articulation of this position came from Richard Gutstadt, director of the ADL. The first priority, according to Gutstadt, was to achieve a unified Jewish stand on released time. He recommended a middle approach, an open and positive endorsement of dismissed time, which would afford rabbis and educators additional hours for religious instruction while avoiding embarrassment for Jewish children. With respect to the formidable problem of public relations, where Jewish separationists were pitted against progressive educators as well as "reactionary" forces, he counseled against both independent resistance implicit in the Congress's position and the passive acceptance of Christian dictates. Gutstadt advocated a third option, indeed one which had been popular with Jewish defenders for over a century: Jews must seek out their "natural allies" among the Christians and present their uneasiness over released time in the context of fundamental American principles rather than Jewish self-interest. If they made no headway on that level, they might attempt interreligious endeavors to tailor the released time program. Successful efforts at injecting interfaith or intercultural values, or softening the sectarian aspects of the program, would profit Jews in what otherwise was a no-win situation. Certainly, a readiness to sit down with Christian leaders would erase the popular image of the Jew as obstructionist. Gutstadt's views, particularly the caveat against alienating Christian America, were warmly seconded by John Slawson, executive vice-president of the AJC.

The conference formulated a Statement of Principles that drew from the positions of the defense agencies. Although it stressed the responsibility of the synagogue and the home to provide children with religious instruction, it endorsed dismissed time. It termed released time "an entering wedge toward the sectarianization of the public school," and it asked local Jewish communities to voice their principled opposition to the program and to insist on certain safeguards. Nevertheless, it refrained from advising boycotts or nonparticipation. Indeed, as critics of the provision pointed out, the very mention of safeguards implied that opponents of released time were prepared to give way. Actually, no more than a compromise could have been hammered out. Opponents of released time admitted that they were too late in expressing meaningful resistance. Having failed to contest the program in its formative stages, Jews could scarcely expect at a much later date to impede its progress or to win over fellow Jews who were enrolled. In 1947, however, NCRAC and SCA, the parent bodies of the conference, amended the statement along stricter lines. They agreed that dismissed was better than released time, but they registered their formal opposition to both. "The utilization in any manner of time, facilities, personnel, or funds of the public school system for purposes of religious instruction should not be permitted."[7]

The primary goal of the conference had been to establish Jewish unity. Toward that end, and to provide guidance and assistance to the local communities, the statement recommended the formation of a Joint Advisory Committee on Religious Instruction and the Public Schools under the aegis of the SCA and NCRAC. It also urged that where released time was in effect the local Jewish community consult with that committee before deciding upon a course of action. The Joint Advisory Committee (JAC) was formally established the following year, and despite constant eruptions of interorganizational friction, it functioned actively for a quarter of a century. Working in tandem with the legal departments of the three major defense agencies, most closely with the Congress, it very quickly broadened its purview to all church–state matters. The JAC never supplanted the defense agencies in legal activity, but as the clearinghouse for community councils all over the country and as the link between religious and secular organizations, it more accurately spoke for the majority of affiliated American Jews.

The conference of 1946 hastened the transfer of leadership in extra-synagogal affairs from the American rabbinate to lay professionals. The process of lay domination had begun in earnest with the establishment of the AJC and ADL. From then on, direction of the national affairs of the Jewish community had shifted increasingly to the defense agencies. Leadership at first was exercised by volunteers, men of the generation of Louis Marshall and Cyrus Adler. They in turn were eclipsed after the war when salaried professionals, often less committed than their predecessors to Judaism as a religion, directed policy. At the conference the new leadership dominated, and the Statement of Principles drew largely from their data and recommendations. To be sure, rabbis representing organizations affiliated with the SCA participated in committee meetings, and statements of policy were always issued under the names of both the SCA and NCRAC. But, as the litigation demonstrates, strategy and operations in the area of church and state became virtually the exclusive province of a handful of lay experts on the agencies' payrolls.

One session of the conference was devoted to a discussion of the legal and constitutional aspects of released time. The expansion of the program had called forth opinions on its constitutionality from state attorneys-general and had generated several lawsuits. By the time the conference convened, two cases had been heard in Illinois courts, *McCollum* v. *Board of Education* and *Latimer* v. *Board of Education,* with the courts finding against the plaintiffs in both.[8] No federal court had yet been involved, but it was not unlikely that the issue would eventually reach the Supreme Court. The real question before the delegates was the propriety and feasibility of Jewish participation in litigation as "friends of the court." Leo Pfeffer of the Congress disclosed that the agencies had privately resolved to stay out of the Illinois cases,[9] but deliberations were still in progress.

At the conference, where a larger group of Jewish representatives had the opportunity to debate the issue openly, the opinions corresponded roughly to those about released time in general. Those who favored a positive approach to released time argued that Jews should accept and comply with the ruling in the New York case of 1927, *Lewis* v. *Graves,* and with the more recent Illinois decisions. One Orthodox attorney, who was a member of New York City's Board of Education and president of the Brooklyn Jewish Community Council, reminded the delegates of the rabbinic injunction that the law of the land was to be obeyed. And hadn't the earlier court decisions clearly stated that the law was not antagonistic to religion and the churches? The outspoken opponents of released time disagreed. Despite a general wariness about plunging into the forum of litigation, some delegates were prepared to support Jewish participation. To be sure, the risks involved in the loss of a suit, particularly after the defeats in New York and Illinois, were clear to all, but, as one Conservative rabbi observed, "you cannot win a suit without taking the chance of losing the suit."

The qualities of an ideal case that would merit Jewish participation were defined by Leo Pfeffer, whose expertise carried considerable weight at the conference. Pfeffer was then assistant director of the Congress's Commission on Law and Social Action, and in a distinguished career that followed with the Congress, and as writer and professor of law, he earned the reputation of a foremost authority on matters of church and state. Pfeffer, a Jew who sent his children to day schools, usually stood for strict separation. His approach was often criticized as "doctrinaire" or "absolutist," but as he retorted: "Absolutes have their rightful place." His principles shaped the long-term policies of the Congress and NCRAC, and under his guidance Jewish litigation in defense of separation was honed to a fine art.[10]

According to Pfeffer, the constitutionality of released time had not been adequately tested by any court, for none had clearly addressed the question of whether released time breached the principle of separation. The *Latimer* case had placed a primary emphasis on the use of public funds for sectarian purposes, but Pfeffer disapproved of that approach. Not only did it inaccurately reflect the essential nature of the opposition, but it ill served the cause of Jewish public relations. Rather, he wanted plaintiffs to focus squarely on the First Amendment rights. If released time violated religious liberty, and of that Pfeffer was convinced, "it is not material whether the expense involved is small or great; a slight infringement of religious liberty is as unconstitutional as a substantial infringement." Misuse of tax monies was an important but only an ancillary argument.

Pfeffer insisted that a case should not be brought until a specific program of released time had been in operation sufficiently long to permit careful analysis. The courts were not interested in theory but in the pragmatic, factual consequences of a program. It would be essential, he explained, to prove that the state was aiding sectarian education, that the school's influence was used to induce the child or his parent to participate in the program, or that school authorities permitted church representatives to solicit children to attend religious classes. Such evidence, he thought, would make a strong case proving that released time and church–state separation were inconsistent.

Interpreting religious freedom to include freedom *from* religion, Pfeffer approved the protection of the rights of atheists and freethinkers. In fact, all three cases of record—the one in New York and the two in Illinois— involved such plaintiffs. Nevertheless, the conferees and Pfeffer himself recognized the unpleasant consequences for the Jewish community in an alliance with nonbelievers. The *McCollum* case, where the complainant had gratuitously attacked religion generally,[11] had evoked an angry backlash. Protestant church groups were funding the defense of released time, and the press was attacking the "godless" character of released time opponents. The issue had polarized public opinion, with believers, the godly, lined up against the ungodly. Jews could not risk being linked with atheists like McCollum any more than they could align themselves publicly with Communists or other leftists. The ideal case required a propitious setting, one where public opinion was neutral if not sympathetic. Intrinsically the *McCollum* case was a strong one—released time classes were conducted on school premises, the way in which the children elected to receive religious instruction was blatantly divisive—but its strength was vitiated by the specter of atheism.

Implicit in Pfeffer's presentation was the fond but perhaps unrealistic hope that it was possible for Jews to contest religious practices in schools without incurring the stigma of godlessness. At the same time, in this as well as in later episodes, the force of public opinion removed the need of any internal showdown between religious and secular Jews over first principles.

The Statement of Principles adopted by the conference said nothing about litigation. An attempt to establish a consensus on released time, it could not afford to strain the agreement that had been hammered out. Besides, the difficulties and risks surrounding litigation, and the real possibility of injury to those who pressed an unpopular cause, inhibited even the ardent foes of released time from proposing immediate action. Rabbi Arthur Gilbert, long active in interreligious affairs, recalled later how inauspicious the 1940s were for legal action by Jews. "The record indicates," he wrote, "that Jewish parents who had protested Christian religious practices in the public schools endured cross burnings on their lawns, harassing phone calls, the threat of economic boycott, and the mass distribution of anti-Semitic hate literature."[12] For the time being, then, the policy on legal action was one of watchful waiting.

The First Test

The signal that ended the period of waiting came a few months later. In February 1947 the Supreme Court handed down its decision in *Everson* v. *Board of Education,* a case that tested the constitutionality of public transportation in a New Jersey county for parochial as well as public school students. Although the justices validated that form of public aid, they did two things to hearten separationists. First, they held that the establishment clause of the First Amendment was equally binding upon the states as on Congress; second, and of greater import, they defined establishment in sweeping terms. The words of Justice Hugo Black permanently stamped all future litigation on church–state relations:

> The "establishment of religion" clause of the First Amendment means at least this: Neither a state nor the Federal Government can set up a church. Neither can pass laws which aid one religion, aid all religions, or prefer one religion over another. Neither can force nor influence a person to go to or to remain away from church against his will or force him to profess a belief or disbelief in any religion. No person can be punished for entertaining or professing religious beliefs or disbeliefs, for church attendance or non-attendance. No tax in any amount, large or small, can be levied to support any religious activities or institutions, whatever they may be called, or whatever form they may adopt to teach or practice religion. Neither a state nor the Federal Government can, openly or secretly, participate in the affairs of any religious organizations or groups and *vice versa*. In the words of Jefferson, the clause against establishment of religion by law was intended to erect "a wall of separation between church and State."[13]

Since the actual ruling appeared at variance to the principles that Black laid down, neither Catholics nor Protestants were completely satisfied. The former resented the principles but, mollified by the specific ruling, determined to take full advantage of public aid. The latter liked the principles but feared the advantages that might accrue to the Catholics. Tensions mounted on both sides. One congressman introduced a constitutional amendment that would have prohibited state aid to sectarian educational institutions, and prominent Protestant leaders of various sects founded Protestants and Other Americans United for Separation of Church and State (POAU). The organization's anti-Catholic bent was primary, but its platform included a broader purpose: "All possible aid to the citizens of any community . . . who are seeking to protect their public schools from sectarian domination."[14]

Jewish separationists, who preferred Justice Wiley Rutledge's minority opinion against aid to parochial schools,[15] weighed the different variables. They, too, worried about the assertiveness of the Catholics on church–state issues after the war. Catholic spokesmen now vigorously defended released time; in their words opposition was "patently Nazi" or "another victory for the atheistic Kremlin and its brutal Communistic doctrine." Furthermore, Jews noted that *Everson* unleashed a flurry of bills in state legislatures and in Congress whose passage would have created additional links between religion and the school system. Protestant outrage, however, was a positive sign, for it opened up a potential reserve of allies, like the POAU, in the struggle against released time. To be sure, many Protestants displayed a glaring inconsistency on separation; that is, they favored religion in the public school but opposed assistance to Catholic schools. But if enlightened Protestants were to shift ground for the sake of principle, they would rupture the Protestant–Catholic alliance on released time and vitiate the strength of that program. Protestant–Catholic animosity might ultimately redound to Jewish advantage, perhaps even erasing the Jew-versus-Christian appearance of the released time situation. Some Jews briefly considered new political ploys—Jewish neutrality while Protestants and Catholics fought each other on church–state matters, or a bargain with Protestants whereby Jews would join in opposition to parochial school aid in exchange for Protestant opposition to released time.[16]

Although Protestant support was very much in doubt, the *Everson* decision boosted the confidence of those Jews who favored participation in a released time suit. Leo Pfeffer, who had recommended Jewish inter-vention in *Everson,* was convinced that Black's fundamental proposition on the neutrality of government toward both religion and nonreligion, "if honestly and sincerely applied," presaged a Supreme Court ruling against released time. Pfeffer's optimism tempered his earlier uneasiness about *McCollum,* and upon learning that the case would be brought before the Supreme Court, he urged Jewish action. Since the Court would determine the issue for all Jewish communities, "we have no alternative but to in-tervene and assist as best we can."[17]

The *McCollum* case challenged the released time system in Champaign, Illinois, which had been in operation since 1940. Under that program classes in religious instruction were given within the school buildings, and Prot-estant and Catholic teachers, approved by the superintendent of schools, were engaged by the Champaign interfaith council. (Jewish classes were discontinued after a few years.) At the beginning of each term the public school teacher distributed enrollment cards, and those pupils who obtained parental consent were released from secular studies for religious instruc-tion. Where a majority elected to participate, Protestant instruction was given in the regular classroom; Catholics, Jews, and nonparticipants were sent to other rooms. Usually, the public school teacher stayed in the class-room during the religious class.

The facts in the case revealed the pressures put upon children by the program. Terry McCollum, a fifth-grader, was a solitary nonparticipant. In his public school, as in most others of Champaign, only Protestant instruction was provided, but Catholic and Jewish children could attend Protestant classes where an interdenominational Protestantism was taught. Terry's teacher urged him to remain in class, but although the boy was amenable, his mother refused her permission. The teacher exiled Terry first to a desk in the hall, where he was teased and harassed by passing children, and then to an unoccuppied room. When his mother complained to the school, he was sent to another fifth-grade class. Caught between parent and teacher, Terry's lot was not an enviable one.[18]

The facts clearly bore out Jewish arguments against released time: the schools were directly involved with the religion classes; the very program fostered religious distinctions; and if Jewish children were able to participate only in Protestant classes, they were likely to learn fundamental Christian charges against Jews. *McCollum* was a strong case, but its attractiveness was marred by the tenor of the petition filed by Terry's mother, Vashti McCollum. A self-styled rationalist and atheist, McCollum joined her legal suit for the invalidation of the program with an attack on religion. Christianity and the New Testament, based on stories that she claimed only proved the "hateful," "intolerant," "selfish," and "antisocial" attitudes of Jesus, bore the brunt of her invective. Holding up the biblical narratives to ridicule, she lambasted the "myth, filth, murder, war, and hate" that appeared in both Old and New Testaments and made them, she said, books unfit for children. She sneered also at the "Jewish God"; the Jewish Bible belonged only in libraries, for "this whole Jewish mythology should be thrown out as unworthy of Twentieth Century culture."[19] Offensive to most Americans, McCollum's militancy seemed likely to jeopardize the outcome of her suit.

Since the AJC and ADL feared that an association with McCollum would expose Jews to public attack, they resisted Pfeffer's determination to intervene. In drawn-out deliberations that tested the newly established Jewish unity, the two agencies held out against action that bore an explicit Jewish label. First they suggested a multisectarian body to assist McCollum, and then they thought of a silent partnership with the ACLU in the preparation and financing of the latter's brief. Pfeffer, however, remained adamant. He announced that the Congress was prepared to file an *amicus* brief on its own, but he pressed for joint action on the part of all the agencies in NCRAC and the SCA. To allay Jewish fears, as well as resentment of McCollum's irreverent statements, he reasoned that the Supreme Court would probably not concern itself with her views on religion. Furthermore, the Jewish brief could be drafted in such a way as to dissociate Jews from irreligion.[20]

The final decision to intervene owed much to the pressure of the local Jewish communities. On their behalf NCRAC voted in June 1947 to file a brief, and the major holdouts, the AJC and the ADL, soon yielded. The agencies also consented to share the costs of McCollum's appeal. The SCA, which at first had planned to file separately as a religious body, was persuaded to join the common endeavor. The secular agencies sorely needed its cooperation for substantiating the claim that they spoke for a religious people. In the end, the decision to intervene allied the secular and religious Jewish groups with the ACLU and the American Ethical Union along with Unitarians, Baptists, and Seventh-Day Adventists. The Jews agreed that with a good brief, whose composition was assigned to Pfeffer, they had at least a fifty–fifty chance before the Supreme Court.[21]

Jewish strategy judged the presentation of a united stand as important as the substance of the Jewish argument. That goal was achieved in the *McCollum* brief, the first in which all major Jewish groups cooperated. Filed in the name of the SCA and NCRAC, which together represented over 80 percent of those affiliated with Jewish organizations, the brief could rightfully claim that it spoke for American Jewry. Some years later Professor Robert MacIver of Columbia University called it an "outstanding collective achievement."[22]

Reading in part like a declaration of faith, the brief[23] postulated the Jewish commitment both to church–state separation—"freedom of religious worship and belief . . . can remain inviolate only when there exists no intrusion of secular authority in religious affairs or of religious authority in secular affairs"—and to the public school—"one of the most precious products of our American democracy." The interests of the *amici* in the defense of freedom of worship and of the American democratic system in no way linked them to McCollum's personal views on religion: "We wish not only to dissociate ourselves completely from the anti-religious views of the appellant, but wish also to deplore the fact that the sponsors of the original petition chose this case as a means of . . . dragging into it the unrelated issues of atheism versus religion." Furthermore, Jewish insistence on religion-free public schools did not stem from a hostility to religion or religious education. Indeed, "in Jewish history and tradition religious instruction has always been regarded as a most sacred responsibility."

Jews, too, the brief said, deplored religious illiteracy, but like thoughtful Christians they deplored even more the divisiveness among the children generated by the released time program. Not only were the children grouped according to religious affiliation, but the instruction they received, reinforced by the authority of the public school, divided them further. Consider, the brief stated, the "stigmatizing effect of teaching Jewish participation in the crucifixion" and its psychological impact upon Jewish and non-Jewish children. Sectarianism in the schools was always harmful to minority religions, and released time classes, a form of sectarianism, fostered antagonism among the major religious groups and even among the various Protestant sects.

The brief did not contest released time in general but focused specifically on the Champaign plan of holding religious classes on school premises. Resting its essential argument on the *Everson* decision, it claimed that nonpreferential aid to all religions, which might be construed as justification of the program, was invalid. Certainly, the nonpreferential approach impinged on the equality of nonbelievers and put them beyond the pale of constitutional protection. Besides, the plan recognized only the traditional Protestant, Catholic, and Jewish groups and ignored less popular sects like Jehovah's Witnesses. The fact that Protestant children stayed in the regular classrooms for religious instruction while Catholics were moved elsewhere showed an obvious preference for the predominant sect of the community.

Only when religion was "wholly exempt from the cognizance of civil society," as Madison had said, was true neutrality on the part of the state guaranteed.

The brief also argued at length on the element of compulsion in the program. The absence of direct sanctions for nonattendance did not make the program completely voluntary. If the child felt that he incurred the displeasure of school authorities by not participating, or if the nonparticipant was subjected to harassment or discomfort, his free choice was appreciably curtailed. That Terry McCollum and his mother were the sole objectors doubtless indicated that many preferred to join the religious classes rather than confront the antagonism of school authorities or the cruelty of classmates. Such pressures only augured worse. Citing Madison again, the brief warned of the possibility of persecution and oppression in the wake of state aid to sectarian dogma or groups.

By referring to opinions of Christian educators and spokesmen, the brief tried to prove that the Jewish point of view was not a parochial one. Furthermore, it made use of studies in social psychology, specifically as evidence of the pressures foisted upon school children. Injecting material not already before the court, it showed how an *amicus* brief could be more than judicial lobbying. Indeed, Justice Felix Frankfurter, whose opinion discussed the pressures on the children for conformity, relied heavily on the evidence of the Jewish *amici*.[24]

The Congress received numerous plaudits for the brief. The *St. Louis Post-Dispatch* called it "a notable document in the history of religious freedom in this country," and the Chicago Civil Liberties Committee honored Pfeffer for his work.[25] From a Jewish perspective the brief signaled a new assertiveness and confidence on the part of postwar Jews and, simultaneously, a newly found unity among organized American Jews. It neither disguised Jewish interests nor buried them in universalist categories. A manifesto of Jewish views, the brief reinforced the public image of Jewish separationism while it spurred Jews on to greater activism in matters of church and state.

At oral argument on the *McCollum* case, it was clear that the justices had read the Jewish brief. Felix Frankfurter seemed particularly impressed by the charge that released time introduced religious conflict into the school system. He and his fellow justices asked numerous questions about the degree of collaboration between religious functionaries and the school under the program and about the curriculum of the released time classes. Their comments, according to knowledgeable analysts, hinted that the Champaign system was likely to be invalidated on the grounds set forth in *Everson*.[26]

The predictions proved accurate. The opinion handed down in March 1948 held that the close ties between the school and the released time classes fell under the ban of the First and Fourteenth Amendments as interpreted in the bus case. Rejecting the plea of released time proponents for a repudiation of both the broad definition of establishment and the application of the First Amendment to state behavior, the Court explicitly reaffirmed its earlier stand. Aid to all religions, Justice Black wrote for the majority, was as unacceptable as the preference of one religion over another. Black tempered his remarks by stating that the court's reasoning did not manifest a hostility to religion: "A manifestation of such hostility would be at war with our national tradition.... For the First Amendment rests upon the premise that both religion and government can best work ... if each is left free from the other within its respective sphere."[27]

The seemingly straightforward decision left a basic issue unclear. Were all released time programs invalid or merely those that made use of school facilities? In a separate opinion Frankfurter added to the ambiguity. Examining the Champaign system within a historical overview of the public school, he maintained that a religion-free school in a heterogeneous society was essential for the avoidance of interreligious divisiveness. The operation of the Champaign system overstepped the appropriate line of separation, but, he suggested, other programs might well be found to be constitutional. Believing in the public school as the key to the preservation of national unity, Frankfurter was particularly disturbed by the divisiveness caused by the released time practice. His concern is not difficult to understand. A Jew who had substituted Americanism for his Jewish identity (and, incidentally, as one whose education had begun in the public school), he desired a society which brooked no distinctions based on religion and schools which did not remind Jews of their differences.

Instead of putting the matter to rest, the decision refueled the controversy over released time. Justice Black commented some years later that few opinions of the mid-century Court stirred wider debate. Roundly acclaimed by separationists, *McCollum* drew bitter responses from those who bemoaned the surrender to godlessness. A popular point of view was articulated by Luther Weigle, dean emeritus of Yale Divinity School, who announced that it was time for "those who believe in God to claim and insist on their full religious freedom." Sharp criticism of the decision also appeared in numerous law and education journals as well as in popular periodicals. Nor did officials in charge of released time programs across the country yield gracefully to the ruling. Although some programs were discontinued and others were modified, most remained just as they were.[28]

From the three major religious groups came three different responses. Jews generally acclaimed the decision, confidently assuming that the Court had disapproved of released time programs in general. Black had not said explicitly that the ruling applied only to Champaign but in fact had strongly implied that more than the use of school buildings had violated the principle of separation. Besides, the lone dissenter, Justice Stanley Reed, had pointed out that the majority's opinion would apply to released time programs both off and on school grounds. Speaking for the SCA and NCRAC, Rabbi William Rosenblum and Henry Epstein announced that the decision was "so sweeping as to make it appear that released time, in and of itself, is inconsistent with the court's opinion." Pfeffer also doubted that released time outside Champaign could stand. He drew support from a St. Louis case decided two months after *McCollum* in which the state court held that the use of school buildings was inconsequential for the invalidation of released time. "The controlling fact," the court there explained, "is that the public schools are used to aid sectarian groups to disseminate their doctrines." The CCAR found another gratifying feature in Black's statement that the decision did not derogate the importance of religion. The rabbis called upon Christians to take up the Court's challenge and cooperate with Jews for strengthening religious education in the places where it belonged—in religious institutions. Overall the Jewish agencies liked to believe that their brief had influenced the Court, and a sense of pride overlay their praise of the opinion.[29]

Protestants divided over *McCollum*. The majority stressed the responsibility of the public school for some sort of religious instruction, and only a minority thought that released time fell under the ban of separation. Some observers saw a real possibility of a Protestant–Catholic alliance, at least with respect to religious trappings in the classrooms. Others focused primarily on the perceived threat of Catholic assertiveness. The *Christian Century* editorialized that resistance to Catholic "aggressions" demanded consistency; Protestants "can hardly resist these aggressions if they practice or condone what they condemn in others." The journal warned that Catholic support of released time was in reality but a tactic in the larger fight to breach the wall of separation and secure parochial school aid, and it gloomily observed that Protestant participants in released time "were innocently engaged in pulling Catholic chestnuts out of the fire."[30]

Whatever their larger objectives, Catholics were the most vehement critics of the Court's ruling. As one analyst observed: "To the spokesmen for Catholicism the McCollum case is what the Dred Scott decision was to the Abolitionists in the years before the Civil War." Prominent leaders, both religious and lay, condemned the decision for its opposition to God, its curtailment of religious freedom, and its misinterpretation of the First Amendment. A cleric who taught history at Seton Hall University warned that the Court's "distorted constitutional interpretation," hinted at radical changes "in the Christian, American way of life." Fourteen ranking Catholic bishops inveighed against the victories of secularism, the "most deadly menace" to the American way of life, in the *Everson* and *McCollum* cases. In a joint statement the prelates claimed that the First Amendment only forbade the establishment of one particular church; to say that the clause meant government indifference to religion contradicted both logic and

history. Popular and legislative sanction and not merely judicial pronouncements, the bishops insisted, were required to execute so sweeping
a reinterpretation. Now the most zealous supporters of religious instruction
and exercises in the schools, Catholics had completely reversed their
nineteenth-century stand. Understandably, they and like-minded Protestants urged a narrow interpretation of the decision, namely, the unconstitutionality of only the Champaign plan.[31]

The Jewish agencies quickly felt the unpopularity of their stand with
most Christian religious groups. A rabbi on the staff of the AJC reported
on a meeting of Protestant and Catholic leaders convened by the National
Conference of Christians and Jews (NCCJ). Ostensibly called to deal with
Protestant–Catholic tensions, it resolved into "a mutual love feast with
both Catholics and Protestants agreeing on the destructive effects of the
McCollum decision." A suggested resolution in condemnation of the ruling
was abandoned only when one of the two Jewish representatives warned
of a possible counterstatement from the Jews. Nevertheless, under pressure
from Catholics and from some Protestant representatives, the NCCJ prepared to sponsor local conferences to discuss both released time and the
Court's decision. Since the Jews interpreted the move as an attempt to
generate Protestant–Catholic accord, they deduced that their community
might well become the "whipping boy," a sacrifice on the altar of Christian
unity. Fearful of appearing at odds with both Christian groups, the Jews
refused to participate. So palpable was Christian hostility that Leo Pfeffer,
the acknowledged villain of the case, had to be smuggled into Minneapolis
when he was invited to lecture at a local synagogue.[32]

An official of the Congress termed the *McCollum* ruling the "Magna
Carta of the secular school system,"[33] but the Jewish agencies understood
that permanent gains had yet to be consolidated. The removal of ambi-
guities and the vindication of the Jewish position could be secured only by
a second favorable Supreme Court opinion. Meantime, continuing to monitor released time programs in the communities, the agencies devised plans
for promoting popular acceptance not only of *McCollum* but of a broadly
interpreted decision. Simultaneously, the JAC applied pressure on Jewish
educators and rabbis, advising those engaged in released time programs
that their activities ran counter to the Jewish consensus. Yet, inhibited by
Christian opinion, the agencies hesitated to suggest that Jews take unilateral action and drop out of the programs. In that very fluid situation, the
JAC continued to look upon released time as its top priority.[34]

Legal Action in New York City

The Jewish agencies would have preferred to delay further litigation until
the *McCollum* ruling, at least with respect to released time programs *on*

school premises, mustered general compliance. Nevertheless, their hand was forced. When Superintendent of Schools William Jansen announced that *McCollum* would cause no change in New York City's program, atheists swung into action. Joseph Lewis, head of the Free Thinkers Society and a perennial, albeit unsuccessful, plaintiff on matters of church and state—he was the Lewis of the released time case of 1927—brought a suit against the city's released time program (*Lewis* v. *Spaulding*). The state supreme court ruled against him, arguing that the crucial differences between the New York and Champaign systems rendered the *McCollum* decision inapplicable. Lewis's case troubled the ACLU and Jewish separationists. It held out little chance of victory, for Lewis was not a resident, taxpayer, or parent of a New York City school child. Jews were particularly concerned about Lewis's militant atheism, which reinforced the image of the "godless" opponents of released time. Since Lewis threatened to carry his suit up to the Supreme Court, the Jewish agencies feared that the gains registered by *McCollum* might well be lost. Accordingly, in the words of Will Maslow of the Congress: "We therefore pleaded with his counsel to discontinue the action. But [Lewis] would agree only on condition that we committed ourselves to an independent suit challenging released time off school premises. With many reservations, we, along with other Jewish and non-Jewish organizations, brought suit on behalf of parents of children attending the public school."[35]

The litigants could hardly have chosen a worse setting. The New York City system of released time was the "pure" system, or the one that flourished with least connection to the public schools. Both the *amici* and the Court had noted in the *McCollum* case that it exemplified a program furthest removed from the Champaign system. In short, the defenders of released time had their best chance with New York. For the same reason Pfeffer preferred to avoid New York and bring a test case from Boston. There, too, religious classes were held off school premises, but in minor administrative details the schools were more involved in the program. Pfeffer reasoned that a gradual rather than extreme follow-up to Champaign would sooner prevent a Supreme Court under public pressure from backtracking on *McCollum*. Nevertheless, the Boston Jewish community was reluctant to institute a suit.[36]

Ironically, even though they had greater misgivings about participation than in *McCollum*, the Jewish defense agencies assumed a broader role in the ensuing case of *Zorach* v. *Clauson*. Coordinating strategy behind the scenes with the ACLU and the Public Education Association, they rounded up the plaintiffs, drew up the legal papers, gathered evidence, and paid the costs. The ideal scenario called for a joint suit by a Protestant, Catholic, and Jew who were parents of school children and who, as active church members, provided their children with private religious instruction. Since no Catholic was found, the sponsors had to make do with an Episcopalian,

Tessim Zorach, and a Jew, Esta Gluck. The plaintiffs had their own criticisms of the released time program—Gluck's children, for example, suffered anti-Semitic slurs for nonparticipation—but the idea of a suit did not originate with them. As Frank Sorauf put it, the situation was one of "litigation in search of litigants." Despite their minor role, the Glucks incurred harassment. Loyal members of the Congress, the parents became targets for angry neighbors and anti-Semitic bigots. The Gluck children lost friends; Esta Gluck's position as president of the PTA grew increasingly untenable.[37]

The sponsors of the Zorach suit canvassed parents, teachers, students, clergy, and school administrators for statements showing the involvement of the public schools with the city's released time program. Their strategy called for the presentation of that evidence, in the form of affidavits, before the courts. The facts proved, the plaintiffs argued, that the very operation of New York's plan brought about results that were undesirable as well as unconstitutional.

The collected depositions talked about children who were ostracized and taunted for nonparticipation, religious and ethnic divisiveness that surfaced in the wake of the program, teachers who actively pressured for participation in religious classes, and other links between the schools and religious instruction. The matter-of-fact tone of the statements masked neither the abusive words of certain teachers and students nor the serious stress caused to some nonparticipants and their families. A Jewish child who did not join in the program was called "Christ killer" and "dirty Jew" by her classmates; in one Jewish family the children asked their mother if they could become Catholics in order to join their classmates in released time; a Protestant father reported that his daughter thought of herself as a "Protestant martyr" because she was one of the few nonparticipants in her class; a teacher told a sick student that "she did not object to looking at the vomit as much as she objected to looking at the student's face because he did not participate in the released time program."[38]

Unfortunately for the plaintiffs, the entire exercise proved futile. Although the witnesses were prepared to undergo cross-examination at the trial, none of the three New York tribunals that ruled on the case—Supreme Court, Appellate Division of the Supreme Court, Court of Appeals—permitted a trial of the facts. The judges ruled that evidence of abuses or maladministration was not inherent in the plan and hence did not affect the issue of constitutionality. The courts focused instead on how regulations governing the New York system differed from the program in Champaign. In the first trial Judge Anthony DiGiovanna, drawing heavily from the case of *Lewis* v. *Spaulding,* listed the differences between the two programs and concluded that the New York plan was "radically dissimilar" from the one in Illinois. He also maintained that the Supreme Court in *McCollum* had not intended to invalidate all released time programs. By a three-to-two vote the Appellate Division agreed with him. Only the minority was disturbed that the public school machinery was employed in helping to provide sectarian classes with pupils. Released time scored a third victory when the highest state tribunal, the Court of Appeals, upheld the program in a six-to-one decision. There the differences between New York and Champaign were again pinpointed, and again the *McCollum* decision was interpreted narrowly. Judge Stanley Fuld, a Jew and the lone dissenter, read the *McCollum* ruling, and Frankfurter's opinion in particular, differently. He maintained that the pressures inherent in the Champaign system no less than the provision of facilities on school premises had breached the wall of separation and led the justices to invalidate that program. The New York plan, Fuld wrote, "is infected with the same constitutional infirmity" and deserved a similar verdict.[39]

The three major Jewish defense agencies filed a joint *amicus* brief with the higher state courts. Both times they challenged the dismissal of the plaintiffs' petition without a trial of the facts. Furthermore, the brief charged that the New York courts erred by sloughing off the complaints as mere administrative abuses. Rather, the so-called abuses were endemic to the program. The heart of the Jewish brief, however, was its broad interpretation of the *McCollum* decision. The agencies emphasized Black's words equating released time practices with state aid to religious groups. Not confining himself to the Champaign system, the justice had written that such practices ran afoul of the limits imposed on the states by the First and Fourteenth Amendments. Therefore, the brief concluded that "any form of released time for sectarian religious education was unconstitutional."[40]

Legal arguments, however, could not compete with the obstacles attending the litigation. In the first place, the *Zorach* case was haunted by the specter of Joseph Lewis. Although the freethinker had withdrawn his suit, the decision in *Lewis* v. *Spaulding* served as a weighty precedent in the rulings by DiGiovanna and the higher courts. More important, Lewis aroused an emotional defense of released time. His personal aim, to undermine the forces of religion,[41] enabled the supporters of the program to present any attack on the program as a blow for atheism. The disclaimers of the Jewish *amici* in both *McCollum* and *Zorach*, Justice Black's denial that his opinion evidenced a hostility to religion, and the fact that both Zorach and Gluck provided their children with religious instruction after school hours—all failed to erase the belief that opponents of released time were no different from Lewis.

Second, the timing of the suit—again, a condition forced by Lewis— was all wrong. The escalation of the cold war and the onset of the McCarthy era prompted Americans to reaffirm their loyalty to religious values in the struggle against atheistic communism. (The pledge of allegiance was amended in those years to include the phrase "under God.") Many grew impatient with the fine points of church–state separation and urged that the scope of the earlier decision be delimited.

Third, the Jewish community appeared less united to the public than it had in *McCollum*. To be sure, there had always been, as our earlier discussion indicated, some Jews who for a variety of reasons participated in and even favored released time. That minority had not necessarily grown, nor had it become more vocal during the *Zorach* proceedings. But its importance was highlighted by the very fact that the defense of released time in New York was led by a twelve-man interfaith body, the Greater New York Coordinating Committee on Released Time of Jews, Protestants, and Roman Catholics, where one-third of the members were prominent Jewish laymen.[42] Their endorsement of the program publicly exposed disunity within the Jewish ranks and undercut the group's strength within the political process.

Finally, as the case made its way through the state courts, another specter, that of a Jewish–Christian confrontation, increasingly worried the Jewish agencies. Even the thirteen New York judges who tried the case divided along religious lines; the two Jews voted against released time, and the five Catholics and five of the six Protestants supported it. Troubled by evidence of popular hostility, the agencies realized that to many Americans the specific question at stake had become a symbol of a larger contest between Jewish secularism (or atheism) and Christian (or American) religion. "The time has come," a New York minister charged his congregation, "for Christian people to rise up and insist that this nation was conceived as a Christian nation."[43] Not surprisingly, Jewish separationists found themselves bereft of allies and on the wrong side of a hotly debated issue.

To avoid a Jewish–Christian confrontation, the defense agencies deliberately sought to minimize the Jewish role in *Zorach*. At the outset, the sponsors of the suit had looked for non-Jewish litigants and attorneys, but the names of plaintiff Zorach and attorney Kenneth Greenawalt (both non-Jews) sounded Jewish to the public. After the defeats in the state courts, the AJC and ADL refused to allow Pfeffer, who had prepared all the legal papers, to share argument with the non-Jewish counsel before the Supreme Court. Similarly, the JAC decided not to submit an *amicus* brief to the highest court. Having learned that the National Council of Churches intended to file in support of the defense, the Jewish agencies thought it wiser to keep silent than to fan the flames of an interreligious controversy.[44] Thus, the Jewish confidence born of the *McCollum* victory quickly evaporated.

Responsibility for interreligious tensions rested partially on the defense agencies themselves. They had envisioned the possibility of a hostile and united Christian front but had done little to prevent it. They educated the public neither on the evils of released time nor on the respectability of the Jewish stand. Most serious, they had failed to convince Americans that believers could at the same time be strict separationists. To be sure, a few individuals attacked released time in popular periodicals or in their local communities, but scattered resistance was incapable of defusing public hostility.[45]

The isolation of the Jewish separationists grew more pronounced as the *Zorach* case proceeded to the higher courts. As a result, a partial paralysis, or "muteness," as one of Pfeffer's associates put it, gripped the Jewish defense structure with respect to both ongoing and new challenges. When, at the same time, the legality of Bible reading and recitation of the Lord's Prayer in New Jersey's schools was tested in the courts, only the Congress filed an *amicus* brief. Pfeffer argued that precisely because of the opposition to the *Zorach* suit it was vital "to demonstrate that the Jewish community is solidly behind the Everson and McCollum decisions and strongly opposes any retreat from those principles." Nevertheless, out of fear of compounding anti-Jewish sentiment, the JAC rejected his plea.[46]

Nor did the Jewish organizations react strongly to what Pfeffer called "the most serious development in the church–state field since the McCollum decision." In 1951 U.S. Attorney-General J. Howard McGrath, a Catholic, roundly criticized Justice Black in an address delivered before the National Catholic Educational Association. McGrath charged that the justice had distorted the meaning of the First Amendment by insisting on an impregnable wall of separation. "If anything," the attorney-general countered, "the state and church must not have any fence between them." Tempers flared, and the influential *Christian Century* called for McGrath's resignation.

The Jewish agencies were equally disturbed by the injudicious remarks of the nation's chief law enforcement official, but they clashed over a proper response. Characteristically, the Congress was most militant and the ADL most conciliatory. With the JAC at an impasse, the Congress proceeded to act alone. Pfeffer, speaking before the University of Chicago Law School, announced that McGrath owed the American people an apology, and the *Congress Weekly,* like the *Christian Century,* came out in favor of the attorney-general's resignation. A few weeks later and under instructions from NCRAC, the JAC considered a letter of protest to McGrath. The attorney-general had at first agreed to a private meeting with a Jewish delegation, but he angrily changed his mind after the Congress's denunciation. Thereupon, the JAC drafted a letter that was signed by the major defense agencies as well as the SCA, the Jewish War Veterans, and the UAHC. Cordial and even deferential in tone, the letter apprised McGrath of the Jewish position. It suggested, but only mildly, that as the chief enforcement officer he was obliged to support the Supreme Court's stand on separation enunciated in *Everson* and *McCollum*.[47] In this episode, outside pressures softened the Jewish response at the same time that they strained interorganizational cooperation.

Aside from general smears against atheists and secularists, Jews were singled out publicly in several Catholic attacks. The official diocesan weekly of St. Louis headlined a report on the activity of the Congress and the ACLU against released time with inflammatory words: "Leftists, Jews to Test After-School Catechism."[48] Another assault was less primitive but just as vicious. In 1951 the CCAR's Committee on Church and State issued its annual report underlining its opposition to released time and to religious holiday observances and Bible reading in the public schools. It also denounced the name-calling tactic of Christian religious groups, noting its danger to the nonconformist religious minority. The report offered nothing substantively new; it reaffirmed positions taken by the organization for over forty years. Nevertheless, in the heat of the *Zorach* case, it called forth a bitter denunciation from Cardinal Spellman's secretary for education. Monsignor John Middleton minced no words: "The 600 Reform Rabbis, in fact, are not advocating the separation of Church and State, but rather . . . are encouraging the secularism that is already eating away the heart of American life." None of the religious practices of which the rabbis complained, he said, violated church–state separation. With respect to Christmas observance Middleton invoked the sanction of majoritarianism: "Are we to closet the historical Christ and obliterate the memory of His existence because the few are displeased?" At the same time he sought to isolate the strict separationists and minimize their importance. He denied that the CCAR was representative of American Jewish or American opinion, and he called upon Jewish parents to prove that the Reform body did not speak for them on matters of religion and public education. Middleton pointedly advised Christians to demand "that *a part of a part* of the American people should not exert an influence contrary to the demands of justice, charity and common sense." Privately Middleton had charged that the Jewish position smacked of religious bias. And, just as anti-Semitism was a "bad thing," so was anti-Catholicism.

A low-key reply to Middleton came from the president of the CCAR in a letter to the *New York Herald-Tribune*. Defending the independence of both religion and religion-free schools, Rabbi Philip Bernstein asserted that the rabbis had the same right as Catholic educators to express their views on public education. Ignoring the CCAR's disapproval of the decision in the bus case, Bernstein stated that he had no objection to equal welfare benefits to pupils in parochial schools. He was prepared, he said, to join with Catholic leaders in drafting and endorsing such legislation.[49] In this instance the usually outspoken organization preferred to alter its previous stand in order to avoid a collision with Spellman's office.

Protestant spokesmen, if less abusive, often sounded much like the Catholics. The influential chaplain of Columbia University, James Pike, openly suggested that it was morally right to flout the *McCollum* decision and proceed with the establishment of released time programs. Despite the counterimperative of respect for law and order, Pike pointed to the "widespread public revolt" and stated that "it is not clear that the Christian conscience has as its final court of appeal the Supreme Court of the United States." Views like Pike's prompted the individual Jewish agencies as well as the JAC to seek informal discussions with Protestant leaders. The motive was to reach a common meeting ground and, if possible, to persuade the Christians to modify their stand on religion and the schools.[50]

The proceedings of one such conference[51] revealed how unrealistic the Jewish objective was. On December 26, 1951, representatives of the Jewish defense agenceies met with officers of the National Council of Churches and members of leading Protestant denominations. A small group, twenty-one in all, they had arranged to discuss what was loosely labeled "church–state issues." As it turned out, the only area of agreement was a tacit criticism of Catholic aggressiveness on public policy.

Rabbi Bernard Bamberger of the SCA opened the four-hour meeting with a frank statement: both Protestants and Jews subscribed to the prin-ciple of separation, but their interpretations of its meaning and application differed. Jews were committed to the religious training of their children but, unlike the Protestants, they strongly opposed religious practices in the public schools such as Bible reading, prayer, religious holiday obser-vances, and released time. The need to counter ongoing efforts to extend those practices was urgent; they breached the wall of separation and en-croached upon the rights of the individual and the family. Bamberger sharply criticized the "use of intimidation to the point of terror in the name of religion" against those who contested the Christian practices. He ended with a challenge to his audience: "The really serious threat to religious liberty . . . does not come from the hoodlums or the lunatic fringe. Much more serious is the fact that high-minded people for exalted motives should embark upon policies . . . that involve a measure of injustice and even duress."

Bamberger had tried to focus the discussion on the issue of the schools, but his counterpart, Dr. Roswell Barnes of the National Council of Churches, followed with an entirely different agenda. He presented a list of ten items; the question of an ambassador to the Vatican came first and religion in the schools came last. With respect to the first issue, from which the Protestants refused to be deflected, Barnes denied that he and his colleagues sought to pressure the Jews, although admittedly they needed Jewish support to prove that Protestant opposition was not sectarian. For their part, the Jews, too, disapproved of diplomatic rep-resentation to the Vatican, but they refused to say so publicly. Rabbi

Bamberger explained that "Jews did not speak out because as a minority group they were afraid to do so, especially since anyone who goes out on a limb on church–state issues is subjected to continuing vilification and attack."

Only one major Jewish agency, the Congress, had openly opposed the ambassadorship,[52] and at the conference Pfeffer promised the Protestants that the organization was prepared to testify at hearings in Washington. His forthright support of the Protestant position permitted Pfeffer to be more outspoken, and he determinedly reverted to the matter of the schools. Why, he asked, should the Jews oppose the Vatican appointment and jeopardize their position with the Catholic community at the same time that the National Council of Churches proposed to intervene in the *Zorach* case on the side of released time? Both issues represented sectarian intrusions into state affairs. Rabbi Irving Rosenbaum of the ADL followed suit, charging that the Protestants compromised their stand on the ambassadorship by their position on religion in the school. He advised them to "come into court with clean hands" and respond consistently on both issues.

The Protestants at the conference denied that they were considering a trade—a retreat on released time in exchange for Jewish support on the Vatican issue. Barnes observed that the two issues differed markedly; whereas the *Zorach* case required a court decision, the Vatican matter did not. Moreover, as another delegate explained, there was a Protestant consensus on the Vatican issue but not on released time. He gently warned the Jews that a survey of Protestant educators indicated that "they are as much concerned about 'organized secularism' as others are shocked by the organized attack against the separation of church and state principle."

The Jews firmly resisted majority pressure with regard to the Vatican, but they made no dent on Protestant views of released time. In the end, although the National Council of Churches was denied permission to file an *amicus* brief, it made its authority felt in the courtroom through Charles Tuttle, its general counsel, who also represented the defense. Even the separationist POAU refused to adopt a statement in criticism of the released time program.[53] Arrayed against the majority of Christian churches, the Jewish organizations could not realistically expect a sympathetic hearing from the courts.

On the eve of the Supreme Court's decision, a staff member of the Congress surveyed the ominous retreat from separation on the national scene. He faulted both the Jews and the Protestants, the former for their silence in the face of the opposition and the latter for their piecemeal, opportunistic support of the separation principle. "Unless these defections are healed," he warned, "there is danger that the retreat from the *McCollum* case will become a rout."[54]

Religion on Trial

The emotionally charged issue of religion versus atheism reverberated in the judicial proceedings. The opinions of the courts, and the briefs of counsel and *amici* in *Zorach,* revealed that the matter of safeguarding religion was at least as important as the substantive legal points. In the course of the proceedings the issue became personalized around the principals in the litigation; the defenders of released time were depicted as the guardians of American religion, the opponents as its would-be destroyers. By the time the case reached the Supreme Court, the religionists held the upper hand.

An early judicial note which sounded the religious argument in favor of released time came in *Lewis* v. *Spaulding.* New York's Supreme Court, pointing to the recognition of God in the preamble to the state's constitution, said: "Historically and inherently the people of our country are predominantly a religious people."[55] At the first *Zorach* trial in 1950, Judge DiGiovanna ventured further. Insisting that separation of church and state meant freedom *of* but never freedom *from* religion, he warned of the evils inherent in the stand of the anti–released time forces. To forbid the right of children to partake of religious instruction amounted to the suppression of religious freedom, akin to practices of totalitarian governments. Perhaps with an eye on the Jewish challengers of released time, DiGiovanna quoted Governor Lehman's words of approval when he signed the law which allowed the program. Nevertheless, the Jewish participants in the case took offense at the judge's words. Since most Jews opposed released time, Pfeffer maintained, the identification of their position with totalitarianism defamed the entire group.[56]

Charles Tuttle, attorney for the Greater New York Coordinating Committee, which as intervenor-respondent directed the defense of released time, purposely sought to depict the issue as a contest between religion and atheism. As counsel for the Greater New York Federation of Churches and the National Council of Churches, Tuttle had fought against released time with *amicus* briefs in the *Lewis* cases of 1927 and 1948 and in *Mc-Collum.* In *Zorach* his arguments in response to the plaintiffs reeked of bitter invective and emotional appeal. Skillfully integrating popular fears aroused by the cold war into a protest against strict separationism, Tuttle fueled what was already an overheated atmosphere.[57]

The theme of the defense, which Tuttle's brief iterated over and over, was the right of parents to secure religious instruction for their children. The brief called it an elemental right, integral to liberty of conscience. The opposition to released time would, however, deny the parents' right to give children "a moment . . . to revere the faith of their fathers." Those parents who rightfully believed that secularism was both a major cause of world unrest and an enemy of American freedom were severely threatened, for secular control of education presaged a "gateless 'wall of separation' between the child and his parent's 'liberty of conscience.' " Released time also stood as a reminder of the limits to the powers of a secular state and its monopoly of education. Like DiGiovanna, Tuttle warned that if the school became a vassal of the state and the citizens it educated mere creatures of the state, all fundamental rights would be at the mercy of totalitarian control. "Such is the appalling lesson of all the systems of Brown, Black and Red Shirts throughout the last ten years." Thus, by the conclusion of the brief, released time had assumed new dimensions. As the symbol of individual rights besieged by shock troop assaults, it stood for true Americanism.

Having likened the opponents of released time to Nazis and Communists, Tuttle refused to recognize any differences between atheists and the plaintiffs. The brief stubbornly insisted that the plea was essentially a replica of Joseph Lewis's suit—an atheistic plan under a changed "frontispiece." The brief invoked the *Holy Trinity* case of 1892, singling out Brewer's phrase, "this is a religious people." It liked even more the "peculiarly appropriate" language of the Texas court in the case of *Church* v. *Bullock* (1908). There the judges had said that no individual, out of personal objections, had the right to deny Bible reading to public school children: "This would be to starve the moral and spiritual natures of the many out of deference to the few." To be sure, the brief omitted Brewer's mention of "a Christian nation" and the Texas court's observation that Christianity was interwoven with the "web and woof of the State government," but to a non-Christian minority ever alert to the dangers of majoritarianism, the broad hints were disturbing.[58]

The opinion of the Court of Appeals bore a marked resemblance to Tuttle's brief. It, too, stressed the religious freedom of parents and the specter of unlimited state authority, and it also found support in Justice Brewer. The court insisted that the government could constitutionally accommodate religion without violating the separation principle. The wall of separation, "which in our 'religious nation' is designed as a reasonable demarcation between friends," must not be built too high. Indeed, invalidation of released time would be tantamount to the creation of "an 'iron curtain' as between foes."

A concurring opinion by Judge Charles Desmond also cited Brewer's words and, going back even further, Chancellor Kent's admonition in the *Ruggles* case of 1811 that religion need not be ignored by the law. Desmond did not mention Kent's affirmation that "we are a christian people" or his view that Christianity was part of the common law. But why should the judge have noted those two cases, where the Christian-state idea loomed so important, to the exclusion of other accommodationist rulings which made no mention of Christianity? Purposefully or unwittingly, he—like Tuttle and like the majority of the Court of Appeals—implied that government accommodation of Christianity was the only alternative to secularism. Such arguments only confirmed the fears that released time was part of a larger struggle of religious Christians to reconquer the schools.[59]

Clearly the defense, and the courts, had inflated the issue of released time in order to regain some of the ground lost in *Everson* and *McCollum,* but the smears of atheism and totalitarianism could not go unanswered. In their briefs, the AJC, Congress, and ADL lashed out against the "intemperate" and "unwarranted" statements and the "false" and "irrelevant" issues that beclouded the legal proceedings.[60] But mere denials of atheism—look at the Jews whose tradition commanded religious instruction, who privately funded after-school religious classes for their children, and whose religious organizations had joined the *McCollum* brief—or of totalitarianism failed to undo the damage. The Jews found themselves in the unenviable position of disputing an image which, despite inaccuracies, had gained popular credence. Having lost the emotional initiative to the other side, their responses smacked of apologetics and their championship of the religion-free public school rang feeble.

Against that background, the Supreme Court's decision upholding New York's program was not unexpected. (No religious *amicus* briefs were filled with the Court, but eight states registered their support of released time. One of them, Oregon, argued along Tuttle's lines that to strike down released time would be a blow to freedom of religion.)[61] Speaking for a majority of six, Justice William Douglas found that the New York plan differed significantly from the Champaign system of the *McCollum* case. Since classrooms were not used for religious instruction, and since pupils were not coerced to attend, the program impinged on neither the establishment nor the free-exercise clause. Separation, Douglas insisted, did not require hostility to religion, and purist separationism ran counter to traditional American habits and public rituals. The justice's oft-quoted words, "We are a religious people whose institutions presuppose a Supreme Being," were used to introduce a broad definition of separation, but, according to Douglas, no law required the government to encourage the weakening of religion. If government did not accommodate the spiritual needs of the people, it would be showing a preference for nonbelievers over believers.[62] The Court specifically denied that it had repudiated *McCollum,* but the decision, a not unexpected response to popular sentiment, was a significant retreat from the spirit of *Everson* and *McCollum.* The ruling may have contributed to a modest increase in released time enrollment, and, of greater concern to separationists, it weakened compliance with the earlier decision that released time classes had to be held off school premises. Perhaps most disturbing, those who supported additional ties between religion and the schools seized upon *Zorach* to validate their demands.[63]

The Jewish defense agencies were disappointed but, although they had counted on Douglas's support, not surprised. They said that the real danger lay in the Court's repudiation of the Jeffersonian wall of separation and its implication that the First Amendment did not consistently mandate separation in all respects. Members of the JAC commiserated that the decision could have been worse. To be sure, the heart of the Jewish argument since 1946, namely, that released time meant coercion, was cut out, but the Court had not repudiated *McCollum*. The agencies expected further trouble, attempts either to extend released time or to inject new religious practices into the schools. Meantime, the task was to prevent a massive retreat on the issue of released time by local Jewish communities.[64]

Fifty years earlier, the fear of a Christian state would doubtless have agitated Jewish leaders. Telltale signs had enveloped the case: innuendos in court briefs and judicial opinions, references to the *Holy Trinity* case, a Protestant–Catholic working alliance in opposition to the Jewish objective, charges like those from Spellman's office, and evidence that defenders of released time entertained more ambitious plans for linking religion and the schools. Yet the passage of time, and the "second disestablishment," had permanently altered both Christian and Jewish behavior. In 1950 no responsible Christian judges or attorneys, even if they meant "Christianity" when they said religion or "Christian" when they said religious people, would have stated publicly that the United States was a Christian nation. Christian hegemony at least in public policy had been toppled, and the subject was not resurrected even in private Jewish deliberations. The Jewish fear of a Christian state remained dormant; it lived on in the tenacity and persistence displayed by Jewish separationists with respect to the schools. Believers as well as nonbelievers—most still worried lest religious incursions into public life undermine the comfort and security of the non-Christian minority.

The issue of released time waned in importance on the Jewish defense agenda of the 1950s, but it left a stumbling block to Catholic–Jewish amity. In 1959 Bishop Lawrence W. Lynch of Chicago addressed a Parents–Teachers Association and called for the need of God in the public school. A religionless school reminded him, Lynch said, of Shylock, who wanted a pound of flesh without the blood that brought vitality. When a local rabbi questioned the remark, the bishop was more specific. He confessed to a "constant displeasure" with the activity of the American Jewish Congress and with "comments of leaders of your faith" in opposition to released time programs.[65] For many years such sentiments blocked Jewish separationist efforts on matters of church and state.

6
The Case of
the Innocuous Prayer

Cures for the "Godless" Public School

As part of an instructional program in moral and spiritual values, the New York State Board of Regents suggested in 1951 that school children begin their day with a short, nonsectarian prayer. Unlike released time or Bible reading, both the program and prayer were new ideas on the postwar educational scene. The Regents' prayer was adopted in some school districts; ultimately it came to the Supreme Court for review in the landmark case of *Engel* v. *Vitale*. The ruling climaxed eleven years of public debate on a broader issue, the use of the classroom to cultivate religious sensibilities and impart rudimentary knowledge about religion. From the Jewish perspective, the full significance of the decision can be understood best only when it is examined within that historical context. Indeed, the setting of the case as well as the ensuing backlash are as important to the story of Jewish activity on public religion as the case itself.

Fueled by the postwar religious revival, criticisms of the "godless" public school abounded. In essence, they said that the school system had failed to shape God-fearing children. Both Christian spokesmen and influential educational organizations like the American Council on Education and the National Education Association deplored the condition of religious illiteracy. Together they vigorously campaigned against secularism and sought devices to fill the void of religionless instruction. The most popular of the proposed solutions, in addition to released time, were the teaching of a "common core" of religious doctrines, the inculcation of "moral and spiritual values," and objective "teaching about religion."[1]

Each of the proposals raised obvious questions. Could the different religions agree on a common core? Could religion or values be taught objectively without sectarian interpretation or indoctrination? Was there any one definition of moral and spiritual values that all would accept? Was the average teacher equipped to present such subject matter free of bias? Religious leaders had their own doubts. Some resented the dilution of sacred teachings or the religious syncretism inherent in the proposals, and some questioned whether a free-floating morality ungrounded in religion could be taught at all. Still others objected to the state's invasion into an area heretofore reserved to the churches and its right to determine the essentials of a moral education. For many Americans discussion of the place of religion in the public school curriculum became the central and most baffling issue of church–state relations.[2]

Unlike the released time plan, where separate classes in religion were taught by clergymen either on or off school premises, the new proposals aimed at the integration of religious values or concepts within the normal curriculum. Reacting against the *McCollum* decision, they sidestepped the issue of religious classes and focused on the captive audience within the classroom. While proponents, particularly among responsible educators, conscientiously steered clear of any gross violation of church–state separation, they regarded a nameless and amorphous nonsectarian religion supported by state schools to be permissible. Their beliefs also reinforced entrenched usages in the schools—Bible reading and prayer, celebration of religious holidays—which strict separationists consistently found offensive. Christmas, for example, assumed greater significance; the popular religious attempt to "put Christ back into Christmas" now drew support from the perceived urgency of retaining religious symbols in the classroom.

The Jewish list of grievances on religion in the schools grew longer, and the newer practices, spawning endless discussions, conferences, and workshops, soon overshadowed the old. As schools around the country instituted programs for the inculcation of religious values and concepts, the strict separationists in control of the Jewish defense structure were hard put to come up with an appropriate stand. Public opinion notwithstanding, they viewed the untried programs as a clear breach of the wall of separation and as a formidable threat to the ideal of a nonreligious public school. One prominent Jewish educator asked: "How much more needs to be introduced to satisfy Christian requirements of the public schools?" In terms of Jewish security and equality the programs appeared to be an entering wedge for blatant sectarianism or for fixed religious distinctions among school children.[3]

The initial fears of the separationists were often substantiated during the 1950s. In some localities—Austin, Texas, or Meridian, Mississippi, for instance—religion, or moral and spiritual values, was synonymous with Christianity or Christian culture, and the programs became ways of indoctrination in the majority faith. True, very few Jews were affected in places like Meridian, but, as Jewish separationists consistently maintained, numbers were meaningless where principle was concerned. The programs themselves sometimes generated a heightened display of religious bias. When a school board in Sierra Madre, California, announced that religious instruction was not a function of the schools, the statement touched off a wave of popular hysteria and bigotry.[4]

Shortly after the *Zorach* ruling, the leading Protestant organization, the National Council of Churches, publicly condemned the inroads of secularism into society and the schools. The Protestants' letter (whose very salutation, "Dear Fellow Christians," offended the CCAR) announced that a heightened awareness of God in the classroom, as in "reverent" Bible readings, was the solution. Those Americans—Jews and Christians—who believed that moral values could be grounded in secular humanism or in an American civil religion were thus excluded from the very debate. Dr. Israel Chipkin of the Jewish Education Committee commented bitterly: "I know that our Christian friends regard this country as Christian. . . . To challenge their position is to be regarded as anti-religious (or even godless). To challenge them in the courts is of course to make them martyrs on behalf of their sectarian faiths."[5]

Jewish separationists mounted attacks on the divisive effects of the programs and simultaneously defended the nonreligious public school against its critics.[6] Nevertheless, some recognized that a summary rejection of the new and popular proposals was woefully inadequate. Public pressure on the Jewish community necessitated a compromise. Within the Jewish community a few voices, rabbinical (Conservative and Reform) and lay, urged at least a willingness to explore the new proposals. The situation exposed considerations that had always challenged the strict separationism of American Jews. An appropriate stand had to be one of a *religious* community, a group which, like its Christian counterparts, worried about the moral and religious climate of society at large. Were that group simply to reject suggestions for nondenominational instruction in or about religion, it would appear to have sacrificed its faith on the altar of secularism. As Jews had learned during the bitter fight over released time, that impression could not be effectively dislodged either by hoisting the flag of separation or by incanting legal and constitutional formulas. The acrimony unleashed by *McCollum* continued to cast a pall on intergroup relations. "Either you are Theists or Atheists," Jewish representatives were told at an interreligious meeting in New York.[7]

Tactically, rabbis who opposed the new programs were in a stronger position than the secular defense agencies. As religious leaders they could more legitimately argue that the Jews, who called themselves a religious people, had valid reasons for resisting seemingly inoffensive forms of public religion. For that reason the JAC reprinted and distributed an article by Morris Adler, a prominent Conservative rabbi, that presented a well-reasoned statement on why Jews, as both Americans and Jews, should stand firm against religion in the classroom. Yet even rabbis had no easy answers. As the CCAR explained: "We want to promote religious and spiritual values and elevate the moral and ethical life of society. How can we best achieve these ends without doing violence to our convictions about the separation of church and state and without encroaching upon personal liberties?"[8]

Talk of compromise increased. Of the major agencies, the ADL was the first to modify its course of action. Its position was adumbrated early on in the remarks of one staff member, Rabbi Irving Rosenbaum, at the 1947 NCRAC conference on sectarianism in the schools. The rabbi condemned what he called the "signal reaction," or the way in which Jewish leaders, constantly using the shibboleth of separation, automatically judged any sort of religion in the school as harmful to Jews. Their fears that religious teaching would breed divisiveness and unequal status for minorities were valid, he argued, only if that teaching was sectarian. A neutral teaching of religion such as recommended by the American Council on Education would, however, be a unifying and beneficial force. Indeed, if Jews refused to acknowledge the legitimacy of the beliefs of different groups, their support of intercultural education (a cause that began in the mid–1930s) was both inconsistent and hypocritical. Moreover, Jewish acceptance of "teaching about religion" would erase their secularist image and end their isolation from Christian religious groups.

The rabbi urged Jews to face the realities. On the issue of Christmas, for example, Americans were hypersensitive. Why else would a liberal Protestant like Daniel Poling expostulate that a ban on the singing of carols "is quite as bad as burning books in Nazi Berlin"? "We must become reconciled to the idea," Rosenbaum explained, "that [Christmas] has become a part of the folkways and mores of America, and that we should be in a most untenable position if we attempted to extirpate it." Perhaps it was wiser to support joint Christmas–Hanukkah celebrations, thus taking Christmas out of the realm of sectarianism and making the joint endeavor an exercise in intercultural education. The implication of his remarks, and one that would be widely debated within the Jewish community after *Engel,* was clear: the Christian nature of American culture put finite limits on the course of rigid separationism.[9]

Following these lines, the ADL diverged from the path of its sister agencies. It took the lead in supporting joint holiday programs in local communities, and it also defended the teaching of moral and spiritual values divorced from religious sanctions. One of its last messages before it withdrew from the JAC advised that a tendency to become "doctrinaire and purist" would only strengthen the enemies of separation. The ADL never retreated from the abstract principle of separation, and indeed to all but strict separationists its divergence was minimal. Nevertheless, its apparent readiness to yield on school-related issues caused a serious rupture in the separationist camp. It meant, among other things, that the JAC had lost its standing as the single Jewish voice to Christian groups on church–state matters.[10]

The ADL's "soft" line drew much support from local Jewish communities, particularly since Christmas celebrations often replaced Bible reading as the primary religious issue in the schools. Indeed, there was ample evidence of animosity and harassment suffered by Jews who questioned Christmas observances. (One family in Chelsea, Massachusetts, was forced to go into hiding in a nearby community. In Hamden, Connecticut, there were swastikas, threats of boycotts, and a sign in the high school that read: "What Eichmann started, we'll finish.")[11] The ADL later modified its position on religious holidays, but the popularity of its position in the 1950s forced the strict separationists to a less rigid stance. Their official statements notwithstanding, they settled for Christmas in the schools but without Christological elements. Leo Pfeffer himself admitted: "It would be fatuous to believe that Christmas can be banished from the public school. It is as much part of the American school culture as Thanksgiving and graduation day."[12]

Within the Jewish community at large, rampant divisiveness quickly erased the overwhelming consensus that had obtained on released time. Although the major agencies circulated statements, pamphlets, and guides on the subject of religion in the schools,[13] they had little control over individual laymen or rabbis who determined policy for specific localities. The first priority of the average Jewish layman was to avoid any public disturbance. He needed the goodwill of his Christian neighbors to keep his business on an even keel and his family unmolested. Why should he antagonize his neighbors unnecessarily by opposing practices that seemed so inconsequential? Besides, as he was wont to say, he himself had been subjected in school to Christian prayers and hymns, Bible reading, and Christmas celebrations, and those experiences had not made him any less a Jew. Resigned to minority status, laymen often criticized rabbis who "stirred up trouble" by their defense of strict separation. The average rabbi shared his congregation's worry about public relations. The spokesman of the congregation to the Christian community, he was often caught between the two. He much more than his congregants was concerned about the principle involved, but his stand was influenced by other variables—personal, professional, and congregational. Since local conditions above all determined the multiple and often contradictory positions of the individual congregations, central agencies like the JAC could hardly keep the ranks in line.[14]

To forge some sort of consensus among the local communities, and, more important, to keep them on the path of strict separation, the JAC planned two regional conferences, followed by an ambitious national conference, to discuss the ideas of "common core," "moral and spiritual values," and "teaching about religion." After the conferences the SCA and NCRAC formulated their conclusions. Their position paper rejected "common core" outright; articles of faith, even if drawn from all religions, violated the principle of separation, and a common-denominator religion watered down that which was spiritually meaningful to each faith. With regard to "moral and spiritual values," the statement distinguished between religious teaching, which remained the responsibility of the home and the church, and the teaching of ethics and citizenship, which, it claimed, the schools were in fact supplying. Schools bore a responsibility "for fostering a commitment to these moral values, without presenting or teaching any sectarian or theological sources or sanctions for such values." The statement agreed that "teaching about religion," or objective instruction on religion's share in the development of social institutions, was required when such material was intrinsic to the subject. But teaching about the *doctrines* of religion opened the door to sectarian pressures on the schools. Therefore, objective and impartial teaching about religious beliefs was "an unattainable objective."[15]

Widely disseminated throughout the community, the JAC's statement was joined by separate pronouncements from the ADL and AJC. On the issues of "common core," "moral and spiritual values," and "teaching about religion," the texts, albeit lower keyed, were very similar. The Jewish groups had not summarily dismissed the new proposals. To some degree, the statements were a compromise: they agreed that the schools had to inculcate moral values (without a religious grounding), and they endorsed at least in theory the "teaching about religion." Over the years the three agencies manifested a genuine willingness to consider all sorts of experiments designed for the improvement of the moral climate in the schools.[16]

While the big three agreed on essentials, they differed sharply on how loudly the Jews should trumpet their minority views in the public arena. All responsible Jewish agencies were alert to popular opinion, but the AJC and ADL, who cooperated closely in many endeavors, reacted more timidly than the Congress. With a constant eye on Christian friendship, they preferred to minimize the "Jewish" component of their opinions. For the sake of interreligious harmony, they shied away from delicate issues which involved no immediate threat to the Jewish community. Where principle was involved, as in the area of church and state, they weighed the advantages of Jewish action against the possibility of Christian antagonism. The Congress, on the other hand, proclaimed that principle came first. At stake was the preservation of Jewish equality as well as constitutional freedoms. Were Jews to heed those critics who warned that complaints about prayer or Christmas in the schools would only foment anti-Semitism, they would be tacitly consenting to a status of second-class citizenship. Following Pfeffer's book *Creeds in Competition,* the Congress also argued that the airing of religious differences was a salutary if not creative force in social evolution.[17]

The Regents' Prayer

The New York Board of Regents, which included members from the three major faiths, issued a short policy statement in 1951 that made front-page news. Postulating that Americans were always a religious people, the Regents announced that the fundamental American belief in God was "the best security against the dangers of these difficult days." Accordingly, the statement advised, it became the responsibility of the school to assist the home and church in nurturing religious commitment and a love of God. In the spirit of the Founding Fathers, who acknowledged their dependence on their Creator as the source of their rights and freedoms, schools had to prepare each child "to follow the faith of his or her father." The Regents made two proposals: the daily recitation of a nonsectarian prayer in the classroom, and the implementation of programs in moral and spiritual values.[18]

The first recommendation, a twenty-two-word prayer that read "Almighty God, we acknowledge our dependence upon Thee and we beg Thy blessings upon us, our parents, our teachers and our country," aroused heated controversy throughout the state. Catholic as well as most Protestant church leaders approved; Jews, some Protestants, and various educational and civic groups passed antiprayer resolutions. The Jewish position, which was shared by the major defense agencies, the SCA, the New York Board of Rabbis, and local community councils, emphasized the violation of separation. Not only might the prayer open the door to other usages destructive of the nonsectarian school, but it was another improper attempt to equate belief in God with good citizenship. Jews also voiced strong misgivings about the divisiveness that the practice would inject into the classroom, since school authority, as in the case of released time, influenced conformity. Besides, the Regents' purpose could scarcely be achieved by rote recitation of an essentially empty formula.[19]

The prayer debate fomented interreligious animosity, and Jewish opposition raised yet again, now from Christian members of parent associations across the state, the accusation that Jews were "communistic and Godless." In New York City, after a stormy public hearing on the issue, the Board of Education hit upon its own compromise; in lieu of the prayer school children would sing the fourth stanza of "America" as well as the first. Even that solution stirred up disagreement. Catholic and Protestant groups desired only the fourth stanza, which they interpreted publicly as a prayer, but the Board of Rabbis insisted that the first and fourth stanzas be sung together as a *patriotic* hymn. Nevertheless, the debate quickly died. By 1955 only 10 percent of the school districts in the state had adopted the Regents' prayer.[20]

During the mid-1950s the Jewish defense agencies were more concerned with the Regents' program on moral and spiritual values than with its nonsectarian prayer. To them the prayer was but a single item in a larger package, one that was far more dangerous to the secular public school than released time or even a separate hour for religious instruction. It encouraged, they said, "the introduction of religion into every phase of school life and in effect makes the public teacher a full time religious missionary."[21] Jewish opposition was loudest in New York City, where, as in other metropolises, Jews were pitted against a politically powerful and well-organized Catholic bloc. The prominent part played by the New York Board of Rabbis, a body established in 1881 to speak for the different wings within Judaism, proved too that rabbinical opposition to nonsectarian public religion was no less strong than that of the secular agencies.

Superintendent Jansen invited representatives of the three major faiths to consider how the Regents' proposal for teaching moral and spiritual values might be implemented. His choice of the Board of Rabbis to speak for the Jews was politically sound. It kept the issue on a religious plane, and it sidestepped the interorganizational rivalry so characteristic of the three major agencies. The episode marks one of the rare postwar occasions on which the secular defense network was officially bypassed in favor of a religious body. From the Jewish point of view, it promised a distinct advantage. Affirmations of the Jewish commitment to religious education coming from a rabbinical group, which spoke for the Orthodox, Conservative, and Reform, enjoyed greater credibility than similar statements from the Congress. Indeed, the board's role as public defender could help to dispel popular views about secularist Jews who conspired to keep religion out of the schools.

Delegates of the Board of Rabbis met with members of the Protestant Council and the Archdiocese of New York for over two years, but they failed to reach a common agreement. Thereupon, New York City's Board of Superintendents formulated its own guide on how to implement a school program of moral and spiritual values. In all subjects—social studies, science, fine arts, industrial arts—they pointed out opportunities for instruction about America's religious heritage and Americans' religious commitment. Again the Board of Rabbis served as the designated representative of the Jews to review the guide, and again the rabbis resisted what they called state intrusion into the area of religious education. Under conflicting pressures from Catholics as well as Jews, the Board of Education drastically revised the guide. Reservations about the amended program remained, but Jews could note with satisfaction that their persistent pressure had blunted the drive for a stronger public religion. The extent to which the moral climate of the schools improved after 1956 was yet another matter.[22]

For the better part of the decade Jewish defense organizations concentrated on the program of moral and spiritual values and virtually ignored the Regents' prayer. When a rabbi in a suburban community sought guidance from the JAC in 1952 on how Jewish children should behave during the recitation of the prayer, the agency refused to take a stand. Yet more frequently recalled is the case about a prayer which even Pfeffer, the strict separationist, called the "most inoffensive, . . . most innocuous religious practice imaginable."[23] Logically the Jewish approach, which fixed on the larger and more serious threat to the secular school, was correct. Not until the case of *Engel* v. *Vitale* was appealed to the higher courts did the seemingly inconsequential prayer command sustained Jewish attention.

In 1958 the school board of New Hyde Park, Long Island, adopted the Regents' prayer for use in the classrooms. School prayers were not new to area residents; some schools adhered to the longstanding custom of reciting the Lord's Prayer and others introduced silent prayer, where children accompanied their prayer with religious gestures like kneeling or crossing themselves.[24] But in this town the move added to a list of grievances against the school board.

New Hyde Park was one of the numerous suburban areas that received a large influx of Jews and Catholics after the war. Religious issues usually pitted the new groups against each other, with Protestants somewhere in the middle. No Jew served on the school board, and local Jewish leaders thought the board members were reactionary and anti-Semitic. One resident wrote that in 1957 the district was "the most turbulent battleground in New York State, if not in the whole country, on the issue of religion in the public schools." A year later, when the board decided that Hanukkah should not be celebrated or discussed in the classroom at a time when it would interfere with the Christmas season, local Jewish leaders denounced the "outrageous and discriminatory" policy. They charged the board with having created community divisiveness and dissension.[25]

The Regents' prayer had been in effect but a few months when Lawrence Roth, a businessman who called himself "a very religious person but not a churchgoer," placed an advertisement in a local paper asking for taxpayer-parents to join him in seeking legal redress. Members of different religions responded, but in the end no orthodox Christian appeared among the litigants. The five parents who became the plaintiffs included two Jews, one Unitarian, one Ethical Culturist, and Roth. They argued that the prayer, even though it was voluntary, involved some measure of coercion, and that despite its nonsectarian form it violated the establishment clause of the First Amendment. The parents were represented by a Catholic lawyer, but guidance of the case rested in the hands of the New York affiliate of the ACLU. The very roster of the participants did not augur well for attracting the support of middle America, and to some it appeared as if it were a Jewish case.[26]

The New York Civil Liberties Union invited Pfeffer's cooperation, but the lawyer thought that litigation over the Regents' prayer, "as non-sectarian as a prayer can be," held out no prospect of success. It would, he said, only provide the courts with another opportunity to expound on religion and patriotism. Pfeffer, who urged that the first legal case over a prayer be a "substantial" one, eagerly anticipated the introduction of a suit, also in a Long Island district, challenging the recitation of the Lord's Prayer. That issue was of national rather than merely state importance, and it involved a sectarian Christian prayer. The lawyer had already plotted the strategy for the case when much to his annoyance the local Jewish community council agreed to the fourth stanza of "America" and the Regents' prayer in lieu of the Lord's Prayer.[27]

The suit against the Regents' prayer, *Engel* v. *Vitale,* went ahead despite Pfeffer. Its sponsors rapidly attracted ridicule as well as anti-Semitism. One of the many hate letters received by Lawrence Roth read: "This looks like Jews trying to grab America as Jews grab everything they want in any nation. America is a Christian nation." Another testified to the prevalent acceptance of the Jew-as-Communist image: "If you dont't like our God, then go behind the Iron Curtain where you belong, Kike, Hebe, Filth!"[28] Anti-Semitism erupted elsewhere too. In North Massapequa, Long Island, the school board, where Jews outnumbered Catholics by a margin of one, resolved to postpone its decision on the adoption of the Regents' prayer until the courts had decided for New Hyde Park. Thereupon, Catholics launched a hate campaign against those who "tabled" God in the schools. Broken windows, obscene phone calls, and a boycott of "anti-Christian" merchants ensued. As in the cases of Christmas celebrations or released time programs, such episodes nurtured Jewish reluctance to support strict separation.[29]

The opinions by the lower courts confirmed Pfeffer's initial misgivings. Writing for the New York Supreme Court, Justice Bernard Meyer held that the Regents' prayer did not constitute religious instruction or show a preference for any one religion. He dismissed the plaintiffs' point that the practice created divisiveness; religious differences were among the facts of life. Meyer expatiated on the respondents' argument that prayer was part of the national heritage. After a lengthy historical survey he concluded that no intent existed at the time of the adoption of the First and the Fourteenth Amendments to exclude the routine of school prayer as long as it was not compulsory. "The Constitution does not require separation in every and all respects," and therefore the prayer fell within the realm of "permissible accommodation."[30]

To a large degree, the constitutional issue that divided opponents and supporters of the Regents' prayer revolved around the rulings in the released time cases. Opponents argued that *McCollum* had set permanent boundaries to accommodation; even in *Zorach* the Court specifically refused to repudiate the earlier ruling. Supporters, like Meyer, cited Douglas's dictum, "We are a religious people," and *Zorach*'s tilt toward accommodationism. One justice of the Appellate Division of New York's Supreme Court, which upheld Meyer's decision, used both *Zorach* and the *Holy Trinity* case to declare that Americans were a religious people and the prayer constitutional. Dissenters, he agreed, might suffer "embarrassment," but "it is the price which every nonconformist must pay."[31]

When the plaintiffs carried the case to the Court of Appeals, they were supported by a joint *amicus* brief filed by the ADL and AJC. One reason for filing, the agencies said, was "to demonstrate to the court that strongly religious groups oppose this practice for reasons of religious freedom." The brief postulated that an attempt by the state to provide for the spiritual needs of the pupils was unlawful. A prayer meaningful for individual denominations depended on form and content, and the form of the Regents' prayer, which was unknown to synagogues, created confusion in the minds of Jewish children. In this brief, too, the released time decisions were the focal point, and the agencies contended that the *McCollum* decision controlled the prayer case. Regardless of whether or not the prayer was compulsory, it fell under the prohibitions of the establishment clause as interpreted by Justice Black. Not only was the Regents' prayer conducted within the school building, but the Regents were *sponsoring* rather than merely *accommodating* religion.[32]

The Court of Appeals upheld the lower courts' rulings by a vote of five to two. Chief Judge Charles Desmond, a Catholic and the author of the religiously slanted concurring opinion in the *Zorach* case, wrote the decision. Since, in his opinion, establishment meant only preferential treatment of one or several sects, Desmond rejected Black's definition in *Everson* and *McCollum*. To call the Regents' prayer a violation of the First Amendment defied all American history. Drawing from *Zorach* and the *Holy Trinity* cases, he added: "Belief in a Supreme Being is as essential and permanent a feature of the American governmental system as is freedom of worship, equality under the law and due process of law. Like them it is an American absolute, an application of the natural law beliefs on which the Republic was founded." Another Catholic member of the majority bitterly criticized the minority opinion. To banish religion entirely from the schools was an attempt to compel conformity by forcing a secularist culture on the children. In short, it was "a Marxist concept," which promoted the cause of atheism.[33]

The plaintiffs appealed to the Supreme Court, but sympathizers like Pfeffer doubted whether the highest court would grant review. In terms of significance and substance the Lord's Prayer and Bible reading outranked the Regents' prayer. It would be more sensible, separationists thought, to use those issues for securing a complete review from the Court on religion and the schools. Writer Paul Blanshard, for example, compared the Regents' prayer case to "an impatient lady at the end of a long theatre queue who insists on rushing to the head of the line and purchasing her ticket before other waiting customers." Nor did the prospect of ultimate victory appear real, since many state attorneys-general had come out in support of the prayer.[34]

When the Court accepted the case, Pfeffer prepared an *amicus* brief for NCRAC and the SCA. Since the AJC and ADL filed in a separate brief, the organized Jewish community, as in the *McCollum* case, closed ranks.[35] In trenchant fashion the NCRAC brief rebutted the various reasons given by the lower courts for upholding the prayer. First, the brief insisted, the prayer was both sectarian and preferential. It showed a preference for theistic religions and for those faiths which sanctioned the practice. Second, despite its voluntary character, it impinged on the right of free exercise. In a school setting where they were under pressure to conform, children of minority groups usually opted to participate. Third, even if free exercise was preserved, the prayer (a meaningless rote recitation) violated the establishment clause as defined in *Everson* and *McCollum*. Finally, a long-standing history of school prayer did not make it constitutional. Indeed, if historical usage determined constitutionality, then the Court in 1954 (*Brown* v. *Board of Education*) could not have outlawed racial segregation in the schools.

As the Jewish agencies always had, the brief denied that exclusion of prayer from the schools betrayed hostility to religion. And again it made a valiant effort to dissociate Jews from the charge of secularism: "The thousands of rabbis and congregations who have authorized the submission of this brief can hardly be characterized as being 'on the side of those who oppose religion.' "

The justices asked many questions of both sides when they heard oral argument, but no observer could confidently predict the verdict.[36] The six-to-one decision invalidating the Regents' prayer, which the Court announced on June 25, 1962, stunned the nation. Again Justice Black spoke for the majority. The prayer, he said, was a religious activity and hence violative of the establishment clause. That clause, which represented the belief that "a union of government and religion tends to destroy government and to degrade religion," meant that "it is no part of the business of the government to compose official prayers for any group of the American people." Neither the nonsectarian nor the voluntary nature of the prayer freed it from those limitations. Along the lines of *McCollum,* Black denied that a ban on public prayer manifested hostility to religion or to prayer. In fact, Black salvaged part of the Regents' program on moral and spiritual values. He said in a footnote that nothing in the decision interfered with encouraging children to recite historical documents (like the Declaration of Independence) or to sing anthems which contained references to God. The justice concluded his opinion with a reference to the entering wedge. Along the lines of Madison's "Memorial and Remonstrance," he said that just because the prayer was relatively insignificant made it no less ominous a breach of principle.[37]

Jewish defense organizations could not have asked for more. Ever since the war they had actively combated religion in the classroom, and *Engel* was an unqualified vindication. That they had contributed to the result in some small measure was equally gratifying. The Court's ruling, the logical culmination of *Everson* and *McCollum,* legitimated the familiar Jewish arguments. Jews had worn the mantle of separationism, but a non-Jewish court had breathed life into those ideals. By upholding strict separation, which had so long been perceived as the sine qua non of American Jewish well-being, the Court also struck a blow for Jewish security. More important, the ruling gave credence to a larger theme that American Jews had been expounding since the birth of the Republic—the identity of Jewish and American interests. What greater comfort for the minority than to know that their perception of Jewish needs coincided with the American way? The Court had stamped their posture as eminently American, and the victory was sweet.

Jewish separationists gleefully explored the legal implications of the *Engel* decision. At the very least, it appeared as if the Court had sounded the death knell for the recitation of the Lord's Prayer and other religious prayers. Logically it followed that devotional reading of the Bible was doomed, as were religious holiday observances. Most important, according to Pfeffer, the decision affirmed that the government could neither pursue religious ends nor employ religious means for secular objectives. Whatever doubts *Zorach* may have cast on the principle of separation appeared to have been laid to rest.[38]

Backlash

The storm unleashed by the *Engel* decision cut short any celebration. Torrents of abuse fell upon the Warren Court for outlawing God in the classroom. Americans expressed their outrage, from former presidents Hoover and Eisenhower to the eleven-year-old who asked, "Does this mean we can't have Christmas plays anymore?" On Capitol Hill congressmen and senators eagerly waited a turn to say nice things about God and religion and nasty things about the ruling and the Court. Whether the Court was out to usurp legislative power, or whether it was in league with Moscow or the devil, it had betrayed the American way of life. One puzzled congressman, recalling his own school days at a time when religious practices were openly Protestant, stated that his Jewish and Catholic classmates "did not seem unduly affected" by prayer recitation. Another suggested that the decision brought new urgency to the proposal for a Christian amendment. The Southerners, still smarting under the Court's rulings on desegregation, were particularly vehement. George Andrews of Alabama summed it up this way: "They put the Negroes in the schools, and now they've driven God out." Within hours of the decision, proposals for amending the Constitution were introduced. The furor in Congress subsided somewhat after President Kennedy, the first Catholic in the Oval Office, counseled public support for the decision. But the idea of a constitutional amendment permitting prayer, which was eagerly supported by a conference of the nation's governors (only Nelson Rockefeller of New York abstained) and by a few state legislatures, persisted.[39]

The press fueled the storm. Highlighting the emotional opposition and initially ignoring expressions of popular support, its treatment was, according to one Jewish communal leader, "little short of catastrophic." Letters to newspapers, more disapproving than editorials, ran over three to one against the ruling. The Jewish defense agencies analyzed press coverage for evidence of anti-Semitism. Among the seventy-seven editorials studied by the JAC in the first three weeks, some commented on the "unholy influence" of a minority. But of two hundred letters (and that was but a sample of the heavy mail to the newspapers), only one could be called anti-Semitic. Others, however, hinted darkly at nefarious designs of "the minority" or advised that Christian teachings were necessary in a Christian country.[40]

The reaction of the major religious groups conformed largely to the post-*McCollum* pattern. The Protestant response was mixed, but hostile opinions from public figures like Billy Graham and James Pike gave the opposition a distinct edge. Criticisms from theologians Reinhold Niebuhr and John Bennett showed that important segments of liberal opinion, among religious leaders as well as Congress, were strangely reticent or openly hostile. Nor did endorsements of the decision necessarily mean that Protestant spokesmen were in accord with the Jewish–ACLU point of view. Prominent Baptists thought that the ruling was proper not because it banned prayer but because it banned state-composed, and even un-Christian, prayer. The National Association of Evangelicals praised the Court for outlawing a state-written prayer but proceeded to uphold voluntary nonsectarian religious practices in the schools. Such supporters of *Engel* were still light years away from the strict separationists.

Most Catholics followed Cardinals Spellman, McIntyre, and Cushing and condemned what they called a frightening trend toward secularism, materialism, and atheism. Some Catholic publications denounced "a well-organized and litigious minority" that denied the rights of the majority, or the assault on American tradition by "small cliques of minorities—

Ethical Culturalists, Humanists, Atheists and Agnostics, assisted by certain secularist Jews and Unitarians." The *Catholic Standard and Times* of Philadelphia openly warned separationist Jews: "It is to be hoped that those who have inexplicably rejected the God-fearing traditions of their fathers—traditions preserved despite centuries of persecution—will stop short of any action which will awaken the dragon of racial and religious hatreds which sleeps restlessly in our midst." Like the Southerners, the Catholics had their own agenda. Aiming for public aid to parochial schools, they stood to lose more than the Regents' prayer if the direction of the Warren Court prevailed.[41]

Jewish defense agencies went on immediate alert. The situation bore ominous signs—a "litigious minority" so long identified with strict separationism and with secularism had been vindicated by the highest court. The fact that the *Engel* ruling could be called a "humanist" or "agnostic" victory at least as much as a Jewish victory did not shield Jews from popular hostility. In addition to unfriendly pieces in the press, other isolated incidents suggested a possible crisis. Lawrence Roth, the initiator of the suit, was the target of anti-Semitic threats even after the decision was handed down. (Although Roth did not identify with any religion, he was not permitted to disavow his Jewishness.) Representative Emanuel Celler, the first defender of the decision in the House, received anti-Semitic mail. In Florida, where the negative response was especially strong, the Miami Council of Churches warned the ADL regional office of serious anti-Semitic repercussions. Talk about a Christian country and the attempt in Congress to resurrect the Christian amendment also indicated that assaults upon public religion, even if the usage was nondenominational, were equated by many Americans with assaults upon Christianity.[42]

For such reasons the *Engel* decision was regarded in some Jewish quarters as a Pyrrhic victory. Although certain community relations councils worked within the Jewish and non-Jewish communities to rally public support for the ruling, the majority decided to keep silent unless the controversy grew alarmingly bitter. Very few Jews sent letters to the press. Some chided Congressman Celler; just because he was a Jew his rush to support the decision was ill-advised. An irate merchant in the Bronx, responding to one of Leo Pfeffer's public statements on the decision, doubtless expressed certain common sentiments when he demanded that "Mr. Pfeffer shut his mouth." He was amazed to see "Jewish leaders obviously and knowingly fanning anti-semitism," and therefore, he advised, "fire Mr. Pfeffer . . . and promote Jewish welfare in harmony with other religious groups."[43]

The Jewish agencies rushed in to mend fences. Individually and through their chapters they looked for friends in government and among Christian leaders. Since the situation called for a united front, the AJC and ADL temporarily suspended their rivalry with the Congress and NCRAC and invited interorganizational consultation. For the purpose of mobilizing the entire community, the JAC scheduled an emergency conference of the members of NCRAC and the SCA.[44]

The conference convened[45] three weeks after the decision, and by then public furor and Jewish panic had abated. The Supreme Court rather than the Jews had borne the brunt of popular antagonism, and although not all Jewish fears were allayed, it appeared clear that an eruption of anti-Semitism was not a real possibility. The conference concentrated on the damage caused by *Engel* to intergroup harmony and, more important, on the fate of pending church–state cases concerning recitation of the Lord's Prayer and Bible reading. Pfeffer explained that although the direction of the Court presaged victories for the separationists, it was totally unrealistic to consider the Court immune to public opinion. Just as the reaction to *McCollum* had spawned *Zorach,* so might the backlash to *Engel* lead to serious judicial qualifications. Pfeffer would have preferred a moratorium on all litigation for several years in order to prepare a favorable "climate of opinion" for Court action. Since that was no longer possible, the urgent task of creating that climate of opinion had to be completed in less than a year. In short, the situation called for a strong public relations campaign, first, in the interest of the pending cases and second, to defuse the clamor for a constitutional amendment. On both scores it was advisable, the conference finally decided, to educate both the Jewish and non-Jewish communities toward an appreciation of the need for religionless schools.

Of central importance to the conferees were the political implications of the *Engel* backlash. To be sure, Protestants might realize in time that only a broad interpretation of *Engel* could stymie Catholic efforts for to parochial schools. In that event they would rally to the side of the Court's ruling, thereby shifting the burden of Catholic antagonism away from Jews. But the danger signs, notably the silence of the liberals and the widespread support for a constitutional amendment, were immediate. Congressional elections within a few short months promised to keep *Engel* alive. As one speaker put it: "This is an issue like motherhood and patriotism; what is closer to a politician's dream than to be on the side of God?" Accordingly, the conference decided to mount a lobbying campaign with political leaders in all ranks of government. Constituent agencies were urged to stimulate a flood of telegrams and letters to James Eastland, chairman of the Senate Judiciary Committee (where an amendment would first be considered), and to seek non-Jewish aid in that campaign.[46]

When the JAC turned to the implementation of the conference's recommendations, the need to block the amendment movement became the first priority. The urgency of the issue was highlighted in a confidential report from Reform Rabbi Richard Hirsch on the opening session of the Senate Judiciary Committee. His account of the testimony taken from senators revealed that the lawmakers, like their constituents, were apprehensive lest the Court's direction cause irreparable damage to the American way of life. Hirsch concluded that Jews had not utilized their resources or energies sufficiently, and he called for an immediate campaign to impress Congress, and particularly the Senate Judiciary Committee, with the opposition to an amendment.

The JAC responded enthusiastically. All national agencies resolved to arouse their constituents; the New York Board of Rabbis encouraged its members to devote sermons to the subject; the UAHC prepared a kit of materials about *Engel*. (One article in the kit, which denied that the United States was a Christian country, proved again that Jewish opposition to public religion rested on the assumption that religion meant Christianity.) The Jewish consensus was "Hands off the Bill of Rights."[47]

A week later Hirsch circulated a report of the second session of the Judiciary Committee. At that hearing James Pike, lawyer and prominent Episcopalian bishop, was the star witness. Denouncing the "religion" of secularism and defending the nonpreferentialist interpretation of the First Amendment, he pleaded impassionedly for preserving religious usages in the classroom. He considered neither Bible reading nor the Lord's Prayer sectarian but rather the common possession of both Jews and Christians. As for the rights of minorities, Pike said: "Our Constitution is meant to protect minorities but is not meant to impose on the majority the outlook of any minority." Again Hirsch urged the need to "educate Congress."[48]

Since the Judiciary Committee planned further hearings, the defense organizations set about preparing their statements. To enhance the prestige of the strict separationists before the committee, Leo Pfeffer rounded up over one hundred deans and professors of law and political science who signed a statement in support of *Engel* and in opposition to any amendment. No further hearings were held, but the issue flared up again when the new Congress convened.[49]

Troubled by the nature of the Jewish campaign, the Catholic journal *America* responded with a vicious anti-Semitic editorial.[50] The very title, "To Our Jewish Friends," set the tone. Often used by critics of the Jews, the phrase reeked of patient tolerance and overbearing superiority. The editorial told readers that "disturbing hints of heightened anti-Semitic feeling" had surfaced since the *Engel* decision. To be sure, it admitted, responsibility for *Engel* had to be shared among Jews and other groups—the ACLU, Ethical Culturalists, humanists, and atheists. Besides, the Jewish community itself included many diverse opinions. But once having planted Jews within a larger company of dubious respectability, the editorial proceeded to suggest that an anti-Semitic outbreak, a backlash solely against Jews, was not only possible but justifiable.

The editorial was not, as most observers concluded, merely a crude response to Jewish participation in the *Engel* case. That had been heard earlier in the previously quoted piece from the *Catholic Standard and Times*. Rather, the powerful Jesuit weekly had scores to settle that had built up during the protracted fight over New York's program of moral and spiritual values and over Sunday laws. More immediately, *America* took fright at the lobbying campaign orchestrated by the Jewish defense network to head off the movement for a constitutional amendment. A careful study of the editorial's very choice of words suggests that the Catholic paper had obtained a copy of Rabbi Hirsch's confidential memorandum which had been the subject of the JAC's recent deliberations. Jewish defense plans in response to that memorandum, when added to the list of earlier Jewish-Catholic clashes, caused Catholic resentment to overboil.

The bitter invective of the editorial cannot be written off as a momentary lapse.[51] Perceiving a genuine threat to Catholic goals, specifically federal aid to parochial schools, *America* painted a dark picture of a virtual plot that knowingly flew in the face of public opinion. The design of the instigators, their efforts to mobilize Jewish "resources" and "expertise," and their centralized control of the larger Jewish community added up to a dangerous cabal. Nor was the editorial a kindly reproach to Leo Pfeffer and his associates. *America*'s true Jewish friends, the periodical explained, were those who disagreed with the minority's efforts "to secularize the public schools and public life from top to bottom." *America* advised that well-meaning but misled majority that it would be "most unfortunate" if the entire Jewish community were to be blamed for the unrelenting pressure tactics. Hence, it behooved responsible Jewish spokesmen to resist the militants and to make it known that the campaign did not genuinely speak for their entire community. The editorial closed with a somber warning: "What will have been accomplished if our Jewish friends win all the legal immunities they seek, but thereby paint themselves into a corner of social and cultural alienation? The time has come for these fellow-citizens of ours to decide among themselves what they conceive to be the final objective of the Jewish community in the United States—in a word, what bargain they are willing to strike as one of the minorities in a pluralistic society."

America's editorial triggered an outburst of denunciation by Christians as well as Jews. Most agreed that it was a none-too-subtle threat if not an outright example of "Jesuit Anti-Semitism." Even the Catholic *Commonweal,* reacting to *America*'s ostensible purpose of combating anti-Semitism, said: "If there is . . . any real danger of anti-Semitism among Catholics, then it is Catholics who ought to be warned." The Protestant *Christian Century* charged *America* with attempting to bully the Jews, and it hoped that Pfeffer and the Congress would refuse to be cowed.[52]

Although *America* may have given voice to private Jewish fears, Jews closed ranks in condemnation of a public Christian threat. Only a forthright response, Pfeffer insisted at a special meeting of the JAC, would prove to Jews and Christians alike that American Jewry was an integral part of the society and no longer in *galut*. The defense agencies, purposely divorcing the issue from the Catholic church and from the *Engel* ruling itself, hastened to formulate dignified replies. Jewish organizations and spokesmen rarely heard on matters of church and state also spoke up. The Jewish Labor Committee was particularly disturbed by the last paragraph in the editorial, and it denied that minorities needed to "bargain" in an equal society. Hasidic leaders joined the chorus. The Lubavitcher rebbe, who disapproved of the *Engel* decision, was outraged by the editorial. He hoped that its anti-Semitic threat would be repudiated by "a higher [Catholic] authority." The Bostoner rebbe recalled that Orthodox Jews in Massachusetts had been the target of equally vehement Catholic invective when they had sought the amendment of Sunday laws. Either we are attacked for our religious concerns, he concluded, or we are accused of defending atheists.[53]

America printed a trenchant rejoinder from the AJC, which was also featured in the national press. Among other things, the agency pointedly asked: Why "this intense preoccupation" with the influence of Jewish separationists? "After all, Jews (religious and secular together) number less than 3 per cent of the total population of whom 37½ per cent are *unchurched* gentiles. Given these statistics, would the problem of secularism within the Christian community be solved even if the 'militant' Jewish organizations were to abandon their positions on the First Amendment?"[54] Nevertheless, *America* stubbornly refused to backtrack. A second editorial two weeks later sloughed off the "ridiculous" charge of anti-Semitism. Claiming that its critics had missed the point, the paper repeated its initial warning. If the Supreme Court decided to strike down Bible reading and the Lord's Prayer in the classroom, cases in which "Leo Pfeffer and his fellow campaigners" were "bending every effort," the entire Jewish community would be blamed for the actions of the militants. The editorial wondered ingenuously at Jewish ingratitude. When a warning is given "to a friend who is about to step into the path of an oncoming ten-ton truck . . . it is rather disconcerting to have your friend turn on you and accuse you of driving the truck."[55]

A Jewish Debate

Jews united against *America,* but not all supported the *Engel* decision. Statements of disapproval came from the different wings of American Judaism. A professor of theology at the Conservative seminary thought the ruling was wrong, and so did a professor of rabbinics at the Reform seminary. Immanuel Jakobovits, Orthodox rabbi of the prestigious Fifth Avenue Synagogue, distanced himself from the pro-*Engel* stand of the New York Board of Rabbis. In a letter to the *Times* the former chief rabbi of

Ireland expressed his dismay at the alliance between teachers of Judaism and the spokesmen of secularism and atheism. The *Times* also reported a statement from Rabbi Menahem Schneerson, the Lubavitcher rebbe, deploring the prayer decision. The Hasidic leader, who faulted the ruling on the grounds of "Halachah [Jewish law] and common sense," stated that it was the duty of all Jews committed to the Torah to work for the reversal of *Engel*. Some of these critics joined a defense of prayer with an attack on Jewish separationists.[56]

By now elements among the Orthodox were actively challenging conventional Jewish defense on church–state matters. The postwar years had witnessed a resurgence of a right-wing Orthodoxy, which claimed an equal voice in the public arena with less observant Jews.[57] Under its influence Jewish disapproval with campaigns against public religion grew. Some Orthodox Jews, like many Christian Americans, saw no middle way between the poles of public religion and a secularist society. As Americans they agreed that public religion sooner than a "naked public square" better served the nation at large, and as Jews they resented the secular agencies' leadership on public policy. On the crucial matter of government aid to parochial schools, they stood closer to Catholics than to nonreligious fellow Jews. Like the Catholics, they feared that the Court's direction in *Engel* augured ill for aid to parochial schools. Mounting a Jewish religious protest against Jewish secularism, they saw no reason to sacrifice the interests of their day schools for what appeared to be no more than abstract principle.[58]

Engel left some Orthodox Jews uncomfortable. They understood that nondenominational formulas were no substitute for religion, but they believed that the inoffensive usages served to develop an awareness of the importance of religion. A hint of Orthodox restiveness surfaced at the convention of the Union of Orthodox Jewish Congregations a few months after the Court's decision. Heated debate erupted on the issues of school prayer and federal aid to religious schools. It was imperative, the chairman of the convention concluded, to strike a proper balance between separation and the growing desire of Americans for religious identification. Clearly, the accommodationists were becoming more articulate. The inevitable break from the unified stand of the SCA and NCRAC came three years later when Orthodox agencies supported aid to parochial school children under the Elementary and Secondary Education Act.[59]

Dissatisfaction with *Engel* gave rise to deeper analyses of the church–state issue and to a debate that had begun in Jewish intellectual circles some ten years earlier. Different from the Orthodox, who had their own specific agenda, the first would-be revisionists faulted a strict separationist stance on various grounds. Will Herberg, who came to the serious study of Judaism in mid-life, was the best known of the early critics. In a provocative essay that appeared in 1952, he accused separationism of contributing both to the religious vacuum in society and to the sharpening of religious cleavage in American life. He expounded on two basic themes. First, absolute separation, never contemplated by the Founding Fathers, was simply the goal of those who sought to replace traditional faiths by "their own non- or anti-religious faith." Second, Jewish leadership, extremist in support of separation, was operating in effect to divorce religion from life. Particularly critical of Jewish opposition to all suggestions for bringing religious values into public education, Herberg had little patience for the traditional fears of the minority group. As he saw it, the customary and "crippling" defensive strategy ill suited the needs of American Jewish existence and survival. "American Jews . . . must rethink the problem of church and state, of religion and life, as it affects the Jew and as it affects the entire nation. We must be ready to abandon ancient fears and prejudices if they no longer conform to reality."[60]

Drawing applause from clergymen of the different faiths, Herberg suggested ways for meeting the problem of religious illiteracy. He warned that unless public education included or, better still, was grounded in religion, it would inevitably turn into "indoctrination with an idolatrous counter-religion." Further, a definitive victory for secularism would be fatal to both Judaism and democracy. During the 1950s Herberg publicly supported aid to parochial schools as well as religion in the public schools. Before long the JAC put Herberg on the agenda; particularly since he enjoyed the respect of Christian intellectuals, the defense agencies felt compelled to inform the public that he did not represent organized Jewry. Herberg, in turn, continued to denounce strict separationism. Speaking at the famous seminar sponsored by the Fund for the Republic on "Religion in a Free Society," he said: "Minorities must not be oppressed, but majorities have their rights as well as minorities. . . . Some balance must be struck somewhere, but such a balance obviously cannot be a matter of 'principle,' nor can it be fixed and frozen in a constitutional provision."[61]

While Herberg spoke primarily to intellectuals, Reform Rabbi Arthur Gilbert aimed at a more popular audience—rabbis and congregants of the average synagogues. Long involved in interreligious work under the auspices of the ADL and the National Conference of Christians and Jews, Gilbert preached against strict separation on the grounds that it significantly impeded intergroup understanding. He thought, for example, that Jews exaggerated the importance of religion in the public schools and that by their constant negative response evoked anger and fear from Christian Americans. Critical also of the secularist defense of Jewish interests, he called on Jews to formulate their position on religious grounds.[62]

In 1958 Gilbert was invited to address the annual convention of the CCAR. Since his subject was the reconsideration of church–state policy, the very invitation pointed to a measure of restiveness within Reform ranks. Challenging his rabbinical colleagues to awaken to the new mood in the land, Gilbert stated that Americans, unlike their forebears at the turn of the century, were less sanguine about the goodness of man and the promise of the future. Many had turned or returned to religion for guidance in the preservation of the nation's ideals. While they gave allegiance to the principle of separation, they would hardly agree that the concept of Americanism was devoid of religious content. For Jews, and the CCAR in particular, to respond with the tired legal phrases that they had mouthed for over fifty years bespoke a callous indifference to the interests of their countrymen. "Our record is stuck in its groove," Gilbert said, and the "summary dismissal of a legitimate concern of the American people . . . is reprehensible."

It was equally unrealistic and misguided, Gilbert said, to insist on absolute separation when neither Protestants nor Catholics subscribed to that interpretation of the First Amendment. Certainly no Christian would consent to removing Christmas celebrations from the schools, and Jewish policy statements to the contrary only convinced Christians of the minority's hostile rigidity. The Jewish stand implicitly indicted Christians for illegal behavior, and, Gilbert insisted, it was high time for rabbis to stop talking like lawyers and to formulate their arguments in terms of their religious tradition.

A mixed response greeted Gilbert's address. One listener seconded Gilbert's criticism. Jews were so boxed in by their rigid stand, he said, that they concerned themselves with "picayune" matters like a cross in Minnesota's centennial emblem and the flag at half-mast on Good Friday in San Francisco. "America will survive whether we have the Ten Commandments [posted] in the schools or not," he added. Another rabbi, who disagreed with the notion that joint Christmas–Hanukkah celebrations in the schools—which Gilbert supported—made for equality, quipped: "Judah Maccabee cannot balance or offset Jesus!" None, however, directly addressed a message implicit in Gilbert's words, namely, the Christian component and mores of American culture fixed a point beyond which separationism could make no dent.[63]

In recognition of divergent currents of thought within the ranks, the CCAR resolved to canvass the opinions of its members before it formulated an overall policy statement. The results of a questionnaire showed that at least part of Gilbert's message was strongly supported by the membership. Although three-quarters of the rabbis rejected any retreat from the strict separationist stand that had characterized the organization over the years, many wanted to ground their approach in religious and theological convictions rather than in legal and constitutional precedents. Accordingly, the statement adopted in 1960 broke new ground. It made no mention whatsoever of Roger Williams, Jefferson, Madison, the First Amendment, or judicial decisions; rather, it invoked Jewish teachings and Jewish history to explain its commitment to separation. The statement reaffirmed older themes—the centrality of the home and the house of worship in the inculcation of moral discipline and religious tenets, the need of separation in order for religion to flourish, the inability of "religious formalities" in the schools to solve critical social ills—but all in a gentler tone than was ever employed. Positing a sympathy with religious forces that strove to counter the inroads of secularism and materialism, it also registered warm approval of attempts to raise moral standards within society. Thus, while uncompromising on principle, the policy statement avoided the anti-Christian animus of which Gilbert had complained. The CCAR signaled two things thereby: first, an awareness of the basic security of postwar Jews, which permitted a less strident defense; and second, a desire to keep open the lines of communication with their Christian compatriots.[64]

After *Engel* the debate intensified, engaging spokesmen from the different branches of American Judaism. Indeed, the prayer decision marked the first time that many prominent Jews argued publicly (albeit in Jewish periodicals) against their own secular organizations and, equally, against separationist rabbis. Ironically, it was victory rather than defeat that generated new levels of dissatisfaction. Had the Court gone the route of *Zorach* rather than *McCollum,* the critics would have been fewer and the criticisms more guarded. Their customary fears about religious equality quieted, Jews now permitted themselves to probe the issue of religion in the public schools from different perspectives.

America contributed to Jewish unease, but it was not the sole stimulus for the debate. In part the critics resented the power of the secular agencies whose posture, which elicited a "knee-jerk reflex" from most Jews, was now stamped with the Court's seal of approval. An epochal victory like *Engel* might well increase their militancy and inflexibility. In part the critics believed that the ruling could polarize Americans, pitting believers against nonbelievers. Their concern about public relations may not have been as crude as the Bronx merchant who wanted to fire Leo Pfeffer, but why, they also asked, should Jews knowingly contribute and abet the divisions between Jew and Christian and between Jew and Jew? And, in part, the critics were genuinely troubled by the implications of the ruling for public religion generally. Admittedly public usages were only watered-down religion, but they at least indicated an awareness and acknowledgment of the importance of religion for the individual and society. The survival of Judaism, like the survival of Christianity, depended on just such an awareness and acknowledgment.

A sampling of the views of several thinkers, all religiously committed Jews, indicates how the lines set by Herberg and Gilbert in the 1950s were etched ever deeper. Each of the three discussed here called for a rethinking of the fixed defense pattern. Each spoke only for himself, but together they touched on the common reservations that some serious Jews held about strict separation.

Michael Wyschogrod, a modern Orthodox Jew and professor of philosophy, felt impelled to urge a reassessment in the wake of the *America* episode. Addressing himself exclusively to an Orthodox audience, he insisted that American Jews required a society where Christians remained true to their faith. Jewish history, particularly persecution at the hands of Nazis and Communists, taught that Jews fared best in "God-fearing" nations. Indeed, the Chofetz Chaim, a renowned Talmudist and moralist in prewar Poland, refused to ride in a carriage whose driver did *not* cross himself before the crucifixes along the roads. Judaism would perish in a secularist world, and Jews, bereft of the security of their faith, would still be regarded as different. Diagnosing the overriding threat to Jews as religious illiteracy, Wyschogrod supported prayer in the schools. To be sure, the recitation of short, nondenominational prayers would hardly solve the larger problem, but a prayer—"the notion of dialogue with God"—could arouse a religious awareness within the individual child. He dismissed the arguments that religious practices in the schools caused emotional distress to Jewish children. Those secure in their Jewish roots would hardly be shocked by the use of Christian religious symbols in a society where the majority was Christian. In essence, then, Wyschogrod adapted *America*'s question to his argument: How long would the Orthodox, against their best religious interests, follow the lead of the secular defense agencies?[65]

Conservative rabbi and theologian Seymour Siegel attacked the defenders of the "non-existent wall of separation of church and state" who "brainwashed" the Jewish community. A supporter of the Regents' prayer, Siegel posited that all cultures, America's in particular, were built around a religious core. A secular state was alien to both Americanism and Judaism. Since religion and the state could not be separated, he endorsed the ideas of a state that recognized the legitimacy of religion and a government that cooperated with all traditional religions. And, just as contemporary Judaism could hope to flourish only in a general culture supportive of religious aims, so did that general culture require symbols, like prayer in the schools, to express its religious commitment. Siegel argued that unquestioned reliance on a secular state rested on erroneous foundations; for one, the conditions that drove nineteenth-century Jews to the defense of a secular state no longer obtained. He also dismissed the argument that public religion widened the gulf between Christians and Jews. Jewish separation from the gentiles was the normative situation in *galut;* to obliterate it bred a "false messianism," which should not be attempted.

"If we completely desacralize our culture," Siegel warned, "we will be in danger of creating a kind of bland, common Americanism which in the end will progressively wear away Jewish consciousness and commitment." Although the first converts to the idea of a post-Jewish and postgentile culture would doubtless be the Jews, theirs was a suicidal course: "We will be digging our own graves—and ironically enough cheering on the grave-diggers and spending money and effort to insure that no one takes away their shovels."[66]

While Siegel argued for Judaism, Reform Rabbi Herbert Weiner took up "The Case for the Timorous Jew." Denouncing the control and intimidation of the community by the militant separationists, he charged that Jewish organizations were not at liberty "to demand in the name of Judaism that every Jew must rejoice when a non-offensive prayer is eliminated from the schools" or to call Jewish dissenters disloyal to both Americanism and Judaism. Nor did the rabbi understand why Jewish agencies, ostensibly committed to intergroup harmony, worked so furiously on issues destructive of that harmony. The rank and file of local Jewish communities—not merely an "infinitesimal" and "cowardly" minority, as described by the defense network—had suffered harassment when they contested religious practices in the schools. From a pragmatic point of view, they wondered whether purist separationism transcended the principle of communal accord and whether dogmatism was always wiser than flexibility and compromise.

Like Siegel but for nontheological reasons, Weiner believed that *galut,* even in America, was real. "A Jew . . . who thinks that he is not surrounded by a majority that considers itself Christian, and involved in a culture and history that is not saturated with Christianity, and with Christian judgments about Jews—is surely fooling himself." Therefore, Jews would do better to accept the limitations, like religious usages in the schools, which were the fate of a non-Christian minority. To do otherwise and aim for an end to Jewish–gentile distinctions was tantamount to the creation of a false messiah.[67]

For Weiner and Siegel *galut* dictated accommodationism. It also put a finite boundary on the pursuit of equality. Jews could aspire to equal status under law, but equality in the form of total assimilation was both unattainable and, from a religious point of view, undesirable. The false messiah of total assimilation, like other false messiahs in Jewish history, promised only disappointment and suffering. It was equally illusory to expect Christian Americans to discard the religious symbols of their culture and totally "de-religionize" their society. Legal victories of separationism notwithstanding, America was still rooted in Christianity. Doubtless most Jews, wedded to the belief that the essentials of Judaism were virtually synonomous with the tenets of Americanism, would not have agreed with the limitations of *galut.* Leo Pfeffer, for example, had urged action against a prayer amendment precisely for the purpose of proving that Jews were not in exile. After *Engel,* talk of *galut* reflected a new dimension in American Jewish intellectual thought.

Serious criticisms of strict separationism went beyond rabbinical and academic circles. The editor of the *Jewish Spectator* denounced the policies of the defense agencies, which, she said, silenced an awareness of religion and bred communal friction. Within the AJC, sharp differences arose among policymaking staff members. Was it appropriate, they asked after *Engel,* for an agency dedicated to the improvement of intergroup relations to ignore the religious element in a pluralist society? Under those influences the AJC modified its strict separationism in 1965 and gave grudging support to the Elementary and Secondary Education Act.[68] Nevertheless, those isolated, independent voices, lacking the support of the NCRAC–SCA network, could not hope to change the bent of the organized Jewish community.

Nor were dissident rabbis representative of the vast majority of their colleagues. The rabbinical associations stood firmly in support of strict separation.[69] Some religious leaders went only so far as to caution against Jewish "extremism." Reform Rabbi Balfour Brickner favored strict separation, but in tune with the modified emphasis of the CCAR he strongly urged Jews to couch their case in a Jewish religious idiom. Conservative Rabbi Arthur Hertzberg argued against "First Amendmentism" and against absolutes of any sort in a pluralist society. But he explicated the conventional Jewish posture more than he criticized it. On a profound emotional level, he said, American Jews did not believe that anti-Semitism in Western civilization was a relic. To ensure their equality and not mere toleration, Jews turned to strict separation only when they felt their equality threatened: "[The] deepest and most messianic need [of the American Jew] is not a completely secular state; it is a truly equal status in American culture." How realistic that "messianic need" was yet another question.[70]

Rabbi Richard Rubenstein, then a Hillel director, was one who saw no reason to change positions at all. Although he agreed that authentic Judaism neither justified secularism nor endorsed a divorce between church and state, he injected a weightier argument in defense of separationism. It was Christian theology, Rubenstein insisted, that forced Jews to a separationist stance. The Jewish role in Christian thought—both as "God-bearers and God-killers"—placed them in an irrevocably abnormal situation. The Holocaust had taught that Jewish–Christian relations "have led and can again lead" to genocide. Because of that abnormality, Jews naturally recoiled from areas where Christianity was privileged and sought to carve out a common meeting ground, like the public school, where their equality was unquestioned. Hence their insistence on the religionless school for the preservation of their rights. Whereas Siegel wrote that the nineteenth-century struggle for political rights was no longer relevant for justifying separationism, Rubenstein believed that in light of the Holocaust Jews could not afford to forget their history.[71]

The Jewish debate resembled talk in Christian intellectual circles. Reinhold Niebuhr explained that the storm of protest which had greeted *Engel* revealed the importance even of an innocuous prayer as a symbol of the nation's religious tradition. He and other critics also examined basics—the intent of the Founding Fathers, the correct interpretation of the First Amendment, the requirements of a pluralist society. One liberal Protestant, Dean Erwin Griswold of the Harvard Law School, roundly criticized the Supreme Court for engaging in "a species of absolutism . . . which is more likely to lead us into darkness than to light." Griswold compared Justice Black's reasoning to a "Fundamentalist theological" approach that was blind to the function of the Constitution in a complex society. Must we cast off all the deeply entrenched religious vestiges in public life, he asked, and permit religious toleration to lead to "religious sterility"?

> This . . . has been, and is, a Christian country, in origin, history, tradition and culture. It was out of Christian doctrine and ethics . . . that it developed its notion of toleration. . . . But does the fact that we have officially adopted toleration as our standard mean that we must give up our history and our tradition? The Moslem who comes here may worship as he pleases, and may hold public office without discrimination. That is as it should be. But why should it follow that he can require others to give up their Christian tradition merely because he is a tolerated and welcomed member of the community?[72]

Griswold didn't mention Jews, but "Moslem" was a convenient euphemism. On Christianity as the source of religious toleration, his views resembled those of Judge John O'Neale in the Sunday law case of 1846.

Like Griswold, educator Robert Ulich, who joined the debate after the Bible-reading case, denied that a majority had to relinquish its heritage for the sake of minorities. Ulich pointedly argued that the Jews could not have survived a history of persecution without the preservation of their rituals and prayers. "May then the loss of the Christian past not jeopardize the future of *this* nation, just as the desertion from the covenant would have jeopardized the survival of the Jews?"[73] The message was clear. Christian Americans had moved over and made ample room for non-Christian minorities. For the minorities to expect the extirpation of all vestiges of a public, Christian-flavored religion was both unnatural and wrong. In line with those Jews who talked about *galut,* Christians like Ulich and Griswold set a limit to the Jewish pursuit of equality.

Engel raised the Jewish debate on church–state relations to a level never before reached. The basics were confronted—history, Jewish theology, the concept of exile, the nature of pluralism, Christian theology. The old theme of the Jew in Christian America reappeared, too. Were Jews in America also in *galut?* What in fact did a Jewish identity in America mean? And if, as Hertzberg said, they were not "co-founders" of the American culture, could Jews dispute Christians (liberal as well as orthodox) who assumed that public expressions of religion were part of the American establishment?[74] Emotionally, Jews could not accept the same conclusions from Christians—they would have been outraged and dismayed had non-Jews reminded them that they were in exile—but serious reassessments at least for internal consumption were in ferment.

7

Scripture in the Schools

Established Practices

Exactly one year after *Engel,* the Supreme Court ruled that Bible reading
and the recitation of the Lord's Prayer in the classroom were unconstitutional. The *Schempp-Murray* decision, capping what the American Jewish
Congress called "A Momentous Year for Church and State," was part of
the *Engel* continuum. Logic alone dictated that if the Court struck down
a nondenominational exercise like the Regents' prayer, sectarian practices
were doomed a fortiori. As the congressional debates and the hearings on
a prayer amendment had revealed, both supporters and opponents of the
Engel decision were fully aware that Bible reading and recitation of the
Lord's Prayer were also at stake. One of the amendments proposed in
1962, anticipating just that outcome, would have permitted both prayer
and Bible reading in the schools. Indeed, the very purpose of the Jewish
campaign against an amendment was to ensure the uninterrupted application of the principles set forth in *Engel* to pending litigation on Bible
reading and the Lord's Prayer.[1]

The spurt of state legislation for Bible reading had petered out before
World War II, but the laws enacted after 1913 stayed fixed. Twelve states
required Bible reading, and although seven of those prohibited sectarian
instruction, they saw no inconsistency in their position. Two dozen states
permitted Bible reading, and one, Mississippi, expressly stated in its constitution that the practice should not be excluded from the schools. In those
instances, the states indirectly exempted Bible reading from the restraints
imposed by the First Amendment and by their own constitutions. Furthermore, in the eight states where Bible reading was prohibited, not all
school districts complied. For example, whereas New York State reported
prohibition of the practice, New York City's Board of Education provided
for Bible reading at school assemblies. On a regional scale, the South
scored highest, but while figures are not exact, it can be assumed that Bible
reading prevailed at least in some communities of most states. Overall, the
authority bestowed by time on a usage as old as the public schools themselves endowed it with a validity that transcended any legal base.[2]

The constitutionality of Bible reading in the classroom had been debated in state courts ever since the *Donahoe* case of 1854, but not until the post-*McCollum* era was Bible reading challenged in the courts on the grounds that, as a religious exercise, it conflicted with the First Amendment. Supporters denied that Bible reading was sectarian instruction. After all, they reasoned, since all the major faiths were rooted in the same Bible, the book was nonsectarian. Where certain conditions were officially imposed on Bible reading—for example, that no comment accompany the readings, that children of parents who objected to the readings could be excused—the practice appeared even more benign.[3] The minority view that Bible reading violated religious freedom grounded itself in the *Minor* (1872) and *Weiss* (1890) cases. No longer, however, were Catholics in the forefront of the opposition. In a dramatic reversal of opinion after *McCollum,* they along with most Protestant groups supported readings in the classroom.

Active Jewish involvement in the matter of Bible reading dated back to the days of Isaac Mayer Wise and Max Lilienthal. Some thirty-five years later, in response to Justice David Brewer, the CCAR picked up the issue and, as discussed earlier, launched an unprecedented campaign that shifted the overall Jewish focus from "Christian state" to Bible reading in the schools. It in turn was overshadowed by the gathering momentum of the released time programs, which became the first priority of the postwar Jewish agencies. Bible reading, however, remained a chronic irritant.

Organized Jews, including all three religious wings represented in the Synagogue Council, overwhelmingly opposed the practice, but they were uncomfortably aware that, as with other features of religion in the schools, the ranks of Christian allies had thinned. In a joint statement of 1948, NCRAC and the SCA objected to Bible reading in the schools (except where the book was studied as literature); however, sobered by the *McCollum* backlash and by resistance on the part of the ADL, they did not publish the statement. For reasons of public relations the agencies also shied away from litigation, and passive acceptance of the school usages characterized the Jewish community for most of the decade. A popular pamphlet issued first in 1958 by Reform's Commission on Social Action addressed the question of Jewish resistance: "Where Bible reading and/ or prayer recitation are practiced, should Jewish parents permit their children to participate in such programs?" Cognizant of communal pressures, the lame reply admitted that the answer depended on local factors and the attitudes of individual children and parents. Only in several places where the status of Bible reading was not yet fixed did Jews resist attempts to introduce the practice.[4]

Jewish spokesmen who charged that Bible reading violated church–state separation listed specific complaints. For one thing, they disputed the notion that the Bible, even the Old Testament, was a nonsectarian book. Legal scholar Milton Konvitz put it succinctly: since Protestants, Catholics, and Jews each used a translation that differed meaningfully from the other two, "there is no such thing as a non-sectarian Bible." Jews doubted too whether true religious neutrality could be achieved merely by stipulating that biblical passages be read without comment. Rabbi Louis Wolsey of the CCAR had explained many years before the war that even tonal inflections, gesticulations, and facial expressions on the part of the teacher conveyed a form of sectarian instruction. Furthermore, Jews charged that children were not adequately protected from even a voluntary exercise, since they were under pressure by their teachers and peers to conform. Justice Frankfurter's words in the released time case, "Non-conformity is not an outstanding characteristic of children," applied here too.

Classroom recitation of the Lord's Prayer, which in numerous places accompanied Bible reading, was rooted in custom rather than law. No state required it, legislation in only four states permitted it, and judicial decisions in several others upheld it. In many schools the recitation went along with body motions; children closed their eyes, or bowed their heads, or folded their hands in certain positions. The Lord's Prayer, too, was considered by many Christians, clergy and educators included, to be nonsectarian. At the amendment hearings in 1962 Bishop James Pike stated that the prayer, like the Bible, "belong to all of us." "Theologically speaking, Jesus was never more Jewish than when he uttered the Lord's Prayer." When a rabbi privately reminded the bishop that "Lord" referred to Jesus and not to God, Pike backtracked. He meant, he explained, that the "theological intent" of the prayer would be acceptable to Jews.[5]

Some Jews shared that well-nigh unshakable impression. It may have been compounded by a popular article in *Life* magazine by the CCAR's president, Philip Bernstein. Writing in 1950 on "What the Jews Believe," the rabbi pointed out the similarity between the Lord's Prayer and the Jewish *kaddish*. In the 1950s, when the prayer was more frequently recited in New York City classrooms, the New York Board of Rabbis issued a strong statement that aimed to correct the Jewish misapprehension. Drawing on Christian sources and scholarship, the rabbis showed that theologically and historically the prayer was bound up solely with Christianity. Despite the similarity of many of its phrases to the Jewish liturgy, it was "essentially and exclusively" a Christian prayer whose recitation was forbidden by Jewish tradition.[6]

For the better part of the decade, signs were unpropitious for a successful challenge of Bible reading. In 1950 the New Jersey Supreme Court upheld the constitutionality of state laws requiring the daily recitation in public schools of at least five verses from the Old Testament and permitting the recitation of the Lord's Prayer. The decision in *Doremus* v. *Board of Education,* like the released time cases, mirrored tensions generated by the cold war. The court commented on the threat of totalitarianism and organized atheism to religious worship, and it stressed the elemental need of a theistic society in America. On the specific issue, Justice Clarence Case ruled that both the Old Testament and the Lord's Prayer were nonsectarian. Invoking the authority of Bernstein's article, the justice said that the Lord's Prayer was neither alien to Jewish or Christian believers nor controversial or dogmatic. "Christ was a Jew and He was speaking to Jews." Narrowly construing both *Everson* and *McCollum*, Case denied that those rulings were relevant here.[7]

Doremus's attorney consulted Leo Pfeffer about an appeal to the Supreme Court, but the latter, concerned primarily with the need of shoring up *McCollum*, advised against it. He feared a judicial retreat, which in turn would also doom the then-pending *Zorach* case. Nevertheless, since the plaintiffs resolutely pressed ahead, Pfeffer saw no alternative but to file an *amicus* brief on behalf of Doremus. The anti-*McCollum* campaign was succeeding, he said, precisely because the groups that supported the ruling were silent. Jews had forthrightly intervened in the released time case, and it behooved them to muster that same strength in defense of the decision. Pfeffer sought but failed to secure Protestant help. Nor could he convince the other Jewish agencies of the importance of intervention. In the end, the Congress filed the solitary brief that spoke for a religious group.[8]

Building an argument primarily on *Everson, McCollum,* and the notable state decisions against Bible reading, the Jewish brief disputed the "fictional and irrelevant" claims that the New Jersey usages were voluntary and that the Bible and the Lord's Prayer were nonsectarian. Even if the practices were acceptable to all religions, they would still fall under the ban of the First Amendment as interpreted by *Everson* and *McCollum*. The Jews were particularly concerned, the brief explained, not out of an antireligious bias. Rather, the persecution the minority had suffered made it sensitive to the dangers of the entering wedge.

The real question was whether the Court felt bound by Justice Black's two historic opinions. When the justices heard argument on *Doremus,* they expressed some reservations about the religious practices, but the final decision, a victory for Bible reading, rested on the grounds that the plaintiffs had no standing to sue. Clearly, the Court preferred not to deal with the volatile issue, but neither was it prepared to backtrack on *McCollum*.[9]

The loss to strict separationists was less severe than anticipated. Perhaps no more could be achieved while the cold war and Joe McCarthy raged. As a voice from middle America explained, the Court deserved commendation for resisting "the organized attack upon religion in our time, when Stalin and his fellow conspirators are preaching godlessness and persecuting Christians."[10]

The *Doremus* defeat of 1952 was partially offset the following year. In a decision, again by the New Jersey Supreme Court, another facet of the Bible issue, that of Bible distribution within the schools, was ruled unconstitutional. Distribution differed from legally sanctioned Bible reading, but where permitted by authorities on school premises and within the school day, it also constituted what the JAC called sectarian intrusion. In this instance, and unlike *Doremus,* the question of sectarianism led to an opposite ruling.[11]

Tudor v. *Board of Education* concerned the activities of the Gideons International, a Protestant missionary society that actively crusaded after the war to circulate copies of the New Testament (bound with selections from the Psalms and Proverbs) in the schools. Under the banner of "Winning Man and Woman for the Lord Jesus Christ," a representative of the society would address the children and urge them to accept a copy of the book. A child who obtained parental consent for the acquisition pledged in turn to read the book. The Gideons were required to secure permission from the school boards before they entered the buildings, but in some cases their involvement went further. In Davenport, Iowa, for example, the local rabbi reported that they injected themselves into school board elections and the politics of the ministerial association.

The evangelical pitch of the Gideon representative and the Protestant flavor of his wares aroused Jewish and Catholic opposition. Separately or together, and sometimes with the help of liberal Protestants, rabbis and priests acted to keep the Gideons out of the schools. The Jewish defense organizations also cooperated. The Congress in 1948 prepared a legal memorandum on the unconstitutionality of Gideon activity in the schools. In Portland, Oregon, the ADL's representative descended upon the editorial offices of one newspaper with an armful of Catholic, Protestant, and Jewish Bibles. He made his point—the multiple versions, proving that each religion had its own interpretation, confirmed that the Bible was sectarian—and the editor, who had originally prepared an endorsement of the Gideons, changed his mind.[12]

Although public disapproval usually sufficed to end the Gideon operation within a school, the practice persisted in Rutherford, New Jersey. Accordingly, a local priest and rabbi brought suit against the society and engaged Leo Pfeffer to represent two parents, a Jew and a Catholic. The opposing sides conferred out of court but failed to settle the dispute. Pfeffer was unimpressed by the Gideon argument that disregard of the Bible had led to the annihilation of the Jews by the Nazis, and his opponents were equally unmoved by Pfeffer's insistence that principle rather than antireligious sentiment motivated the plaintiffs.[13] At the trial three rabbis testified that the Gideon Bible was unacceptable to Jews; the New Testament was a sectarian book, and many of its teachings were in direct conflict with

Judaism. Pfeffer, who liked to marshal arguments from the social sciences, also brought in three experts to testify on the negative effects of the distribution process on school children. The psychological point had been raised in the Jewish brief in *McCollum,* but, Pfeffer proudly explained, this was the first instance in which expert support for the argument was introduced into a trial.[14]

The trial court decided against the plaintiffs, but the situation brightened when the case moved to the state supreme court. The judges agreed unanimously that the Gideon Bible was indeed a sectarian book and that its distribution violated the principle of no religious preference.[15] Since the Supreme Court refused to review the case, *Tudor* technically applied only to New Jersey. Nor did the ruling end the efforts of the Gideons in the schools. Nevertheless, the Congress warmly applauded the decision and noted two important "firsts." One was the scientific evidence, which Pfeffer later claimed was particularly instrumental in influencing the higher court, and the other was the alliance of Catholics and Jews. To be sure, as was stated earlier, Jews and Catholics had joined as plaintiffs in the *Bullock* (Texas, 1908) and *Herold* (Louisiana, 1915) Bible-reading cases. But, according to Pfeffer, *Tudor* marked "the first instance of active cooperation between diocesan authorities of the Catholic Church and a national Jewish organization in prosecuting litigation involving . . . religion in the public schools."[16]

Interagency Flare-up: The Miami Case

The story of Jewish involvement in church–state litigation is interlaced with frequent eruptions of interorganizational sniping and acrimony. Divisiveness followed an almost standardized formula: Pfeffer and the Congress would attempt to lead the organized defense network into new forays, and the ADL and AJC would raise objections. For whatever reason—public relations in local communities, interreligious harmony, protection of the Jewish image, overtaxing of Jewish resources—the latter sought to curb the Congress's initiative. Disagreement arose over principles and tactics, but much sprang from sheer jealousy. The ADL and AJC were keenly aware that Pfeffer's hard work, his ever-growing stature in the legal profession, and his alliances with groups like the ACLU had enhanced the reputation of the Congress. And each success that the Congress chalked up strengthened its control over the agencies affiliated with NCRAC and the SCA. The Congress had cornered the Jewish market on church–state relations, leaving the ADL and AJC forever in second place in an area of vital concern to American Jews. As for Pfeffer and the Congress, their acknowledged leadership in church–state matters strengthened their assertiveness and independence. They grew less patient with would-be restrainers and less receptive to criticism from sister agencies or local communities.

The Bible issue had its share of interagency differences. The ADL, for example, grumbled about the Congress's unilateral actions in *Doremus* and *Tudor*.[17] When the ADL and AJC resigned from the Joint Advisory Committee tensions persisted, but the clashes were no longer confined to JAC meetings. In the Miami Bible-reading case of 1960 a particularly bitter dispute was aired publicly throughout the Jewish community.

Over the years the Miami offices of the big three had received complaints from Jewish parents and students about the blatant sectarianism in Miami's schools—religious symbols including a picture of Jesus in school buildings, inspirational messages by Christian clergymen, mandatory attendance at holiday celebrations that reenacted the nativity and crucifixion themes. Since Miami's Jews had no Jewish community council, the standard agency for handling communal issues, the national organizations wielded greater influence. But without a strong local agency it became more difficult to forge a Jewish consensus. For the same reason, efforts at interreligious friendship, particularly important in Bible Belt country, lacked direction; rabbis were not included in the Ministerial Association of Miami. The overall setting contributed to a strong fear of anti-Semitism on the part of local Jews as well as the ADL and AJC. Indeed, in deference to the Jews the Florida affiliate of the ACLU (FCLU) withheld court action on religion in the schools where Jews alone had agreed to file charges.[18]

In April 1959 Pfeffer was told that the FCLU had found its case. On behalf of a parent, Harlow Chamberlin, who was a self-proclaimed agnostic, the FCLU proposed to challenge Bible reading and the recitation of the Lord's Prayer in the schools of Dade County. Actually, it was a package suit which included many other usages—religious holiday celebrations (Jewish as well as Christian), religious symbols, hymns and baccalaureate services, and religious tests for teachers. Pfeffer not only agreed to cooperate, but he prepared to mount a parallel case. The purpose was to show that religious people as well as agnostics opposed the sectarian practices. The Congress would not have chosen to contest all issues in an omnibus case, but "the die was cast for us" and its complaint had to follow the FCLU's lead. Pfeffer subsequently insisted that the Congress's announcement of its intent to Jewish community leaders in Miami aroused no opposition and that the ADL and AJC cooperated in mapping out strategy for the litigation.[19]

Pfeffer's statement was not entirely accurate. Intense opposition from local Jews as well as from the Congress's rivals had greeted his actions, and only one attorney of the ADL, acting in a private capacity, cooperated readily with Pfeffer and Chamberlin's lawyers. The interagency dispute escalated rapidly. Publicly, the Congress was accused of jeopardizing the future of the Jewish community throughout the South. Even if its suit succeeded, one ADL leader reportedly charged, "it would be the story of the operation being a success but the patient dying."[20]

In the summer of 1960 the ADL and AJC widely circulated an indictment of the Congress for its "irresponsible" action: "This was the wrong case, in the wrong place at the wrong time." Claiming that the FCLU's defense of a nonbeliever and a parallel Jewish case were objectionable to the Jewish leaders of Miami, the agencies charged that the Congress's suit would be at best a gratuitous duplicate of the Chamberlin case. More likely, it would turn the legal issues into a Jewish–Christian fight. Reluctantly and only for reasons of "conscience" and commitment to the principle of separation, the ADL said, did it continue to support the litigation of the FCLU and the Congress. It much preferred its own approach: negotiations with school authorities to diminish the offensive sectarian practices.[21]

Under the barrage of accusations that it had dragged an unwilling community into a potentially dangerous situation, the Congress modified its initial claim. It now admitted that it had encountered opposition in Miami but only from those associated with the ADL and AJC. It explained that informal discussions between Jewish groups and the school board on the objectionable practices held out no prospect of success. Indeed, one member of the board had warned that concessions would be tantamount to "living under the dictatorship of a minority group." Accordingly, the Congress stepped in to represent four parents, three Jews and one Unitarian. Their suit, the *Reznick* case, was consolidated for trial with Chamberlin's in *Chamberlin* v. *Dade County,* and Pfeffer served as chief counsel.

While its own integrity was under attack, the Congress countered with a story that rocked the foundations of its opponents' credibility. It charged that the ADL and AJC had sought to buy their way into the *Chamberlin* case; offering to provide three thousand to five thousand dollars toward legal costs, they had asked the FCLU that one official from each agency be named as co-counsel in the suit. The FCLU had retorted that control of the case "was not for sale." The ADL's version of the story admitted that an approach had been made to the FCLU, but it categorically denied that either side had interpreted the offer as a means of buying control.[22] The ADL's distinction was hardly significant. Even if its account was accurate, its righteous protestations against the Congress now rang hollow. The same charges—that the Congress failed to secure community clearance and that Jewish involvement in a suit, particularly on behalf of an agnostic, would exacerbate intergroup tension—applied to the offer by the ADL and AJC to help Chamberlin. Furthermore, an attempt to preempt the Congress in the Chamberlin case suggests that opportunism at least as much as principle (i.e., a commitment to a "softer" approach on separation) determined their stand on this matter.[23]

Irrespective of who was bending the truth, it was clear that the Congress had erred politically. It may have announced its intention of filing a suit to various local and national Jewish bodies, as it claimed, but it never solicited advice or consultation. Its high-handed presentation of a fait accompli aroused queries and resentment from community leaders, even loyal followers of Pfeffer, in various cities. As a prominent communal worker in Cleveland explained, input from other agencies was essential in a case that would doubtless affect Jews throughout the country. Meantime, the ADL and AJC seized the opportunity to foment criticism of the Congress in the local communities. Under those pressures the Congress circulated an explanatory report, and it belatedly sought (and received) official approval from the JAC for its action. However, when the Congress's budget was discussed at a committee meeting of the Large Cities Budgeting Conference in 1960, the agency was mildly rebuked for its failure to obtain local agreement to the suit. It was made to sign a new ground rule which insisted that national agencies obtain "prior consent from the local Jewish community" before involving themselves in a problem of community relations.[24]

Charges and countercharges precluded any interagency discussion of the substantive issues. Was Bible reading in the schools a practice of value for American Jews and American Judaism? Should Jews out of a concern for communal harmony accommodate to the customs of the schools? Did a Bible Belt setting dictate the need for a strategy different from that, say, in New Jersey? The closest the contending parties came to the subject of principle was a private comment by the Congress in defense of its action. The agency insisted that the fear of adverse public relations was outweighed by the need for Jews to fight their own battles and by the long-term goal of shoring up the principle of separation.[25]

Predicting a heated courtroom battle, the press gave wide coverage to the case. Outraged Floridians focused on the preservation of Bible reading, and civic groups, women's organizations, and councils of churches loudly campaigned for its retention. A petition was circulated door-to-door; a bumper sticker proclaimed "Keep the Bible in the Public Schools"; editors received numerous letters and phone calls against the plaintiffs. One Presbyterian women's group called the suits "un-American, un-Biblical, and undesirable." The women realized that "technically and officially" the government was committed neither to Christianity nor to the Bible, but "the very fabric of American life is founded upon Christianity and spiritual principles." In the hope of calming tempers, some local rabbis approached the Protestant Ministerial Association and offered to compromise. The Christian group refused, stating that the matter should be left to the courts.[26]

Tension rose when the trial began. The scene at the courthouse, Frank Sorauf recounts, was reminiscent of the famous Scopes trial of 1925. "Supporters of Bible-reading were first in line every day before the trial commenced, and so a phalanx of white-shirted, blue-trousered, Bible-toting young men occupied the front two rows of the spectators' sections." The attorney for the school board, "a colorful, stentorian barrister of the old, old school . . . played skillfully to the sympathetic crowds in a performance some journalists—inevitably perhaps—likened to that of William Jennings Bryan."[27] Outside the court, a Presbyterian church held an all-night vigil at which the Bible was read, and the Council of Churches directed church groups and Sunday schools to pray for the victory of the school board. The trial also figured in a county school board election whose theme was "keep religion in the schools." The Jewish candidate, who was a member of the American Jewish Congress, was bitterly attacked for his connections to groups that were "utterly liberal" and that defended Communists. "Thank God we have a Christian Republican candidate," the director of the Council of Churches said at a public meeting.

Christian opposition to the suit, even from several prominent individuals who were known as friendly to the Jews, set the defense agencies to wondering whether the reaction could be called anti-Semitic. The ADL didn't think so. It reasoned that Dade County (despite the influx of northern Jews into Miami Beach) was still Bible Belt country, where religious viewpoints were at least as deeply rooted as racial segregation. One knowledgeable ADL official explained: "People live in a Christian world here and by that they mean that it is a Protestant world and to have Bible reading . . . is every bit as ingrained and as natural . . . as segregated social facilities would be. Consequently, the tremendous reaction of surprise, confusion, indignation on even the part of persons who are no wise consciously anti-Semitic."

The level of public criticism intensified Jewish unhappiness with the suit. A Jewish columnist for the *Jewish Floridian* wrote that "the American Jewish Congress is going it alone in Dade County with the Jewish community at large having to pay the price." The Congress insisted, however, that the decibel level of local hostility was much lower. It also noted with satisfaction the support it had received from out-of-state papers and, unexpectedly, from some important Catholic and Protestant periodicals.[28]

Fortunately for the Congress, the publicity aided its search for witnesses. The trial had opened with apparently little evidence to sustain certain allegations of the plaintiffs, but once the hearings began Pfeffer easily rounded up volunteers who were prepared to offer testimony. During the first week of the trial in July 1960, students and parents told how Jewish pupils were a captive audience for Christological practices. One Jewish student, the editor of the high school newspaper, related that despite repeated requests to be excused, she was compelled to attend religious programs. When she wrote an editorial against religious discrimination, it was disallowed by school authorities. The most dramatic testimony from student witnesses at the trial described the annual Easter play, which reenacted the crucifixion—replete with wooden cross and blood (ketchup).[29]

The trial recessed after one week, and both sides discussed the terms of a possible settlement recommended by the counsel for the school board and the superintendent of schools. Under the proposed terms some practices would be discontinued and others modified, but Bible reading from the Old and New Testaments (without sectarian comments) and the Lord's Prayer (or a nonsectarian prayer at the teacher's option) stood. The school board rejected the terms of its own officials. On the eve of the trial it had agreed to excuse students from Bible reading at a parent's request, and it was unwilling to retreat further. Nonetheless, with scrupulous attention to the opinion of Miami's Jews, the JAC discussed the proposed settlement. Some members thought that the case was sufficiently strong to fight up to the Supreme Court, but representatives from Miami, hoping that the school board might reconsider its decision, urged adoption of the initial proposal. The final resolution was a compromise: the JAC formally supported the continuation of litigation, but it agreed that if the Jewish community of Miami preferred a settlement, that position should prevail.[30]

Since no settlement was reached, the trial resumed. At this stage, as was his wont, Pfeffer brought in expert witnesses—an educator, a psychiatrist, a psychologist, and three clergymen—who testified to the Christian character of the religious practices and the conflicts generated among children by sectarian exercises. Refusing to hear testimony on the issues of coercion and free choice, the circuit court handed down a mixed decision in April 1961. Judge J. Fritz Gordon enjoined several practices contested by the plaintiffs, notably the nativity and crucifixion plays, but he upheld Bible reading and the recitation of the Lord's Prayer with the proviso that objectors could be excused. Denying that the United States was "a Godless nation," Gordon advised a commonsense approach: "It would seem to this court that the Golden Rule should be observed by those selecting verses from the Bible to be read so that the Old Testament when agreeable would be used and only verses not highly controversial would be read."[31] Sentiment ran high on both sides for an appeal to the Supreme Court, but by that time the primary focus on the Bible-reading issue had shifted to the *Schempp* case.

The Philadelphia Story

The *Schempp* case originated in 1957 in Abington Township, a suburb of Philadelphia. The Schempps, a Unitarian family in a religiously mixed, upper-middle class community challenged the Pennsylvania law of 1949 which required the daily reading of ten verses from the Bible. The procedure in the Abington high school called for a student to read from the Bible, usually the Protestant version, over a public address system. At the conclusion, the students in their separate classrooms would rise, bow their heads, and recite the Lord's Prayer. The prayer, although not required by law, was standard usage throughout the state. Ellory, the oldest Schempp child, objected to the morning exercises. He read the Koran during Bible reading, and he refused to stand for the Lord's Prayer. At his request he was permitted to sit in a school office during the ceremonies, but after some months he was required to remain in the classroom.[32]

The ACLU backed the Schempps, but the Congress had reservations about the case. To be sure, the dreaded label of "agnostic" or "atheist" did not apply; the Schempps were churchgoers and the children attended a Sunday school. Nevertheless, Pfeffer preferred a case involving Jewish and Catholic parents that would explicitly challenge the constitutionality of the Lord's Prayer. As always, he sought to register Jewish religious interest along with the interest of other minorities and to underscore the sectarian nature of the practice in question. A year later, and only at the urging of its Philadelphia branch, the Congress became officially involved and filed an *amicus* brief with the lower court.[33]

The Schempps, father and children, testified at the trial in 1959. So did two expert witnesses, Dean Emeritus Luther Weigle of the Yale Divinity School for the Abington school district, and Dr. Solomon Grayzel, a Jewish scholar, for Schempp. Weigle affirmed that the Bible was nonsectarian. On the other hand, Bible reading solely from the Old Testament would be a sectarian practice, since "Holy Bible," the term used in the state law, was incomplete without the New Testament. Grayzel spoke about the crucial differences between the Jewish and Christian Bibles and the utter unsuitability of the New Testament for Jewish children. The concept of Jesus as the son of God was "practically blasphemous" to Judaism, and verses in the New Testament heaped ridicule and scorn upon the Jews. He explained, for example, that the Good Samaritan story in Luke 10, although of Jewish origin, had been emended when inserted in the New Testament. As "a slap at the Jews of that day who refused to join the Christian church," the word Samaritan had been substituted for Israelite. Grayzel dwelt in particular on the account of the crucifixion in Matthew 27, which related how Jews had refused to exchange Jesus for Barabbas. He said that verse 25—"Then answered all the people, and said: 'His blood be on us, and our children' "—"had been the cause of more anti-Jewish riots throughout the ages than anything else in history."[34]

The federal district court ruled that the Pennsylvania law constituted an establishment of religion as well as a violation of free exercise. The daily Bible readings, religious ceremonies which indoctrinated the children with "a religious sense," amounted to a "promotion of religious education." "Inasmuch as the 'Holy Bible' is a Christian document, the practice aids and prefers the Christian religion." Since recitation of the Lord's Prayer was not required by law, its constitutionality was judged by the court as part of the Bible-reading exercise. The decision was an unqualified victory for the separationists, and it was hailed as a sign that *McCollum* rather than *Zorach* was increasingly accepted as the law of the land.

The school board appealed to the Supreme Court. While the appeal was pending, the Pennsylvania legislature hastened to amend the law. It now permitted children to be excused from the morning exercises upon written request of their parents. When the case reached the highest court, the justices vacated the first ruling and, in light of the recent amendment, remanded the case to the district court.[35] In preparation for the second hearing the Jewish Community Relations Council of Greater Philadelphia (JCRC) swung into action.

Unlike the situation in Miami where no Jewish community council existed, Philadelphia's Jews were well organized. The JCRC, founded in 1939, represented over thirty organizations, including the local branches of all major national Jewish agencies. It also was a respected member of the Philadelphia Fellowship Commission, a body called the "powerful conscience of the city," which was dedicated to the pursuit of intergroup harmony. Proud of its civic standing and its activities, and boasting of its own committee on church–state matters, the JCRC would not meekly defer to directives of a national defense agency. At the beginning, many Jewish leaders had been irritated by the Congress's involvement in the *Schempp* case. They did not consider Bible reading a top priority, and they feared a setback to their efforts for interreligious amity. Not until after the initial decision did the JCRC join the challenge to Bible reading. From then until the case went again to the Supreme Court a second time, Jewish interest in *Schempp* was represented exclusively, and successfully, by Philadelphia Jewry. The sequence of events reveals how local statements and strategy— low-key, less legalistic, and more finely attuned to the sentiments of the larger community—differed from the conventional pattern of the Congress.[36]

When the amendment permitting excused absences was under consideration, the JCRC discussed a proper response. Obviously, if the courts upheld Bible reading, voluntary attendance was preferable to mandatory. Yet to accede to the amendment, or even to keep silent, could be interpreted as an admission that Bible reading belonged in the schools. Advice from the national agencies was mixed, but in the end the JCRC urged the governor to veto the measure. Most of its letter enlarged on Frankfurter's argument in *McCollum* that nonconformity was not an outstanding characteristic of children. It also maintained that the right to be excused did not legitimate the practice itself.[37] By its letter the JCRC committed itself to the public defense of strict separation. Tacitly, it also affirmed its independence of the national agencies.

The JCRC stepped up its activity in 1960. It circulated a strong statement in opposition to Bible reading that was reported in the national press and disseminated throughout the country. It presented its position astutely, in a manner calculated to appeal to the "Philadelphia spirit" of the Fellowship Commission and yet unlikely to offend believers. The statement neither emphasized the "secular" school nor belabored the rights of atheists. Affirming that the ethical and moral concepts underlying American democracy derived from religion, it argued nonetheless that Bible reading, with or without the right to be excused, was religious instruction that had no place in the schools. Religious freedom could flourish, it insisted, only if it was free of governmental interference or regulation. Furthermore, the practice was of scant aid to believers, for Bible reading without comment or the appropriate mood and ritual gestures was an empty exercise.[38] When *Schempp* again came before the district court, the JCRC repeated the same arguments in an *amicus* brief. Unanimously endorsed by its constituent groups, the decision to file did not ruffle either the Jewish or non-Jewish community. Marking the first time that a local Jewish community council filed independently of a national agency in church–state litigation, it demonstrated the able leadership and tight organization of Philadelphia's Jewry.[39]

At issue in the second trial was whether the amendment which provided for excuses sufficed to make Bible reading constitutional. Edward Schempp, the father, testified that he had not sought excuses for his children. Since their classmates tended to regard religious differences as "atheism," and since atheism had connotations of communism, immorality, and "un-Americanism," he preferred that the children not be labeled as "odd balls." The court vindicated his stand. Reiterating its first decision, it also ruled that there was little difference between compulsory and voluntary attendance at exercises conducted on school premises by school authorities. The amended law still violated the establishment clause of the First Amendment, and therefore the court enjoined Bible reading, with or without the Lord's Prayer, in the Abington high school.[40]

The Abington school board convened a public meeting to decide whether it should appeal to the Supreme Court. Knowing that a heated discussion was inevitable, and aware of anti-Jewish remarks unleashed by the decision, the JCRC carefully planned its strategy. It issued a thoughtful statement on why Bible reading in the schools was bad religion, bad education, and bad for communal unity, but it decided not to turn the meeting into an open battle by urging Jews to attend or to speak. The strategy of restraint seemed to have worked. To be sure, some common biases—the equation of religion with patriotism, the claim that "this is a Christian country," the need to abide by the majority's wishes—were aired. But perhaps because the defenders of public religion did not feel threatened by a Jewish campaign, the meeting was orderly and far less emotional than expected. The school board's final decision to appeal the case was pre-dictable, but, more important, a serious communal rift was averted. Jewish agencies in various cities, which closely monitored events in Philadelphia, concurred on the skillful manner in which the JCRC had handled the case against Bible reading in the court and the community.[41]

As the case made its way to the Supreme Court, the national agencies, still smarting under the *Engel* backlash, prepared for the decision. They confidently expected a favorable judgment, but they sought to avoid the appearance of a narrow "Jewish" victory. Anticipating an even stormier reaction should the Court outlaw Bible reading and the Lord's Prayer, they planned ambitious educational campaigns for averting hysteria in the local communities. The plans revealed the perceived need of education for Jews as well as for non-Jews.[42]

The Supreme Court heard *Abington Township School District* v. *Schempp* in conjunction with *Murray* v. *Curlett,* a suit originating in Baltimore that challenged Bible reading and the recitation of the Lord's Prayer. The two were not identical. Unlike the situation in Abington where Bible reading was mandated by state law and the prayer recitation was a customary accompaniment, a school board rule in Baltimore required the daily reading of a chapter from the Bible "and/or" the Lord's Prayer. The litigants differed, too. The Schempps were churchgoing Unitarians; Madalyn Murray, who sought to enjoin a practice in her son's school, was a flamboyant self-proclaimed and self-advertising atheist. More aggressive than Vashti McCollum, she delighted in scandalizing the public by her antireligious remarks, for which she and her son reaped public scorn and abuse. Her conduct also explained why Pfeffer and the Congress initially backed away from the case and why the JAC was less than comfortable as her "friend in court." An atheist's suit in a Southern city which had reacted bitterly to *Engel* inevitably aroused considerable public hostility. Not surprisingly Murray's challenge to Bible reading and prayer lost in the lower courts. The Superior Court of Baltimore was harshly condemnatory: "While the present petitioners clamor for religious freedom, their ultimate objective is religious suppression."[43]

The Jewish defense agencies formally supported Schempp and Murray before the Supreme Court. NCRAC and the SCA filed an *amicus* brief; the ADL, now squarely opposed to Bible reading, joined with the AJC in a separate brief. The Jewish briefs were the only ones from a religious group. Along with those of the American Ethical Union and the American Humanist Association they stood opposed to briefs of nineteen state attorneys-general on behalf of Bible reading.[44]

Pfeffer, who filed for the SCA and NCRAC, developed the themes familiar since 1947. He maintained that Bible reading and prayer, even if they were nonsectarian, and even if they did not show a preference for

Protestantism, violated the establishment clause. Here again echoes of the Jewish pursuit of legal equality—which a minority could realistically hope to achieve only if benefits were withheld from all groups—resounded. Citing the expert testimony amassed in Miami, Pfeffer's brief also claimed violation of the free exercise clause, because permission to be excused did not make the practices truly voluntary.

Since the attorneys opposed to Murray insisted that the school exercises aimed to further moral and spiritual values and not religion, Pfeffer's brief devoted several pages to the consideration of "Religion as a Means and an End." A novel departure from the tried Jewish approach, it suggested clearly defined guidelines on the interplay of government with religion. In light of the Court's suggestions in *Schempp* and in later cases of similar guidelines or tests on church–state separation, this new Jewish argument is particularly noteworthy. The brief said that according to the Court's decisions, the First Amendment required a secular government. Hence, although the state might incidentally affect religion in acts related to its secular pursuits, it was constrained from pursuing religious ends or from purposely utilizing religious means to accomplish a secular end. It followed therefore that even if Baltimore had sought to implement a secular purpose, its choice of religious means made the exercise invalid.

Both Jewish briefs insisted that their opposition to religious exercises in the schools was not prompted by a hostility to religion. That argument had been raised ever since *McCollum,* but in *Schempp* it was joined to a positive statement: "Nothing in the Constitution of the United States requires the school authorities to remove all matter relating to religion from the school curriculum. It is not contended that, for example, the Bible may not be studied in the public schools as a work of literature. . . . Nor is it contended that the influence of religion and religious institutions upon history may not be studied." Venturing even further, the NCRAC–SCA brief admitted that a certain kind of prayer—the "right of individual children to engage in private or individual prayer of their own choice during public school hours in a manner which does not interfere with the regular conduct of public school operations"—was also legitimate. The legal ramifications of silent prayer would come to a head in the 1980s, and at that time mainline Jewish defense spoke differently. In the *Murray–Schempp* brief, however, the statement was a gesture of accommodation to non-Jewish critics of *Engel* and at least as much to Jewish critics of strict separation.[45]

When the Court heard oral argument, the main issue was whether the school exercises were religious ceremonies or nonsectarian usages for the teaching of moral principles. The attorneys for the schools attempted to minimize the religious character of daily practices which took so little time during the school day, but the justices refused to ignore principle. All signs indicated that the Court would adopt the reasoning of *McCollum* and

Engel, and even the eight-to-one lineup (Potter Stewart was the lone dissenter) was predictable.[46]

With the uproar over *Engel* in mind, Chief Justice Warren selected Tom Clark to write the opinion. An opinion by Clark, who was considered a conservative in comparison to Black, was likely to arouse less public opposition.[47] Since the majority included a Catholic (William Brennan) and a Jew (Arthur Goldberg), the ruling was a felicitous gesture of interreligious agreement. The justices were also careful to stress the close identification of religion with American life. An education was incomplete, they said, without a study of the role of religion in civilization. They vehemently denied that the decision established a "religion of secularism"; the invalidation of state-sponsored exercises in no way precluded the objective study of religion and the Bible in the schools.

The Court defined free exercise to mean the prohibition of religious coercion. Accordingly, the majority could not construe its right of free exercise as a validation of the school practices; the free exercise clause "has never meant that a majority could use the machinery of the State to practice its beliefs." The Court's primary focus, however, was on the establishment clause, and continuing the line of broad interpretation, it easily found that the religious exercises were unconstitutional. To argue that the practices were relatively minor constituted no defense against a possible entering wedge. "The breach . . . that is today a trickling stream may all too soon become a raging torrent."

Clark outlined a test of neutrality for determining the constitutionality of a legislative enactment: "What are the purpose and primary effect of the enactment? If either is the advancement or inhibition of religion then the enactment exceeds the scope of legislative power as circumscribed by the Constitution." Rather, "there must be a secular legislative purpose and a primary effect that neither advances nor inhibits religion." The Court called for a "wholesome" neutrality on the part of government toward religion, a concept that legal analysts were quick to dissect. But even if, as some claimed, the Court preferred a "benevolent neutrality" geared to accommodation and involvement rather than strict neutrality, the opinion was a historic victory for separationists. Rounding out the Court's approach to the establishment clause which was first formulated in *Everson,* it highlighted, as the Congress claimed, the legal acceptance of religious pluralism and the successful "social revolution" of those committed to religious and cultural equality.[48]

Indeed, Justice Brennan in a concurring opinion addressed just that point. Discussing the pluralistic nature of American society and its impact on judicial interpretation, he wrote: "Today the Nation is far more heterogeneous religiously, including as it does substantial minorities not only of Catholics and Jews but as well of those who worship according to no version of the Bible and those who worship no God at all. In the face of such profound changes, practices which may have been objectionable to no one in the time of Jefferson and Madison may today be highly offensive to many persons."[49]

A Gallup poll released two months after the decision revealed that 70 percent of the public disapproved of the decision and only 24 percent approved. Nevertheless, the hostility with which Protestants had greeted the 1962 ruling did not surface. American Catholics were disappointed, but they too were far more restrained than in response to *Engel*. Only three of the five cardinals condemned the decision, and *America* refrained from inflammatory editorials. In Congress, despite a new round of amendment proposals, the response was also lower keyed. One congressman called for "mental tests" for the justices, but vilification of the Court and noncompliance with the decision were confined mostly to Southerners still bitter over the civil rights decisions.

Surveys done by the Jewish defense agencies agreed that the reaction was comparatively mild. Overall, newspaper editorials and letters to the editor showed an opposition far less militant than in 1962. Nor did the Jewish surveys discover any anti-Semitic slurs. (Only one article in *Commonweal* criticized the "large Jewish-secular minority" who, with the support of many Protestants, were not committed to the historical forms of the American religious heritage.) The reaction was all the more gratifying because *Engel* had dealt with a practice in only 10 percent of the schools of one state, whereas *Murray* and *Schempp* concerned practices in the majority of the nation's schools. Several reasons explained the milder tone: the civil rights crisis, which deflected attention from church–state affairs; the belief after *Engel* that the ruling was inevitable; and the year-long preparations of Jewish and Christian proseparation forces for cushioning the expected decision.[50]

The Integrity of the Bill of Rights

Despite *Engel* and *Schempp*, Bible reading and prayer in the schools were not permitted to die without a struggle. Attempts to inject new life into the practices shifted the action from the Court to Congress, where constitutional amendments to topple the recent rulings were proposed. The initial movement for an amendment had suffered a setback in the immediate aftermath of *Engel*, but it persisted. Congressman Frank Becker of New York, a Republican, a Catholic, and one of the sponsors of an amendment in 1962, introduced his same proposal as soon as the 88th Congress convened. Six months later, determined to capitalize on public dissatisfaction with *Schempp*, he filed a discharge petition to bring his resolution from the House Judiciary Committee to the floor of Congress. He also substituted a broader version for his original proposal, one designed to unite the sixty congressmen who had introduced similar resolutions. The second version, known as the Becker Amendment, cut through parties and sections, and it secured the powerful backing of the proreligion and anti-Court forces.[51]

The first section of the Becker Amendment permitted the "offering, reading from, or listening to prayers or biblical scriptures" on a voluntary basis in public schools or places. The second allowed "making reference to belief in, reliance upon, or invoking the aid of God or a Supreme Being" in public documents, ceremonies, and institutions. The third specified that "nothing in this article shall constitute an establishment of religion." The implications were far-reaching. Not only could states or Congress overturn the Court's decisions on public religion, but the test oath clause of Article VI was threatened as well. Politically the Becker Amendment became a magnet for the conservative coalition in Congress, especially critics of the Court's decisions on racial integration and reapportionment. While it encouraged noncompliance with those rulings, it fueled the propaganda machine of the radical right.[52]

As Becker plotted his campaign in the fall and winter of 1963–64, grassroots support continued to swell. The important Judiciary Committee, which dealt with major domestic issues, received more mail in favor of an amendment than on any other subject. State legislators introduced resolutions for an amendment, and new organizations cropped up to mobilize popular support. One group described itself as "ministers and Christians of ALL churches who love Jesus Christ, the Holy Bible, and their nation's youth more than life itself!" Another, the fundamentalist group Project Prayer, drew well-publicized support of Hollywood movie and television performers. So sure was Becker of public support that he planned on canvassing in person the districts of those congressmen who had not signed the discharge petition. His crusade appeared formidable if not unbeatable. After all, how many of his colleagues were prepared to vote against God—especially in an election year?[53]

But for the fact that the preponderant majority of correspondents were women, letters to Congress in support of the Becker Amendment represented a cross section of American society. They revealed that the amendment movement was backed by both Protestants and Catholics from urban as well as rural regions. They proved, too, that many Christian leaders were distanced from their followers. Although the major Protestant groups had endorsed the *Engel* and *Schempp* decisions, the rank and file in the churches had not been totally persuaded. Nor was there unity among Catholics. Some spokesmen (like *America*) who had vigorously opposed the Court's rulings now voiced disapproval of an amendment.[54]

The Jewish defense agencies had monitored developments on the amendment issue ever since 1962, and as Becker's discharge petition continued to gain signatures they grew more restive. In January 1964, when the JAC alerted all its constituents to the need to defeat the discharge petition, it touched off a massive publicity campaign.[55] Following directives from the defense agencies or acting on their own, individuals and local Jewish groups across the country joined in. They organized mail and phone drives, circulated fact sheets, and drew up petitions. They wrote to their representatives and to the House Judiciary Committee, they paid personal visits to congressmen, and they lobbied with state legislatures. Synagogues and communities pressed the issue from pulpits and in discussions with Christian opinion leaders. National groups responded independently, and a few sent letters to all members of the House. Speaking for rabbis and congregations, strong statements were issued by the Reform and Conservative commissions on social action. The strategy behind all the efforts was to bolster the resistance to the discharge petition or, if a congressman had signed it, to induce him to remove his name.

A few individual responses stand out. One letter was from a Jew in Baltimore to his congressman. He was "shocked," the writer stated, that his representative (a Jew) had signed the discharge petition. Noting the "terrifying tale" of persecutions attendant upon state-sponsored religion, he cited authorities from Jesus to John Kennedy who counseled against "the public display of religiosity." In Detroit a statement from over a dozen rabbis was circulated among the local Christian clergy. Different from the standard legalistic approach employed by Jews, it argued solely in religious terms: the Becker Amendment was a misguided effort that "distorts rather than bolsters" religion and that could seriously damage religion's function in society. Even an academic institution, the Hebrew Union College, contributed to the campaign. It publicized a letter of 1915 from James Cardinal Gibbons to a Reform rabbi in which the famous prelate had registered his opposition to Bible reading in the schools. The implication was clear: Catholics more prestigious than Frank Becker would have applauded the *Schempp* decision and resisted the amendment.[56]

A theme common to most statements warned against tampering with the Bill of Rights, which, they said, had so well protected Americans for 172 years. The United Synagogue held that the First Amendment was virtually sacrosanct and "unamendable." The Baltimore Jew who chided his congressman wrote: "The Bill of Rights was specifically designed to exempt religion and other rights from political pressures. . . . These rights may not be submitted to vote." Leo Pfeffer warned that the integrity of the entire Bill of Rights was challenged, jeopardizing other liberties along with religious freedom: "If this amendment is adopted it will set a precedent for further assaults on the Bill of Rights whenever the Supreme Court hands down a decision protecting civil liberties." The theme of untouchability, which became the centerpiece of a special leaflet issued by the JAC entitled "Save the Bill of Rights," was not new; it had figured prominently in the response of the Jewish defense agencies to the amendment movement of 1962.[57] However, since the 1962 episode had been short-lived, the idea was developed fully only in 1964.

The amendment issue united the overwhelming number of American Jews, even some who had previously opposed a strict separationist stand. True, a minority view in the Union of Orthodox Jewish Congregations advised a passive approach, not to oppose the amendment but to keep alert to, and protest against, abuses involving public school prayer. It was more important, one such opinion held, to resist the secularist stand of Jewish organizations, posturing under the mask of neutralism, than to fight religion in the schools.[58] But except for a few right-wingers, the Becker Amendment temporarily silenced the critics who had deliberated the pros and cons of strict separation in the aftermath of *Engel*.

At first Chairman Emanuel Celler of the Judiciary Committee, a Reform Jew and a strong opponent of an amendment, kept the proposals pigeon-holed. Unabated public pressure and the progress of the discharge petition forced his retreat. Rather than risk a debate on the House floor where the amendment would doubtless pass, he scheduled committee hearings for April. The hearings bought him time, for by then Celler had the invaluable aid of a small ad hoc committee representing the major religious groups, which operated quietly but effectively to wreck Becker's crusade. When the word came down from Celler's office that the amendment proposals "must be killed" before they reached the floor of Congress, that committee stepped up its activity.[59]

Dean M. Kelley, director of the Department of Religious Liberty of the National Council of Churches, called a meeting in mid-March of two dozen staff members of Protestant and Jewish organizations to discuss "possible actions to preserve the Bill of Rights in its present form." The three major Jewish defense agencies were invited, as were representatives of NCRAC and the SCA. (Whereas almost all of the Protestants were ministers of different denominations, Jews of the secular agencies, rather than of the Reform, Orthodox, and Conservative rabbinical groups, were regarded—as they were in litigation—as the primary spokesmen for the community.) Kelley's committee worked on the assumption that the anti-amendment forces had but one chance, namely, to keep the bills bottled up until the end of the congressional session and Frank Becker's scheduled retirement. It decided that its prime function within the limited time was to acquaint Congress, and members of the Judiciary Committee in partic-ular, with the existence of a large body of *religious* opinion in opposition to an amendment. To secure a flow of mail offsetting that of supporters of the amendment, it laid plans to concentrate on religious leaders and press (including Catholics), to encourage anti-amendment statements from plenary conventions of the major churches, and to mobilize grassroots support within each denomination. Kelley also hoped to arrange meetings between clergymen and members of Congress, and for underscoring the point of religious opposition, the wearing of clerical collars at such meetings was advised.

Assignments were divided among the members of the ad hoc committee. Pfeffer's task, for example, was to draw up a statement on the inviolability of the Bill of Rights to be signed by leading constitutional scholars.[60] The committee, however, saw no reason to discuss or direct the flourishing campaigns of the Jewish organizations. Despite a hands-off policy, Kelley's committee benefited the independent Jewish efforts. It served to erase the view in Washington circles that the amendment issue pitted Jew against Christian, a notion which at first worked *for* the amendment's success.[61] The only way to neutralize the image of a Jewish issue was to demonstrate Christian religious opposition to the amendment.

For three weeks before the hearings Kelley's committee, and a parallel group in Washington that represented virtually the same organizations, mobilized opposition to the amendment. They formulated arguments for use in letters and personal visits to congressmen, and they served as links of communication between religious leaders, local religious communities, and Congress. In close contact with Celler both before and during the hearings, Kelley supplied names of both Protestant and Catholic leaders, as well as individual congressmen, who were prepared to testify against the amendment. By ending the near-monopoly that Becker's camp had enjoyed over the flow of mail to Congress, the committees disproved the contention of one pro-amendment witness that his clerical opponents were "generals without armies."

On a different level entirely, and one that usually escapes notice, the work of the committees was a major interfaith achievement. For the Jews it represented a signal triumph. Prominent Protestant leaders had invited them to cooperate, a move that in itself testified to their acceptance and respectability in the larger society.

Perhaps the most dramatic feat of Kelley's committee was the mobilization of the country's legal scholars against an amendment. The tactic was first employed in 1962 by Leo Pfeffer, who had submitted an anti-amendment statement signed by 110 deans and professors of law and political science to the Senate Judiciary Committee. Yet the appeal and eloquence of the 1964 memorandum, which Pfeffer drafted under the title "Our Most Precious Heritage," made it stand out above the earlier effort. Unlike its prototype, the new version was sponsored by representatives of the different faiths: Paul Freund of Harvard (Jewish), Wilber Katz of Wisconsin (Protestant), and Robert Drinan of Boston College (Catholic). It differed in substance, too. The 1962 statement had warned against tampering with the Bill of Rights, but it concentrated on a defense of separation and the *Engel* ruling. The second one, with Catholics and other critics of the prayer decisions in mind, downplayed the legal cases and argued for a broader principle. It may well be, the short statement said, that the prayer decisions will be judged unwise by the American people, but "we are convinced that it would be far wiser for our nation to accept the decisions than to amend the Bill of Rights in order to nullify them." Jefferson's words in the Virginia statute on religious freedom applied here, too: "We are free to declare, and do declare, that the rights hereby asserted are of the natural rights of mankind, and that if any act shall be hereafter passed to repeal the present, or to narrow its operation, such act will be an infringement of natural right." If, however, Congress experimented with the religion clauses, it threatened the security of the other clauses as well.

Pfeffer easily gathered 223 signatures. The statement proved sufficiently strong to draw even prominent critics of the prayer decisions to the anti-amendment side. Dean Griswold of Harvard, for example, refused to entertain a remedy that entailed a violation of "the center and core of our governmental system." The legal experts' defense of the Bill of Rights had a significant impact on the hearings. As one member of the Judiciary Committee commented: "We have just been hit by 223 bricks."[62]

Representatives of eight national Jewish organizations—ADL, Congress, UAHC, CCAR, United Synagogue, SCA, Union of Orthodox Jewish Congregations, Jewish War Veterans—appeared at the hearings of the Judiciary Committee. Six were rabbis. Pfeffer, identified as an attorney from New York, officially testified as an independent expert, but all knew of his affiliation with the Congress. In a united show of opposition to the amendment, the Jewish witnesses countered the defamatory charges of amendment supporters. They also stressed the inviolability of the Bill of Rights, the cornerstone of American Jewish security. Referring to the historical experiences of the Jews and to the nineteenth-century experience of American Catholics, they insisted that minority rights must not be subjected to majority votes.

Religious identification and arguments were central to Jewish testimony, even on the part of the non-rabbis. Pfeffer mentioned that he regularly attended religious services and that his children studied at religious schools; Seymour Graubard of the ADL and Daniel Heller of the Jewish War Veterans recalled personal discomfort as Jews when confronted with Christian ceremonies in school. Most insisted that rote practices watered down and weakened religion. Rabbi Maurice Eisendrath of the UAHC doubted that such usages elevated public morality. Challenging Bishop Fulton Sheen, who had endorsed the use of the motto "In God We Trust" as a school prayer, the rabbi asked: "If we plastered stickers proclaiming, 'In God We Trust,' on all the public buildings and recited it hourly in every public school, would we be saved?" In a moving statement, Rabbi Joachim Prinz of the Congress also denied the moral value of state-sponsored religion. Speaking of his personal experiences in Germany, where he had served as a rabbi and had later endured solitary confinement in a Nazi prison, he told how he, like all German children, had received nine years of religious instruction in public school. Raised in a Catholic village, Prinz had routinely made the sign of the cross at the start of each school session. "It did not make of me a good Christian," he commented wryly, but only "a rabbi who knows how to make the sign of the cross." He affirmed that the German school system, which encouraged public prayer, had no visible moral effect. It "has not made of the German nation a nation that was able to prevent the coming of Hitler and the tortuous death of millions of Christians and Jews."

The witnesses defended the Supreme Court and a school system free of legalized religious exercises. They denied that the Court's rulings banned prayer in general from the schools, and all were prepared to accept silent prayer or meditation. Rabbi Moses Feuerstein, president of the Union of Orthodox Congregations, elaborated on that compromise position which had been endorsed at the Union's convention. Concerned with the "spiritual deprivation" suffered by most American children, he suggested that each child who so desired carry a prayer card, to be provided by his parents or house of worship, to be read silently during the allocated moments. The silent prayer would provide the pupils with a religious orientation, thus fulfilling the Jewish teaching on the desirability of a religious discipline for children of all faiths. At the same time it would permit each to pray in the authentic idiom of his own faith.[63]

Except for Feuerstein, whose testimony did not appear to offend anyone, the witnesses were subjected to intensive grilling by the pro-amendment congressmen on the Judiciary Committee. How consistent were the strict separationists who supported *Engel* and *Schempp* but who found nothing wrong with chaplaincies, tax exemptions for religious institutions, and the mention of God in the national motto and the pledge to the flag? Did they who were so concerned with the rights of minorities in a pluralistic society respect the right of the majority to free exercise of their religion? Was silent prayer in essence qualitatively different from formal, nonsectarian prayers? At times only the intervention of the chairman or a member of the committee saved a witness from intense discomfort.

The Jewish position was noted in testimony from the pro-amendment group. Becker, the first witness at the hearings, sneered at the "cynics," "secularists," and "atheists" who lacked patriotism as well as religiosity. In that context, he singled out the Congress and one of its officers, Shad Polier. He pointedly reminded his listeners, and Polier's organization, that the Court in the *Holy Trinity* case had ruled that the United States was a Christian nation. Careful to avoid any semblance of anti-Semitism, Becker praised the pro-amendment position of two Jews (he erred about one) which had come to his attention. A few days later Pfeffer publicly protested

Becker's charges. It behooved the congressman and his following, the Jewish lawyer advised, to remember the biblical injunction against bearing false witness![64]

Another witness at the hearings raised the Christian-nation theme; he referred to both *Holy Trinity* and *United States* v. *Macintosh*. But overall the testimony was free of anti-Jewish innuendo except for the remarks of a Charles Winegarner, an official of the Citizens Congressional Committee. There was something wrong, Winegarner contended, when schools permitted communist propaganda but considered it a crime to pay tribute to God. "It was Christ who said when his detractors [read Jews] tried to trap him with legal technicalities: 'The letter killeth, the spirit giveth life.' " He pleaded that "those who deal in tablets of stone must not be permitted to repeal or erase this law of the heart." Blaming "insignificant minorities" for all sorts of antisocial deeds—from undoing the Constitution to sex perversion—he pleaded that the American way of life should not be discarded to satisfy "an intense and obnoxious microscopic minority." Columnists Rowland Evans and Robert Novak exposed Winegarner's anti-Semitic views, and they also revealed that he was the nephew of the notorious Jew baiter Gerald L. K. Smith, who directed and financed the Citizens Congressional Committee. Other extremists were allied with the amendment drive; the John Birch Society and the Christian Crusade, which sought the impeachment of Earl Warren, rallied to the support of God and Frank Becker.[65] The right-wing presence, however, neither erupted into an anti-Semitic campaign nor cowed Jews into maintaining silence on the amendment issue.

By the end of May the tide of congressional opinion was turning. Testimony at the hearings exposed the confusion that could result from an amendment. Simultaneously, strong protests from the mainline churches and energetic publicity campaigns by anti-amendment groups began to neutralize the pressure of Becker's crusade. Soon after the hearings concluded, Kelley's committee reported that several congressmen had removed their names from the discharge petition. No report was filed by the Judiciary Committee, and Congress adjourned without any discussion of a prayer amendment. Although the 1964 platform of the Republican party supported an amendment, Becker virtually conceded by mid-August that his amendment was dead.[66]

Along with other active opponents of the Becker Amendment, the Jewish defense network had scored well. During an interview with a professor of political science, Becker blamed Leo Pfeffer, who coincidentally lived in the congressman's district, for having been "the archvillain" most responsible for his defeat.[67] Nevertheless, the Jewish agencies could not relax their guard. In the summer of 1964 Dr. Martin Marty, a prominent Protestant scholar, told a Jewish audience: "Last spring's spectacle in the House Judiciary Committee . . . has not begun to play its last stand." Indeed, the drive for a prayer amendment, highlighted by the efforts of Senators Everett Dirksen and Jesse Helms and calling forth repeated Jewish protests, survived well into the 1980s.[68]

In both *Engel* and *Schempp* the Court left the door open for objective teaching about religion in the schools. Many educators and Christian clergymen took up the challenge, seeking ways to plant religion firmly in the academic curriculum within proper constitutional limits. Encouraged by established educational bodies and by new organizations created precisely for that purpose, schools and other groups launched experiments for developing the proper courses and teaching materials. The National Council of Churches was supportive, and so were some prominent Catholics. A reprise of the debates in the 1950s on moral and spiritual values, conferences, and workshops abounded on all facets of the subject. Some hoped that exploring the issue would foster dialogue and cooperation among religious groups. It was time, Rabbi Arthur Gilbert stated, that cooperation be substituted for litigation as the way of resolving interreligious disputes.[69]

Yet for the remainder of the decade the Jewish community—rank and file as well as professional leaders—held back. Although Pfeffer's brief in *Schempp* had spoken of the legitimate study of the Bible as a literary subject, the implications of that statement were ignored. The suspicions on the part of the overwhelming majority of American Jews were summed up in the oft-cited remarks of Dr. Robert Gordis, a prominent Conservative rabbi. Gordis wrote in 1962 that "the danger of the 'camel's head in the tent' is not imaginary. It cannot be denied that there are those who would regard teaching about religion merely as the opening wedge for the teaching *of* religion." Most Jews saw no need to alter the position first enunciated by the JAC in 1957 (*Safeguarding Religious Liberty*) and only slightly revised in 1962:

> We believe that the public schools must and should teach, with full objectivity, the role that religion has played in the life of mankind and in the development of our society, when such teaching is intrinsic to the regular subject matter being studied. Beyond this, we believe that the public school is not equipped to teach the doctrines of religion in a factual, objective, and impartial way. While such factual, objective and impartial study . . . may not be inconsistent with the principle of the separation of Church and State, we believe there is reason for concern lest the introduction of such teaching . . . engender pressures upon school personnel from sectarian groups, compromise the impartiality of teaching and the integrity of the public education system to other grave consequence.[70]

It was evident that the judicial victories for separation had not expunged the entrenched Jewish fear of an aggressive Christianity. To compromise meant to regress, possibly to turn the clock back to the pre-*McCollum* school situation. The Jews had learned in the 1950s how "teaching about religion" was used in some places as a guise for instruction in Christianity. Even now most American Jews were not fully convinced of the sincerity of interreligious understanding. At a workshop on church–state relations one rabbi advised that the Jewish position should be "love me outside the school." Jewish leaders were also aware of the high degree of noncompliance with the Court's rulings and of the persistent clamor for a prayer amendment. It was not unrealistic, therefore, to question how objective Americans were, and would be, about the study of religion.[71]

A few days after the *Schempp* decision Sidney Vincent, associate director of the Cleveland Jewish Community Federation and respected figure in the Jewish defense network, spoke at the plenary session of NCRAC. He shocked his audience by questioning the soundness of NCRAC's position. In *Safeguarding Religious Liberty* the organization had declared that "the American democratic system is founded in large part on ethical and moral concepts derived from the great religions of mankind," but, without considering how those principles were to be transmitted, it adopted a rigid stance against any religious intrusion into the schools. Suggesting certain approaches that might be employed in the classroom without violating separation, Vincent stressed the introduction of moral education into the curriculum by way of selected texts. Not doctrine, he insisted, but an awareness and infusion of moral issues and religious values into secular subjects should be the goal of the Jewish community. The address aroused heated debate and some bitter rejoinders. Several critics saw it as a proposal in support of a theistic orientation; one participant called it an ill-conceived way of promoting interreligious amity; still another remarked that even if the goal was commendable, the lack of properly trained teachers made it unrealistic. Shad Polier of the Congress affixed the separationist seal of disapproval. He found it strange "that, at a moment marking the successful outcome of a struggle to which the Jewish community had devoted a major part of its energies for so long, a struggle that it recognized as a struggle for freedom, . . . a proposal should be advanced which . . . would be a negation of that struggle."[72]

At NCRAC committee meetings on church–state matters at the end of the 1960s the consensus was to maintain a guarded approach. The abstract aim of an objective study of the Bible and religion was admittedly inoffensive, but the Jewish agencies still considered it an unattainable goal. Their function, particularly on the local scene, was primarily one of policing the specific ways in which the courses were taught.[73]

"It is not too optimistic to suggest," Pfeffer wrote shortly after *Schempp,* that "this may well be the last major battle . . . in the area of religion in the public schools."[74] In large measure he predicted accurately. In the wake of *Engel* and *Schempp,* which more than other decisions legitimated the secular public school, much of the subsequent litigation looked like marginal or mere mopping-up operations.

8
Sabbaths and Symbols

Sunday Laws Intact

Justice Oliver Wendell Holmes once remarked: "Sunday laws, no doubt, would be sustained by a bench of judges, even if every one of them thought it superstitious to make any day holy."[1] The great jurist could have included legislators as well. Until the mid–1950s, the age-old pattern of state laws and municipal ordinances that forbade certain activities on Sunday remained virtually unchanged. The overwhelming number of states retained some form of Sunday laws. Very few had repealed their Sunday laws, and only three had adopted a one-in-seven rest day. Patterns of enforcement were erratic and inconsistent, and the regulations themselves often defied the canons of logic. Why, Leo Pfeffer asked about New York's laws, permission to sell bread but not meat, gasoline but not antifreeze, beer but not butter? A few states provided full exemptions for Sabbatarians; others allowed only partial exemptions (e.g., exemption for servile labor but not retailing).

Protestants were still the principal defenders of the regulations. To be sure, popular observance of Sunday as a holy day was no longer commonplace, and nineteenth-century Protestant pressures for preserving the holiness of the Sabbath, except for a weaker Lord's Day Alliance, had largely dissipated. But even if honored in the breach, the sanctity of the Christian Sabbath was too firmly entrenched by time and usage to permit casual tampering with its protective legal shield. State courts usually invoked the doctrine of police power and, sidestepping religious reasons, validated Sunday laws as health measures. Nevertheless, the Christian origins and flavor of the legislation were ineradicable. As Frank Yost, a professor at a Seventh-Day Adventist college, argued, if Sunday laws were not religious laws, the pleas of Sabbatarian minorities for equal treatment would not have been rejected.[2]

Nor had the Jewish position on Sunday laws changed since the 1920s. Jews agitated for exemptions on behalf of Sabbath observers but not against Sunday laws per se. They recognized the religious nature of the laws that bred inequality for non-Christians, but—afraid of inciting anti-Jewish sen-

214

timent—they concentrated on the narrower, more realistic, objective of exemptions instead of repeal.[3]

In New York, the state with the largest Jewish population, the fight for relief from the discriminatory legislation was led by the Orthodox. After the death of Louis Marshall and until the war's end, the principal spokesmen came from the Jewish Sabbath Alliance, Young Israel, and the Union of Orthodox Jewish Congregations. Unable to counter the apathy of most Christians, and unable to lobby successfully with legislators or Christian groups, they failed repeatedly. Perhaps, the editor of the *Jewish Forum* suggested, Jews "lack the conviction that this country politically is not a Christian country." At Pfeffer's urging, the American Jewish Congress joined the campaign for a fair Sabbath law in 1945, and other secular and Zionist organizations followed suit. (On this matter the Orthodox did not spurn the aid of the "secularists.") Simultaneously, the Congress began its defense of the rights of Sabbatarians, Seventh-Day Adventists as well as Jews, who were denied unemployment benefits in different cities when they refused to accept jobs involving work on Saturdays. The other major agencies were content to leave that issue to the American Jewish Congress, for as the legal director of the ADL explained, "the Congress got into it even before we were aware of it."[4]

Just as most Christians were apathetic about Sunday laws, so were most Jews. The religious revival of the postwar years did not herald a mass return to Orthodoxy, and traditional Sabbath observance, except among the very religious, was a thing of the past. Jews may have kept certain Sabbath rituals, but few felt bound by Jewish *halakha* (as evidenced by the parking lots in Orthodox as well as Conservative suburban synagogues for Sabbath worshipers). Rabbis urged congregants to avoid social functions on the Sabbath, and they appealed to national Jewish organizations not to schedule conventions for Saturday. Some also protested the Saturday schedule of football games by Brandeis University. The problem of Sabbath laxity was recognized by all branches of American Judaism. Calling for a stricter observance of the Sabbath, the Union of Orthodox Rabbis declared in 1952 that "it was not necessary to violate the Sabbath in order to achieve success in the business and professional world." A survey of Conservative lay leaders in 1953 revealed that only one-third frequently attended Sabbath services. Those findings led to two moves within Conservative Judaism, one to reaffirm the centrality of Sabbath observance and one to relax minor regulations in Jewish law on Sabbath behavior.[5] According to all signs, American Jews who identified as religious observers were defining their own code of appropriate Sabbath practices.

Doubtless the laws that mandated Sunday closings, and official usages that ignored Jewish sensibilities, accounted in many instances for nonobservance of the traditional Sabbath. Merchants who could not afford the economic losses entailed in keeping closed on two days, or prospective applicants for the civil service who were required to take tests or to work on Saturdays, faced grave problems.[6] More often than not, economic pressures triumphed over religious scruples. And, as Jews increasingly abandoned or tailored their Sabbath rituals to accommodate to the marketplace, the more difficult it became for the observant minority.

Jewish nonobservance similarly impeded the fight against Sunday laws. Aware that most Jews did work on Saturdays, legislators refused to acknowledge inequities in the laws. When Louisiana's legislature resolved to hold primary elections on Saturdays, a united Jewish community, viewing the measure as somehow more discriminatory than Sunday laws, urged a veto by the governor. Governor Earl Long was unimpressed. The Jews had no right to protest, he said, since "they do not observe their Sabbath anyway." *Jewish Life,* the Orthodox magazine which reported the story, drew the obvious moral: so long as Jews desecrated their own Sabbath, they could not expect Christian respect for them or their Sabbath.[7]

With little to gain by exemptions, most Jews, especially in smaller cities, worried little about the recognition of Sunday as a holy day. Rather, concern about public relations within the community overshadowed any theoretical objection to old laws which had little or no impact. Where churches were in a position to threaten boycotts of stores that opened on Sundays, and where Jews were invited to join interfaith committees to protect Sunday observance, agitation against Sunday laws was an imprudent course. As late as 1963 the Jews of North Carolina insisted that the ADL refrain from action on a Sunday bill in their state even though the measure allowed no exemptions. They claimed that none of North Carolina's three thousand Jews kept their stores closed on Saturdays, and that "if we are going to need [Christian] favors, let's not use them up with 'this kind of nonsense.' "[8]

The Congress endeavored to rally Jewish sentiment by defining the issue in terms of equal rights. For all intents and purposes, however, the ranks of the Sunday law protesters drew only Sabbath-observing Jews. Under the direction of Orthodox agencies and the Congress, they were the ones who regularly lobbied in state capitals and brought suits in state courts. The ADL and AJC supported legislative exemptions for Sabbatarians, and they monitored developments within communities, weighing in particular any manifestations of anti-Semitism. Nevertheless, they stayed aloof from litigation until the end of the decade.[9]

Throughout the 1950s Pfeffer and the Congress followed a two-pronged approach, one to achieve relief through legislative action, the other to contest the laws in the courts. Logically, the two prongs were contradictory. The legislative side admitted the constitutionality of the regulations so long as they included the desired exemptions; the judicial thrust led to a challenge of the constitutionality of the Sunday law principle. Only insofar as both approaches aimed at relieving the burdens on Sabbatarians were they complementary. Pfeffer, the strict separationist, would have preferred to scrap all Sunday laws; they were violations, he iterated, of the principle of separation. Although he conscientiously fought for exemptions on pragmatic grounds, he aspired to more inclusive judicial victories. Even if Sunday laws were health measures—and he seriously questioned that premise, since those who were permitted, for example, to sell newspapers and cigarettes on Sundays did not enjoy a day of rest—they still amounted to unconstitutional abridgments of religious freedom. The time seemed ripe for litigation, because the broad interpretation of separation in *Everson* and *McCollum* suggested that the courts might reevaluate Sunday laws in a different light. Pfeffer pinned his hopes on the New York kosher butchers case of 1948, a possible "wedge by which much of the Sunday legislation of the United States may be overthrown."[10]

On a Sunday morning in November 1948 Sam Friedman and Sam Praska, kosher butchers in a predominantly Jewish neighborhood on the Lower East Side, were served summonses for selling uncooked meat. The butchers had not heeded a prior police warning to close their shops on Sundays, nor was this their first Sunday law violation. This time, however, counsel for the defense, Pfeffer, announced the Congress's intention of fighting the case to the Supreme Court. At the trial the butchers were convicted and fined ten dollars. Friedman admitted having sold the meat but, as his answers to the judge's questions revealed, he did not consider his actions a crime. ("I thought," he explained, that "when you make a holdup, that is a crime.") His defense—that he was a Sabbath observer who did not labor on that day, that the conduct of his business caused no disturbance to Sunday observers, and that violations of Sunday laws by large chain stores, amusement centers, and radio and television companies went unpunished—was not persuasive. Indeed, evidence attesting to large-scale commercial activities on Sunday, which was gathered for Pfeffer by members of Young Israel, was held irrelevant. Prevented from deviating from the narrow question of the sale of meat, Pfeffer could only retort: "There may be a serious question whether it is more important for people to eat meat than to see a burlesque show on Sunday."

The defense argued several points in its appeal to New York's higher courts, but they boiled down to one central issue. If exemptions were not provided for those who observed other days as holy time, the Sunday law stood as an unconstitutional violation of the establishment clause. Frankly admitting that proper exemptions would eliminate the need for judicial action, Pfeffer proceeded nevertheless to build up the case of unconstitutionality. The law, from its historical inception to the present, reflected religious motivation; its text and workings disproved the contention that it was a health measure; *Everson* and *McCollum,* both defining the meaning of separation, called for a new interpretation. The counsel stated: "While we have no desire to attack the Sunday law except as it affects those observing a day other than Sunday as holy time, it may well be that the constitutional deficiencies which render the law void against them, render it void against all." If we are unsuccessful before the court, he continued, we submit that the Sunday law "is in its entirety an unconstitutional law." Professor Alvin Johnson, a friend and a steadfast opponent of Sunday laws, was more impressed with the argument for unconstitutionality than for exemption. He understood, however, that Pfeffer had adopted "a shotgun charge,—that if one shot does not strike your objective, another one will."[11]

The appeal in *Friedman* had the support of Orthodox organizations as well as the SCA, the New York Board of Rabbis, and the Jewish War Veterans. In an *amicus* brief filed for all those agencies, the Congress argued forcefully for the equality of observers of the Sabbath. The issue of majority and minority was irrelevant in matters of religion; the "Sabbaths of the Christian, Jewish and other religions have equal standing under American tradition and constitutional principles." Drawing corroboration from Congressman Johnson's report on Sunday mails and even from John Stuart Mill's essay *On Liberty,* the brief waxed eloquent on the principle of religious liberty. It argued that even if construed as health measures, Sunday laws violated the liberty of Jews and Christian Sabbatarians.

It is interesting that whereas Pfeffer, the counsel for the butchers, concentrated on the establishment clause, the *amicus* brief prepared by his own organization focused on free exercise. Instead of urging the invalidation of Sunday laws, it argued merely that exemptions be made for those who observed another day of rest. Only then would "grave constitutional doubts as to the validity of the entire Sunday law" be avoided. Implicitly, it hinted at a trade-off: if Sabbatarians received full exemptions, legal challenges of the Sunday laws would be dropped. Having chosen that route, the *amici* mentioned neither the establishment clause nor the principles set down in *Everson* and *McCollum.*[12]

An opposing Jewish *amicus* brief, the first time that Jewish groups were formally arrayed against each other in church–state litigation, was also filed. In this instance four kosher butcher unions of New York City spoke for the defense. They contended that the Sunday law was not a religious, but a welfare measure which promoted the health of the kosher butcher and provided him with a five-day work week. For that same reason the unions opposed the passage of a fair Sabbath law. Most startling, the same butchers were apparently financing the (Protestant) Lord's Day Alliance![13]

The state courts turned down the *Friedman* appeal. Sticking closely to precedent, New York's highest court insisted that Sunday laws were health measures which in no way constituted an establishment of religion or a denial of equal protection of the laws. Nor was it the court's duty to review the motives or question the wisdom of the legislature: "A plea that a statute imposes inconvenience or hardship upon a litigant should be addressed to the Legislature." When the Supreme Court refused to review the case for want of a substantial federal question, anti–Sunday law agitation in New York took the route advised by the Court of Appeals. For more than ten years pressure was brought to bear on state lawmakers in a struggle marked by partisan wrangling and Jewish–Catholic acrimony.[14]

As for the Supreme Court's inaction, Will Maslow of the Congress commented cynically that it was "another indicator of the increasing practice of that court of ducking important issues." Despite the defeat in New York, the Congress took pride in the case of the kosher butchers. Pfeffer later explained: "Every one of the innumerable challenges to Blue Laws brought in courts all over the country during the ensuing 25 years was based on one or more of the claims asserted and rejected in the *Friedman* case." Having pioneered toward that end, the Congress was prepared to assist in similar litigation in other states. It confidently predicted that it was only a matter of time until the Supreme Court, helped by decisions in the states, would invalidate Sunday laws.[15]

The Commercialization of Sunday

"Which has contributed more to the present fuss over Sunday closing laws," the ADL's legal director wondered facetiously in 1958, "Henry Ford or the Fourth Commandment?" Indeed, by the mid-1950s the automobile explosion that accompanied the development of suburbia had turned Sunday laws into "one of the country's hottest issues." The stream of retail stores that opened along well-trafficked highways appealed to the now more mobile shoppers by keeping open on Sundays and by discounting standard prices. Consumer appetite was whetted by double-page spreads in Sunday newspapers touting the wares—furniture, TVs, appliances—that were available that day in bargain centers on the outskirts of the city. But although Americans saw the chance to combine a Sunday afternoon drive with attractive bargains, they were loath to discard traditional beliefs about the holiness of Sunday. A survey of greater Detroit residents, for example, revealed that although most were unwilling to support legislation for Sunday closings, a majority still believed that "Sunday shopping is usually or always morally wrong."[16]

The rapid commercialization of Sundays brought new life and new participants into the struggle that had previously been confined mainly to Sabbatarians and their religious opponents. A survey conducted by the JAC in 1958 and innumerable reports from local and regional ADL representatives revealed the new forces at work across the country. The data proved how the economic issue divided groups within the same community. Downtown merchants sought stronger observance of the traditional rest day, and their suburban competitors agitated for the right to stay open on seven days. Labor divided too. Usually unions favored closing laws in order to preserve a reduced work week, but some supported Sunday openings as a way of earning overtime pay. Economic interests in favor of Sunday laws often made common cause with religious groups. It was the Chamber of Commerce of Oshkosh and not a church that campaigned to "put the Sabbath back in your life." The Minnesota Retail Federation also mouthed pious words: "[Sunday] is, and should be, a day of rest for everybody. . . . Commercializing Sunday could become a national shame." Since it was difficult to avoid conflicts between the spiritual and economic, some churches grew increasingly uncomfortable over a marriage with the business interests. Nevertheless, Protestants made use of the ad hoc alliance for shoring up the Christian Sabbath or for their own partisan purposes. For the Lord's Day Alliance it meant stronger efforts in most states; for some Protestants it offered a way of "keeping up with the Catholics" in religious zeal.

Many businessmen now sought the solution for an economic problem in laws whose original purpose was religious. Pressures mounted for stiffer laws and for stricter enforcement; since a great number of the new stores were outside city limits, state legislation rather than municipal ordinances became a primary focus. Efforts for stricter legislative enforcement were supplemented by voluntary closing movements in different cities. A "Respect Sunday" group, initiated by downtown merchants and endorsed by the Ministerial Association, sprang up in Indianapolis. Using a high-powered public relations firm, the group conducted a door-to-door campaign soliciting merchants not to sell, and families not to buy, on Sundays. Cleveland had a similar organization, "Sunday, Inc.," and St. Louis boasted of a Catholic-sponsored campaign called "Don't Shop on Sunday."[17] The voluntary efforts promised to rally public support against legislative or judicial challenges to traditional laws. They also bore serious implications for Jewish–Christian relations.

Jews now became more involved as well. Jewish retailers, like their Christian counterparts, clashed with one another in the contest between downtown firms and highway stores. Often the profit motive erased religious lines and allied Jews with Christians against other Jews and Christians. Some Jews demanded enforcement of the Sunday laws; some cooperated actively in interfaith voluntary enforcement organizations. Jewish city merchants in New Jersey, who led the campaign for strict laws, even registered opposition to exemptions for Sabbath observers! There were also Jews who were not Sabbath observers who demanded legislative relief for Sabbatarians out of a desire to keep open on Sundays. A Conservative rabbi of St. Paul denounced that subterfuge in his community: "I challenge anyone to find more than two Jewish businesses in St. Paul that are closed on Saturday . . . outside the kosher butcher shops. I ask simply are we worthy of being defended on this issue?" In principle the Jewish community relations councils (JCRCs) consistently opposed the laws as sectarian and in violation of freedom of conscience, but the economic dimension made a shambles of Jewish unity.[18]

The fundamental issue was one that was raised but not addressed at a meeting of NCRAC. If Sunday laws became an issue of economic rather than religious interest, did Jews qua Jews have a stake any longer in the matter? Were they, a group which largely abided by the American definition that they were a religious community, prepared to invoke the protection of the religion clauses of the Constitution for nonreligious reasons? The questions were not merely theoretical. In Pittsburgh, for example, the anti–Sunday closings group naturally expected assistance from the Jewish community. But was there a proper *Jewish* response? Should Jews confine their concern to the rights of Sabbatarians or should they oppose Sunday laws on broad libertarian grounds and fight for Christians and Jews who were not closed on Saturdays?[19]

Divisiveness over Sunday laws plagued both the Jewish and the Christian communities, but the broadened issue raised special problems for the Jewish minority. One concerned the attempts of downtown stores, aiming to offset the appeal of Sunday shopping, to make Friday night a shopping night. Outside the large metropolises, Friday evening services had come to supersede Saturday services in importance; thus, Jews in cities like Fort Wayne, Indiana, and Louisville, Kentucky, were torn apart still further. In Fort Wayne, the rabbis opposed Friday night openings, but the Jewish merchants divided. In Louisville, where the community's sentiment ran against late Friday openings, Jews hesitated about taking a public stand. The ADL counseled inaction. If the Jews opposed Friday night openings, they might be asked: "What makes the Sabbath Eve more sacrosanct than the Sabbath Day and if you insist on Friday night closing, why don't you logically ask that the stores be closed until sundown on the Sabbath?" Christians unsympathetic to traditional Sabbath observers would hardly have understood the sociological evolution of Jewish religious behavior in America.[20]

A second problem was that of community relations. The Jewish fear of arousing Christian hostility on the issue of Sunday laws had not disappeared. Rather, it was compounded now in the face of the religious–economic alliance of the pro-Sunday forces. Since the religious component of that alliance had become more aggressive, Jews in some communities were unable to resist the pressure to join interfaith enforcement groups. Although Jews themselves divided on the issue, Sunday law advocates in some cities portrayed them as the chief offenders. Where the image of "the Jew" was superimposed on the Sunday law question, and where Christian groups appealed specifically to Christians, obvious anti-Semitic feelings surfaced. In Pittsburgh, Protestant and Catholic Sunday observers, goaded by the radio message "See you in Church on Sunday," threatened strikes, pickets, and boycotts against all businesses that opened on Sunday. It was unrealistic to expect such campaigns to make exceptions for Sabbath observers who kept closed on Saturdays. Some Jews, out of economic self-interest, may have deviated from the anti–Sunday law policy of the JCRCs, but their defection did not automatically endear them to the defenders of a Christian Sabbath. Recognizing their isolation from both Protestants and Catholics, Ohio's Jews chose not to become involved on either side in the Sunday closing campaign.[21]

A new and significant component in the Sunday law controversy appeared in the form of Catholic activism. Displacing the Protestants, who until the 1950s had been *the* defenders of Sunday and Sunday laws, Catholics became the aggressive guardians of the American Protestant Sabbath. Their opposition to Sunday law amendments, the chancery office in New York City explained, derived from Catholic religious beliefs and American traditions. Leo Pfeffer offered a different explanation: adjustment to America and the desire to break the Protestant–humanist monopoly over the direction of American culture accounted for the Catholic stand. Whatever the reasons, a survey by the Congress concluded that the Catholic church in most communities had become the most influential protagonist of Sunday legislation.[22]

The Sunday issue exacerbated Jewish–Catholic tensions. Since the end of the war the two groups had clashed on church–state issues such as released time, moral and spiritual values, school prayers, an ambassador to the Vatican, and government aid to parochial schools. Often Catholic spokesmen and periodicals singled out the Jews as the secularist, atheistic menace to the American way of life. For their part Jews saw a Catholic threat to the wall of separation. An early AJC memorandum likened the Catholic concept of a wall to "a beautifully kept low hedge, pierced in twenty-four place and intended to be a mere visual link of demarcation instead of an impassable barrier." Now, on the Sunday issue, one Catholic newspaper asserted that a Christian nation had to keep its holy days holy. It said in defense of Sunday closings: "There are minority groups who may not like what we are doing. Are we going to give each one of them the veto power—something like the Russians have in the U.N. Security Council?"[23] (One doubts whether the mention of the Russians, which triggers an association to the Jew–Communist charge, was unconscious.) Not surprisingly, in cities like New York and Boston, Catholic political power continued to impede Jewish efforts at Sunday law reform.

Given the sensitivity of the issue and the divisions within the Jewish community, national organizations were hard put to articulate policy. All had followed the loose rule of thumb of favoring exemptions for Sabbath observers, but now the problem spawned many questions. For one thing, should the agencies limit their efforts to the attainment of exemptions or should they fight all Sunday laws as unconstitutional? Second, if exemptions were the goal, who should be exempt? Those who kept closed on a day other than Sunday or only those who "conscientiously"—and how would that be proved—observed the Sabbath? Were *businesses* that were closed on Sundays for religious reasons to be exempted or *employees* who opted for a rest day other than Sunday? If only employees, then theoretically, as the Catholic lay organizations of New York maintained, businesses could well be operated on seven days.

Each major defense agency continued to advocate exemptions for Sabbath observers. The AJC, which liked to recall the efforts of Louis Marshall on behalf of Sabbatarians, came out in favor of those who conscientiously believed in a rest day other than Sunday. It opposed the enactment of new Sunday laws, but if such laws appeared imminent, it called for the inclusion of exemptions. To avoid strife within the communities, President Irving Engel suggested the formation of interfaith advisory commissions to cope with the Sunday problem. The Congress, on the other hand, held on to two goals, exemptions and the unconstitutionality of all Sunday laws. In this manner it begged a basic question: If Sabbath observers received appropriate exemptions, would the Congress still consider the laws to be unconstitutional? Meantime, Congress members in different states lobbied for exemptions.[24]

Differences of opinion abounded within the agencies. A poll taken of the National Civil Rights Committee of the ADL in 1957 is illustrative. Of the thirty members, seventeen voted to oppose Sunday laws which did not exempt Sabbatarians, five voted to oppose the laws unconditionally, one voted to oppose the laws if they were couched in religious terms, six said that the ADL should take no position, and one had no opinion. (The final decision followed the majority of seventeen.) The ADL's regional boards were divided as well: the Chicago executive voted for opposition to all Sunday closing laws; the Southeastern board, by a narrow margin, voted to oppose laws that contained no exemptions; the Northern California board voted unanimously to oppose all closing laws, but the Southern California board, opposed in principle, voted to accept exemptions. Here again, regional differences and the autonomy of the local synagogues and communities accounted for the variations.[25]

The resolution adopted by NCRAC and the SCA in 1957 was also a compromise. It stated that Sunday laws violated the principle of religious freedom by compelling people to conform to a law which was intrinsically religious. It opposed the "enactment or expansion" of Sunday laws, but it was prepared to settle for less: "We urge that at the very least Sunday observance laws be amended to exempt . . . persons whose religious convictions compel them to observe a day other than Sunday as a religious day of rest." The resolution affirmed its support of legislation requiring a day of rest, but it suggested that the choice of the day be left to the individual. In principle the defense organization went beyond a negative on Sunday laws. Divorcing the issue from religion and religious choice, it gave its approval to the idea of a one-in-seven rest day.[26]

In 1958 moves for stricter enforcement of Pennsylvania's Sunday law aroused Jewish concern. The law of 1794 had been modified over the years, but the flavor of the original act remained. Phrases like "Christian Sabbath," "worldly employment," and "profanation of the Lord's Day" still proclaimed the religious origins and purposes of the law. Now, in the middle of the twentieth century the state looked back to that eighteenth-century religious law to remedy a modern, largely economic situation. Rabbi Harold Silver of Pittsburgh described in two sermons devoted to the topic— itself an indicator of the significance of the issue for Jews—how the problem had spread across the state, "like an enveloping cloud, first in the eastern half of Pennsylvania, then in the central portion, and now here in Allegheny County." The rabbi proceeded to argue the unconstitutionality of all Sunday laws; exemptions for Orthodox Jews might appear to be an equitable solution, but that did not touch the root of the problem. "Under our Federal Constitution," Silver said, "the State has *no right* to legislate on this particular matter regarding Jewish . . . or Christian Sabbath observance."[27] However, as a Harrisburg conference of the state's major Jewish communities would prove, Silver's stand was too extremist for most Jews.

Representatives of eight communities who met at the state capital in September 1958 shared common experiences. The rapid commercialization of Sunday divided Jews in all cities according to economic interests, and no longer could they be counted on to oppose Sunday laws. The president of the Merchants Association who appealed for Sunday closings in Scranton was Jewish; a Jewish district attorney in Pittsburgh prosecuted Jewish violators of Sunday laws even though they were Sabbath observers; Jews in Philadelphia, rather than Catholics or Protestants, appeared to be the prime agitators on both sides. The gloomy picture of Jewish disunity was compounded by the realities: repeal of Sunday laws was impossible, further exemptions were unlikely, and interreligious tensions were on the rise.

Clearly, NCRAC's official stand did not mesh with the economic interests within the communities. Nor were the divided communities prepared to speak out, as NCRAC had, against the expansion of Sunday laws. Although legislative action for stricter enforcement was anticipated, none of the JCRCs would advise that Jews risk Christian hostility, particularly on a losing proposition, by calling for the liberalization of the law. Furthermore, if liberalization became a Jewish issue, it might well boomerang and result in more onerous laws. At an impasse, the conferees opted for the status quo. They would neither campaign for repeal nor seek further exemptions unless there was a movement to strengthen the law. Tacitly admitting the uselessness of NCRAC's stand, they agreed that local communities would decide policy in specific situations. The only positive result of the conference was the establishment of a closer working relationship among the communities and between them and the JAC.[28]

A few months later the JAC succeeded in rallying the major Jewish communities of Pennsylvania to oppose a bill that significantly increased the penalties for Sunday violations. Asking the state legislature to exempt Sabbath observers, the Jewish plea was in keeping with the decisions made at the Harrisburg conference. Pfeffer prepared a statement which was presented to a committee of the lower house by the JCRC of Philadelphia and three other communities. Very similar to a polished court brief, it challenged the constitutionality of Sunday laws, calling them an establishment of religion and a violation of religious liberty. It went on, however, to add two points. First, each person could be required to keep his business closed one day a week, but the choice of the day should be his. Second, under any circumstances, the law should provide exemptions for those who observed any other day as a religious day of rest.[29] The "shotgun" approach of *Friedman*—the erection of multiple targets in order to increase the chances of hitting at least one—was still operative.

Two other Jewish statements took a narrower approach. The Pennsylvania Regional Board of the ADL, emphasizing the need for government impartiality toward all religions, called only for exemptions. The Rabbinical Association of Philadelphia also argued exclusively for the religious needs of Sabbath observers. In a nonlegal but more eloquent statement, Rabbi Moses Burak described the importance and beauty of the Sabbath for Jews and the economic sacrifice required of a Jewish businessman who fulfilled his religious duty. He also insisted that a law which ignored the observer's need for exemptions was discriminatory and fostered inequality: "We ask that the Jewish community be granted the same religious freedom in observing its Sabbath as is granted to our Christian brothers in regard to their Sunday. Even as you do not say to the Christian community 'If you want to observe Sunday, you must also stay closed on Saturday,' so, you should not say to Sabbath observers—'If you stay closed on Saturday, you must also stay closed on Sunday.' "[30]

The Jewish statements, along with one from the Seventh-Day Adventists, failed to sway the lower house. Ironically, the forces in favor of the bill were headed by a Jew, a wealthy businessman and owner of department stores in Philadelphia, who feared that the success of highway shopping would kill the downtown area. Jewish efforts for exemptions by legislative action continued, but by the time the new law took effect in September 1959, the focus of attention had turned to the courts.[31]

The "Shomer Shabbos" Cases

With little debate the Jewish defense agencies agreed to limit their involvement in Sunday litigation. They would take a stand only where religious rather than commercial interests were directly concerned and where
the equal rights of Sabbath-observing litigants were at stake. Some individual Jewish businessmen may have sympathized with a discount chain
(Two Guys from Harrison) that brought an anti–Sunday closing suit out
of economic motives alone, but the agencies held a narrower view. An
economic point of departure was far afield from action appropriate to
Jewish groups. Even if argued in civil libertarian terms, a blatant economic
motive could lend credence to anti-Semitic stereotypes. Only by ignoring
crass materialism could Jews hope to challenge the Protestant and Catholic
defenders of a religious day of rest. Besides, a religious focus could sooner
attract the not insignificant support of rabbinical groups.[32]

In 1959 a suit in Massachusetts, *Crown Kosher Super Market* v. *Gallagher,* challenged the religious discrimination inherent in Sunday laws. So
determined was Herbert Ehrmann, attorney for the plaintiffs, to preserve
a religious appearance that in the early stages of the case he refused to
permit supporting briefs from secular Jewish agencies. Doubtless the outspoken stand and political clout of the Catholics sharpened his concern—
indeed, the Archdiocesan Council of Catholic Men filed an *amicus* brief
in support of the laws—and Ehrmann insisted on religious allies, Jewish
and Christian, only.[33]

Ehrmann's client was a food market in Springfield which catered to the
needs of Orthodox Jews within a radius of thirty miles. Owned and operated
by Orthodox Jews, Crown Kosher closed at sundown on Friday and remained closed throughout Saturday. The shopping habits of its clientele
explained why over one-third of the market's weekly sales were made on
Sunday. Crown Kosher regularly kept open on Sundays until Springfield
moved to enforce the state law. After the police chief threatened to arrest
all employees if the market flouted the law, and after the market was
convicted in state courts, Crown Kosher, some of its customers, and the
rabbi responsible for its *kashruth* brought suit in a federal court. In the
course of the proceedings Ehrmann charged that just as the plaintiffs were
concerned primarily about religious issues so was the state. He argued that
the Massachusetts Sunday law, the "Lord's Day Act," still aimed at im-
posing a Christian Sabbath. How else, but for the purpose of noninterference with church services, could one explain the hours restricting retail
sales and recreational activities? Furthermore, the law made no exemptions
for Sabbatarians.[34]

Rumor had it that the court would express its sympathy with the plaintiffs but would hold, as the Supreme Court had in *Friedman,* that no

substantial federal question was involved. To the delight of Ehrmann, by then the president of the AJC, and his supporters, the court found the Sunday law unconstitutional. The decision, written by Calvert Magruder, a highly respected judge, stated that the law violated both religion clauses of the First Amendment. Emphasizing the hardships imposed on Orthodox Jews, Magruder attacked the condition of religious inequality created by the statute: "What Massachusetts has done ... is to furnish special protection to the dominant Christian sects which celebrate Sunday as the Lord's Day, without furnishing such protection in their religious observances to those Christian sects and to Orthodox and Conservative Jews who observe Saturday as the Sabbath, and to the prejudice of the latter group."[35]

The decision revived efforts throughout Massachusetts both for and against Sunday closings. It also unleashed a storm of Catholic protest. The *Boston Pilot* angrily charged that the ruling was subversive of the good order of the community and discriminatory in favor of those who observed a day other than Sunday. It advised religious Christians to resist changes in the law for the sake of preserving Christian worship and observance. Richard Cardinal Cushing, warning that the American Sunday would fast become like Sunday in godless Russia, expressed his outrage. He urged that the traditional day of rest be defended against attack by those "who would destroy religion in the name of democracy." Similar sentiments were echoed in *America* by Father Robert Drinan, who pointed out the social dangers inherent both in "unqualified" religious freedom and in the doctrine that the state must be "a total stranger to the faith of its people." To be sure, Catholics sympathized with those who observed another day of rest, he said, but the hardships they bore were no different from the economic penalty imposed on supporters of parochial schools.[36]

The Jewish organizations refused to respond to the Catholic assault. They prudently chose to keep silent and let the decision, which, they said, stood as a victory for religious liberty and not for the Jews, speak for itself. At the same time they grew more optimistic about the chances of toppling the Sunday laws in the Supreme Court.[37]

Attention shifted back to Pennsylvania where suits testing the constitutionality of the new law cropped up in various parts of the state. But despite the victory in *Crown Kosher,* not all Jews were prepared to participate. A report from Erie County, for example, related that even merchants who were adversely affected shied away from legal action. One observer explained that the new law intensified the Jewish feeling of "difference," a feeling heightened by public reaction to the issues of Bible reading and Sunday laws. "Implicit in many of the editorial and pulpit discussions," he said, "is the belief that Jews have prospered in a 'Christian society' and owe it to their neighbors not to insist upon their rights in matters deemed fundamental to the Christian majority." In Philadelphia, however, a suit which was begun before the law took effect mustered overwhelming local and national Jewish support. Abraham Braunfeld and four other retailers, all Orthodox Jews who closed their shops from sundown Friday until sundown Saturday, were mobilized by Congress members in a suit that charged discrimination under the statute.[38] Known in Jewish circles as the "shomer Shabbos" (Sabbath observer) case, *Braunfeld* v. *Gibbons* (later *Braunfeld* v. *Brown*) along with *Crown Kosher* ultimately reached the Supreme Court.

All the Jewish agencies had agreed to confine their involvement to cases of Sabbatarians, but they differed over the proper range of arguments. Should they adopt a broad approach, one that argued the points of religious establishment and economic discrimination as well as religious liberty, or should they restrict themselves to religious liberty alone? The AJC and ADL favored the latter course, which better fitted their policy of accepting Sunday laws so long as they provided proper exemptions for Sabbatarians. The Congress, which by now stood against all Sunday laws, preferred a wider range of attack. It turned out that the distinction was virtually meaningless. As *amici* on Braunfeld's behalf, the AJC and ADL moved beyond their official policy statements and like the Congress also attacked Sunday laws on the grounds of religious establishment.[39] Nevertheless, the primary emphasis on religious liberty and free exercise set off the Jewish from the commercial cases (*Two Guys from Harrison* v. *McGinley, McGowan* v. *Maryland*), where the establishment clause was the cardinal element.[40]

The *Braunfeld* case opened in a federal district court in Philadelphia. In oral argument and written briefs, both sides addressed the religious issue. The attorney for Philadelphia, in support of a motion for dismissal, flatly denied that the law collided with the First Amendment. The Supreme Court had ruled that only when a statute interfered *directly* with a First Amendment right could the court intervene, and here the law in no way impinged on the freedom of the retailers to observe their Sabbath. Whether or not the original Sunday laws were enacted to protect the Christian Sabbath was irrelevant. The present statutes were civil regulations, and the Jewish complaint concerned indirect and economic, but not religious, interference. One of the attorneys again raised the point that the economic loss to Orthodox Jews was analogous to that of parents who sent their children to parochial schools. Yet, he said, the choice of parochial schools did not invalidate public school taxes.

For the plaintiffs, attorney Theodore Mann contended in his oral presentation that the Sunday law "tends to diminish the effective exercise" of his clients' religion. Stressing the centrality of the biblically ordained Sabbath in the life of the Orthodox Jew, he described how observant Jews behaved on the Sabbath. Indeed, their deportment was the model to which early legislatures aspired when they enacted Sunday laws for American Christians. The lawyer claimed that at least one of his clients would be forced out of business if compelled to obey both the Sunday law and his religious law. Was it fair, he asked, for Pennsylvania to choose Sunday, the day of rest of but one of several religions, and thereby impose a crippling handicap on non-Christians? Mann's arguments were buttressed by Pfeffer, who spoke as attorney for the Rabbinical Association and Board of Rabbis of Philadelphia. Urging a broad interpretation of religious freedom in order to preserve the equality of a minority faith, he said: "The history of religious liberty in this country has been in large measure the history of a struggle against attempts to put an economic burden . . . upon the practice of unpopular or minority religions."

Both plaintiffs and defendants invoked numerous precedents, from the pre–Civil War *Specht* case to the recent butchers case. With respect to the latter, the defendants enjoyed an advantage. While they had merely to insist that *Braunfeld,* like *Friedman,* failed to raise a substantial federal question, their opponents, in order to keep the suit alive, had to prove how the two cases differed. The exact opposite held true with respect to *Crown Kosher.* That opinion gave the plaintiffs a weighty precedent, while the Sunday law supporters were forced to argue that Pennsylvania's law differed qualitatively from that of Massachusetts.[41]

The district court dismissed the complaint of Braunfeld and the others, and the case, along with *Two Guys, McGowan,* and *Crown Kosher,* was accepted for review by the Supreme Court. *Amicus* briefs were filed by the Jewish agencies, one by the AJC and ADL for *Crown Kosher* and one by NCRAC and the SCA for both *Crown Kosher* and *Braunfeld.* Although the setting was the Supreme Court instead of a state court, and although the First Amendment was now binding upon the states, the underlying Jewish arguments had not changed substantially since the nineteenth century. The briefs talked at length about the Christian nature and purpose of the statutes, which were not eradicated by calling them police or health regulations, and about the inviolability of religious freedom. They also pressed for religious equality. Pointing to the inferior status foisted upon non-Christians by the laws, the AJC and ADL argued that court dicta on a "Christian nation," like Justice Brewer's remarks in *Holy Trinity,* which were still nurtured by institutions like Sunday laws, were no longer acceptable. A twentieth-century emendation to the plea for freedom of religion appeared in the SCA–NCRAC brief. Now the agencies insisted that they would speak out even if Jews were not specifically involved: "We would be concerned even if Braunfeld and the proprietors of Crown Kosher were not Jews or observers of the seventh day of the week as the Sabbath. We believe that the principle of religious liberty is impaired if any person is penalized for adhering to his religious beliefs . . . so long as he neither interferes with the rights of others nor endangers the public peace or security."[42]

In May 1961 the Supreme Court dealt a severe setback to the Sunday law challengers when it upheld the statutes of Pennsylvania, Maryland, and Massachusetts. In all four (two "religious" and two "commercial") cases the decisions rejected the arguments based on the establishment clause. Eight of the nine justices agreed that the laws were health measures and that a secular law which happened to coincide with a religious purpose did not make that law religious. Having disposed thereby of the two discount house cases, six justices joined in denying that religious liberty, the heart of the Jewish cases, was violated by Sunday laws. They employed the age-old reasoning: the laws neither interfered with the minority's beliefs nor forbade anything commanded by the Jewish religion. According to Chief Justice Earl Warren, Sunday laws only made the practice of Orthodox Jewish beliefs more expensive. To be sure, states could enact one-in-seven rest day laws, or they could provide exemptions for Sabbatarians, but, he said, they were liable thereby to stir up other constitutional or administrative problems.

Justice William O. Douglas, the lone dissenter in the two discount house cases, claimed that the laws, which served and satisfied Christians, constituted an establishment of religion. He stressed the unfairness to Orthodox Jews, and in language similar to that employed by the Jewish litigants before the district court he argued that the economic sanctions carried by the statutes violated the religious freedom of Jews. Justices William Brennan and Potter Stewart also dissented in the religious liberty cases. They asserted that the right of religious freedom transcended the "convenience" of a state health measure; it certainly outweighed the majority's suggestion that Sabbatarians who worked on Sundays held an advantage over their competitors. Sunday laws were a "clog upon the exercise of religion," a state-imposed burden upon Orthodox Jews. Without provisions for exemptions, "their effect is that no one may at one and the same time be an Orthodox Jew and compete effectively with his Sunday-observing fellow tradesmen."[43]

Jewish optimism in the wake of Magruder's opinion in *Crown Kosher* had obviously been misplaced. Pfeffer called *Braunfeld* "the nadir of free exercise," but he attempted to find bright spots in the otherwise bleak picture. He saw an advance over *Friedman,* where the Court had refused to review the issue; moreover, the door to further litigation was left open. Nor did the cases undo previous victories of the separationists. Although only three justices who had participated in *Everson* and *McCollum* were still on the bench, the Court unanimously upheld the broad interpretation of the First Amendment, and even Justice Douglas saw fit to explain that his dictum in *Zorach,* "We are a religious people," was not meant to approve government measures on behalf of religion.[44]

Catholics, on the other hand, read a far different interpretation into the rulings. According to Father Drinan, the decisions repudiated the "doctrinaire interpretation" of the First Amendment by the Congress and the

ACLU, and despite Black's definition of separation, "the state may provide for the common good in a manner which may indirectly aid a religion or even prefer one religion over another." Shortly after the decisions, however, Catholic intransigence on modifications of Sunday laws ebbed; Drinan, for example, came out in favor of exemptions for Sabbatarians. Whether or not it reflected the new spirit generated by Pope John XXIII and Vatican II, or, at the other extreme, a desire to cultivate Orthodox Jewish support for aid to parochial schools, the change in attitude abetted Jewish efforts to obtain legislative relief. Within the next decade broad exemptions for Sabbatarians were secured in New York, Pennsylvania, and Massachusetts, the home states of *Friedman, Braunfeld,* and *Crown Kosher.*[45]

It would seem logical to assume that Jews, especially the Orthodox, were united in opposition to the Sunday decisions. Yet in this instance, too, opinion was much divided. Usually the Orthodox lamented the injustice of Sunday laws to minorities, but a few, mostly right-wingers, believed that a divorce of Sunday laws from religious considerations entailed greater dangers, namely, the triumph of materialism and the "subjugation of the religious heritage as an irrelevant, rather than focal, factor in the life of man and society." Writing for an Orthodox periodical under the title "Is America a Christian Country?" one rabbi agreed with the Court's rulings. The Orthodox who defended Sabbath laws in Israel, he stated, could not in all good conscience plead for the abolition of Sunday laws in America. Nor could the traditional Jew who believed that religion should govern all human activities deny American Christians the right to breathe their religious beliefs into the law. To insist on separation between religion and government in a country whose core was Christian contradicted the tenets of Judaism: "To assert that the influence of Christianity should stop at the chambers of the legislature is to deny to the Christian faith what we claim for our own." He suggested, however, that the Orthodox make a concentrated effort to secure full exemptions for Sabbath observers. Their activity would prove to the Christian that Jewish opposition to Sunday laws was not motivated solely by economic interests and that Jews were not challenging the laws as they applied to non-Sabbatarians. "The goal is freedom of worship, not disestablishment."[46]

Hitherto unschooled in the tactics of political lobbying, Orthodox Jews, right-wingers like Agudath Israel as well as the Rabbinical Council, were spurred by the decisions to push vigorously for legislative redress. The desire to break the secularist monopoly of Jewish defense and create a public Jewish image distinct from the big three accompanied the new assertiveness. Indeed, many of the Orthodox believed that such an association on the issue of Sunday laws actually impeded the drive for exemptions. Marvin Schick, a political scientist and an advocate of government accommodation of Orthodox interests, described how the fight for exemptions in New York took a positive turn only with Orthodox participation. He told that when legislative hearings were scheduled in 1962 on the issue of exemptions, the Congress and several dozen Orthodox leaders appeared in Albany. "The hearings got off dully, with Dr. Leo Pfeffer dominating the scene, speaking and deciding who would speak and in what order; it was not until some bearded rabbis made their plea in broken English (and if my memory serves me right, one spoke in Yiddish) that the advocates of fair play made any impact on legislators who were not Jewish and not from New York City." An Orthodox delegation met shortly thereafter with Governor Nelson Rockefeller, leading the governor to comment that he understood for the first time how onerous the closing laws were to Sabbatarians. The implication was obvious: pressure for exemptions by Jews who themselves did not observe the Sabbath was useless if not counterproductive.[47]

By 1966 the National Jewish Commission on Law and Public Affairs (COLPA), an Orthodox legal agency serviced by young Orthodox lawyers, was fully entrenched, raising the image and the political clout of the Jewish traditionalists. From the beginning its commitment to the protection of Sabbath observers—their rights under Sunday laws and their defense against discrimination in employment—was paramount. While the secular agencies also participated in those matters, they were poles apart from COLPA on its other main objective, government aid to parochial schools. Agudath Israel rejoiced in its autonomy. Freed from a "distorted reverence" for the powers of the Jewish establishment, it would dispense with the "hired-Kaddish" (a person hired by a mourner to recite the obligatory memorial prayer) and fight its own battles.[48]

The Supreme Court did not repudiate *Braunfeld*, but it appeared to have second thoughts about the conflict between Sunday laws and religious liberty. In 1963 it decided in *Sherbert* v. *Verner* that a state could not deny unemployment benefits to a Seventh-Day Adventist who refused to take a job requiring work on Saturdays. Now, two years after *Braunfeld*, the Court admitted that economic penalties on Sabbatarians constituted a violation of the free exercise clause, and that only a "compelling state interest" could justify such infringements. Legal analysts have said that the Court's efforts to reconcile *Sherbert* with *Braunfeld* were at best strained, but they were more impressed by the Court's positive embrace of religious freedom and its retreat from the older principle of secular regulation.[49]

The Jewish agencies, whose *amicus* briefs on behalf of *Sherbert* were built on the free exercise argument, were delighted with the decision. Pfeffer hailed it as another sign that religious pluralism had come of age. True, the constitutionality of Sunday laws stood, but if legislative exemptions were secured and if enforcement of the old laws continued to abate, the 1961 decision might not have to be overruled.[50] The Christian Sabbath, a hotly disputed issue since colonial times, had finally burned out.

A Rash of Symbols

"If Christian faiths are to be permitted to display their symbols upon public lands, then the same privilege must be given to non-Christian faiths, or there does exist a discrimination and a preference." With those words the city attorney of San Rafael, California, ruled in 1957 that it was unlawful to erect a forty-eight-foot cross on public property. He noted realistically that if other groups sought permission to erect religious symbols, their requests would doubtless be contested or denied. Before World War II, except for an occasional Hanukkah menorah in the schools, Jews never sought to parade their religious symbols publicly. They were, however, sensitive to Christian displays that put the non-Christian in a less than equal position. As early as 1880 the *American Israelite* had lashed out at a proposal introduced in Congress for paintings on the Capitol walls depicting the life of Jesus.[51]

From 1955 on the Jewish defense agencies recognized "a wave of . . . efforts to put up religious monuments in public places." A survey conducted by the JAC in 1958 disclosed that the trend was intensifying. Displays were both privately and governmentally sponsored, both permanent and temporary. Conventional seasonal displays like nativity scenes and Easter pageants, usually on school grounds, were most common. More recent were projects of a permanent nature: crucifixes in two of Indiana's public parks (one dedicated by the celebration of a Catholic Mass); the adoption in Minnesota of a centennial emblem which featured a cross (to mark, it was said, the significant role of the missionaries in the early history of the state); attempts in various states to display plaques of the Ten Commandments in classrooms, on courthouse lawns, and in city halls.[52] The overall issue posed a serious challenge to the defense bodies. Publicly supported Christian symbols and displays not only violated the principle of separation, but they proclaimed perhaps more convincingly than words that America was in fact a Christian nation.

The JAC formally opposed the presence of religious symbols on public property, stating that such displays divided communities and produced intergroup hostility. Yet many Jews were reluctant to protest religious displays, particularly when they were of long standing. Even Jews who did not grasp the ramifications of church–state separation well understood the problems of interreligious communal tensions. They may also have thought it was not the symbols, but protests by Jews against their display that caused the friction. Indeed, on this seemingly trivial matter, Christians resisted changes. Explaining the situation in suburbia, one New Jersey rabbi said: "Most of the suburban communities in which we live are but recently settled by Jews, and the resentment against the 'invasion' is at high voltage." For the newcomers to suggest the removal of long-accepted religious symbols, which the Christians defined as nonsectarian signs of goodwill, would ignite an explosive issue. Garnering scant support from Christian religious groups, and opting for a low profile, most JCRCs remained passive. Despite some offers of assistance from the ACLU, they showed little inclination for confrontational tactics. As one JCRC executive reported, each time a new situation developed, the majority of Jews swallowed their discomfort and agreed to do nothing.[53]

Some Christians did not hesitate to remind the few who did protest that America was a Christian nation. So said an Oklahoma court in upholding the erection of a chapel on public property; so said Mayor Richard Daley in defense of an elaborate crèche in Chicago's city hall. The archbishop of St. Paul, referring to objections to the cross in Minnesota's emblem, also warned: "If today's pressure removes the cross from the emblem that marks the past, tomorrow's pressure will attempt to tear it from our churches and homes."[54] The issue of religious displays corroborated the views of those who realized that certain public religious rituals could not be extirpated even in a secular society. It also confirmed the criticism leveled by some Jews against strict separationism: American legal safeguards notwithstanding, Jews living in a society whose culture was Christian were still in *galut*.

As in the volatile matter of religious holiday celebrations in the schools, the separationist agencies were far ahead of the local communities in arguing the unconstitutionality of religious displays. While the agencies equally opposed displays of the Hanukkah menorah, some local communities happily adopted the solution of joint displays at Christmas time. Supporters of joint celebrations regarded a lighted menorah alongside a large Christmas tree as a sign of Jewish respectability and acceptance. A rabbi of East Orange, New Jersey, described the impact of the joint display at the city hall: "A tremendous surge of pride on the part of Jews—adults and children alike—that, at last, in a community known for its anti-Semitism over the years, Judaism had come into its own and was accorded public recognition on the basis of equal respect." He insisted that the same level of respect could not have been won without the use of those symbols.[55]

According to a Congress report of 1956, the courts had broken their silence on the matter of religious displays only once. In 1952 a Louisiana court upheld the right of the Knights of Columbus to erect a statue to Mother Cabrini on a state highway. It reasoned that a religious statue would be unconstitutional but that the statue honored Mother Cabrini as a public figure who had served the welfare of the community at large.[56] The judicial record further deterred the Jews from pioneering in litigation on religious displays.

On September 12, 1956, Mayor Jesse Collyer appeared before the school board of Ossining, New York. Spokesman for a citizens' crèche committee in the community of fifteen thousand, he requested permission to erect a crèche on the high school lawn for the Christmas season. The purpose was "to put Christ back into Christmas." When the board approved the mayor's request, a number of citizens objected. What irked them in particular was the choice of a school site. Pointing to the availability of space at nearby churches, they urged the board to reconsider its action. Defenders of the display countered that any publicly owned property was an appropriate place for a religious symbol. Tensions rose within the village; one periodical wrote that "many residents began to treat the issue as if it meant being for or against God." At a public meeting in November the board reversed itself, voting to comply with the suggestion of the state's Department of Education to look for an alternative site. Since the faction in favor of a school display now grew more indignant, the board reversed itself a second time, again permitting the construction of the crèche on school grounds.[57]

Ossining's Jews divided along lines of principle versus intergroup amity; one Jewish merchant, who served on the crèche committee, gave the largest single contribution for the display. At first, the local rabbi tried to ignore any special interest of Jews in the public endorsement of Christian symbols. Noting the division within his congregation, he argued lamely that the display was an offense to all citizens and not merely to Jews. Willingly or unwillingly, however, Jews were dragged into the controversy. When a Jew, attorney Stanley Estrow, assumed a leading role in opposition to the display, he was singled out as a newcomer who was acting on behalf of "pressure groups of New York City." Not only did Estrow become the tool of the evil, foreign-dominated metropolis, but the common anti-Semitic device of distinguishing between good and bad Jews (here, established residents as opposed to newcomers and commuters) surfaced. A Protestant minister also reminded Ossining residents that theirs was a Christian community and a Christian nation. The local JCRC was alerted, but in light of Jewish disunity, the idea of a suit was dropped. Some may have rationalized that the board, aware of the friction it had caused, would act differently the following year.[58]

The Congress was eager to take on the challenge. Not only did the incident highlight the wave of religious displays, but it represented another facet of the problem that dominated the agenda of Jewish separationists in the 1950s, namely, religious practices in the schools. Research by the Congress revealed that the precise question of whether the placing of religious symbols in a public *school* was constitutional had never been litigated.[59] Religious symbols in schools, rather than on public property generally, narrowed the issue to controllable proportions. Indeed, the Supreme Court's decision in *McCollum* suggested a strong legal foundation: just as released time classes on school premises had been banned, so might religious symbols. Furthermore, a successful suit would be likely to strengthen general acceptance of Justice Black's broad definition of sep-

aration and simultaneously weaken the advantage scored by accommodationists under *Zorach*. In a decade abounding with schemes for school
prayers and programs of moral and spiritual values, a separationist victory
bearing on religion and the schools would be especially significant. Besides,
the Jewish community needed reassurance on two scores: first, that separationism was the correct route for Jewish defense; and second, that
insistence on equal rights through the divorce of church and state did not
necessarily cause an anti-Jewish backlash.

A year later, when Ossining's board of education again granted permission for the erection of a crèche on school grounds, opponents reluctantly decided that they had no alternative but to initiate legal action. The
rabbi now emerged as a forceful figure, determined to go along with litigation. Warned by a Protestant colleague that his agitation might hurt the
economic welfare of his congregants, he would not be dissuaded. The
exasperated minister concluded that the Jewish leader was the dupe of
trouble-making city residents.[60]

When the suit was filed, the crèche committee referred to the plaintiffs—a group that included Jews, Christians, Ethical Culturists, and nonbelievers—as the "dissident ten," a "militant minority" standing in
opposition to the majority's belief that the birth of Jesus "was the most
important single event in the history of the world." Except for those few,
"our non-Christian neighbors" were not offended by the display. The committee charged that most dissidents were not residents of Ossining, and it
cavalierly suggested that they "avoid gazing at the crib, if somehow it
offends their sensibilities."[61]

By this time the situation had engaged the attention of national religious
groups. Envisioning the possibility of serious intergroup friction accompanying litigation, the Board of Social and Economic Relations of the
Methodist Church decided to measure the level of community conflict that
had developed in the village. Under the direction of Reverend Dean M.
Kelley, a survey was conducted of the opinions and actions of Ossining's
lay and religious leaders. Unlike other episodes that raised communal
tensions in the 1950s, the Ossining controversy received dispassionate study
while it was still under way.

The survey documented the divisions among Jews and it also calculated
that Christian opinion ran two to one in favor of the display on school
grounds. Quoting a few interviewees, it revealed some sharp words that
were leveled at "Jewish troublemakers." Nevertheless, the anticipated
storm did not break out. There were neither boycotts of Jewish businesses
nor more extreme measures. The study suggested that a half-page ad by
a Jewish merchant asking the town to receive the final verdict peaceably
might well have contributed to the soothing of tempers. Conflict in Ossining, the survey concluded, "was limited to verbal exhanges, pointed avoidances, and wounded sensibilities." Hardly comparable to bombings and

cross-burnings that went on elsewhere, the "verbal exchanges" and "pointed avoidances" were, however, troublesome enough to Jewish opponents of the display.[62]

Leo Pfeffer, attorney for the plaintiffs, moved for an injunction against the board in 1957. He charged that a religious display on public property violated the separationist principle as enjoined by the state and federal constitutions and as defined in *Everson* and *McCollum*. Although the crèche committee insisted that the nativity scene was a historical event, it was rather a celebration of a religious belief. The crèche, a distinctive Christian symbol unacceptable to non-Christians and nonbelievers, showed a preference for one religion over another. In no way could it be called nonsectarian. Since the issue at stake was separation, it made no difference how much or how little the public display cost the government. Nor did the Christian beliefs of the majority validate the display: "Religious freedom is not a matter of balloting or the counting of hands."

The memorandum of law submitted by the Congress went beyond strict points of constitutional law. Similar to earlier briefs, it drew on psychological data, arguing that children who attended the school were a captive audience to the influence of a religion in which they did not necessarily believe. Indeed, few official acts "could more effectively propagandize on behalf of a particular religious affiliation." Other and more appropriate sites were available, but the adamant refusal of the school board to place the crèche elsewhere proved that it purposely sought to invoke the authority of the school for the propagation of sectarian beliefs.[63]

The memorandum emphasized the importance of religious symbolism. Psychology taught that the propagation of religious doctrine depended in no small measure on the use of symbols. State courts had acknowledged that fact, as had the Supreme Court. In the flag-salute case the highest court had stated: "Symbolism is a primitive but effective way of communicating ideas. . . . The State announces rank, function, and authority through crowns and maces, uniforms and black robes; the church speaks through the Cross, the Crucifix, the altar and shrine, and clerical raiment."[64] The power of symbols was compounded by displays which implied official sanction and which, the memorandum continued, operated to induce conformity on the part of the beholder.

Supporting briefs and statements were presented by the New York Civil Liberties Union, the Westchester Ethical Culture Society, the New York Board of Rabbis, and the JCRC of Northern Westchester–Putnam. Pfeffer also introduced affidavits from Jews and Protestants, both residents and nonresidents of Ossining. Two ministers joined three prominent rabbis (one from each branch of Judaism) in testifying that the crèche was inconsistent with Jewish teachings. Expert witnesses, two educators and a psychologist who had offered testimony in *Tudor,* stressed the adverse effects of the display not only on intergroup relations but, more important, on the children. The latter perceived the display to be the school's preference for, and endorsement of, Christianity. As such, the experts said, it caused psychological injury to many Jewish children.[65]

Despite a star-studded cast of supporters, the court denied Pfeffer's motion for an injunction. Since the board had promised not to install the crèche before the holiday recess and to remove it before classes reconvened—a move agreed to only after the suit was begun—Judge Frank Coyne ruled that the allegations of harm to the children were not at issue. The question of constitutionality would have to be decided by a trial, but in his opinion strict separation was neither desirable nor demanded by the Constitution: "The Constitution does not demand that every friendly gesture between the church and state should be discountenanced nor that every vestige of the existence of God be eradicated." Pfeffer, who admitted that he would have advised against litigation had the board at the outset set a time limit on the display, now prepared for the trial of *Baer* v. *Kilmorgen*.[66]

The trial, which took place in September 1958, was an exercise in frustration for the plaintiffs. Repeating the same arguments, Pfeffer's attempts to buttress the points made in his memorandum were utterly stymied. He called upon rabbis, ministers, and biblical scholars to testify that the nativity scene depicted a religious belief rather than a historical event, but objections to his line of questioning were repeatedly sustained. Nor did the court admit opinions from the rabbis or the experts in education and psychology.

Judge Elbert Gallagher's decision was, therefore, no surprise. The court dismissed the argument about the impact of a religious display on the children, because the crèche in 1957 was not erected while school was in session. Besides, since religious symbolism was inescapable during the Christmas season, Gallagher saw little difference in impact between a symbol on public as opposed to private property. Contentions that the crèche constituted an establishment of religion or a denial of religious freedom were equally untenable. The judge strongly defended government accommodation of religion: "If such accommodation violates the doctrine of absolute separation between Church and State, then it is time that that doctrine be discarded once and for all."[67]

The Ossining community regarded the decision as a standoff. Gallagher's words implied that the crèche could not be displayed while school was in session, and thus the plaintiffs scored at least partially. The defendants won the right to erect a crèche on school grounds, but their victory was narrowed by the stipulation on time. There was even talk that the crèche committee would consider alternative sites for the display in order to keep it over a longer period of time. If that turned out to be true, Pfeffer said, the plaintiffs would have won decisively. The following Christmas, however, the crèche returned to the school lawn for its limited stay.[68]

The plaintiffs were eager to appeal the case, and so were Pfeffer's colleagues at the Congress. Pfeffer himself was opposed, despite hints at the outset that he was prepared to carry the case to the Supreme Court. Since the school board had yielded on the issue of time, the heart of his case for the nonsectarian school had been eviscerated. If the crèche existed only while school was in recess, the issue became one of religious displays on public property generally. On that broader matter the attorney believed that success was extremely unlikely. He duly filed an appeal for his clients, but it was not pursued.[69] Not until 1984 in *Lynch* v. *Donnelly* did the Supreme Court rule on public religious displays.

The Congress drew one positive conclusion from the episode. Referring to Dean Kelley's study, it insisted that the Ossining community had not been traumatized by the litigation. From that lesson, it said, timid Jews could learn that their fears of publicly defending constitutional liberties were exaggerated.[70] The Congress, however, ignored the stark truth of Judge Gallagher's decision. Religious symbolism during the Christmas season *was* inescapable, and even if every public display was banned, Jews could not hope to erase all visual reminders of an American culture steeped in Christian traditions.

Afterword

Despite the judicial victories of the 1960s, the zeal of Jewish strict separationists did not abate. Ever loyal to the ideal of the religion-free public school, they pressed on, campaigning against silent prayer and meditation, religious baccalaureate services and holiday observances, the use of school facilities by religious groups, and the teaching of "scientific creationism." Similarly, efforts continued as before on behalf of the rights of Sabbath observers and against the public display of Christian symbols. Jewish separationists still denounced official statements in which the United States was called a Christian nation, and venturing further, they also cast suspicion on plans that bore the label "Judeo-Christian," a euphemism, they said, for old-fashioned Christianity.[1] Holding fast to a broad interpretation of the establishment clause, they treated each new challenge as a threat to religious equality. And each success that they scored boosted their confidence a notch higher.

An unchanged stand on separation found ready justification, and not merely on grounds of abstract principle. For one thing, full compliance with the Court's rulings on released time, Bible reading, and prayer was never achieved. More important, the political activities of the New Christian Right of the 1970s and 1980s and the accommodationist tendencies of the post–Warren Supreme Court lent credence to the wisdom of a tried and rigid defense posture. A few years ago, in response to agitation for public school education in moral and spiritual values, NJCRAC (now the National Jewish Community Relations Advisory Council) circulated conclusions first hammered out in 1954 on the teaching of a "common core" religion, the objective teaching about religion, and the teaching of moral values. Indeed, the overall guidelines of the defense network on church–state matters, *Safeguarding Religious Liberty*, which were formulated in 1957 and minimally revised over the years, have not been altered since the third version of 1971.[2]

Organizational unity on separation persisted, too. Only on aid to parochial schools, an issue that generated stormy public debates in the 1970s, did consensus break down. Deviating from the official stand of the NJCRAC–SCA, the Orthodox affiliates (the Rabbinical Council of America and the Union of Orthodox Jewish Congregations) favored government aid, in the form of tuition tax credits or reimbursement to religious schools for the expenses of their secular programs.[3] Nevertheless, neither that nor the questions raised after *Engel* about secularist leadership and tactics caused any major rupture, and the two Orthodox organizations stayed firmly within the unified defense network. The activities of COLPA, a legal agency devoted exclusively to the special interests of observant Jews, permitted them to agitate for government aid outside the conventional defense network. Allied in support of COLPA with right-wing groups like Agudath Israel, which had never been affiliated with NJCRAC or the SCA, the Rabbinical Council and Orthodox union enjoyed the advantages of both the secular and Orthodox defense worlds.[4]

Reinforcement of a strict separationist posture was provided by *Lynch* v. *Donnelly* (1984), in which the Supreme Court upheld the erection of a municipal crèche in Pawtucket, Rhode Island. An analysis of this well-known case shows not only how two "constants" discussed throughout this study—Jewish sensitivity to public opinion and Jewish reliance on the establishment clause—had scarcely changed in forty years. It also reveals how easily Jews were reminded of their vulnerability in a Christian society.

The suit, initiated by the ACLU along with several taxpayers of Pawtucket, challenged the constitutionality of a nativity scene, which since the war had been a feature of the city's annual Christmas display. Although the city argued that the entire display was secular rather than religious, the plaintiffs won in the lower courts. The federal district court found that the crèche violated the establishment clause; the court of appeals agreed that the city's purpose was sectarian and that displaying the crèche, a symbol of one faith, discriminated against the others.[5]

Albeit an issue on which Jewish opposition had long been public, the defense agencies received mixed signals about active involvement. Many of Rhode Island's Jews opted for a low profile. Living in a state which was 60 percent Catholic, some asked whether participation was worth a religious backlash or a possible defeat of Jewish candidates in the elections of 1982. They raised other cogent questions: Was it wise to agitate about a fixed city custom when Christmas was in fact a legal holiday? Could Jews in good conscience argue against crèches without first contesting public displays of Hanukkah menorahs? Why risk the hate campaigns of anti-Semites, especially if most Christians approved (or at least did not disapprove) of such displays? Was it right to jeopardize Christian support of Israel on a matter that did not threaten vital Jewish interests? But, as others retorted, on an issue that constituted a flagrant violation of the establishment clause, how could visible Jewish support of separation not be part of the record?[6]

When the Supreme Court accepted the case for review, the big three took action. The Congress and the ADL filed a joint brief; the AJC filed together with the powerful National Council of Churches. Both briefs insisted that the crèche was a fundamental religious symbol whose appearance alongside other Christmas trappings did not make it any less religious. They charged that the municipal act failed to meet any of the guidelines set by the Court on the boundaries between church and state and, by showing the government's preference of one religion over the others, severely impaired the protection of religious minorities by the establishment clause. One brief said that the crèche sent "a clear message of isolation to Jewish citizens."[7]

Unlike their experience in previous litigation, the Jewish *amici* were pitted against the federal administration. In keeping with his wooing of the New Christian Right, Ronald Reagan approved intervention in the Pawtucket case. Solicitor-General Rex Lee appealed to the Court in an *amicus* brief to save a traditional public celebration that in no way threatened First Amendment rights. Justifying a narrow interpretation of both separation and establishment, he argued that the government was not required to ignore popular sentiments about religious holidays. Not accommodationists, Lee maintained, but those who contrived to exclude religion from public life and who worked for "the establishment of irreligion" ran afoul of the Constitution and the American historical experience. He reminded Jews that they, too, shared in government friendship, and here he referred to presidential messages in commemoration of Jewish holidays and Jewish Heritage Week. If the decision went against display of the crèche, he hinted that such marks of recognition would doubtless be invalidated. Lee refrained from calling America a Christian nation, but his abridged quotations from Justice Joseph Story and Dean Erwin Griswold, men who had denied the equality of other religions to Christianity, were pointedly clear. At oral argument he maintained that the crèche was constitutionally inoffensive because no one was forced to look at it. When asked by one justice whether a government-sponsored voluntary Christmas mass would also be constitutional, Lee was obliged to answer "yes."[8]

The majority opinion attested to the influence of the administration's brief. Chief Justice Warren Burger also took a historical route, recounting the numerous instances of government accommodation of religion. He condemned a rigid, absolutist approach to the establishment clause; he too made mention of Story and of presidential messages to the Jews. To be sure, the five justices in the majority admitted that the crèche was a religious symbol, but they denied that it amounted to an unconstitutional endorsement of Christianity or that it reflected adversely on the status of minorities. The Court, as Mr. Dooley had observed almost a century earlier, followed the election returns. In *Lynch* it may have anticipated Reagan's reelection.

Four justices vehemently disagreed. Not only was the crèche a religious symbol, they said, but it bore a specifically Christian meaning. Justice

William Brennan chided the Court for its regressive opinion: "By insisting that such a distinctively sectarian message is merely an unobjectionable part of our 'religious heritage,' the Court takes a long step backwards to the days when Justice Brewer could arrogantly declare for the Court that 'this is a Christian nation.' . . . Those days, I had thought, were forever put behind us."[9]

The tenor of the decision rather than the legality of any crèche caused widespread Jewish dismay. Nat Hentoff in the *Washington Post* wondered at the Court's display of "religious chauvinism." He recalled how the immigrant Jewish elders in the Boston ghetto of his youth had admonished the children, "Do not forget that you are in a Christian country." Could he have refuted them, "those survivors of the passionate followers of Christ in Russia and Poland," in the wake of *Lynch?* The theme of betrayal was pervasive. The implication of *Lynch,* the president of the American Jewish Congress stated, was that the Jewish community "is now a religious stranger in its own home." Norman Redlich, dean of New York University's law school, vented his anger and frustration along similar lines. In this country, he said, Jews should not be required to accommodate to the dominant religion. "We do not ask to be tolerated. We belong here. When government at any level lends it support to a Christian religious observance, Jews and other non-Christians are automatically excluded." Redlich quoted a Jewish student who had told him, "I feel as if we have been betrayed."[10]

The defense agencies called emergency meetings to consider strategy. They were understandably apprehensive. As Leo Pfeffer explained, Burger could just as easily have validated the nativity scene by agreeing with Pawtucket that the display was primarily secular. Instead, he went out of his way to endorse Christianity, even asserting twice that the crèche commemorated a "historic" and hence universally true religious event. And so the questions mounted. Was religious freedom threatened? Had the Pawtucket case, as one rabbi put it, bored a dangerous hole in the wall of separation? How much had Jews lost in their quest for equality? No one expected an immediate reversion to Justice Brewer, but were the gains under the establishment clause, for which Jewish defenders had labored so long, to be whittled away? Richard John Neuhaus, long the enemy of the "naked public square," insisted that a minority had no right to keep a majority from expressing the religious component of its culture. But most American Jews in 1984 would hardly have agreed with his view that "the minority . . . should not want to be protected from the public evidence that it is in fact a minority."[11]

As predicted, *Lynch* gave rise to a rash of public placements of menorahs as well as crèches. Orthodox Jews, notably of the Lubavitch group, tried to neutralize the Christmas season with displays of their own. Their efforts were contested by the separationist Jewish agencies in the community and the courts. On that divisive issue the Union of Orthodox Jewish

Congregations registered a mild qualification to official Jewish policy. It did not repudiate NJCRAC's opposition to religious displays, but it refused to support litigation against the private sponsorship of menorahs on public property. The menorah in turn had its day in court. In a rather curious decision of 1989 the Supreme Court held that a menorah alongside a Christmas tree was constitutional but that a crèche was not. The decision may have raised more questions than answers. As one lawyer quipped, it only served to deny the claim that the United States was a Christian nation![12]

In the last two decades the Jewish agencies have supplemented their almost obsessive concentration on the establishment clause with a broader emphasis on free exercise. Previously, free exercise had taken second place in Jewish defense; in most litigation it was ancillary, a victim of violations of the establishment clause. In the *Torcaso* case (1961), where a notary public was denied his commission because he refused to swear a belief in God, Pfeffer, attorney for Torcaso, challenged the state's test oath first as violative of the establishment clause and only second as an abridgment of religious freedom. Jews again downplayed free exercise on the matter of ritual slaughter, which was threatened at the end of the 1950s by legislative crusades for "humane" slaughter. Instead of seeking exemption on religious grounds, their main thrust was to prove that ritual slaughter was not inhumane. Only with respect to Sabbatarians and a religious census by the government did free exercise assume significant proportions.[13]

After 1965, when Christianity was no longer synonomous with public religion[14] and when the major battles on schools and Sunday laws had been fought, Jewish organizations expanded their horizons. The Orthodox, particularly ultrareligious groups like Agudath Israel, worked steadily for government accommodation of the interests of observant Jews.[15] Their activity paralleled but did not account for the shift by the major defense agencies. Staffed by professionals who were more committed to Judaism than their immediate predecessors, those agencies increasingly affirmed that free exercise included the protection of religious behavior, in diverse and multiple forms, so long as that behavior did not clash with a compelling state interest. Picking up on the Court's reasoning in *Sherbert,* they were saying that an overzealous application of the principle of secular regulation could well run afoul of the free exercise clause. The defense organizations now aligned themselves with the cause of religious pluralism, and they coupled the older "thou shalt not" command to government with a "thou mayest" nod to both Jewish and non-Jewish minorities.

The new approach enlarged dramatically upon earlier episodes of Jewish concern for nonconformists. In *Pierce* v. *Society of the Sisters* (1925), Louis Marshall had argued against prescribed conformity in an *amicus* brief on behalf of Catholic parochial schools, but that case technically did not involve religious freedom. On the eve of World War II, the CCAR supported Jehovah's Witnesses on the flag salute issue, but it remained merely a sympathetic bystander.[16] Even in the Sunday law cases of 1961 the argument was more an attack on penalties for Jewish religious beliefs than an affirmation of religious pluralism.

The broader approach was best explained in an *amicus* brief filed in 1971 by the SCA and Congress supporting the right of the Amish to keep their children out of public high schools. The Jewish brief found the justification for diversity and pluralism in the First Amendment:

> Concededly the beliefs of the Old Order Amish are unconventional and their practices do not conform to generally accepted standards. Their clothes, like those of some Hassidic Jews, may seem strange to most Americans. Their simple, agricultural life in a highly industrialized nation and era, may seem even stranger. But the First Amendment ban on laws respecting an establishment of religion or prohibiting its free exercise manifested an intention to accord constitutional protection to the nonconforming and unconventional religions, those which are not part of the general establishment. Indeed, the philosophy underlying the First Amendment was that religious diversity was not something to be merely suffered but to be welcomed.[17]

Noncomformity was again defended when the Jewish organizations, secular as well as religious, upheld the right of an Orthodox Jew in the air force to wear a yarmulke while on duty.[18]

To be sure, government accommodation of variant religious practices blurred the line between the strictures of no establishment and the right of free exercise. Indeed, it contradicted the strict interpretation of establishment which Jews themselves had usually defended. But the new emphasis better suited the reality of a pluralist setting. An exclusively negative focus on minority usages was outdated, a relic of the era when America was, or at least aspired to be, a homogeneous Protestant society.

Today, loyal separationists claim that the unrelenting Jewish fight against government identification with religion has contributed in large measure to the security, confidence, and sense of "at-homeness" of American Jews.[19] That the judicial decisions which have broadened the separationist principle were rendered by Christian judges confirmed the deeply rooted belief in the identity of Jewish and American interests. Some critics, like those who spoke up in the post-*Engel* debate, may have thought that an unchanged strict approach was one-sided. It showed great concern for the future of Jews but largely ignored questions about the future of Judaism. Its exponents did not consider whether their stand reinforced the pervasive secularism within the Jewish community. Nor did they admit that on the issue of secularism the community stood apart from most Americans who have continued to identify as believers and churchgoers. Nevertheless, the strict separationists, whose overriding priority has been the attainment of religious equality for the non-Christian minority, still predominate, and the rank and file readily follow. Their message is concise: so long as Jews desire to be considered equal partners in the American enterprise, they bear the open-ended responsibility of preserving the separation of church and state.

Notes

ADL	Anti-Defamation League
AH	*American Hebrew*
AI	*American Israelite*
AJC	American Jewish Committee
AJYB	*American Jewish Year Book*
BDAI	Board of Delegates of American Israelites
CCAR	Central Conference of American Rabbis
CLSA	Commission on Law and Social Action
Congress	American Jewish Congress
ISR	*Israelite*
JAC	Joint Advisory Committee
JCRC	Jewish Community Relations Council
JM	*Jewish Messenger*
NCCJ	National Conference of Christians and Jews
NCRAC	National Community Relations Advisory Council
NJCRAC	National Jewish Community Relations Advisory Council
OCC	*Occident*
PAJHS	*Publications of the American Jewish Historical Society*
SCA	Synagogue Council of America
UAHC	Union of American Hebrew Congregations

ARCHIVAL COLLECTIONS
(other than files of ADL, AJC, and Congress)

Files of JAC	American Jewish Historical Society
Jacob H. Schiff Papers	Jewish Theological Seminary
Louis Marshall Papers	American Jewish Committee
Minutes and *Proceedings* of the BDAI	American Jewish Historical Society

INTRODUCTION

1. John F. Wilson, *Public Religion in American Culture* (Philadelphia, 1979), pp. 8–14; Richard P. McBrien, *Caesar's Coin* (New York, 1987), p. 12.

2. *OCC* 13 (1856): 571–72.

3. Charles E. Silberman, *A Certain People* (New York, 1985), p. 349.

4. Jerold S. Auerbach, *Rabbis and Lawyers* (Bloomington, Ind., 1990).

5. *Everson* v. *Board of Education*, 330 U.S. 1 (1947).

6. Leonard W. Levy, *The Establishment Clause* (New York, 1986), pp. 176–77.

7. Milton R. Konvitz, "Church and State: How Separate?" *Midstream* 30 (Mar. 1984): 37.

8. Peter Y. Medding, *The Transformation of American Jewish Politics* (New York, 1989), p. 2.

9. Robert T. Handy, *A Christian America,* 2d ed. (New York, 1984), ch. 7.

10. *AH,* 2 Mar. 1888.

11. David Biale, *Power and Powerlessness in Jewish History* (New York, 1986), pp. 193–95.

CHAPTER 1

1. Salo W. Baron, *The Jewish Community,* 3 vols. (Philadelphia, 1942), 1:ch. 1.

2. Ibid., vol. 2; Jonathan I. Israel, *European Jewry in the Age of Mercantilism* (Oxford, 1985), ch. 8; Jacob Katz, *Out of the Ghetto* (Cambridge, Mass., 1973), chs. 2, 9.

3. Katz, *Out of the Ghetto,* pp. 38–41; idem, *Emancipation and Assimilation* (Westmead, Eng., 1972), pp. 24–27.

4. Lewis S. Feuer, *Spinoza and the Rise of Liberalism* (Boston, 1966), pp. 65–75, 98–99, 116–17, 134–35, 174–77; Israel, *European Jewry,* p. 219.

5. Jacob R. Marcus, *The Colonial American Jew,* 3 vols. (Detroit, Mich., 1970), 2:chs. 54, 59; 3:ch. 70.

6. Katz, *Out of the Ghetto,* pp. 28–30; idem, *Exclusiveness and Tolerance* (New York, 1961), pp. 156–61; Israel, *European Jewry,* p. 63; Morris U. Schappes, ed., *A Documentary History of the Jews in the United States,* 3d ed. (New York, 1971), pp. 11–13.

7. Katz, *Emancipation and Assimilation,* p. 4; idem, *Out of the Ghetto,* pp. 31–33.

8. Marcus, *The Colonial American Jew,* 2:856–60.

9. Ibid., 2:chs. 51, 52, 54; 3:1237–39.

10. On Lopez see numerous references in Marcus, *The Colonial American Jew;* on Recife, see, in same work, 1:79–81, 360–61.

11. In 1663 the Sephardic congregation in London forbade the conversion of gentiles to Judaism under penalty of excommunication. That interdiction was carried over to America. See Marcus, *The Colonial American Jew,* 2:964.

12. Francis N. Thorpe, comp., *The Federal and State Constitutions,* 7 vols. (Washington, 1909), 1:49–57, 7:3783–84. Examples of twentieth-century cases in which the Supreme Court used "Christian" in the sense of civilized are *Lone Wolf* v. *Hitchcock,* 187 U.S. 553 (1903), and *Tee-Hit-Ton Indians* v. *United States,* 348 U.S. 272 (1955).

13. Thorpe, *Federal and State Constitutions*, 1:519–20, 3:1841, 4:2445, 6:3207; Marcus, *The Colonial American Jew*, 1:424.

14. Marcus discusses in detail the political rights of Jews in each colony in *The Colonial American Jew*, 1: part V. See also Abram V. Goodman, *American Overture* (Philadelphia, 1947); Richard B. Morris, "Civil Liberties and the Jewish Tradition in Early America," *The Jewish Experience in America*, ed. Abraham J. Karp, 5 vols. (Waltham, Mass., and New York, 1969), 1:404–23; Stanley F. Chyet, "The Political Rights of the Jews in the United States: 1776–1840," *Critical Studies in American Jewish History*, vol. 2 (Cincinnati and New York, 1971), pp. 28–29.

15. Sanford H. Cobb, *The Rise of Religious Liberty in America* (New York, 1970), p. 377; Henry S. Commager, ed., *Documents of American History*, 7th ed. (New York, 1963), p. 31; Marcus, *The Colonial American Jew*, 1:449–50; cf. Goodman, *American Overture*, pp. 133–45. On a blasphemy charge against a twentieth-century Jew, Horace Kallen, see Leonard W. Levy, *Treason Against God* (New York, 1981), p. 5.

16. Marcus, *The Colonial American Jew*, 1:400, 409–10, 418, 464–65; Thomas J. Curry, *The First Freedoms* (New York, 1986), p. 58.

17. Schappes, *Documentary History*, pp. 1–2; Goodman, *American Overture*, pp. 12–14. On the Puritan use of biblical law see Bernard J. Meislin, *Jewish Law in American Tribunals* (New York, 1976), pp. 4–13.

18. Goodman, *American Overture*, pp. 121–23; Marcus, *The Colonial American Jew*, 1:442; Edwin Wolf II and Maxwell Whiteman, *The History of the Jews of Philadelphia from Colonial Times to the Age of Jackson* (Philadelphia, 1975), pp. 12–13.

19. "The Fundamental Constitutions of Carolina," *Old South Leaflets* 7, no. 172 (Boston, n.d.), pp. 393–413; Marcus, *The Colonial American Jew*, 1:363, 463–68; Milton R. Konvitz, *Judaism and the American Idea* (Ithaca, N.Y., 1978), pp. 124–31; Loren P. Beth, *The American Theory of Church and State* (Gainesville, Fla., 1956), pp. 28–30.

20. Mark DeWolfe Howe, *The Garden and the Wilderness* (Chicago, 1967), pp. 5–12; Oscar S. Straus, *Roger Williams* (New York, 1936), pp. 172–76; Marcus, *The Colonial American Jew*, 1:430; Maxwell H. Morris, "Roger Williams and the Jews," *American Jewish Archives* 3 (1951): 24–27.

21. Marcus, *The Colonial American Jew*, 1:315–16, 432–33; Salo W. Baron, *Steeled by Adversity* (Philadelphia, 1971), p. 87.

22. Morris, "Civil Liberties and the Jewish Tradition," p. 409; Robert T. Handy, *A Christian America*, 2d ed. (New York, 1984), pp. 13–14.

23. Morris, "Civil Liberties and the Jewish Tradition," p. 417; Schappes, *Documentary History*, pp. 2–13; Marcus, *The Colonial American Jew*, 1:436–38, 3:1307; Leon Huhner, "Francis Salvador," *The Jewish Experience in America*, ed. Abraham J. Karp, 5 vols. (Waltham, Mass., and New York, 1969), 1:282.

24. Naomi W. Cohen, *Encounter with Emancipation* (Philadelphia, 1984), pp. 131, 138–39.

25. Marcus, *The Colonial American Jew*, 1:ch. 23; Schappes, *Documentary History*, pp. 26–30.

26. Beth, *American Theory of Church and State*, p. 58; Anson P. Stokes, *Church and State in the United States*, 3 vols. (New York, 1950), 1:228–30; Handy, *A*

Christian America, pp. 15–19; Marcus, *The Colonial American Jew,* 3:1167; Curry, *First Freedoms,* pp. 96–98.

27. Curry, *First Freedoms,* ch. 5; J. Franklin Jameson, *The American Revolution Considered as a Social Movement* (Boston, 1956), p. 85; Bernard Bailyn, *Pamphlets of the American Revolution,* vol. 1 (Cambridge, Mass., 1965), pp. 150–69.

28. Curry, *First Freedoms,* pp. 96–104, 145; William A. Blakely, ed., *American State Papers on Freedom in Religion,* 4th ed. (Washington, 1949), pp. 103–12; Stokes, *Church and State,* 1:240–44, 375–78; Jonathan D. Sarna, "The Impact of the American Revolution on American Jews," *Modern Judaism* 1 (1981): 152–53.

29. Sidney E. Mead, "Christendom, Enlightenment, and the Revolution," *Religion and the American Revolution,* ed. Jerald C. Brauer (Philadelphia, 1976), pp. 29–54; Handy, *A Christian America,* pp. 15–16, 19–23; Howe, *Garden and the Wilderness,* ch. 1; Cushing Strout, *The New Heavens and New Earth* (New York, 1974), pp. 78–87.

30. Arthur Hertzberg, *The French Enlightenment and the Jews* (New York and Philadelphia, 1968), ch. 9; Marcus, *The Colonial American Jew,* 3:1166–68, chs. 72–74; Samuel Rezneck, *Unrecognized Patriots* (Westport, Conn., 1975), pp. 4–7, 239.

31. Morris, "Civil Liberties and the Jewish Tradition," pp. 421–22; Marcus, *The Colonial American Jew,* 3:1259–64, 1270–71, ch. 74; Rezneck, *Unrecognized Patriots,* esp. pp. 5–6, 239–41, 246; "Jews and the American Revolution," *American Jewish Archives* 27 (1975): 121–22; Schappes, *Documentary History,* pp. 63–69.

32. Schappes, *Documentary History,* p. 3; see, for example, Donald Kagan, rev., *Botsford and Robinson's Hellenic History,* 5th ed. (New York, 1969), p. 79, and P. A. Brunt, *Italian Manpower* (London, 1971), pp. 239–44; Hertzberg, *French Enlightenment and the Jews,* p. 346; Simon Wolf, *The American Jew as Patriot, Soldier, and Citizen* (Philadelphia, 1895); Cohen, *Encounter with Emancipation,* p. 283.

33. Chyet, "Political Rights of the Jews," pp. 53–54.

34. The texts of the state constitutions appear in Thorpe, *Federal and State Constitutions,* and are excerpted and analyzed with reference to Jewish rights by Chyet, "Political Rights of the Jews." See also Cobb, *Rise of Religious Liberty,* p. 505; Leonard W. Levy, *The Establishment Clause* (New York, 1986), pp. 26–39, 47–51.

35. Levy, *The Establishment Clause,* pp. 26–39, 47–49. Varying tallies of provisions touching on religion appear in Stokes, *Church and State,* 1:ch. 5; Cobb, *Rise of Religious Liberty,* pp. 499–500, 503–4, 507; Morton Borden, *Jews, Turks, and Infidels* (Chapel Hill, N.C., 1984), pp. 11–13; Schappes, *Documentary History,* p. 66.

36. Max J. Kohler, "Phases in the History of Religious Liberty in America with Special Reference to the Jews—I," *PAJHS* 11 (1903): 68–69; Borden, *Jews, Turks, and Infidels,* p. 11; Levy, *The Establishment Clause,* p. 61.

37. John W. Pratt, *Religion, Politics, and Diversity* (Ithaca, N.Y., 1967), ch. 4; Howe, *Garden and the Wilderness,* p. 44.

38. The older accounts in Cobb, *Rise of Religious Liberty,* pp. 483–99, and Stokes, *Church and State,* 1:366–97, are supplemented more recently by William L. Miller, *The First Liberty* (New York, 1986), part 1; Levy, *The Establishment*

Clause, pp. 51–60; Curry, *First Freedoms,* pp. 134–38. See also Myron Berman, *Richmond's Jewry* (Charlottesville, Va., 1979), p. 38; Chyet, "Political Rights of the Jews," pp. 38–39.

39. Samuel E. Morison, ed., *Sources and Documents Illustrating the American Revolution,* 2d ed. (Oxford, 1961), pp. 149–51; Joseph L. Blau, ed., *Cornerstones of Religious Freedom in America* (Boston, 1949), pp. 74–87.

40. Kohler, "Phases in the History of Religious Liberty," pp. 62–63, 67–68, 71; Borden, *Jews, Turks, and Infidels,* pp. 13–14; Curry, *First Freedoms,* p. 145; Cobb, *Rise of Religious Liberty,* pp. 497–98; Robert M. Healey, "Jefferson on Judaism and the Jews," *American Jewish History* 73 (1984): 359–60.

41. Schappes, *Documentary History,* pp. 80–81; Levy, *The Establishment Clause,* p. 59.

42. Cobb, *Rise of Religious Liberty,* pp. 497–98; Berman, *Richmond's Jewry,* p. 33.

43. Schappes, *Documentary History,* pp. 66–67. Francis Salvador of South Carolina served in the Provincial Congress that drew up the state's first constitution, but his name did not figure in those deliberations. Huhner, "Francis Salvador," pp. 286–89.

44. Schappes, *Documentary History,* pp. 63–66, 68–69; Wolf and Whiteman, *History of the Jews of Philadelphia,* pp. 146–52.

45. Schappes, *Documentary History,* pp. 68–69; Chyet, "Political Rights of the Jews," p. 41.

46. Chyet, "Political Rights of the Jews," pp. 58–59, 64; Chester J. Antieau, Arthur T. Downey, and Edward C. Roberts, *Freedom from Federal Establishment* (Milwaukee, Wis., 1964), pp. 106–10.

47. Pratt, *Religion, Politics, and Diversity,* pp. 101, 111–16; Stokes, *Church and State,* 3:143–49; Curry, *First Freedoms,* p. 148; Isaac M. Fein, *The Making of an American Jewish Community* (Philadelphia, 1971), p. 23; Max J. Kohler, "Phases in the History of Religious Liberty—II," *PAJHS* 13 (1905): 14–17.

48. Hyman B. Grinstein, *The Rise of the Jewish Community of New York* (Philadelphia, 1945), pp. 337–38.

49. 3 Howard 609 (1845).

50. Stokes, *Church and State,* 1:482.

51. Max Farrand, ed., *The Records of the Federal Convention of 1787,* rev. ed., 4 vols. (New Haven, Conn., 1966), 2:468; Borden, *Jews, Turks, and Infidels,* pp. 18–19; Curry, *First Freedoms,* p. 196.

52. Miller, *First Liberty,* p. 207; Herbert J. Storing, *The Complete Anti-Federalist,* 7 vols. (Chicago, 1981), 4:248–49; Jonathan Elliot, ed., *The Debates in the Several State Conventions on the Adoption of the Federal Constitution,* 2d ed., 5 vols. (Philadelphia, 1907), 4:192–99.

53. Michael Kammen, ed., *The Origins of the American Constitution* (New York, 1986), p. 205; Farrand, *Records,* 3:310.

54. Storing, *The Complete Anti-Federalist,* 1:64, 3:107, 206, 4:242, 248, 6:14; Elliot, *Debates,* 2:44, 4:192, 195, 199, 215; Borden, *Jews, Turks, and Infidels,* p. 18; Kammen, *Origins of the American Constitution,* pp. 292–93.

55. Storing, *The Complete Anti-Federalist,* 1:22–23, 4:242.

56. Curry, *First Freedoms,* p. 208; Strout, *New Heavens and New Earth,* pp. 93–94.

57. For interpretations published prior to 1986 see Elizabeth B. Clark, "Church–State Relations in the Constitution-Making Period," *Church and State in America, A Bibliographical Guide,* ed. John F. Wilson, 2 vols. (Westport, Conn., 1986–87), 1:151–89.

58. Curry, *First Freedoms,* pp. 199–209, 217–18; Strout, *New Heavens and New Earth,* pp. 79–82; Gerard V. Bradley, *Church–State Relationships in America* (New York, 1987), chs. 3–6.

59. Jacob R. Marcus, ed., *American Jewry* (Cincinnati, 1959), p. 62; Borden, *Jews, Turks, and Infidels,* pp. 4–5, 20–22; letters of Jewish congregations to George Washington, Schappes, *Documentary History,* pp. 77–84; Fein, *Making of an American Jewish Community,* p. 21.

60. On emancipation in France see Hertzberg, *French Enlightenment and the Jews,* esp. ch. 9.

61. Marcus, *The Colonial American Jew,* 2:971–74; idem, *Early American Jewry,* 2 vols. (Philadelphia, 1953), 2:486–88; Sarna, "Impact of the American Revolution on American Jews," p. 155.

62. Marcus, *American Jewry,* pp. 148–67.

63. Grinstein, *Rise of the Jewish Community of New York,* pp. 336–39, 348; Marcus, *Early American Jewry,* 2:490–91.

64. Post-Revolutionary changes are traced in Marcus, *Early American Jewry,* and in Joseph L. Blau and Salo W. Baron, eds., *The Jews of the United States, 1790–1840,* 3 vols. (New York and Philadelphia, 1963).

65. Marcus, *American Jewry,* p. 52.

66. Cf. David Thelen, "Introduction," part II, *Journal of American History* 74 (1987): 797.

67. Max J. Kohler, "The Fathers of the Republic and Constitutional Establishment of Religious Liberty," appendix to Luigi Luzzatti, *God in Freedom* (New York, 1930), p. 670.

68. Schappes, *Documentary History,* p. 153; *ISR,* 19 Dec. 1856.

69. Schappes, *Documentary History,* p. 80; Blau and Baron, *The Jews of the United States,* 1:9, 11–14, 60, 64, 112, 2:317; Leo Pfeffer, *Church, State, and Freedom* (Boston, 1953), p. 224; Irving Brant, *The Bill of Rights* (Indianapolis, Ind., 1965), pp. 406, 418.

70. Borden, *Jews, Turks, and Infidels,* pp. 76–79; *OCC* 7 (1849–50): 563–67.

CHAPTER 2

1. Robert T. Handy, *A Christian America,* 2d ed. (New York, 1984), ch. 2; Timothy L. Smith, *Revivalism and Social Reform* (Baltimore, Md., 1980); Clifford S. Griffin, *Their Brothers' Keepers* (New Brunswick, N.J., 1960); Martin E. Marty, *Righteous Empire* (New York, 1977), ch. 7; Winthrop S. Hudson, *Religion in America,* 2d ed. (New York, 1973), ch. 6; John R. Fitzmeier, "Religion, Politics, and the Rise of the Denomination in Early Nineteenth-Century America," and Louis P. Masur, "Religion and Reform in America," *Church and State in America, A Bibliographical Guide,* ed. John F. Wilson, 2 vols. (Westport, Conn., 1986–87), 1:191–250.

2. Hudson, *Religion in America,* pp. 67–74; Handy, *A Christian America,*

pp. 37, 47–48; William L. Miller, *The First Liberty* (New York, 1986), pp. 250–52; Marty, *Righteous Empire,* p. 71; Elizabeth B. Clark, "Church–State Relations in the Constitution-Making Period," *Church and State in America, A Bibliographical Guide,* ed. John F. Wilson, 2 vols. (Westport, Conn., 1986–87), 1:161; Smith, *Revivalism and Social Reform,* ch. 2.

3. Miller, *First Liberty,* pp. 263–65; Griffin, *Their Brothers' Keepers,* ch. 7; Handy, *A Christian America,* p. 50; Anson P. Stokes, *Church and State in the United States,* 3 vols. (New York, 1950), 2:20–25; Joseph L. Blau, ed., *Cornerstones of Religious Freedom in America* (Boston, 1949), pp. 119–22; Seymour M. Lipset and Earl Raab, *The Politics of Unreason* (New York, 1973), pp. 39–47.

4. Handy, *A Christian America,* p. 42; *OCC* 6 (1848–49): 64–65, 186–93, 7 (1849–50): 564, 11 (1853–54): 224–26.

5. Public prayers offered by Rabbi Morris Raphall were a case in point. *ISR,* 20 Apr. 1855; Bertram W. Korn, *Eventful Years and Experiences* (Cincinnati, 1954), pp. 98–118.

6. Timothy L. Smith, "Evangelical Christianity and American Culture," *A Time to Speak,* ed. A. James Rudin and Marvin R. Wilson (Grand Rapids, Mich., 1987), p. 72; Handy, *A Christian America,* p. 52; *ISR,* 9 Apr. 1858. On the missionaries and the Jews see articles by Jonathan D. Sarna: "The American Jewish Response to Nineteenth-Century Christian Missions," *Journal of American History* 68 (1981): 35–51; "American Christian Opposition to Missions to the Jews," *Journal of Ecumenical Studies* 23 (1986): 225–35; "The Freethinker, the Jews, and the Missionaries," *AJS Review* 5 (1980): 101–14; also George L. Berlin, *Defending the Faith* (Albany, N.Y., 1989), ch. 1; idem, "Solomon Jackson's *The Jew,*" *American Jewish History* 71 (1981): 10–28.

7. *Israel Vindicated,* pp. v–viii, 3, 93–94; Berlin, "Solomon Jackson's *The Jew,*" p. 21; *OCC* 1 (1843–44): 145–52.

8. Isaac Leeser, *The Claims of the Jews to an Equality of Rights* (Philadelphia, 1841), pp. 11, 15–16, 51, 79, 82; *OCC* 3 (1845–46): 42.

9. Stanley F. Chyet, "The Political Rights of the Jews in the United States: 1776–1840," *Critical Studies in American Jewish History,* vol. 2 (Cincinnati and New York, 1971), pp. 66–78; Naomi W. Cohen, *Encounter with Emancipation* (Philadelphia, 1984), pp. 75–77; Morton Borden, *Jews, Turks, and Infidels* (Chapel Hill, N.C., 1984), pp. 42–50, 53; Leon Huhner, "The Struggle for Religious Liberty in North Carolina with Special Reference to the Jews," in his *Jews in America after the American Revolution* (New York, 1959), pp. 1–35.

10. Isaac M. Fein, "*Niles' Weekly Register* on the Jews," *The Jewish Experience in America,* ed. Abraham J. Karp, 5 vols. (Waltham, Mass., and New York, 1969), 2:98.

11. See references to Borden and Huhner in n. 9.

12. Edward Eitches, "Maryland's 'Jew Bill,'" *American Jewish Historical Quarterly* 60 (1971): 258–79; Joseph L. Blau and Salo W. Baron, eds., *The Jews of the United States, 1790–1840,* 3 vols. (New York and Philadelphia, 1963), 1:33–37, 45, 48–52; Isaac M. Fein, *The Making of an American Jewish Community* (Philadelphia, 1971), pp. 25–35.

13. E. Milton Altfeld, *The Jew's Struggle for Religious and Civil Liberty in Maryland* (Baltimore, Md., 1924), pp. 108–27, 138–91.

14. Blau and Baron, *The Jews of the United States,* 1:41–42; Eitches, "Mary-

land's 'Jew Bill,'" pp. 268–69; Morris U. Schappes, ed., *A Documentary History of the Jews in the United States,* 3d ed. (New York, 1971), pp. 168–71; see also *Israel Vindicated,* pp. 98–99.

15. Lewis Abraham, "Religious and Ecclesiastical Law," *AI,* 28 Nov. 1879. In the case of *Torcaso* v. *Watkins,* 367 U.S. 488 (1961), Jewish defense organizations filed *amicus* briefs supporting the right of an atheist to hold office in Maryland.

16. Unless otherwise noted, all references to the background, settlement, communal practices, and religion of the German immigrants appear in my book *Encounter with Emancipation,* ch. 1, pp. 109–14, 129–39, 159–80, 212.

17. Selma Stern-Taeubler, "The Motivation of the German-Jewish Emigration to America in the Post-Mendelssohnian Era," *Essays in American Jewish History* (Cincinnati, 1958), pp. 252–55; *OCC* 6 (1848–49): 65.

18. Jacob R. Marcus, "The Americanization of Isaac Mayer Wise," in his *Studies in American Jewish History* (Cincinnati, 1969), p. 182; Stern-Taeubler, "Motivation of the German-Jewish Emigration," pp. 259–61; Howard M. Sachar, *The Course of Modern Jewish History,* rev. ed. (New York, 1977), pp. 108–12.

19. Jacob Katz, *Out of the Ghetto* (Cambridge, Mass., 1973), chs. 3, 9; idem, *Tradition and Crisis* (Glencoe, Ill., 1961), chs. 23, 24. On some who thought that loss of communal stability was too high a price to pay for separation see Salo W. Baron, "Church and State Debates in the Jewish Community of 1848," *Mordecai M. Kaplan Jubilee Volume,* ed. Moshe Davis (New York, 1953), pp. 57–68.

20. Moses Mendelssohn, *Jerusalem,* translated with introduction and commentary by Allan Arkush (Hanover, N.H., 1983), pp. 3–6, 33–70, 77–78; Alexander Altmann, *Moses Mendelssohn* (University, Ala., 1973), pp. 472, 513–31; Katz, *Out of the Ghetto,* p. 59.

21. Max J. Kohler, "Phases in the History of Religious Liberty in America with Special Reference to the Jews—I," *PAJHS* 11 (1903): 56; *ISR,* 16 Feb. 1855; Richard B. Morris, "The Jews, Minorities, and Dissent in the American Revolution," *Migration and Settlement: Proceedings of the Anglo-American Jewish Historical Conference,* July 1970 (London, 1971), p. 164.

22. Blau and Baron, *The Jews of the United States,* 3: 810–11.

23. *ISR,* 20 July 1855, 19 Dec. 1856.

24. *ISR,* 16 Apr. 1858.

25. The most recent and incisive study of the Reform movement is Michael A. Meyer, *Response to Modernity* (New York, 1988), chs. 6–7.

26. *ISR,* 13 Apr. 1855; David Philipson, *Max Lilienthal* (New York, 1915), p. 105. Examples of American Jews who wrote of the American–Judaic connection are Oscar S. Straus, *The Origin of the Republican Form of Government in the United States of America* (New York, 1885), and Milton R. Konvitz, *Judaism and the American Idea* (Ithaca, N.Y., 1978).

27. Jerold S. Auerbach, *Rabbis and Lawyers* (Bloomington, Ind., 1990).

28. *ISR,* 20 Nov. 1854, 28 Jan. 1859; Arnold M. Eisen, *The Chosen People in America* (Bloomington, Ind., 1983), p. 20.

29. *OCC* 5 (1847–48): 500.

30. Bertram W. Korn, *American Jewry and the Civil War* (Philadelphia, 1951), pp. 8–9; Naomi W. Cohen, "Pioneers of American Jewish Defense," *American Jewish Archives* 29 (1977): 116–50.

31. *OCC* 7 (1849–50): 565–66, 13 (1855–56): 466, 570; Jonathan D. Sarna,

Jacksonian Jew (New York, 1981), pp. 132–35; idem, "Jewish–Christian Hostility in the United States," *Uncivil Religion,* ed. Robert Bellah and Frederick Greenspahn (New York, 1987), p. 13.

32. Cohen, *Encounter with Emancipation,* pp. 72–75; *ISR,* 15 Dec. 1854; *OCC* 2 (1844–45): 496–510.

33. *Asmonean,* 22 Mar. 1850; Cohen, *Encounter with Emancipation,* p. 86; cf. Jacob Katz, *Emancipation and Assimilation* (Westmead, Eng., 1972), pp. 94–95.

34. *OCC* 4 (1846–47): 267–68, 7 (1849–50): 2–3, 14 (1856–57): 310–11; 15 (1857–58): 93–94, 16 (1858–59): 531–36; Cohen, "Pioneers of American Jewish Defense," pp. 126–29, 136–38, 144–46.

35. Cohen, *Encounter with Emancipation,* pp. 129–41.

36. Handy, *A Christian America,* p. 51; Ray A. Billington, *The Protestant Crusade* (New York, 1938); Evarts B. Greene, *Religion and the State* (Ithaca, N.Y., 1959), pp. 110–11.

37. Korn, *Eventful Years and Experiences,* ch. 3; *OCC* 12 (1854–55): 557–63, 13 (1855–56): 274–82; *Asmonean,* 17 Nov. 1854, 27 Apr., 4 May, 15 June 1855; *ISR,* 20 July 1855, 21 Nov. 1856, 20 May 1859.

38. Edgar Mortara, a little Jewish boy of Bologna, Italy, was forcibly abducted by papal authorities in 1858 after a servant confessed to having had him secretly baptized. American Jewish protests soared when, that same year, a Jewish patient in a Catholic hospital in St. Louis was baptized involuntarily.

39. Cohen, *Encounter with Emancipation,* p. 218; *ISR,* 9 Dec. 1859, 27 Jan. 1860.

40. Minutes and reports of the BDAI; Max J. Kohler, "The Board of Delegates of American Israelites, 1859–1878," *PAJHS* 29 (1925): 75–135; Allan Tarshish, "The Board of Delegates of American Israelites (1859–1878)," *PAJHS* 49 (1959): 411–27.

41. Unless otherwise noted, all material on the Swiss episode comes from Cohen, *Encounter with Emancipation,* pp. 101–8.

42. *Asmonean,* 7 Feb. 1851.

43. *OCC* 15 (1857–58): 433.

44. *OCC* 3 (1845–46): 564–65, 5 (1847–48): 500–501, 13 (1855–56): 567, 17 (1859–60): 103–4.

45. Carl Zollman, "Religious Liberty in American Law," *Selected Essays on Constitutional Law,* 5 vols. (Chicago, 1938), 2:1121–30, 1133–45; William A. Blakely, ed., *American State Papers on Freedom in Religion,* 4th ed. (Washington, 1949), p. 653; Stokes, *Church and State,* 3:576; *OCC* 7 (1849–50): 162. Some courts differed on the applicability of the common law maxim. See, for example, Stokes, *Church and State,* 3:565–78; *Bloom* v. *Richards,* 2 Ohio St. 387 (1853). In 1917 the highest court in England finally overthrew the doctrine. Max J. Kohler, "The Doctrine That 'Christianity is Part of the Common Law,' and Its Recent Judicial Overthrow in England with Particular Reference to Jewish Rights," *PAJHS* 31 (1928): 105–26.

46. David B. Ernst, "Church–State Issues and the Law: 1606–1870," *Church and State in America, A Bibliographical Guide,* ed. John F. Wilson, 2 vols. (Westport, Conn., 1986–87), 1:338–39; *People* v. *Ruggles,* 8 Johnson 290 (1811); Mark DeWolfe Howe, *The Garden and the Wilderness* (Chicago, 1965), p. 29; John W. Pratt, *Religion, Politics, and Diversity* (Ithaca, N.Y., 1967), pp. 141–42; 1861 case

excerpted in Albert M. Friedenberg, *The Sunday Laws of the United States and Leading Judicial Decisions Having Special Reference to the Jews* (Philadelphia, 1908), pp. 34–35.

47. Joseph Story, *Commentaries on the Constitution of the United States,* 3 vols. (Boston, 1833), 3:722–28.

48. *Vidal v. Girard's Executors,* 2 Howard 127 (1844); Stokes, *Church and State,* 3:560–65; Richard E. Morgan, *The Supreme Court and Religion* (New York, 1972), pp. 36–40.

49. Herbert Friedenwald, "Material for the History of Jews in the British West Indies," *PAJHS* 5 (1897): 59; Max J. Kohler, "Civil Status of the Jews in Colonial New York," *PAJHS* 6 (1897): 98–99; idem, "Phases in the History of Religious Liberty in America—II," *PAJHS* 13 (1905): 9; Pratt, *Religion, Politics, and Diversity,* pp. 138–44, 150–56; Albert M. Friedenberg, "Calendar of American Jewish Law Cases," *PAJHS* 12 (1904): 92.

50. *Lawyers Reports Annotated* 42 (1897): 553–68; Frank Swancara, *Obstruction of Justice by Religion* (Denver, Colo., 1936), chs. 2–4; B. H. Hartogensis, "Denial of Equal Rights to Religious Minorities and Non-Believers in the United States," *Yale Law Journal* 39 (1929–30): 666–71.

51. *People v. Samuel Jackson,* 3 Parker's Criminal Reports 590 (1857); *Jewish Times,* 16 July 1869. The *Jewish Messenger,* discussing the case of an oath for a Jewish juror, advised that Jews cover their heads and use their own Bible. 25 Feb. 1876.

52. William A. Blakely, ed., *American State Papers Bearing on Sunday Legislation,* rev. ed. (Washington, 1911), part I, pp. 414–18, 425–33; Leo Pfeffer, *Church, State, and Freedom* (Boston, 1953), pp. 227–37; Chyet, "Political Rights of the Jews," p. 64; *OCC* 17 (1859–60): 178; Zollman, "Religious Liberty in American Law," 2:1146.

53. Blakely, *Sunday Legislation,* pp. 176–79, 222–68, 269–95; *OCC* 2 (1844–45): 509; Schappes, *Documentary History,* p. 246.

54. Jacob R. Marcus, ed., *American Jewry* (Cincinnati, 1959), pp. 294–302.

55. Cohen, *Encounter with Emancipation,* pp. 79–81; Carl Zollman, *American Church Law* (St. Paul, Minn., 1933), p. 146.

56. Schappes, *Documentary History,* pp. 280–81; *Asmonean,* 4 May 1855; Cohen, *Encounter with Emancipation,* pp. 85–86; *ISR,* 10 July 1857.

57. *OCC* 3 (1845–46): 565, 7 (1849–50): 151, 11 (1853–54): 21, 13 (1855–56): 572–73, 17 (1859–60): 127; *ISR,* 20 Nov. 1854, 19 June 1857; Blakely, *Sunday Legislation,* pp. 265–66.

58. *OCC* 17 (1859–60): 103–4, 19 (1861–62): 106; Friedenberg, *Sunday Laws,* pp. 33–37.

59. Friedenberg, "Calendar of American Jewish Cases"; idem, "Jews and the American Sunday Laws," *PAJHS* 11 (1903): 105–7; Bernard J. Meislin, *Jewish Law in American Tribunals* (New York, 1976), pp. 162–63; Jacob B. Lightman, "The Status of Jews in the American Sunday Laws," *Jewish Social Service Quarterly* 11 (1934): 228; John Samuel, "Some Cases in Pennsylvania Wherein Rights Claimed by Jews Are Affected," *PAJHS* 5 (1897): 35–37; see *Town Council of Columbia v. Duke and Marks* (1833) in Blau and Baron, *The Jews of the United States,* 1:24–26.

60. Cohen, *Encounter with Emancipation,* pp. 188–90; Kerry M. Olitzky, "The

Sunday-Sabbath Movement in American Reform Judaism," *American Jewish Archives* 34 (1982): 75–88. Religious laxity and nonobservance among Jews continued to rise, but the movement to substitute Sunday for Sabbath services made little headway.

61. See also *Commonwealth* v. *Wolf* (1817) in Blau and Baron, *The Jews of the United States,* 1:22–24. Christian Sabbatarians used the same argument. Hartogensis, "Denial of Equal Rights," p. 675.

62. The decision in *City Council of Charleston* v. *Benjamin* (1846) is reprinted in *OCC* 5 (1849–50): 594–99. See also *OCC* 6 (1848–49): 39–40; Cohen, *Encounter with Emancipation,* pp. 83–84; Borden, *Jews, Turks, and Infidels,* pp. 111–15.

63. *OCC* 6 (1848–49): 217–24, 256–61, 265–74, 299–300, 7 (1849–50): 151–65.

64. Zollman, "Religious Liberty in American Law," 2:1118; *OCC* 3 (1845–46): 564–65, 4 (1846–47): 298, 7 (1849–50): 468–69, 16 (1858–59): 272; H. Frank Way, "The Death of the Christian Nation," *Journal of Church and State* 29 (1987): 517.

65. *OCC* 5 (1847–48): 112–17, 164–68, 204–6, 16 (1858–59): 269–74.

66. *OCC* 15 (1857–58): 293, 16 (1858–59): 275, 19 (1861–62): 452–53; *ISR,* 1 Oct. 1858; Way, "Death of the Christian Nation," p. 517. *Ex parte Newman,* 9 Cal. 502 (1858); *Ex parte Andrews,* 18 Cal. 579 (1861); *JM,* 30 July 1858; Meislin, *Jewish Law in American Tribunals,* pp. 157–61.

CHAPTER 3

1. Bertram W. Korn, *American Jewry and the Civil War* (Philadelphia, 1951), esp. chs. 6, 7; *OCC* 20 (1862–63): 485, 593.

2. James D. Richardson, comp., *A Compilation of the Messages and Papers of the Presidents,* 20 vols. (New York, 1897), 7:3226; *JM,* 21 Nov. 1862; *OCC* 20 (1862–63): 457–62; Korn, *American Jewry and the Civil War,* ch. 4; idem, "Congressman Clement L. Vallandigham's Championship of the Jewish Chaplaincy in the Civil War," *American Jewish Historical Quarterly* 53 (1963): 188–91; James G. Heller, *Isaac M. Wise* (New York, 1965), pp. 357–58.

3. William F. Deverell, "Church–State Issues in the Period of the Civil War," *Church and State in America, A Bibliographical Guide,* ed. John F. Wilson, 2 vols. (Westport, Conn., 1986–87), 2:6–8; Anson P. Stokes, *Church and State in the United States,* 3 vols. (New York, 1950), 3:582–83.

4. *Congressional Globe,* 36th Cong., 2d sess., p. 304; William A. Blakely, ed., *American State Papers Bearing on Sunday Legislation,* rev. ed. (Washington, 1911), p. 341; *Proceedings of the National Convention to Secure the Religious Amendment to the Constitution,* 1872 (Philadelphia, 1872), pp. vi–ix.

5. Stokes, *Church and State,* 3:585; *OCC* 22 (1864–65): 485–87; *Congressional Globe,* 38th Cong., 2d sess., p. 1272.

6. *JM,* 15 Jan. 1869, 27 Jan., 10 Feb. 1871; BDAI, *Proceedings,* 1870, p. 8; *Proceedings of the National Convention,* 1872, pp. xiv–xv; *OCC* 22 (1864–65): 439–40; *ISR,* 24 Feb., 3 Mar. 1865.

7. *Proceedings of the National Convention,* 1872, p. xv.

8. *National Perils and Opportunities* was the title of the published sessions of the General Christian Conference (New York, 1887).

9. *OCC* 21 (1863–64): 219–22, 22 (1864–65): 368–69, 432–45, 481–91, 529–33, 23 (1865–66): 313–19.

10. *OCC,* 22 (1864–65): 481; *JM,* 16 Dec. 1864, 3, 10 Mar., 5, 19 May 1865, 13 Nov. 1868, 25 June 1869.

11. *ISR,* 19 Feb. 1864, 3–31 Mar., 14 Apr. 1865; *AI,* 29 June 1877. See also *Jewish Times,* 5 Mar. 1869 and Rabbi David Einhorn, *War with Amalek!* (Philadelphia, 1864), pp. 6–8.

12. BDAI, *Proceedings,* 1865, pp. 6–8; BDAI, Minutes, 21 Dec. 1864; *OCC* 22 (1864–65): 481–85.

13. BDAI, Minutes, 26 Mar. 1865; *Congressional Globe,* 38th Cong., 2d sess., p. 742; BDAI, *Proceedings,* 1865, pp. 6–8.

14. Blakely, *Sunday Legislation,* pp. 342–43, 346; Stokes, *Church and State,* 3:586; *Proceedings of the National Convention,* 1872, p. 66, 1874, pp. 100–103.

15. *JM,* 7 Jan., 11, 25 Feb. 1870; BDAI, *Proceedings,* 1870, p. 8; Benny Kraut, "Francis E. Abbott," *Studies in the American Jewish Experience,* vol. 1, ed. Jacob R. Marcus and Abraham J. Peck (Cincinnati, 1981), p. 99; Morton Borden, *Jews, Turks, and Infidels* (Chapel Hill, N.C., 1984), p. 71; *ISR,* 25 Mar. 1870; *AI,* 4 Aug. 1876; S. Hirsch, in *AI,* 17 Feb. 1871; *Jewish Times,* 4 July 1873, 11 Dec. 1874; Max B. May, *Isaac Mayer Wise* (New York, 1916), p. 211.

16. In *Jewish Times,* 28 Apr. 1871, and *AI,* 16 Dec. 1870.

17. *Jewish Times,* 4 July 1873; *JM,* 1 Mar. 1872.

18. *Proceedings of the National Convention,* 1873, pp. 9–10, 46, 54–55, 1874, p. 32; *JM,* 21 May 1874; Blakely, *Sunday Legislation,* p. 348; Joseph L. Blau, ed., *Cornerstones of Religious Freedom in America* (Boston, 1949), pp. 217–18. See also *JM,* 18 Mar. 1870; *ISR,* 17, 24 Feb. 1871.

19. *Jewish Times,* 23 Feb. 1872; Kraut, "Abbott," pp. 90–93, 99–101; Stokes, *Church and State,* 3:592–94; UAHC, *Proceedings* 3 (1876): 245.

20. Reprinted in *AI,* 26 Nov. 1880.

21. Dennis L. Pettibone, "Caesar's Sabbath: The Sunday Law Controversy in the United States, 1879–1892," Ph.D. thesis (University of California, Riverside, 1979), p. 61.

22. Philip Schaff, "Church and State in the United States," in *Papers of the American Historical Association,* vol. 2, no. 4 (New York, 1888); see also James M. King, "The Christian Resources of Our Country," *National Perils and Opportunities,* pp. 259–69, and John Jay in *New York Times,* 16 Apr. 1890.

23. *AI,* 9 May 1879.

24. Pettibone, "Caesar's Sabbath," intro., pp. 19–29; Sydney E. Ahlstrom, *A Religious History of the American People* (New Haven, Conn., 1972), pt. 7; Robert T. Handy, *A Christian America,* 2d ed. (New York, 1984), pp. 74–75, 90–94.

25. BDAI, *Proceedings,* 1869, p. 9; *JM,* 29 June 1866, 8 Jan. 1869, 4 Mar., 9 Sept. 1870, 19 May 1876, 12 Jan. 1877, 15 Aug. 1879, 23 Jan. 1880, 19 Feb. 1886, 4 Oct., 13 Dec. 1895, 6 Aug. 1897.

26. *AI,* 21 Apr., 15 May 1876, 12, 26 Jan. 1877, 9 May, 11 July, 7 Nov. 1879, 16 Mar., 16 Apr., 24 Dec. 1880, 8 July 1881, 15 Apr. 1887, 20 Apr. 1888, 26 Dec. 1889, 16 Aug. 1895. The paper reprinted similar opinions by Christians.

27. *AI,* 7 Nov. 1879; M. Harris in *AI,* 6 June 1901; T. Schanfarber in *AI,* 12 Apr. 1906.

28. UAHC, *Proceedings* 3 (1876): 244–45; *AI,* Apr.–June 1876, 26 Jan., 16, 23 Mar. 1877.

29. Moshe Davis, *The Emergence of Conservative Judaism* (Philadelphia, 1963), pp. 169–70; *AH,* 2 Dec. 1881, 26 Jan., 25 May 1883, 1 July 1887, 16 Aug. 1895.

30. *Jewish Times,* 15 May 1873; *JM,* 14, 21 Jan. 1876; UAHC, *Proceedings* 19 (1892): 3013.

31. *AI,* 28 Apr.–9 June 1876; Albert M. Friedenberg, "The Jews and the American Sunday Laws," *PAJHS* 11 (1903): 107; *JM,* 19 May, 11 Aug. 1876.

32. *JM,* 19 May 1876; *AI,* 12, 26 May 1876; David Einhorn, "America, Whither Are You Going?" *American Jewish Archives* 28 (1976): 22–23; UAHC, *Proceedings* 3 (1876): 245; Ahlstrom, *Religious History of the American People,* p. 858.

33. See Justice Field's opinion in the Supreme Court case of *Soon Hing* v. *Crowley,* 113 U.S. 703 (1885); H. Frank Way, "The Death of the Christian Nation," *Journal of Church and State* 29 (1987): 517; Pettibone, "Caesar's Sabbath," p. 58.

34. Pettibone, "Caesar's Sabbath," pp. 1–10, 57–59, 336.

35. Ibid., pp. 330–38; on exemptions see Albert M. Friedenberg, *The Sunday Laws of the United States and Leading Judicial Decisions Having Special Reference to the Jews* (Philadelphia, 1908), pp. 22–24.

36. *Jewish Times,* 11 Aug. 1871. In another case the court held that a Jew who closed at sundown on Friday but reopened after sundown on Saturday forfeited his exemption. *JM,* 8 Jan. 1869.

37. *Frolickstein* v. *Mayor of Mobile,* 40 Ala. 725 (1867); *City of Shreveport* v. *Levy,* 26 La. Annual Reports 671 (1874); Friedenberg, *Sunday Laws,* pp. 24–25, 29.

38. 122 Mass. 40 (1877); *JM,* 12 Jan. 1877; *AI,* 12, 26 Jan. 1877; *Commonwealth* v. *Starr,* 144 Mass. 359 (1887); *AH,* 1 July 1887.

39. For the earlier law see Albert M. Friedenberg in *Jewish Comment,* 5 Aug. 1910, and BDAI, *Proceedings,* 1869, p. 5; *Penal Code of the State of New York, 1882* (Albany, N.Y., 1882), p. 55.

40. The *New York Times* reported almost daily in December 1882 on the enforcement of the new Sunday law, which, according to accounts, gripped Christians, too, in "a cold chill." See esp. 3, 9, 10, 20 Dec. 1882; Pettibone, "Caesar's Sabbath," pp. 301–2; Arnoux's decision in *Anonymous,* 12 Abbott's New Cases 455 (1882).

41. *JM,* 29 Dec. 1882, 12 Jan. 1883, 26 June 1885, 12 Jan. 1888, 13 Dec. 1895; *AH,* 29 Dec. 1882, 26 Jan., 3 Aug. 1883, 28 Mar. 1884, 7 June 1901; BDAI, *Proceedings* 10 (1883): 1402–3, 1419, 11 (1884): 1563, 12 (1885): 1788; Friedenberg in *AH,* 1 Jan. 1909; idem, "Jews and American Sunday Laws," p. 111n; *New York Times,* 25 Dec. 1882.

42. Leo Pfeffer, *Church, State, and Freedom* (Boston, 1953), p. 230; Friedenberg, "Jews and American Sunday Laws," pp. 112–13.

43. Sidney E. Mead, *The Lively Experiment* (New York, 1963), p. 66; David Tyack, "The Kingdom of God and the Common School," *Harvard Educational Review* 36 (1966): 448–49; David Tyack, Thomas James, and Aaron Benavot, *Law and the Shaping of Public Education* (Madison, Wis., 1987), p. 162; Robert Michaelsen, *Piety in the Public School* (New York, 1970), ch. 2; Timothy L. Smith, "Parochial Education and American Culture," *History and Education,* ed. Paul Nash (New York, 1970), p. 202.

44. Tyack et al., *Law and the Shaping of Public Education,* pp. 164–65; David B. Tyack, "Onward Christian Soldiers," *History and Education,* ed. Paul Nash (New York, 1970), pp. 216–19; references to Michaelsen and Smith in n. 43; Timothy L. Smith, "Protestant Schooling and American Nationality," *Journal of American History* 53 (1967): 679–95; Rush in Philip B. Kurland and Ralph Lerner, eds., *The Founders' Constitution,* 5 vols. (Chicago, 1987), 1:656; Lawrence A. Cremin, *American Education, The National Experience* (New York, 1980), p. 532; idem, *The American Common School* (New York, 1951), pp. 19–21, 44–48, 66–71.

45. 38 Me. 376 (1854); Alvin W. Johnson and Frank H. Yost, *Separation of Church and State in the United States* (Minneapolis, 1948), pp. 41–42; Way, "Death of the Christian Nation," pp. 518–19.

46. Diane Ravitch, *The Great School Wars* (New York, 1974), chs. 5, 6; John W. Pratt, *Religion, Politics, and Diversity* (Ithaca, N.Y., 1967), ch. 7; Michaelsen, *Piety in the Public School,* p. 124.

47. *OCC* 17 (1859–60): 15, 92; *Asmonean,* 6 Dec. 1850; Floyd S. Fierman, "The Jews and the Problem of Church and State in America Prior to 1881," *Educational Forum* 15 (1951): 335–41; see esp. Lloyd P. Gartner, "Temples of Liberty Unpolluted," *A Bicentennial Festschrift for Jacob Rader Marcus,* ed. Bertram W. Korn (Waltham, Mass., and New York, 1976), pp. 157–82. There is evidence that a few Jewish schools appealed for state funding, saying that if Catholic schools received such aid, the Jewish schools should too.

48. Hyman B. Grinstein, *The Rise of the Jewish Community of New York* (Philadelphia, 1945), pp. 235–37, 239; Fierman, "Jews and the Problem of Church and State," pp. 335–36; *OCC* 1 (1843–44): 413; for the anti-Jewish character of textbooks see Ruth M. Elson, *Guardians of Tradition* (Lincoln, Neb., 1964), pp. 81–87.

49. Gartner, "Temples of Liberty," pp. 166, 169–73; Fierman, "Jews and the Problem of Church and State," p. 336; *ISR,* 8–29 Dec. 1854; Davis, *Emergence of Conservative Judaism,* pp. 130–33.

50. Gartner, "Temples of Liberty," pp. 174–75; David Philipson, *Max Lilienthal* (New York, 1915), p. 122; CCAR, *Yearbook* 3 (1892): 126–29.

51. Michaelsen, *Piety in the Public School,* pp. 109–12, 117–22; Tyack, "Onward Christian Soldiers," pp. 220–33; Carl Zollman, *American Church Law* (St. Paul, Minn., 1933), pp. 94–95, 100–101; Way, "Death of the Christian Nation," pp. 519–20.

52. Gartner, "Temples of Liberty," pp. 175–76; Naomi W. Cohen, *Encounter with Emancipation* (Philadelphia, 1984), p. 92.

53. Michaelsen, *Piety in the Public School,* pp. 89–98.

54. Ibid., p. 103; Philipson, *Lilienthal,* ch. 6, pp. 474–87; UAHC, *Proceedings* 1 (1874): 85–86.

55. Heller, *Wise,* p. 620; Fierman, "Jews and the Problem of Church and State," p. 339; Michaelsen, *Piety in the Public School,* pp. 100–102.

56. *The Bible in the Public Schools,* reprint, intro. by Robert G. McCloskey (New York, 1967), pp. 54, 409–11; Michaelsen, *Piety in the Public School,* pp. 96–103; Philipson, *Lilienthal,* pp. 474–87 reprints Lilienthal's own description of the trial.

57. *Board of Education of Cincinnati v. Minor,* 23 Ohio St. 211 (1872); Johnson and Yost, *Separation of Church and State,* pp. 59–60.

58. *AI,* 10 Dec. 1875, 21 Jan., 21 Apr., 16, 30 June 1876, 10 June 1887, 20 May 1897, 15 Sept. 1892; *Jewish Times,* 22, 28 Jan., 18 Feb. 1870; *JM,* 25 June, 19 Nov. 1869, 31 Oct. 1873, 26 Jan. 1877, 23, 30 July 1886, 11 Feb. 1887, 25 Apr. 1890. 17 Feb., 29 Sept., 24 Nov. 1893, 28 Feb., 12 June 1896, 22 Feb. 1901.

59. *AH,* 14 May 1886, 3 Feb., 2 Mar. 1888. Cf. Rabbi H. Berkowitz on instruction in morality, *AI,* 5 Dec. 1889.

60. *Board of Education of Cincinnati* v. *Minor,* 23 Ohio St. 211; *AI,* 12 May 1876, 15, 22 Aug. 1889, 10 Apr. 1890, 15 Sept. 1892.

61. See, for example, E. P. Hurlbut, *A Secular View of Religion in the State, and the Bible in the Public Schools* (Albany, N.Y., 1870), pp. 38–40; Samuel T. Spear, *Religion and the State* (New York, 1876), pp. 383–84.

62. Michaelsen, *Piety in the Public School,* pp. 109–14; Tyack, "Onward Christian Soldiers," pp. 233–40. States entering the union after 1876 were generally required to provide for public schools "free from sectarian control." Zollman, *American Church Law,* p. 77.

63. *AI,* 25 Aug. 1876; Emma Felsenthal, *Bernhard Felsenthal* (New York, 1924), pp. 265–68, 306; Philipson, *Lilienthal,* pp. 123–24; Michaelsen, *Piety in the Public School,* p. 103.

64. *JM,* 9 Aug. 1889; Richard L. Rubenstein, "Church and State: The Jewish Posture," *Religion and the Public Order, 1963,* ed. Donald A. Giannella (Chicago, 1964), pp. 147–69; Milton Himmelfarb, "Secular Society? A Jewish Perspective," *Daedalus* 96 (1967): 220–30; Arthur Hertzberg, Martin A. Marty, and Joseph N. Moody, *The Outbursts That Await Us* (New York, 1963), pp. 140–53.

65. *AI,* 20 May 1881.

66. Handy, *A Christian America,* pp. 95–130; statement of Methodist conference, *New York Times,* 8 Apr. 1890; Josiah Strong, *Our Country,* ed. Jurgen Herbst (Cambridge, Mass., 1963), pp. 96–97, 106.

67. Blakely, *Sunday Legislation,* pp. 364–66; idem, *American State Papers on Freedom in Religion,* 4th ed. (Washington, 1949), pp. 264–67; *Church of the Holy Trinity* v. *United States,* 143 U.S. 457 (1892).

68. UAHC, *Proceedings* 17 (1890): 2636, 18 (1891): 2671, 2823, 2833, 21 (1894): 3355–56, 22 (1895): 3459; Blakely, *Sunday Legislation,* pp. 227–32, 295–96, 345; *AI,* 25 May, 7, 14 Dec. 1888, 3 Jan., 14 Mar., 26 Dec. 1889, 23 Jan., 6 Feb. 1890.

69. *Miscellaneous Documents of the Senate,* 50th Cong., 2d sess., Doc. 43 (Washington, 1889), pp. 14, 44–50, 94, 120–25; Pettibone, "Caesar's Sabbath," pp. 330–38; *New York Mail and Express,* cited in *AH,* 16 Aug. 1889, also said that Jews and Catholics were alien in a Protestant country.

70. Charles M. Snow, *Religious Liberty in America* (Washington, 1914), p. 305; *AI,* 21 July 1892; *Congressional Record,* 52d Cong., 1st sess., pp. 5999, 6051, 6053–54; Blakely, *Sunday Legislation,* pp. 370–77; idem, *Freedom in Religion,* pp. 298–303; Stokes, *Church and State,* 3:158–61. Lewis Abraham testified against the Sunday closing. *AI,* 5 May 1892.

71. UAHC, *Proceedings* 19 (1892): 3012–14, 3079–80; Simon Wolf, *Selected Addresses and Papers* (Cincinnati, 1926), p. 170.

72. CCAR, *Yearbook* 3 (1892): 42–45; Shlomith Yahalom, "American Judaism and the Question of Separation Between Church and State," Ph. D. thesis in Hebrew (Hebrew University of Jerusalem, 1981), pp. 109–12.

73. Blakely, *Sunday Legislation,* p. 344; UAHC, *Proceedings* 21 (1894): 3354–

55 (the Senate committee's hearings were not published); *AI,* 10 Apr. 1890, 1–15 Feb., 15 Mar., 3 May 1894; *JM,* 30 Mar. 1894; *AH,* 1 Mar. 1894.

74. House of Representatives, *Hearing Before the Committee on the Judiciary,* 11 Mar. 1896 (Washington, 1896), esp. pp. 5, 19–21, 24, 28, 42. At hearings in 1910 on the same issue, representatives of the NRA pointedly argued that the nation could not be governed by the wishes of the Jews. Blakely, *Sunday Legislation,* p. 345.

75. *AI,* 26 Mar., 16 Apr. 1896; UAHC, *Proceedings* 23 (1896): 3648, 3705–6.

76. UAHC, *Proceedings* 23 (1896): 3648, 3705–6, 27 (1900): 4123. The focus on proclamations was probably in response to the Court ruling of 1892 which cited religious terms in proclamations as proof of the Christian character of the nation. In 1900 Simon Wolf, a loyal Republican, criticized McKinley's Thanksgiving proclamation for including the words "In the year of our Lord."

77. *AI,* 13 June 1901.

CHAPTER 4

1. John Higham, *Strangers in the Land,* 2d ed. (New York, 1973), ch. 10; see also Naomi W. Cohen, *Not Free to Desist* (Philadelphia, 1972), ch. 7; Nathan C. Belth, *A Promise to Keep* (New York, 1979), ch. 4.

2. Cohen, *Not Free to Desist,* chs. 8–9; *AJYB* 38 (1936–37): 224–26, 39 (1937–38): 250–52, 41 (1939–40): 211–12, 42 (1940–41): 289–90; Dov Fisch, "The Libel Trial of Robert Edward Edmondson: 1936–1938," *American Jewish History* 71 (1981): 79–102.

3. CCAR, *Yearbook* 39 (1929): 59; Louis I. Newman, *The Sectarian Invasion of Our Public Schools* (San Francisco, 1925), p. 51; Stephen H. Goldfarb, "American Judaism and the Scopes Trial," *Studies in the American Jewish Experience,* vol. 2, ed. Jacob R. Marcus and Abraham J. Peck (Lanham, Md., 1984), pp. 42–44; Robert T. Handy, *A Christian America,* 2d ed. (New York, 1984), p. 130; Shlomith Yahalom, "American Judaism and the Question of Separation Between Church and State," Ph.D. thesis in Hebrew (Hebrew University of Jerusalem, 1981), pp. 223–37; Supreme Court of the United States, October Term 1967, *Epperson* v. *Arkansas, Brief of American Civil Liberties Union and American Jewish Congress as Amici Curiae;* Leo Pfeffer, "Jews and Jewry in American Constitutional History," *Jews, Judaism, and the American Constitution* ([Cincinnati,] 1982), pp. 26–27.

4. The "other ways" not discussed here included efforts toward the creation of a meaningful interfaith movement and nascent support of religious pluralism.

5. *AJYB* 17 (1915–16): 348–49; Naomi W. Cohen, *Encounter with Emancipation* (Philadelphia, 1984), pp. 238–46, ch. 7.

6. J. Schiff to T. Roosevelt, 31 July 1904, Schiff Papers; Ben Halpern, "The Roots of American Jewish Liberalism," *American Jewish Historical Quarterly* 66 (1976): 209.

7. G. Allentuck to author, 26 Aug. 1987.

8. Material for this and the next paragraph has been culled from Jonathan Frankel, *Prophecy and Politics* (Cambridge, Eng., 1981), esp. pp. 1–4, 49–74, 107–32; George Fischer, *Russian Liberalism* (Cambridge, Mass., 1958), pp. 46–47, 76–

80, 119–23, 203–4; Robert M. Seltzer, "Jewish Liberalism in Tsarist Russia," *Contemporary Jewry* 9 (1987–88): 47–66; Ben Halpern and Jehuda Reinharz, "Nationalism and Jewish Socialism," *Modern Judaism* 8 (1988): 219–48.

9. Charles S. Bernheimer, ed., *The Russian Jew in the United States* (Philadelphia, 1905); Michael Weisser, *A Brotherhood of Memory* (New York, 1985); Arthur A. Goren, *New York Jews and the Quest for Community* (New York, 1970); Arthur Gorenstein, "A Portrait of Ethnic Politics," *PAJHS* 50 (1961): 202–26; Halpern, "Roots of American Jewish Liberalism," pp. 207–8.

10. Naomi W. Cohen, "The Ethnic Catalyst," *The Legacy of Jewish Migration*, ed. David Berger (New York, 1983), pp. 131–48; Judah L. Magnes, *Evidences of a Jewish Nationality* (New York, 1908); Louis D. Brandeis, "The Jewish Problem and How to Solve It," *The Zionist Idea*, ed. Arthur Hertzberg (New York and Philadelphia, 1960), pp. 517–23.

11. CCAR, *Yearbook* 22 (1912): 108–18; 24 (1914): 212; *AI*, 9 July, 17 Sept. 1903.

12. Esther L. Panitz, *Simon Wolf* (Rutherford, N.J. 1987), pp. 121–23; U.S. Immigration Commission, *Reports*, vol. 41 (Washington, 1911), p. 277; Cohen, *Encounter with Emancipation*, pp. 228–31, 271–75; *AI*, 1 Jan. 1903.

13. UAHC, *Proceedings*, 30 (1903): 5027–51; Panitz, *Simon Wolf*, pp. 121–27; U.S. Immigration Commission, *Reports*, 41:265–76.

14. *Brief for Petitioner, In the Matter of Hersh Skuratowski*, U.S. District Court, Southern District of New York, 1909. On racial classification see the *Annual Reports* of the Commissioner General of Immigration. The report for 1932 still included that category.

15. For a full account of the abrogation episode see my article "The Abrogation of the Russo-American Treaty of 1832," *Jewish Social Studies* 25 (1963): 3–41.

16. Annual reports of the AJC in the *AJYB* for the 1920s; Charles Reznikoff, ed., *Louis Marshall, Champion of Liberty*, 2 vols. (Philadelphia, 1957), 2:930; Richard D. Horn, "Church–State Issues in the Twenties and Thirties," *Church and State in America, A Bibliographical Guide*, ed. John F. Wilson, 2 vols. (Westport, Conn., 1986–87), 2:192; Cohen, *Not Free to Desist*, pp. 215–18.

17. Marc L. Raphael, *Profiles in American Judaism* (San Francisco, 1984), pp. 117, 122, 136–40, 147–48, 150–52; reports of the Social Justice Committee in *Proceedings* of Rabbinical Assembly, 1930–40; Israel Goldstein, *My World As a Jew*, 2 vols. (New York, 1984), 1:72–73.

18. Cohen, *Not Free to Desist*, chs. 1, 2; CCAR, *Yearbook* 28 (1918): 146; AJC, Minutes of the Executive Committee, Nov. 16, 1924, AJC archives; Deborah D. Moore, *B'nai B'rith and the Challenge of Ethnic Leadership* (Albany, N.Y., 1981), ch. 5; Belth, *A Promise to Keep*, ch. 2.

19. Handy, *A Christian America*, ch. 5, pp. 134–51; Cohen, *Encounter with Emancipation*, pp. 194–202; William A. Blakeley, ed., *American State Papers on Freedom in Religion*, 4th ed. (Washington, 1949), pp. 269–74; idem, *American State Papers Bearing on Sunday Legislation*, rev. ed. (Washington, 1911), p. 344; *AI*, 15 Aug. 1907, 9 July 1908; R. C. Wylie, "Our System of Public Education, Is It Christian or Secular?" *National Reform Documents* 4 (1901): 2–61; David J. Brewer, *The United States a Christian Nation* (Philadelphia, 1905).

20. *Church of the Holy Trinity* v. *United States*, 143 U.S. 457 (1892); for mention of "Christian nation" see, for example, *Beecher* v. *Wetherby*, 95 U.S. 517 (1877),

Buttz v. *Northern Pacific Railroad,* 119 U.S. 55 (1886), *Davis* v. *Beason,* 133 U.S. 333 (1890).

21. Robert T. Miller and Ronald B. Flowers, eds., *Toward Benevolent Neutrality,* 3d ed. (Waco, Tex., 1987), pp. 48–55; Blakely, *Sunday Legislation,* pp. 487, 508–9; Brewer, *The United States a Christian Nation,* p. 11; Harold M. Stephens, "The School, the Church, and the State," *Marquette Law Review* 12 (1927): 223–24; *Lynch* v. *Donnelly,* 465 U.S. 668 (1984).

22. Simon Wolf, *Selected Addresses and Papers* (Cincinnati, 1926), pp. 171–72; Marshall's piece, originally printed in *Menorah* 20 (1896): 1–19, is reprinted in Reznikoff, *Louis Marshall,* 2:936–49.

23. *New York Times,* 26 Feb. 1906; *AI,* 9, 16 Nov. 1905, 5, 12 Apr., 19 July 1906.

24. UAHC, *Proceedings* 33 (1907): 5749, 34 (1908): 5990, 6071, 35 (1909): 6169, 6184–87; CCAR, *Yearbook* 19 (1909): 85; *Harper's Weekly,* 30 Jan. 1909; *AI,* 11, 18 Feb., 4 Mar., 15 July 1909.

25. *A Reply to Justice Brewer's Lectures "The United States a Christian Nation"* (Philadelphia, 1908).

26. Ephraim Frisch, *Is the United States a Christian Nation?,* paper read before the Southern Rabbinical Association, 25 Dec. 1906; Joseph Lewinsohn in *AI,* 12 Sept. 1907; Rudolph Coffee in *AI,* 9 July 1908; Max J. Kohler in *AH,* 1 Apr. 1910; Albert M. Friedenberg in *Reform Advocate,* 15 Jan. 1910, in *Jewish Comment,* 3 Nov. 1905, 29 Jan. 1909. See also A. Kraus in *AI,* 26 Oct. 1899, and essay by Marshall cited in n. 22. A later answer to Brewer appeared in an address by Rabbi M. P. Jacobson of Shreveport in 1913. *Is This a Christian Country?* (Shreveport, La., 1913), esp. pp. 13–14.

27. *AJYB* 3 (1901–2): 16, 9 (1907–8): 554; Alvin W. Johnson and Frank H. Yost, *Separation of Church and State in the United States* (Minneapolis, 1948), p. 47.

28. *AH,* 2 Feb. 1906; *AI,* 22 Feb. 1906; UAHC, *Proceedings* 31 (1905): 5352; Hassler, *A Reply to Justice Brewer's Lectures,* p. 28.

29. *Weiss* v. *District Board,* 76 Wis. 177 (1890); Johnson and Yost, *Separation of Church and State,* pp. 69–71; Robert Michaelsen, *Piety in the Public School* (New York, 1970), pp. 110–12.

30. Wylie, "Our System of Public Education," p. 54; *New York Times,* 8 Apr. 1890; on public opposition in Wisconsin see Wilber G. Katz, *Religion and American Constitutions* (Evanston, Ill., 1964), pp. 36–37; Donald E. Boles, *The Bible, Religion, and the Public Schools,* 3d ed. (Ames, Iowa, 1965), pp. 110, 112; CCAR, *Yearbook* 26 (1916): 148–49.

31. CCAR, *Yearbook* 14 (1904): 32; Joseph Fink, *Summary of C.C.A.R. Opinion on Church and State* (Philadelphia, 1948), p. 5. More recent surveys of CCAR activity are Eugene Lipman, "The Conference Considers Relations Between Religion and the State," *Retrospect and Prospect,* ed. Bertram W. Korn (New York, 1965), pp. 114–28, and Lance J. Sussman, "Rhetoric and Reality," *In Celebration,* ed. Kerry M. Olitzky (Lanham, Md., 1989), pp. 72–95.

32. *AI,* 27 Apr. 1905; M. Heller in *AI,* 18 May 1905; *Menorah* 38 (1905): 170–74, 307–8; UAHC, *Proceedings* 32 (1906): 5515–25.

33. The Harding case led the following year to a Jewish boycott of the schools and a compromise by the Board of Education. Leonard Bloom, "A Successful

Jewish Boycott of the New York City Public Schools," *American Jewish History* 70 (1980): 180–85; T. Schanfarber in *AI*, 5, 12 Apr. 1906; *AH*, 8 Feb., 23 Mar., 6 Apr., 2 June 1906; Eugene Markovitz, "Henry Pereira Mendes," *American Jewish Historical Quarterly* 55 (1966): 383; *Menorah* 42 (1907): 19–20; *AJYB* 9 (1907–8): 510–11; H. Friedenwald to B. L. Levinthal, 10 Dec. 1907, Christmas file, AJC archives.

34. Fink, *Summary of C.C.A.R. Opinion*, p. 5; CCAR, *Yearbook* 15 (1905): 137–38, 16 (1906): 150.

35. CCAR, *Yearbook* 16 (1906): 150–71, 17 (1907): 90–93, 19 (1909): 85–87, 508.

36. *CCAR, Yearbook* 16 (1906): 152–53; criticism of National Council of Jewish Women by T. Schanfarber, *AI*, 12, 19 Apr. 1906. Dr. Cyrus Adler, spokesman for Conservative Jews, also believed that the campaign would cause anti-Jewish prejudice. Cyrus Adler, *Selected Letters*, ed. Ira Robinson, 2 vols. (Philadelphia, 1985), 1:139.

37. M. Heller in *AI*, 27 Apr. 1905; CCAR, *Yearbook* 17 (1907): 92–93, 19 (1909):84, 21 (1911): 108–13, 24 (1914): 137–38, 25 (1915): 423–29, 26 (1916): 79–83, 85, 426–81. While the *AI* defended schools without Bible reading or instruction in morality, the *JM* suggested that "chapters of ethical import," inoffensive to all, could be chosen. *JM*, 22 Feb. 1901.

38. See debates and annual reports of the CCAR's Committee on Church and State in the *Yearbook*, vols. 14–17, 25 (1915): 120–24, 427–29, 27 (1917): 168–70; Fink, *Summary of C.C.A.R. Opinion*, p. 6; *AI*, 10 Mar., 30 June 1910.

39. *AI*, 12 Apr. 1906, 23 July, 6 Aug. 1908, 10 Feb. 1910.

40. CCAR, *Yearbook* 26 (1916): 148–49; memo, 31 Mar. 1941, Church and State/History, Box 44, RG 347–10, AJC files; Alvin W. Johnson, *The Legal Status of Church–State Relationships in the United States* (Minneapolis, 1934), pp. 26–30, chs. 3–5; Nathan Schachner, "Church, State, and Education," *AJYB* 49 (1947–48): 22–24; Boles, *Bible, Religion, and the Public Schools,* chs. 3–4. To the chagrin of some observers, Jewish principals and teachers compounded the hardships by their eagerness to accept Christian trappings and indeed the very concept of a Christian nation. Isaac Rosengarten, "The Jewish Teacher in the New York Public Schools," *Jewish Forum* 1 (1918): 320–21.

41. Carl Zollman, *American Church Law* (St. Paul, Minn., 1933), pp. 94–95, 101; Johnson and Yost, *Separation of Church and State*, ch. 4.

42. *Church* v. *Bullock*, 104 Tex. 1 (1908); Johnson and Yost, *Separation of Church and State*, pp. 52–53.

43. *Ring* v. *Board of Education*, 245 Ill. 334 (1910). A case in Louisiana went beyond the usual definition of sectarian. Three parents, two Jews and one Catholic, challenged readings from the Protestant Bible as well as recitations of the Lord's Prayer. The court responded with a singular line of reasoning. Distinguishing between the "Rabbinical Bible" and the "Christian Bible," it accepted the Jewish complaint about the use of the New Testament. The Catholics, however, were not in the same position; their Bible differed from the Protestant version but at bottom both were "the Bibles of the Christians." The exercises, however, were invalidated. *Herold* v. *Parish Board*, 136 La. 1034 (1915).

44. CCAR, *Yearbook* 40 (1930): 49.

45. CCAR, *Yearbook* 12 (1902): 112–15; Yahalom, "American Judaism and the Question of Separation," pp. 112–25.

46. Local communities found their own ways of resisting Sunday laws. *AH*, 11 May 1906; *AJYB* 15 (1913–14): 242; M. Harris in *AI*, 1 May 1902.

47. T. Schanfarber in *AI*, 12 Apr. 1906; *Maccabaean* 2 (1902): 23–24; I. Levitan in *Jewish Comment*, 25 June 1915; "The Jewish Sabbath in America," *Maccabaean* 2 (1902): 16–18.

48. Naomi W. Cohen, "The Challenges of Darwinism and Biblical Criticism to American Judaism," *Modern Judaism* 4 (1984): 122–23, 127–29, 145–46; CCAR, *Yearbook* 23 (1913): 210–11.

49. CCAR, *Yearbook* 16 (1906): 150, 17 (1907): 89–90, 24 (1914): 135–36; Johnson and Yost, *Separation of Church and State*, p. 254.

50. Blakely, *Sunday Legislation*, p. 556; idem, *Freedom in Religion*, p. 260 and seq.; Albert M. Friedenberg, *The Sunday Laws of the United States and Leading Judicial Decisions Having Special Reference to the Jews* (Philadelphia, 1908); idem in *AH*, 1 Jan. 1909; Anson P. Stokes, *Church and State in the United States*, 3 vols. (New York, 1950), 3:161; *AI*, 24 Dec. 1908, 7 Jan., 10 June 1909; M. Harris in *AI*, 6 June 1901; Peter Wiernik, *History of the Jews in America* (New York, 1912), pp. 327–28; *AJYB* 11 (1909–10): 104.

51. *AH*, 7 June 1901, 13 Feb. 1903. A Jewish–Irish clash at the turn of the century is examined in Leonard Dinnerstein, "The Funeral of Rabbi Jacob Joseph," *Anti-Semitism in American History*, ed. David A. Gerber (Urbana, Ill., 1986), pp. 275–301.

52. Wiernik, *History of the Jews*, p. 327; Friedenberg in *AH*, 1 Jan. 1909. A list of Supreme Court cases in which Sunday laws were upheld as valid exercises of the police power is in *Petit* v. *Minnesota*, 177 U.S. 164 (1900). Recurrent suits by Jews failed to dent the accepted constitutionality of Sunday legislation. Cf. *State* v. *Weiss*, 97 Minn. 125 (1906).

53. Friedenberg, *Sunday Laws*, pp. 29–30, 32; Friedenberg in *AH*, 1 Jan. 1909; Stokes, *Church and State*, 3:172; B. H. Hartogensis, "Denial of Equal Rights to Religious Minorities and Non-Believers in the United States," *Yale Law Journal* 39 (1929–30): 674–75.

54. UAHC, *Proceedings* 35 (1909): 6168, 6183–84, 37 (1911): 6533–34.

55. *AI*, 21 Nov. 1907, 12 Aug. 1909; M. Harris in *AI*, 6 June 1901, 1 May 1902.

56. *JM*, 7 June 1901.

57. Friedenberg in *AH*, 1 Jan. 1909, in *Jewish Comment*, 5 Aug. 1915; *AH*, 7 June 1901, 20 Feb. 1903; Leo Pfeffer, *Church, State, and Freedom* (Boston, 1953), p. 230; Chester Inwald, "Sabbath, Sunday and State," *Jewish Horizon* 12 (1949): 11.

58. Yahalom, "American Judaism and the Question of Separation," pp. 120, 122–23, 128; Friedenberg in *AH*, 1 Jan. 1909; Reznikoff, *Louis Marshall*, 2:923–28; *AJYB* 10 (1908–9): 143, 11 (1909–10): 59, 105–6, 12 (1910–11): 104, 15 (1913–14): 242, 16 (1914–15): 139; 26 (1924–25): 25; on the work of the Jewish Sabbath Alliance see Benjamin K. Hunnicutt, "The Jewish Sabbath Movement in the Early Twentieth Century," *American Jewish History* 69 (1979): 196–225; Bernard Drachman, "The Five Day Working Week," *Jewish Forum* 8 (1925): 486–90.

59. *AJYB* 28 (1926–27): 23–24, 29 (1927–28): 21, 30 (1928–29): 26–27; Yahalom, "American Judaism and the Question of Separation," pp. 122–27; *The Synagogue*

Council of America, Its Origins and Activities (New York, 1931), pp. 1–2, 8–9; CCAR, *Yearbook* 42 (1932): 65, 44 (1934): 42.

60. United Synagogue of America, *Fourth Annual Report,* 1917, pp. 20–21; Yahalom, "American Judaism and the Question of Separation," pp. 138–40, 231–37; *AJYB* 20 (1918–19): 368, 24 (1922–23): 23, 26 (1924–25): 25–26, 27 (1925–26): 28, 28 (1926–27): 27–29.

61. CCAR, *Yearbook* 41 (1931): 44, 43 (1933): 39, 44–47, 51, 47 (1937): 54, 50 (1940): 93; Sussman, "Rhetoric and Reality," pp. 91–92.

62. *AJYB* 28 (1926–27): 42; Michaelsen, *Piety in the Public School,* pp. 170–91; Johnson, *Legal Status of Church–State Relationships,* pp. 129–47; Pfeffer, *Church, State, and Freedom,* ch. 10; Stokes, *Church and State,* 2:495–534; Morris Fine, "The Released Time Plan of Religious Education," *Contemporary Jewish Record* 4 (1941): 14–20.

63. "The Jewish Position on Released Time and Bible Reading," Aug. 1960, pp. 14–17, Religion and Schools/AJC statements, Box 266, RG 347–10, AJC files; Reznikoff, *Louis Marshall,* 2:970; Michaelsen, *Piety in the Public School,* pp. 177–78.

64. Newman, *Sectarian Invasion of Our Public Schools,* p. 18; Stokes, *Church and State,* 2:528; Fine, "Released Time Plan of Religious Education," p. 16.

65. Stokes, *Church and State,* 2:495–97.

66. See annual reports of the Committee on Church and State in the *Yearbook* of the CCAR, esp. 32 (1922): 45, 34 (1924): 80–90, 35 (1925): 45–76, 36 (1926): 37–41, 83–84, 86–95; *AI,* 18 Aug. 1927.

67. Newman, *Sectarian Invasion of Our Public Schools,* passim.

68. Walter M. Howlett, "Released Time for Religious Education in New York City," *Religious Education* 37 (1942): 104, 106–7; CCAR, *Yearbook* 50 (1940): 85; Fine, "Released Time Plan of Religious Education," p. 20; Pfeffer, *Church, State, and Freedom,* pp. 316–17; Frank J. Sorauf, "The Released Time Case," *The Third Branch of Government,* ed. C. Herman Pritchett and Alan F. Westin (New York, 1963), p. 121. Before 1940 released time for New York City was supported by an interfaith committee, but it was rejected by the New York Board of Jewish Ministers, the very agency that had appointed the Jewish members on the committee. The episode well illustrates how interfaith pressures caused individual rabbis to deviate from their own group.

69. John W. Pratt, *Religion, Politics, and Diversity* (Ithaca, N.Y., 1967), pp. 272–80; Fine, "Released Time Plan of Religious Education," pp. 18, 20–21; *Jewish Education* 12 (1941): 130–32, 162–65; "Public School Time for Religious Education," *Reconstructionist,* 16 Feb. 1940; Ben Edidin of the Jewish Education Committee in "Released Time in New York City, A Symposium," *Religious Education* 38 (1943): 20–22.

70. CCAR, *Yearbook* 51 (1941): 120–21; Pfeffer, *Church, State, and Freedom,* p. 321.

71. Johnson, *Legal Status of Church–State Relationships,* pp. 130–34; *Lewis v. Graves,* 245 N.Y. 195 (1927).

72. CCAR, *Yearbook* 50 (1940): 90, 94, 51 (1941): 87, 52 (1942): 81–83; Joshua Trachtenberg in *AJYB* 43 (1941–42): 29 and 45 (1943–44): 138–39; Morris D. Waldman, "America and the Jewish Community," *Contemporary Jewish Record*

4 (1941): 256–57; G. George Fox, "Religious Education but Not in Public Schools," *Religious Education* 36 (1941): 213.

73. CCAR, *Yearbook* 50 (1940): 84–86, 93, 213, 51 (1941): 92–93; "Released Time in Chicago," *Religious Education* 36 (1941): 112–16.

74. F. Ernest Johnson, "Religious Education in Public Schools," *Contemporary Jewish Record* 3 (1940): 459–69; SCA, Conference on Religious Education and the Public School, Mar. 1944, pp. 10–12, 22, Religion and Schools/Conferences, Box 267, RG 347–10, AJC files; CCAR, *Yearbook* 50 (1940): 85, 54 (1944): 106.

75. Fox, "Religious Education but Not in Public Schools," pp. 214–16.

76. CCAR, *Yearbook* 53 (1943): 75–77. Unless otherwise noted, the material for the remainder of this section comes from SCA, Conference on Religious Education and the Public School, Mar. 1944.

77. The public stand of the defense agencies was mixed. The Congress opposed released time; the AJC and ADL opposed its introduction but did not advocate its repeal where it was in operation. Memo by A. H. Pekelis, Legal Status of "Released Time," 10 July 1945, Congress files.

78. Letter by Dr. Alexander Dushkin of the Jewish Education Committee in *Congress Weekly,* 1 May 1942.

OVERVIEW

1. Lucy S. Dawidowicz, *On Equal Terms* (New York, 1982), ch. 7; Murray Friedman, *The Utopian Dilemma* (Washington, 1985), ch. 2.

2. Charles H. Stember and Others, *Jews in the Mind of America* (New York, 1966), pp. 7–10.

3. See thoughtful comments by Murray Friedman, "A New Direction for American Jews," *Commentary* 72 (1981): 37–39.

4. Alexander H. Pekelis, "Full Equality in a Free Society: A Program for Jewish Action," *Law and Social Action,* ed. Milton R. Konvitz (Ithaca, N.Y., 1950), pp. 218–59. On the AJC see Naomi W. Cohen, *Not Free to Desist* (Philadelphia, 1972), part 2; on the ADL see Jill D. Snyder and Eric K. Goodman, *Friend of the Court, 1947–1982* (New York, 1983) and Nathan C. Belth, *A Promise to Keep* (New York, 1979). A brief comparison of the agencies is provided in Jerome A. Chanes, "The Voices of the American Jewish Community," *Survey of Jewish Affairs, 1989,* ed. William Frankel (Oxford, 1989), pp. 122–24.

5. Richard E. Morgan, *The Politics of Religious Conflict* (New York, 1968), p. 68.

6. The work of the Congress—rationale, tactics, allies—is skillfully analyzed in Frank J. Sorauf, *The Wall of Separation* (Princeton, N.J., 1976), esp. ch. 3; see also Will Maslow, "The Legal Defense of Religious Liberty: The Strategy and Tactics of the American Jewish Congress," paper presented at the annual meeting of the American Political Science Association, 1961; "Private Attorneys-General: Group Action in the Fight for Civil Liberties," *Yale Law Journal* 58 (1949): 589–98; Leo Pfeffer, "Amici in Church–State Litigation," *Law and Contemporary Problems* 44 (1981): 83–110; Morgan, *Politics of Religious Conflict,* pp. 77–81.

7. Workshop on Religion and the Public Schools, 16 Jan. 1948, Religion and Schools/AJC 1947–62, Box 265, RG 347–10, AJC files.

8. NCRAC, *Report on the Jewish Community Relations Agencies* (New York, 1951), pp. 77–80, 132–33, 192–94; Abraham G. Duker, *Jewish Community Relations* (New York, 1952), pp. 9–12, 34–35; Cohen, *Not Free to Desist,* p. 339.

9. In the 1950s a community on Long Island decided to post a nondenominational version of the Ten Commandments in every classroom. Since the content of the Christian Decalogue differed from the Jewish, and since Jews disagreed with Christians and Protestants disagreed with Catholics over the numbering of the commandments, the compromise version, which deviated from all standard texts, pleased no religious group. Leo Pfeffer, "Religious Confusion in Education," *American Judaism* 11 (Summer 1962): 8–9.

10. Cf. Wilber G. Katz, *Religion and American Constitutions* (Evanston, Ill., 1964), p. 46.

11. Friedman, *Utopian Dilemma,* p. 31.

12. Seymour Siegel, "Church and State," *Conservative Judaism* 17 (1963): 6–7.

13. Harold R. Rafton, "The Christian Amendment," *Unitarian Register,* Dec. 1958, Church and State/Christian Nation, AJC vertical files; National Council of Churches, *Information Service,* 22 Jan. 1955, *J.T.A. News,* 5 May 1955, Jesus Christ Authority-Congress files; *Newsweek,* 21 June 1954; *Christian Amendment, Hearings Before a Subcommittee of the Committee on the Judiciary, United States Senate, 83 Cong. 2 Sess. on S.J. Res. 87* (Washington, 1954), pp. 2–3, 15, 43, 52–54, 64–65.

14. *Religious News Service,* 20 May 1954, Jesus Christ Authority-Congress files; *New York Times,* 22, 23 May 1954; Rafton, "Christian Amendment"; *Christian Amendment Hearings,* pp. 18, 21, 31, 43, 64–65.

15. *New York Times,* 27 May 1954; J. Cohen to W. Maslow, 7 July 1953, S. Bolz to L. Pfeffer, 27 May 1954, L. Pfeffer to D. Petegorsky, 2 June 1954, Statement of the SCA and the NCRAC to the Senate Committee on the Judiciary in Opposition to S.J. Res. 87, 17 May 1954, Jesus Christ Authority-Congress files; *Christian Amendment Hearings,* pp. 5, 9–13, 31–33, 47, 69–82, 85–87.

16. Efforts for a Christian amendment persisted. See items for 1950s in Jesus Christ Authority-Congress files. The attempt in 1959 was sponsored by seven congressmen, more than had ever done so. *AJYB* 61 (1960): 40.

17. Arthur Gilbert, "Minority Jewish View on Religion and the State," *Jewish Digest* 8 (Aug. 1963): 38–39.

18. See, for example, Robert F. Drinan, *Religion, the Courts, and Public Policy* (New York, 1963), p. 230.

19. One regional director of the ADL recounted how aid to Israel became a quid pro quo for a Jewish retreat on separationism. Alexander F. Miller in *ADL Oral Memoirs* 5 (1987): 239, ADL files. An overview of Jewish–Catholic relations on separation is David G. Singer, "One Nation Completely Under God?" *Journal of Church and State* 26 (1984): 473–90.

20. Leo Pfeffer, "The Case for Separation," *Religion in America,* ed. John Cogley (New York, 1958), p. 60; *Everson* v. *Board of Education,* 330 U.S. 1 (1947), *McCollum* v. *Board of Education,* 333 U.S. 203 (1948). Black reiterated his interpretation of establishment in *Torcaso* v. *Watkins,* a case that invalidated a religious test for officeholding in Maryland. 367 U.S. 488 (1961). Leo Pfeffer and an attorney of the ACLU represented the plaintiff, an atheist who refused to swear a belief in

God in order to serve as a notary public, and the ADL and AJC filed an *amicus* brief on his behalf.

21. Statement of the SCA and the NCRAC Submitted to the Subcommittee on Constitutional Rights of the Senate Committee on the Judiciary, 9 Nov. 1955, Box 5, JAC files.

CHAPTER 5

1. Quoted by Conrad H. Moehlman in "Is the Public School 'Godless'?" *Congress Weekly,* 3 Mar. 1952, p. 20.

2. NCRAC–SCA, Joint Conference on Religious Instruction and the Public School, 11–12 Nov. 1946, NCRAC files. Unless otherwise noted, all material for this section is taken from the transcript of this conference.

3. For varying estimates on the extent of the program, see Leo Pfeffer, *Church, State, and Freedom* (Boston, 1953), p. 318, ch. 10; Milton Konvitz, "Whittling Away Religious Freedom," *Commentary* 1 (1946): 11–12.

4. Joseph H. Lookstein, "Religion and the Public Schools," *Jewish Education* 21 (1949): 39.

5. See also NCRAC–SCA, Conference on Sectarianism in the Public Schools, 10–12 June 1947, p. 47, Box 8, JAC files.

6. Pfeffer, *Church, State, and Freedom,* p. 322.

7. Statement of Principles on Released Time Practices in the Public Schools Adopted in 1947 by NCRAC and SCA, Box 11, JAC files.

8. Pfeffer, *Church, State, and Freedom,* p. 340; *New York Times,* 27 Jan. 1946. In 1947 a district court of appeals in California upheld released time. Donald E. Boles, *The Two Swords* (Ames, Iowa, 1967), pp. 29–34.

9. See also Minutes of NCRAC–SCA Meeting on Religious Instruction in the Public Schools, 17 Jan. 1946, Box 1, JAC files.

10. Pfeffer's career is outlined in his "Autobiographical Sketch," *Religion and the State: Essays in Honor of Leo Pfeffer,* ed. James E. Wood, Jr. (Waco, Tex., 1985). See also Leo Pfeffer, "The Case for Separation," *Religion in America,* ed. John Cogley (New York, 1958), pp. 90–91.

11. Pfeffer, *Church, State, and Freedom,* p. 343. When the ADL was approached by the Chicago Action Council, a group of left-wingers that had stimulated McCollum's suit, the Jewish agency refused its support. R. Gutstadt to A. Benesch, 21 Aug. 1945, I. Minkoff to NCRAC Executive Committee, 31 Dec. 1947, ADL files.

12. Arthur Gilbert, *A Jew in Christian America* (New York, 1966), p. 137.

13. 330 U.S. 1 (1947).

14. *Congressional Record,* 80th Cong., 1st sess., p. 4479; Richard E. Morgan, *The Supreme Court and Religion* (New York, 1972), pp. 90–93; Boles, *Two Swords,* pp. 11–12; L. Pfeffer to C. Posner, 15 Jan. 1948, CLSA binder, Congress files.

15. CCAR, *Yearbook* 57 (1947): 121–22, 59 (1949): 77; Leo Pfeffer, "A Little Case over Bus Fares," *Congress Weekly,* 21 Mar. 1947, pp. 5–7.

16. JAC, Minutes, 4 Mar. 1947, Box 1, NCRAC–SCA, Conference on Sectarianism, p. 36; Morgan, *Supreme Court and Religion,* pp. 81–90; Boles, *Two Swords,* pp. 14, 16; CCAR, *Yearbook* 57 (1947): 121.

17. NCRAC–SCA, Conference on Sectarianism, pp. 103–10, 126–51; Pfeffer, "Autobiographical Sketch," p. 492; L. Pfeffer to D. Petegorsky, 4 Apr. 1947, Released Time–Ill./McCollum, Congress files.

18. Pfeffer, *Church, State, and Freedom,* pp. 342–47.

19. Ibid., pp. 345–46; NCRAC–SCA, Joint Conference on Religious Instruction and the Public School; Supreme Court of Illinois, September Term 1946, *McCollum* v. *Board of Education, Abstract of Record,* pp. 22–37.

20. L. Pfeffer to D. Petegorsky, 4 Apr. 1947, to S. Polier, 5 May 1947, S. Polier to L. Pfeffer, 2 May 1947, J. Cohen to M. Brenner et al., 6 May 1947, Minutes of Special Legal Committee, 12 May, 10 June 1947, B. Miller to L. Pfeffer, 22 Oct. 1947, Released Time–Ill./McCollum, Congress files; Minutes of NCRAC–SCA Joint Committee, 4, 20 Mar. 1947, Box 1, JAC files.

21. L. Pfeffer to B. Miller, [June 1947,] 5 Sept. 1947, D. Petegorsky to W. Maslow, 18 June 1947, Minutes of Special Legal Committee, 10 June 1947, Minutes of Legislative Information Committee, 10, 17 July 1947, S. Polier to H. Epstein, 15 July 1947, Minutes of NCRAC–SCA Joint Committee, 21 July 1947, Released Time–Ill./McCollum, Congress files; Leo Pfeffer, *Creeds in Competition* (Westport, Conn., 1958), p. 68.

22. L. Pfeffer to B. Miller, 2 Sept. 1947, Released Time–Ill./McCollum, Congress files; NCRAC, *Report on the Jewish Community Relations Agencies* (New York, 1951), p. 79.

23. Supreme Court of the United States, October Term 1947, *McCollum* v. *Board of Education,* SCA and NCRAC, *Brief of Amici Curiae and Motion.*

24. Will Maslow, "The Legal Defense of Religious Liberty: The Strategy and Tactics of the American Jewish Congress," paper presented at the annual meeting of the American Political Science Association, 1961, pp. 14, 16; Samuel Krislov, "The Amicus Curiae Brief," *Yale Law Journal* 72 (1963): 711.

25. Released Time–Ill./McCollum, Congress files.

26. W. Maslow to JAC et al., 24 Dec. 1947, Released Time–Ill./McCollum, Congress files.

27. 333 U.S. 203 (1948); *Congress Weekly,* 19 Mar. 1948, pp. 3–4.

28. Clippings, Released Time–Ill./McCollum, Congress files; C. Herman Pritchett, *Civil Liberties and the Vinson Court* (Chicago, 1954), p. 12; Boles, *Two Swords,* p. 64; Gordon Patric, "The Impact of a Court Decision: Aftermath of the McCollum Case," *Journal of Public Law* 6 (1957): 455–64; Pfeffer, *Church, State, and Freedom,* p. 352; Pfeffer, in "The Fight Against Released Time," *Standard* 35 (1948): 9, said that disregard of the decision was worst in the South.

29. *New York Times,* 10 Mar., 12 Mar. (Pfeffer's letter) 1948; L. Pfeffer to O. Cohen and H. Barron, 11 Mar. 1948, Released Time–Ill./McCollum, Congress files; *Congress Weekly,* 15 Mar. 1948; "McCollum Case," Ill./CI [1949], AJC files; Leo Pfeffer, "Religion, Education and the Constitution," *Lawyers Guild* 8 (May–June 1948); Theodore Leskes, "Released Time—Not Just an Hour," *Committee Reporter* 6 (1949): 7; CCAR, *Yearbook* 58 (1948): 105–6; Pfeffer, "Autobiographical Sketch," p. 494.

30. Pfeffer, *Creeds in Competition,* pp. 73–74; "Protestants: Come Clean!" *Christian Century,* 16 June 1948, p. 592.

31. *New York Times,* 21 Nov. 1948; *Religious News Service,* 15 Dec. 1948, Congress files; Robert F. Drinan, "The Lawyers and Religion," *America,* 5 Mar.

1949, pp. 593–95; idem, *Religion, the Courts, and Public Policy* (New York, 1963), pp. 80–81; Joseph H. Brady, *Confusion Twice Confounded,* 2d ed. (South Orange, N.J., 1955), p. 190; John C. Murray, "Law or Professions?" *Law and Contemporary Problems* 14 (1949): 23–43; Pfeffer, *Creeds in Competition,* pp. 68–69.

32. A. Rosenbaum to J. Slawson, 21 May 1948, Religion and Schools/1947–62, Box 265, RG 347–10, AJC files; JAC, Minutes, 28 June 1948, Box 1, JAC files; Samuel Walker, *In Defense of American Liberties* (New York, 1990), pp. 219–20.

33. Shad Polier, "Observations on Church–State Problems in America and the Interest of the American Jewish Community," *Journal of Jewish Sociology* 1 (1959): 74–75.

34. CLSA, *Reports,* 3 May 1948, Comments on the McCollum Decision, Released Time–Ill./McCollum, Congress files; S. Hirsh to Domestic Affairs Committee, 13 Jan. 1949, Religion and Schools/Released Time 40–61, Box 271, Re-Statement of Views on Released Time, 7 June 1949, Religion and Schools/Released Time/AJC, Box 271, RG 347–10, AJC files; JAC, Minutes, 28 June, 27 July 1948, 1 Feb. 1950, Box 1, JAC files; S. Rabkin to A. Forster, 22 Mar. 1948, ADL files.

35. *New York Times,* 10 Mar. 1948, and Pfeffer's letter to *Times,* 12 Mar. 1948; *Lewis* v. *Spaulding,* 193 Misc. 66 (N.Y. 1948); Frank J. Sorauf, "The Released Time Case," *The Third Branch of Government,* ed. C. Herman Pritchett and Alan Westin (New York, 1963), pp. 122–24; idem, *The Wall of Separation* (Princeton, N.J., 1976), pp. 48–51; Maslow, "Legal Defense of Religious Liberty," p. 8. Vashti McCollum claimed credit for persuading Lewis to withdraw his suit. V. McCollum to B. Miller, 21 Apr. 1949, Released Time–Ill./McCollum, Congress files.

36. JAC, Minutes, 28 June 1948, Box 1, JAC files; L. Pfeffer to O. Cohen and H. Barron, 11 Mar. 1948, W. Maslow to JAC et al., 24 Dec. 1947, Released Time–Ill./McCollum, Congress files; Sorauf, "Released Time Case," pp. 127–28; B. Herzberg to H. Epstein, 19 Nov. 1948, Religion and Schools/Released Time/AJC, Box 271, RG 347–10, AJC files.

37. L. Pfeffer, memos on Strategy Committee Meetings, 14 July 1948, 28 June 1950, L. Pfeffer to S. Polier, 22 Nov. 1948, to K. Greenawalt, 28 Aug. 1950, Released Time–N.Y./Zorach, Congress files; Sorauf, "Released Time Case," pp. 122, 124–27.

38. Pfeffer, *Church, State, and Freedom,* pp. 356–67; Sorauf, "Released Time Case," pp. 132–34.

39. *Zorach* v. *Clauson,* 198 Misc. 631 (N.Y. 1950); 303 N.Y. 161 (1951); 278 App. Div. 573 (N.Y. 1951); Sorauf, "Released Time Case," pp. 123–24, 129–33.

40. Supreme Court of the State of New York, Appellate Division-Second Department, 1950, *Zorach* v. *Clauson, Amici Curiae Brief, Submitted on Behalf of the AJC, the AJ Congress, and the ADL;* Court of Appeals of the State of New York, 1951, *Zorach* v. *Clauson, Amici Curiae Brief Submitted on Behalf of the AJC, the AJ Congress, and the ADL.* The New York Board of Rabbis also filed on the side of Zorach. Sorauf, "Released Time Case," p. 131.

41. L. Pfeffer to K. Greenawalt, 28 Aug. 1950, Released Time–N.Y./Zorach, Congress files.

42. The Jewish members were Edward S. Greenbaum, Daniel Gutman, Maximilian Moss, and Sol Tekulsky.

43. Sorauf, *Wall of Separation,* p. 222; *New York Times,* 2 July 1951.

44. Pfeffer, "Autobiographical Sketch," pp. 498–99; JAC, Minutes, 10 Jan. 1952, Box 1, JAC files.

45. J. Leonard Azneer, "The Attitude of American Jewish Leaders with Reference to Selected Problems of Religion in Public Education," Ph.D. thesis (University of Pittsburgh, 1959), pp. 28–29; J. Cohen to R. Lederer, 2 Oct. 1950, Box 10, JAC files; Solomon B. Freehof, "Religion and the Public Schools," *Religious Education* 43 (1948): 207–9; Leo Pfeffer, "Judgment by Attack and Default," *Congress Weekly,* 25 June 1951, p. 8.

46. Phil Baum, "Church and State Today: A Survey," *Congress Weekly,* 3 Mar. 1952, pp. 3–5; JAC, Minutes, 19 Sept. 1951, Box 1, JAC files; Pfeffer, *Church, State, and Freedom,* p. 385. Again in 1951, when Jews of Jersey City protested the erection of a public nativity scene, the JAC, this time with the Congress's consent, agreed to inaction. JAC, Minutes, 11 Dec. 1951, Box 1, JAC files.

47. JAC, Minutes, 8 May, 8 June 1951, J. Cohen to JAC, 28 June 1951, Box 1, JAC files; CCAR, *Yearbook* 61 (1951): 115–16; *New York Times,* 31 Mar., 11 May 1951; *Christian Century,* 11 Apr. 1951, p. 451; *Congress Weekly,* 4 June 1951, pp. 3–4.

48. *St. Louis Register,* 10 June 1949, Box 1, JAC files.

49. CCAR, *Yearbook* 61 (1951): 109–20; 57 (1947): 120–21; 62 (1952): 161–62; Religion and Schools/CCAR 51–53, Box 266, M. Jung to J. Slawson et al., 15 Nov. 1950, Religion and Schools/1947–62, Box 265, RG 347–10, AJC files.

50. Baum, "Church and State Today," p. 3; JAC, Minutes, 8 June, 28 July, 19 Sept., 20 Nov. 1951, 10 Jan., 13 Mar. 1952, Box 1, JAC files; Notes on Off-the-Record Meeting with Top Protestant Leadership, 21 Jan. 1952, Church–State/Conferences, Box 44, RG 347–10, AJC files.

51. Summary of Informal Discussions between Jewish and Protestant Leaders on Church–State Issues, 26 Dec. 1951, Box 1, JAC files.

52. *New York Times,* 20 Nov. 1951.

53. Pfeffer, *Church, State, and Freedom,* p. 331; Sorauf, "Released Time Case," p. 139.

54. Baum, "Church and State Today," p. 3.

55. 193 Misc. 66 (N.Y. 1948). Twenty years before, in *Lewis* v. *Graves,* the court had said that "Neither the Constitution nor the law discriminates against religion." 245 N.Y. 195 (1927).

56. 198 Misc. 631 (N.Y. 1950); L. Pfeffer, memo, 28 June 1950, to D. Petegorsky, 2 Feb. 1951, Released Time–N.Y./Zorach, Congress files.

57. L. Pfeffer to K. Greenawalt. 28 Aug. 1950, Released Time–N.Y./Zorach, Congress files; Sorauf, "Released Time Case," pp. 121–23, 128.

58. Court of Appeals, State of New York, 1951, *Zorach* v. *Clauson, Brief for Intervenor-Respondent, The Greater New York Coordinating Committee on Released Time of Jews, Protestants and Roman Catholics.*

59. *Zorach* v. *Clauson,* 303 N.Y. 161 (1951).

60. Summary of Recent and Current Issues before the JAC [Jan. 1952], Box 1, JAC files. See n. 40 for citations to the Jewish briefs.

61. Sorauf, "Released Time Case," p. 139; *Zorach* v. *Clauson,* 343 U.S. 306 (1952).

62. Cf. Douglas's later remarks on religious freedom and on Americans as a

religious, and a Christian, people. William O. Douglas, *The Bible and the Schools* (Boston, 1966), p. 4.

63. Sorauf, "Released Time Case," pp. 145–48; idem, "*Zorach* v. *Clauson*," *American Political Science Review* 53 (1959): 782–91. Justice Black, now in the minority, held that in *Zorach* the Court abandoned the principle of government neutrality on religion. Pritchett, *Civil Liberties and the Vinson Court*, pp. 12–14. In 1956, when the Bureau of the Census announced that it would include the question "What is your religion?" in the next national census, Pfeffer saw the influence of Douglas's opinion at work. *Church, State, and Freedom*, rev. ed. (Boston, 1967), pp. 261–64.

64. L. Pfeffer to D. Sawyer, 21 Mar. 1952, Released Time–N.Y./Zorach, Congress files; "Breached but Not Demolished," *Congress Weekly*, 12 May 1952, pp. 3–4; JAC, Minutes, 5 May 1952, M. Brenner and S. Kramer to NCRAC membership, 16 May 1952, communal reports on released time, Box 11, JAC files; CCAR, *Yearbook* 63 (1953): 61, 66 (1956): 46, 67 (1957): 38.

65. L. Lynch to H. G. Perlmutter, 6 Feb. 1959, Released Time–Ill./McCollum, Congress files.

CHAPTER 6

1. The influential report of the American Council on Education, "The Relation of Religion to Public Education" (1947), was reprinted in *Religious Education* 42 (1947): 129–63; a summary of the Council's report of 1953 appeared in *Religious Education* 48 (1953): 67–72.

2. Leo Pfeffer, *Church, State, and Freedom*, rev. ed. (Boston, 1967), pp. 350–63; Robert F. Drinan, *Religion, the Courts, and Public Policy* (New York, 1963), pp. 43–50; NCRAC–SCA, Conference on Sectarianism in the Public Schools, June 10–12, 1947, Box 8, JAC files; CCAR, *Yearbook* 63 (1953): 61–68; *AJYB* 55 (1954): 54.

3. I. Chipkin to M. Kertzer, 21 Nov. 1951, Religion and Schools 1935–53, Box 265, RG 347–10, AJC files. A study of Jewish opinions in the 1950s also confirmed that the recent proposals were receiving equal if not more attention from individual communal leaders. J. Leonard Azneer, "The Attitude of American Jewish Leaders to Selected Problems of Religion in Public Education," Ph.D. thesis (University of Pittsburgh, 1959).

4. CCAR, *Yearbook* 63 (1953): 66, 65 (1955): 46, 66 (1956): 45, 47, 67 (1957): 40; Marvin Braiterman, *Religion and the Public Schools* (New York, 1964), p. 2; Pfeffer, "Outlook in Church and State," p. 9; Abraham G. Duker, "The Community and Education," *Congress Weekly*, 8 Jan. 1951, p. 15; *Congress Weekly*, 12 Dec. 1955, p. 3.

5. *New York Times*, 16 Nov., 13 Dec. 1952; CCAR, *Yearbook* 63 (1953): 54; I. Chipkin to M. Kertzer, 21 Nov. 1951, Religion and Schools 1935–53, Box 265, RG 347–10, AJC files.

6. The entire issue of *Congress Weekly* for 3 Mar. 1952 dealt with aspects of the church–state problem; see especially articles by Moehlman and Polier.

7. Azneer, "Attitude of American Jewish Leaders," pp. 9–13; Arthur Gilbert,

"Should There Be Religion in the Schools?" *National Jewish Monthly* 71 (1957): 24.

8. Morris Adler, "Religion and Public Education," *CCAR Journal,* no. 9, Apr. 1955, pp. 8–13; CCAR, *Yearbook* 62 (1952): 160. Two other rabbinical critiques of the new proposals were Robert Gordis, "Education for a Nation of Nations," *Religion and the Schools* (New York, 1959), pp. 10–13, and Israel Goldstein, "Moral Training Through the School," *Congress Weekly,* 23 Feb. 1953, pp. 8–9.

9. NCRAC–SCA, Conference on Sectarianism, pp. 51, 216–39, 399–402.

10. Pfeffer, *Church, State, and Freedom,* pp. 493–98; William D. Silverman and Samuel D. Soskin, "Joint Holiday Observances in the Public Schools," *CCAR Journal,* no. 9, Apr. 1955, pp. 23–28; *Congress Weekly,* 7 Nov. 1955, p. 4; CCAR, *Yearbook* 67 (1957): 41; Benjamin Epstein in *ADL Bulletin* 12 (Oct. 1955): 6–7; Frank N. Trager, "The Big Blooming Buzzing Confusion," *Religious Education* 46 (1951): 82–89; JAC, Minutes, 29 Jan., 8 May 1951, 10 Jan. 1952, 21 Oct. 1953, S. Rabkin to J. Cohen, 16 Apr. 1952, Box 1, JAC files. The AJC also left NCRAC in 1952.

11. ADL, Statement of Principles on Religious Holiday Observances, 1950, Box 1, JAC files; Pfeffer, *Church, State, and Freedom,* pp. 479–87; *Jewish Spectator* 27 (Sept. 1962): 4. The JAC convened a special conference in 1949 that dealt exclusively with the Christmas–Hanukkah issue. For one local community's experience see Eugene J. Lipman and Albert Vorspan, eds., *A Tale of Ten Cities* (New York, 1962), pp. 231–52.

12. S. Graubard to Special Committee, 26 Sept. 1962, ADL files; address by Jules Cohen at the National Conference of Jewish Communal Service, 28 May 1956, J. Cohen to L. Ruchames, 15 Jan. 1958, Box 2, JAC files; Pfeffer, *Church, State, and Freedom,* p. 490.

13. JAC, Minutes, 26 Feb. 1953, Box 1, JAC files; see, for example, Congress, introduction to a study manual, Church and State 1958, Congress files, and Braiterman, *Religion and the Public Schools* (published by the UAHC).

14. NCRAC–SCA, Conference on Sectarianism, pp. 281–82; Simon Greenberg, "A Jewish Educator's View," *American Education and Religion,* ed. F. Ernest Johnson (New York, 1952), pp. 52–54; Azneer, "Attitude of American Jewish Leaders," pp. 169–77.

15. JAC, Conferences (Regional), Cincinnati 1954, St. Louis 1954, Box 4, Summary of a National Conference Looking Toward the Formulation of a Statement of Principles, 25–27 Oct. 1954, Box 2, JAC files; SCA–NCRAC, *About Three Current Approaches to the Teaching of Religion in the Public Schools,* reprinted in a pamphlet, SCA–NCRAC, *Religion and the Public School,* compiled Jan. 1956. The statement was also incorporated into an extensive position paper printed as SCA–NCRAC, *Safeguarding Religious Liberty* (New York, 1957).

16. AJC, *Religion in Public Education* (New York, 1955), pp. 7–10, 13–14; ADL, *Religious Education and the Public Schools* (New York, 1955), pp. 6–9; JAC, Minutes, 12 Sept. 1955, A. Feldman and M. Brenner to JAC, 27 Oct. 1955, 7 May 1957, Box 1, I. Goldaber to JAC, 25 Aug. 1955, Box 7, JAC files.

17. *Congress Weekly,* 19 Dec. 1955, pp. 4–5; *Congress Bi-Weekly,* 12 Nov. 1962, p. 4, 16 Feb. 1959, p. 4; Leo Pfeffer, *Creeds in Competition* (Westport, Conn., 1958), esp. ch. 9.

18. *New York Times,* 1 Dec. 1951.

19. Leo Pfeffer, *Church, State, and Freedom* (Boston, 1953), pp. 395–99; JAC, Minutes, 24 Dec. 1951, Box 1, M. Brenner and S. Kramer to Jewish Community Leaders, 22 Jan. 1952, statements of organizations on Regents' prayer, Box 10, JAC files; statement of ADL regional board, Prayer–General 1951–61, Congress files.

20. A. Vorspan to JAC, 3 June 1952, Prayer–General 1951–61, Congress files; CLSA, Fact Sheet on Statement of NYC Board of Superintendents on "Moral and Spiritual Values and the Schools," 20 Oct. 1955, Box 7, JAC, Minutes, 1 Dec. 1952, Box 1, JAC files; Leo Pfeffer, "Court, Constitution and Prayer," *Rutgers Law Review* 16 (1962): 736–37; *Congress Weekly,* 26 Jan. 1953, p. 4.

21. CLSA, Fact Sheet.

22. Statements of the New York Board of Rabbis, Roman Catholic Archdiocese of New York, and Protestant Council of the City of New York, May 1954, Board of Superintendents, "Moral and Spiritual Values and the Schools," 14 June 1955, Box 7, JAC files. The revised guide and pertinent organizational statements were compiled by the JAC in "The NYC Board of Education Guide to Superintendents and Teachers on 'The Development of Moral and Spiritual Ideals,'" Box 7, JAC files. See also *Congress Weekly,* 8 Oct. 1956, pp. 4–5; Richard B. Dierenfield, *Religion in American Public Schools* (Washington, 1962), p. 42; Drinan, *Religion, the Courts, and Public Policy,* p. 63.

23. JAC, Minutes, 13 Mar. 1952, Box 1, JAC files; L. Pfeffer to S. Gaber, 2 Feb. 1959, Prayer–General 1951–61, remarks by Pfeffer in Report of JAC conference, 16 July 1962, Prayer–N.Y./Engel, Congress files.

24. Prayer–General 1951–61, Congress files; JAC, Minutes, 2 Jan., 24 Oct. 1950, 29 Jan. 1951, Box 1, JAC files.

25. Paul Blanshard, *Religion and the Schools* (Boston, 1963), pp. 27, 30–33, 252; *Congress Weekly,* 4 Feb. 1957, p. 2, 11 Nov. 1957, p. 2; T. Leskes and S. Rabkin to CRC Offices, 21 June 1957, ADL files; J. Cohen to JAC, 28 Nov. 1958, Box 10, JAC files.

26. *New York Times,* 28 June 1962; Blanshard, *Religion and the Schools,* pp. 27–29; Frank J. Sorauf, *The Wall of Separation* (Princeton, N.J., 1976), p. 43; H. Lazere to W. Maslow, 10 March 1959, Prayer–General 1951–61, Congress files.

27. L. Pfeffer to S. Polier, 21 Oct., 24 Nov., 18 Dec. 1958, to S. Gaber, 2 Feb. 1959, Prayer–General 1951–61, Congress files; JAC, Minutes, 22 Dec. 1958, Box 1, JAC files; L. Pfeffer to S. Polier, 3 Apr. 1959, to A. Vorspan, 21 Apr. 1959, A. Vorspan to *National Jewish Post,* 20 Apr. 1959, Prayer–N.Y., Congress files.

28. *New York Times,* 26 June 1962; hate mail reproduced in Blanshard, *Religion and the Schools,* pp. 30–32.

29. H. Chabot to J. Robison, 16 Nov. 1959, L. Pfeffer to P. Perlmutter, 28 Oct. 1959, Prayer–General 1951–61, Congress files.

30. *Engel* v. *Vitale,* 18 Misc.2d 659 (N.Y. 1959). The decision affected the standing of the Lord's Prayer. Because the ruling stressed the nondenominational character of the Regents' prayer, the New York State Department of Education interpreted that to mean that denominational prayers like the Lord's Prayer were invalid. C. Brind to S. Polier, 24 Jan. 1961, Prayer–General 1951–61, Congress files; S. Rabkin and T. Leskes, joint memorandum, 21 Nov. 1960, ADL files.

31. *Engel* v. *Vitale,* 11 App. Div.2d 340 (N.Y. 1960).

32. A. Forster to National Civil Rights Committee, 9 June 1961, ADL files; Court of Appeals, State of New York, *Engel* v. *Vitale, Brief of AJC and ADL, Amici Curiae,* 1961.

33. *Engel* v. *Vitale,* 10 N.Y.2d 174 (1961); Blanshard, *Religion and the Schools,* pp. 36–37.

34. Blanshard, *Religion and the Schools,* pp. 37–38; Pfeffer, "Court, Constitution and Prayer," p. 738.

35. Supreme Court of the United States, October Term 1961, *Engel* v. *Vitale, Brief of SCA and NCRAC as Amici Curiae; Brief of AJC and ADL as Amici Curiae.*

36. S. Rabkin to ADL Regional Offices, 6 July 1962, ADL files; Bernard Schwartz, *Super Chief* (New York, 1983), pp. 440–41.

37. *Engel* v. *Vitale,* 370 U.S. 421 (1962). See also S. Rabkin to ADL Regional Offices, 6 July 1962, ADL files; Pfeffer, "Court, Constitution and Prayer," pp. 738–42; Blanshard, *Religion and the Schools,* p. 47. In a concurring opinion Justice Douglas retreated from his decision in *Zorach.*

38. S. Rabkin to ADL Regional Offices, 6 July 1962, ADL files; Pfeffer, "Court, Constitution and Prayer," pp. 743–51; remarks by Pfeffer in JAC, Report of Conference, 16 July 1962, Prayer–N.Y./Engel, Congress files.

39. *Congressional Record,* 87th Cong., 2d sess., 26–27 June 1962; Schwartz, *Super Chief,* p. 442; Blanshard, *Religion and the Schools,* ch. 3; Conference of JAC, 16 July 1962, background papers, Prayer–N.Y./Engel, Congress files; *New York Times,* 27 June 1962.

40. Conference of JAC, 16 July 1962, background papers, Prayer–N.Y./Engel, Congress files; Report of JAC conference, 16 July 1962, address by S. Vincent, Prayer–N.Y./Engel, Congress files.

41. Conference of JAC, 16 July 1962, background papers, Prayer–N.Y./Engel, Congress files; Blanshard, *Religion and the Schools,* pp. 58–66; Public Reaction to the *Engel* v. *Vitale* Decision, 11 Sept. 1962, Religion and Public Schools/Prayer/AJC, AJC vertical files; S. Bernards et al. to A. Miller, 16 July 1962, ADL files.

42. *New York Times,* 28 June 1962; Conference of JAC, 16 July 1962, background papers, Prayer–N.Y./Engel, Congress files; S. Bernards et al. to A. Miller, 16 July 1962, ADL files.

43. Conference of JAC, 16 July 1962, background papers, M. Kellett to AJ Congress, 17 Nov. 1962, Prayer–N.Y./Engel, Congress files.

44. NCRAC, news release, 28 June 1962, CLSA to Division Leaders, 6 July 1962, Prayer–N.Y./Engel, Congress files; A. Rosen to A. Miller, 3 July 1962, S. Rabkin to ADL Regional Offices, 9 July 1962, ADL files; Leo Pfeffer, "State-Sponsored Prayer," *Commonweal,* 27 July 1962, pp. 417–19; E. London to Division and Chapter Presidents, 6 July 1962, CLSA binder, Congress files; P. Jacobson to J. Levine, 13 July 1962, Box 3, JAC files.

45. This and the next two paragraphs are based on Report of JAC conference, 16 July 1962, Prayer–N.Y./Engel, Congress files.

46. See also P. Jacobson to All Constituent Agencies, 20, 25 July 1962, Box 10, JAC files.

47. JAC, Minutes, 26 July 1962, Box 1, P. Jacobson to All Constituent Agencies, 27 July 1962 (with Hirsch report), Box 3, JAC files.

48. P. Jacobson to All Constituent Agencies, 3 Aug. 1962 (with Hirsch report),

Box 10, JAC files; Joseph Fisher, "The Becker Amendment," *Journal of Church and State* 11 (1969): 427–34. The edited record of the hearings was printed later as *Prayers in Public Schools and Other Matters, Hearings before the Committee on the Judiciary,* U.S. Senate, 87th Cong., 2d sess., 26 July, 2 Aug. 1962.

49. Statements of Jewish agencies and of legal authorities in the printed *Hearings,* pp. 94–105, 135–39, 164–66.

50. 1 Sept. 1962, pp. 665–66.

51. Blanshard, *Religion and the Schools,* p. 70.

52. Folder on *America* in Prayer–N.Y./Engel, Congress files; Albert J. Menendez, ed., *The Best of Church & State* (Silver Spring, Md., 1975), p. 18; *Commonweal,* 7 Sept. 1962, pp. 483–84; *Christian Century,* 5 Sept. 1962, pp. 1057–58.

53. JAC, Minutes, 27 Aug. 1962, Box 1, JAC files; CLSA, *Reports,* 17 Sept. 1962, Congress files; *New York Times,* 27, 28, 31 Aug. 1962; J. Pat to editors, *America,* 10 Sept. 1962, Prayer–N.Y./Engel, Congress files; letter of M. Schneerson to *Jewish Forum* 45 (Nov.–Dec. 1962): 4; undated letter by L. Horowitz, Religion and Public Schools/Prayer/Jews, AJC vertical files.

54. *America,* 8 Sept. 1962, pp. 679–80; *New York Times,* 2 Sept. 1962.

55. *America,* 15, 22 Sept. 1962, pp. 708, 713, 760, 768–69.

56. Letter from S. Siegel to *Jewish Spectator* 27 (June 1962): 30; Jakob J. Petuchowski, "Logic and Reality," *Jewish Spectator* 27 (Sept. 1962): 19–20; *New York Times,* 4 July, 27 Nov. 1962; letter from M. Schneerson to *Jewish Forum,* p. 4; *Jewish Life* 29 (Aug. 1962): 5–7, 30 (Oct. 1962): 9–21.

57. Marc L. Raphael, *Profiles in American Judaism* (San Francisco, 1984), ch. 9; Murray Friedman, *The Utopian Dilemma* (Washington, 1985), pp. 31–35.

58. William W. Brickman, "Public Aid to Jewish Day Schools," *Tradition* 3 (Spring 1961): 151–85; Naomi W. Cohen, "Schools, Religion, and Government: Recent American Jewish Opinions," *Michael,* vol. 3, ed. Lloyd P. Gartner (Tel Aviv, 1975), pp. 364–65, 366–69. The right-wing Agudath Israel charged the defense agencies with conducting a "vendetta against yeshivas." *Jewish Week,* 19 Jan. 1974, Jewish Day Schools, Congress files.

59. J. Cohen to S. Weiss, 7 Dec. 1962, Box 3, JAC files; *AJYB* 67 (1966): 129, 139. An Orthodox group, Young Israel, dissociated itself from the Congress's stand on separation in June 1962. Milton R. Konvitz, "Inter-Group Relations," *The American Jew: A Reappraisal,* ed. Oscar I. Janowsky (Philadelphia, 1964), p. 99.

60. Will Herberg, "The Sectarian Conflict over Church & State," *Commentary* 14 (1952): 450–62.

61. Letters from readers, *Commentary* 15 (1953): 99–103; Will Herberg, "Religious Education and General Education," *Religious Education* 48 (1953): 135–41; idem, "Religion, Democracy and Public Education," *Religion in America,* ed. John Cogley (New York, 1958), pp. 139–40; T. Adams and M. Brenner to JAC, 2 Jan. 1958, Box 1, JAC files.

62. Drinan, *Religion, the Courts, and Public Policy,* p. 53; Arthur Gilbert, "Religion and the Free Society," *Reconstructionist,* 3 Oct. 1958, pp. 10–12. For Gilbert's support of programs in moral and spiritual values, see his "Should There Be Religion in the Schools?" *National Jewish Monthly* 71 (1957): 8; CCAR, *Yearbook* 67 (1957): 41.

63. CCAR, *Yearbook* 68 (1958): 53–64.

64. CCAR, *Yearbook* 69 (1959): 63–65, 70 (1960): 38–42. The Congress also

felt impelled to search for a Jewish rationale, and the CLSA *Reports* of 1 May 1962 harked back to the words of the prophet Jeremiah (29:7).

65. Michael Wyschogrod, "Second Thoughts on *America*," *Tradition* 5 (Fall 1962): 29–36.

66. Letter from S. Siegel to *Jewish Spectator*, p. 30; Seymour Siegel, "Church and State," *Conservative Judaism* 17 (Spring–Summer 1963): 1–12.

67. Herbert Weiner, "The Case for the Timorous Jew," *Midstream* 8 (1962): 3–14.

68. *Jewish Spectator* 27 (May 1962): 5–7, (Sept. 1962): 3–5; *Congress Bi-Weekly*, 12 Nov. 1962, p. 13; staff seminar, 9 Oct. 1962, Dom–AS/Church–State, AJC files; David Danzig (of the AJC) in *Commonweal*, 28 Sept. 1962, pp. 6–8; *AJYB* 67 (1966): 139; Milton Himmelfarb, "Church and State: How High a Wall?" *Commentary* 42 (1966): 23–29; on the Jewish neoconservative critique of strict separation see Noah Pickus, "'Before I Built a Wall,'" *This World*, no. 15 (Fall 1986): 28–43.

69. Two representative rabbinical opinions are Robert Gordis, letter to *New York Times*, 16 July 1962, and Seymour J. Cohen, "Religious Freedom and the Constitution," *Conservative Judaism* 17 (1963): 13–38.

70. Balfour Brickner, "The Main Issue," address, 14 Sept. 1962, Prayer–N.Y./Engel, Congress files; Arthur Hertzberg, "Church, State, and the Jews," *Commentary* 35 (1963): 277–88. See Hertzberg in *Commonweal*, 28 Sept. 1962, pp. 8–10 and in *The Outbursts That Await Us* (New York, 1963), ch. 3.

71. Richard L. Rubenstein, "Church and State," *Religion and the Public Order, 1963*, ed. Donald A. Giannella (Chicago, 1964), pp. 147–69.

72. Reinhold Niebuhr, "The Court and the Prayer," *New Leader,* 9 July 1962, pp. 3–4; Erwin N. Griswold, "Absolute Is in the Dark," *Utah Law Review* 8 (1963): 167–82.

73. Paul A. Freund and Robert Ulich, *Religion and the Public Schools* (Cambridge, Mass., 1965), p. 40; Milton Himmelfarb, "Secular Society? A Jewish Perspective," *Daedalus* 96 (1967): 223.

74. Hertzberg, "Church, State, and the Jews," pp. 284, 288.

CHAPTER 7

1. CLSA *Reports,* 1 Jan. 1964; *Congressional Record,* 87th Cong., 2d sess., Index: s.v. S.J. Res. 207.

2. John H. Laubach, *School Prayers* (Washington, 1969), pp. 30–33; Leo Pfeffer, *Church, State, and Freedom,* rev. ed. (Boston, 1967), p. 445; Donald E. Boles, *The Bible, Religion, and the Public Schools,* 3d ed. (Ames, Iowa, 1965), p. 60; Frank J. Sorauf, *The Wall of Separation* (Princeton, N.J., 1976), p. 297.

3. Boles, *Bible, Religion, and the Public Schools,* chs. 3–4; Pfeffer, *Church, State, and Freedom,* pp. 445–56, 450–55; Laubach, *School Prayers,* p. 32; AJC, "The Doremus Case," [1951,] Religion and Schools/Bible-Reading, Box 266, RG 347–10, AJC files.

4. Statement of M. Brenner at NCRAC executive committee meeting, 15 Jan. 1952, Church–State/Organizations/Resolutions and Statements, Box 44, RG 347–10, AJC files; Leo Pfeffer, *Church, State, and Freedom* (Boston, 1953), p. 386,

rev. ed., pp. 449–50; AJC, "The Doremus Case"; JAC, Minutes, 24 Oct. 1950, Box 1, JAC files; CCAR, *Yearbook* 61 (1951): 114–15; Marvin Braiterman, *Religion and the Public Schools* (New York, 1958), p. 65. Three times during the 1950s the JCRCs of California were instrumental in preventing the passage of a Bible-reading bill. Files on local communities, Box 8, JAC files.

5. Boles, *Bible, Religion, and the Public Schools,* pp. 49, 57; NCRAC–SCA, Conference on Sectarianism in the Public Schools, 10–12 June 1947, p. 41, Box 8, memorandum of R. Hirsch in P. Jacobson to All Constituent Agencies, 3 Aug. 1962, Box 10, JAC files; Braiterman, *Religion and the Public Schools,* p. 38.

6. *Life,* 11 Sept. 1950, p. 162; CCAR, *Yearbook* 61 (1951): 114; Statement of the New York Board of Rabbis, Prayer–General 1951–61, Congress files.

7. *Doremus* v. *Board of Education,* 5 N.J. 435 (1950).

8. L. Pfeffer to S. Polier, 13 Dec. 1950, 14 Mar. 1951, to J. Eisenberg, 13 Mar. 1951, to W. Maslow, 17 July 1951, W. Maslow to L. Pfeffer, 5 July 1951, H. Levy to L. Pfeffer, 16 July 1951, Bible-Reading/N.J.–Doremus, Congress files; JAC, Minutes, 19 Sept. 1951, Box 1, JAC files.

9. Supreme Court of the United States, October Term 1951, *Doremus* v. *Board of Education, Brief of the American Jewish Congress, Amicus Curiae;* CCAR, *Yearbook* 62 (1952): 152; CLSA *Reports,* 7 Feb. 1952; *Doremus* v. *Board of Education,* 342 U.S. 429 (1952).

10. *Youngstown* (Ohio) *Vindicator,* 6 Mar. 1952, Box 8, JAC files.

11. Form letter by W. Rosenblum and M. Brenner, 28 Sept. 1948, ADL files; Boles, *Bible, Religion, and the Public Schools,* p. 93.

12. Pfeffer, *Church, State, and Freedom,* rev. ed., pp. 456–57; NCRAC–SCA, Conference on Sectarianism in the Public Schools, 10–12 June 1947, pp. 77–89, Box 8, J. Cohen to JAC, 31 Mar. 1952, JAC, "Legal Memorandum in Opposition to Distribution in the Public Schools of the Protestant Version of the New Testament by the Gideons, International," [1948,] and JAC, "Supplement to Legal Memorandum," [1952,] Box 2, JAC files; L. Pfeffer to O. Dudkin, 20 Mar. 1953, Bible-Reading/Gideons–Rutherford, Congress files.

13. Pfeffer, *Church, State, and Freedom,* rev. ed., p. 458; L. Pfeffer to W. Maslow, 17 June 1952, to D. Petegorsky, 18 Mar. 1953, to S. Bols, 14 Dec. 1953, Bible-Reading/Gideons–Rutherford. The Catholic parent later withdrew when his child transferred to a parochial school.

14. Testimony of witnesses quoted in *Tudor* v. *Board of Education,* 14 N.J. 31 (1953); L. Pfeffer to D. Petegorsky, 6 May 1953, Bible-Reading/Gideons–Rutherford, Congress files; Sorauf, *Wall of Separation,* p. 119.

15. Boles, *Bible, Religion, and the Public Schools,* pp. 92–94. The broader issue of whether nonsectarian religious material, or religious material of any kind, might be distributed was raised in a brief filed by the SCA and NCRAC. It claimed that even if the Rutherford authorities used school machinery for distributing *Jewish* religious literature, the act would still be unconstitutional. Superior Court of New Jersey, Appellate Division [1953], *Lecoque and Tudor* v. *Board of Education, Brief of Amici Curiae.*

16. CCAR, *Yearbook* 65 (1955): 45, 66 (1956): 46; Leo Pfeffer, "An Autobiographical Sketch," *Religion and the State,* ed. James E. Wood, Jr. (Waco, Tex., 1985), p. 513; Leo Pfeffer, "The Gideons March on the Schools," *Congress Weekly,* 10 Oct. 1953, pp. 7–9, 21 Dec. 1953, pp. 3–4.

17. JAC, Minutes, 19 Sept. 1951, Box 1, JAC files; S. Rabkin to J. Cohen, 21 Jan. 1952, Bible-Reading/Gideons–Rutherford, Congress files.

18. H. Lazere to Congress Staff, 23 Dec. 1960, Miami Religion-in-the-Schools Case, Congress files.

19. H. Lazere to L. Pfeffer, 3 Apr. 1959, H. Heiken to L. Pfeffer, 18 Apr. 1959, Bible-Reading/Fla., Congress files; S. Rabkin to ADL Regional Offices, 2 Aug. 1960, P. Jacobson to S. Vincent, 9, 17 Aug. 1960, Box 10, JAC files.

20. H. Lazere to Congress Staff, 23 Dec. 1960, Miami Religion-in-the-Schools Case, Congress files.

21. S. Rabkin to ADL Regional Offices, 2 Aug. 1960, S. Fineberg and T. Leskes to CRCs, 16 Aug. 1960, B. Roth to J. Mintzer, 28 Nov. 1960, to CRCs, 9 Feb. 1961, ADL memorandum, Dec. 1960, W. Maslow, "AJCongress and the Miami Case," Box 10, JAC files.

22. S. Rabkin to ADL Regional Offices, 2 Aug. 1960, Congress, "Miami Story," Box 10, JAC files. The counsel involved in the *Chamberlin* case, who had originally told the "not for sale" story, later backtracked. He confirmed the ADL version in writing, but he explained to the Congress that he preferred not to figure in an interagency dispute. H. Heiken to B. Roth, 14 Dec. 1960, H. Lazere to L. Pfeffer, 15 Dec. 1960, Miami Religion-in-the-Schools Case, Congress files.

23. J. Mintzer to R. Kohler, 17 Nov. 1960, B. Roth to J. Mintzer, 28 Nov. 1960, W. Maslow, "AJCongress and the Miami Case," Box 10, JAC files.

24. S. Vincent to I. Minkoff, 2 Aug. 1960, to P. Jacobson, 15, 18 Aug. 1960, I. Levine to P. Jacobson, 19 Aug. 1960, J. Mintzer to R. Kohler, 17 Nov. 1960, ADL memo, Dec. 1960, Congress, "Miami Story," Box 10, JAC files.

25. W. Maslow, "AJCongress and the Miami Case," Box 10, JAC files.

26. ADL memo, Dec. 1960, W. Maslow, "AJCongress and the Miami Case," Box 10, JAC files; H. Lazere to Y. Rosenberg, 18 Jan. 1960, to L. Pfeffer, 24, 26 Feb., 11 Mar. 1960, *Religious News Service*, 30 Oct. 1959, Bible-Reading/Fla.; H. Lazere to Congress Staff, 23 Dec. 1960, Miami Religion-in-the-Schools Case, Congress files; Sorauf, *Wall of Separation,* pp. 151–52, 200. Sorauf also discusses the hostility vented on two of the litigants.

27. Sorauf, *Wall of Separation,* pp. 280–81.

28. S. Rabkin to ADL Regional Offices, 2 Aug. 1960, ADL memo, Dec. 1960, Congress, "Miami Story," Box 10, JAC files; *Congress Bi-Weekly,* 2 Jan. 1961, p. 3; *AJYB* 62 (1961): 89–90.

29. ADL memo, Dec. 1960, Congress, "Miami Story," Box 10, JAC files; Pfeffer, *Church, State, and Freedom,* rev. ed., pp. 487–90.

30. JAC, Minutes, 27 Oct. 1960, Box 1, Congress, "Decision in Miami," Terms of Proposed Settlement of Miami Suit, 25 Oct. 1960, Box 10, JAC files.

31. Congress, "Miami Story," Box 10, JAC files; Sorauf, *Wall of Separation,* pp. 119–20; text of decision (17 Fla. Supp. 183 [1961]) in P. Jacobson to NCRAC Members, 27 Apr. 1961, Congress, "Decision in Miami," Box 10, JAC files; S. Rabkin to ADL Regional Offices, 27 Apr. 1961, ADL files.

32. *Schempp* v. *School District of Abington Township,* 177 F.Supp. 398 (1959); Paul Blanshard, *Religion and the Schools* (Boston, 1963), pp. 99–100, 103; Sorauf, *Wall of Separation,* p. 134.

33. M. Klinger to S. Polier, 1 Aug. 1957, L. Pfeffer to S. Gaber, 27 Mar.,

20 May 1958, to S. Polier, 13 Apr. 1958, news release, 16 Jan. 1959, Bible-Reading–Pa./Schempp, Congress files.

34. 177 F.Supp. 398; Supreme Court of the United States, October Term 1962, *Abington Township* v. *Schempp, Brief for Appellees.*

35. 177 F.Supp. 398; L. Pfeffer to S. Polier, 29 Sept. 1959, memorandum by S. Rabkin and T. Leskes, 2 Oct. 1959, memorandum by P. Hartman and T. Leskes, 29 Dec. 1960, Bible-Reading–Pa./Schempp, Congress files; *School District of Abington Township* v. *Schempp,* 364 U.S. 298 (1960).

36. Eugene J. Lipman and Albert Vorspan, eds., *A Tale of Ten Cities* (New York, 1962), pp. 204–30; Minutes of Religious Freedom Committee, JCRC, 16 May 1957, Box 8, JAC files.

37. S. Rabkin to M. Fagan, 12 Nov. 1959, P. Jacobson to M. Fagan, 17 Nov. 1959, Box 8, JAC files; JCRC, Guide for Parents, 1 Nov. 1960, Bible-Reading–Pa./Schempp, Congress files.

38. JCRC, Statement on the 1959 Pennsylvania Bible Reading Law, 1 Apr. 1960, J. Cohen to CRCs, 11 Apr. 1960, to P. Jacobson, 20 Apr. 1960, P. Jacobson to J. Cohen, 15 Apr. 1960, Box 8, JAC files. The JCRC also prepared a guide for parents. Since it recognized the pressures for conformity, it did not presume to advise parents to seek excuses for their children. By its sympathetic offer of assistance, the JCRC strengthened its hold over the rank and file of the Jewish community. JCRC, Guide for Parents, 1 Nov. 1960, Bible-Reading–Pa./Schempp, Congress files.

39. Lipman and Vorspan, *Tale of Ten Cities,* pp. 226–27; U.S. District Court for the Eastern District of Pennsylvania, *Schempp* v. *School District of Abington Township, Brief of JCRC of Greater Philadelphia as Amicus Curiae* [1961].

40. Decision printed in *Legal Intelligencer,* 2 Feb. 1962, Box 3, JAC files; memorandum by S. Rabkin and T. Leskes, 14 Feb. 1962, Bible-Reading–Pa./Schempp, Congress files.

41. JCRC, Some Arguments Against the Practice of Bible Reading and Prayers, 5 Mar. 1962, *Religious News Service,* 13 Feb. 1962, M. Joslow to L. Pfeffer, 19 Feb. 1962, J. Cohen to P. Jacobson et al., 5 Mar. 1962, Bible-Reading–Pa./Schempp, Congress files; J. Cohen to CRCs, 5 Feb. 1962, memorandum by J. Cohen, 13 Mar. 1962, Box 8, JAC, Minutes, 11 Jan. 1960, Box 1, JAC files.

42. Notes on Program re Church–State, 9 Nov. 1962, N.Y./CI/Rel/Prayer, E. Lukas to M. Cohn, 14 Mar. 1963, CRS-D 63 Church–State/Prayer Decision, AJC files; P. Jacobson to All Constituent Agencies, 19 Mar. 1963, Bible-Reading–Pa./Schempp, Congress files.

43. Sorauf, *Wall of Separation,* pp. 131–33, 215; Helen H. Ludwig, "The Baltimore Lord's Prayer Court Case," Background Reports, NCCJ, Nov. 1962, *Religious News Service,* 7 Mar. 1963, Bible-Reading–Md., Congress files; JAC, Minutes, 23 Oct. 1962, Box 1, JAC files; Blanshard, *Religion and the Schools,* pp. 104–6; Marc D. Stern to author, 6 Aug. 1987.

44. A. Forster to National Civil Rights Committee, 4 June 1962, ADL files; Supreme Court of the United States, October Term 1962, *Murray* v. *Curlett, School District of Abington Township* v. *Schempp, Brief of American Jewish Committee and Anti-Defamation League of B'nai B'rith as Amici Curiae, Brief of Synagogue Council of America and National Community Relations Advisory Council as Amici Curiae.*

45. The Union of Orthodox Jewish Congregations had already indicated its support of silent prayer, and even Pfeffer no longer urged a unified stand in opposition. JAC, Minutes, 18 June 1963, NCRAC files.

46. *Religious News Service,* 27 Feb. 1963, Bible-Reading–Md., Congress files; Blanshard, *Religion and the Schools,* p. 113; Bernard Schwartz, *Super Chief* (New York, 1983), p. 466; Leo Pfeffer, "The Schempp–Murray Decision on School Prayers and Bible Reading," *Journal of Church and State* 5 (1963): 172.

47. Schwartz, *Super Chief,* pp. 467–68; *Abington Township School District* v. *Schempp,* 374 U.S. 203 (1963).

48. CLSA *Reports,* 1 Jan. 1964, Congress files.

49. 374 U.S. 203, at 240; Arthur Gilbert, "Religious Freedom and Social Change in a Pluralistic Society," *Religion and the Public Order, 1964,* ed. Donald A. Giannella (Chicago, 1965), p. 116.

50. S. Rabkin to Special Committee on Church and State, 15 July 1963, ADL files; CLSA *Reports,* 15 July, 1 Oct. 1963, Congress files; AJC, "Bible Reading after the *Schempp–Murray* Decision," Dec. 1963, *Dialogue,* May 1964, p. 4, Religion and Public Schools/Prayer/NCCJ, AJC vertical files; Laubach, *School Prayers,* pp. 138–39. For the impact of *Schempp* on the Florida (*Chamberlin*) case, see Laubach, *School Prayers,* pp. 103–4.

51. *Congressional Digest* 43 (1964): 268–69; *New York Times,* 11 Sept. 1963; memorandum from I. Terman, 21 Feb. 1964, Religion and Public Schools/Prayers/AJC, AJC vertical files; Laubach, *School Prayers,* p. 47.

52. *School Prayers, Hearings Before the Committee on the Judiciary, House of Representatives, 88 Cong. 2 Sess.* (Washington, 1964) (hereinafter referred to as *Hearings*), p. 22; memorandum from I. Terman, 21 Feb. 1964; Donald E. Boles, *The Two Swords* (Ames, Iowa, 1967), p. 117; *Dialogue,* May 1964, Religion and Public Schools/Prayers/NCCJ, AJC vertical files.

53. Memorandum from I. Terman, 21 Feb. 1964; poster in Bible-Reading–Pa./Schempp, E. London to Chapter and Division Presidents, 13 Feb. 1963, *Religious News Service,* 15 May 1964, Bible-Reading/General, Congress files.

54. Memorandum from I. Terman, 21 Feb. 1964; *Dialogue,* May 1964, pp. 4, 6, Religion and Public Schools/Prayers/NCCJ, AJC vertical files; CLSA *Reports,* 15 Feb. 1964, Congress files; Joseph Fisher, "The Becker Amendment," *Journal of Church and State* 11 (1969): 436, 455.

55. S. Rabkin to Special Committee on Church and State, 16 Dec. 1963, 2 Jan. 1964, ADL files; E. London to Chapter and Division Presidents, 13 Feb. 1963, P. Jacobson to Constituent Agencies, 16 Jan. 1964, Bible-Reading/General, Congress files. Unless otherwise noted, material for the following three paragraphs comes from Bible-Reading/General, Feb.–June 1964, Congress files.

56. Gibbons's letter also proved advantageous when it was used during the committee hearings to expose an erroneous statement in Becker's own testimony. *Hearings,* p. 220.

57. P. Jacobson to All Constituent Agencies, 20 July 1962, Box 10, 25 July 1962, Box 3, JAC files.

58. Reuben Gross, "The Mask of Neutralism," *Jewish Life* 31 (May–June 1964): 40–44; Gross in *Jewish Observer* 1 (Sept. 1964): 11–12

59. A. Wurtzel to L. Pfeffer, 26 Mar. 1964, Bible-Reading/General, Congress files. Minutes and reports of Kelley's committee and of the parallel committee in

Washington, which are the basis of the next three paragraphs, are in Bible-Reading/ General, Congress files, and in CRS/Church and State/Prayer Amendment/NCC, AJC files. See also Laubach, *School Prayers,* pp. 48–49.

60. On behalf of the committee Pfeffer also wrote to faculty of divinity schools. L. Pfeffer to L. Silberman, 2 Apr. 1964, Bible-Reading/General, Congress files.

61. Memorandum from R. Millenson, 12 Mar. 1964, CRS/Church and State/ Prayer Amendment/Becker, AJC files; William M. Beaney and Edward N. Beiser, "Prayer and Politics," *Journal of Public Law* 13 (1964): 498.

62. L. Pfeffer to P. Freund, R. Drinan, and W. Katz, 7 May 1964, Bible-Reading/General, Congress files; Laubach, *School Prayers,* pp. 65–67; *Hearings,* pp. 2483–84; *Prayers in Public Schools and Other Matters, Hearings Before the Committee on the Judiciary, U.S. Senate, 87 Cong. 2 Sess.* (Washington, 1962), pp. 166–67.

63. Testimony in *Hearings,* pp. 923–38, 977–86, 1239–65, 1425–49, 1627–31, 1996–2000, 2013–22, 2120–23, 2308–14. See also Graubard in *ADL Bulletin* 41 (Nov. 1984): 4–5. The only Jewish statements in favor of an amendment that were read into the record were one from the Lubavitcher rebbe and another, which was introduced by Becker, from a Dr. Jonas Simon. *Hearings,* pp. 2003–11, 2034–35.

64. *Hearings,* pp. 224–28; Laubach, *School Prayers,* pp. 49–50; Congress, news release, 27 Apr. 1964, Bible-Reading/General, Congress files.

65. *Hearings,* pp. 1140, 1038–42; *New York Herald Tribune,* 12 May 1964; *Group Research Report,* 1 May 1964, Bible-Reading/General, Congress files; Boles, *Bible, Religion, and the Public Schools,* pp. 324–27.

66. Report of Kelley's committee, 15 July 1964, L. Pfeffer to W. Maslow, 18 Aug. 1964, Bible-Reading/General, Congress files; Laubach, *School Prayers,* ch. 4; Boles, *Bible, Religion, and the Public Schools,* pp. 327–30.

67. *Hearings,* p. 923; L. Pfeffer to W. Maslow, 18 Aug. 1964, Bible-Reading/ General, Congress files.

68. NCRAC, *Report of the Twentieth Anniversary Plenary Session,* 25–28 June 1964, p. 36; Rodney K. Smith, *Public Prayer and the Constitution* (Wilmington, Del., 1987), pp. 266–79.

69. Nancy Fuchs-Kreimer, "Religious Studies in the Public Schools," *Analysis,* no. 59, Oct. 1976; Arthur Gilbert, "Reactions and Resources," *Religion and Public Education,* ed. Theodore R. Sizer (Boston, 1967), pp. 43–46, 57–58; 65–80; idem, "Religious Freedom and Social Change," pp. 118–20.

70. Quotes in Gilbert, "Reactions and Resources," pp. 47–48; Seymour Cohen in symposium, *Religious Education* 59 (1964): 448–51.

71. Gilbert, "Reactions and Resources," pp. 61–63; JAC, Conference on Church and State–Workshop on Religion in the Schools, 17 Oct. 1966, ADL files.

72. "Bible Reading and the Recitation of the Lord's Prayer in Public Schools," NCRAC, *Report of the Plenary Session,* 27–30 June 1963, pp. 24–36.

73. Fuchs-Kreimer, "Religious Studies in the Public Schools," p. 4; JAC, Workshop, 17 Oct. 1966, S. Rabkin to Law Committee, 13 May 1968, P. Hartman and J. Lichten to L. Waldman, 10 June 1968, L. Silberman to Steering Committee– Commission on Church–State, 9 May 1969, ADL files. Eventually questions relating to the content of "objective" courses reached the courts. Marc D. Stern, *Religion and the Public Schools* (New York, 1986), pp. 3–4.

74. Pfeffer, "Schempp–Murray Decision," p. 175.

CHAPTER 8

1. Quoted in Milton R. Konvitz, "Inter-Group Relations," *The American Jew: A Reappraisal,* ed. Oscar I. Janowsky (Philadelphia, 1964), p. 83.

2. Chester J. Antieau, Phillip M. Carroll, and Thomas C. Burke, *Religion Under the State Constitutions* (Brooklyn, N.Y., 1965), pp. 76–79; Leo Pfeffer, *Church, State, and Freedom* (Boston, 1953), pp. 230–38; Frank H. Yost, "Sunday Laws Are Religious Laws," *Congress Weekly,* 3 Mar. 1952, pp. 12–14.

3. See, for example, CCAR, *Yearbook* 66 (1956): 50; Isaac Rosengarten, "Attempts at Sabbath Legislation in Albany," *Jewish Forum* 29 (1946): 24.

4. Rosengarten, "Attempts at Sabbath Legislation," pp. 23–25; Melvin Hyman, "Sabbatarians and the Sunday Blue Laws Controversy in New York State," Ph.D. thesis (New York University, 1975), pp. 49–55; Leo Pfeffer, "Sunday Law and Sabbath Observance," *Congress Weekly,* 13 Feb. 1950, p. 9, also 20 Apr. 1954, p. 4; S. Rabkin to M. Friedman, 14 Nov. 1955, ADL files.

5. *AJYB* 54 (1953): 102, 55 (1954): 82–84, 56 (1955): 232–34; Arthur Hertzberg, *The Jews in America* (New York, 1989), pp. 300–301.

6. Pfeffer, "Sunday Law and Sabbath Observance," p. 9; Rosengarten, "Attempts at Sabbath Legislation," p. 23.

7. *Jewish Life* 25 (Aug. 1958): 8–9.

8. M. Feigenbaum to A. Forster, 3 July 1953, S. Rabkin to P. Lerman, 28 July 1955, D. Lebenthal to S. Rabkin, 19 Mar. 1963, to J. Finger, 11 June 1963, ADL files.

9. Pfeffer, "Sunday Law and Sabbath Observance," p. 9; Jerome Lefkowitz, "Sunday Blue Laws," *Congress Bi-Weekly,* 28 Dec. 1959, p. 13; S. Rabkin to F. Grossman, 7 May 1957, ADL files. The ADL has full correspondence on developments in the various states; see also Church–State/Sunday Closing Laws, Box 45, RG 347–10, AJC files.

10. Letter from Pfeffer to *New York Times,* 19 June 1951; Pfeffer, "Sunday Law and Sabbath Observance," p. 11; idem, "Are Sunday Laws Religious Laws?" *Liberty,* 1958, CLSA binder, Congress files; Chester Inwald, "Sabbath, Sunday and State," *Jewish Horizon* 12 (Sept. 1949): 8, 12.

11. Pfeffer, *Church, State, and Freedom,* pp. 236–41; Leo Pfeffer, "The Fading of the Blue Laws," *Congress Monthly* 42 (Sept. 1975): 7–9; Supreme Court (NY) Appellate Division—First Department, *People* v. *Friedman, Brief of Defendants–Appellants,* 30 Dec. 1949; A. Johnson to L. Pfeffer, 31 Dec. 1950, Sunday Laws/Kosher Butchers Case, Congress files.

12. Court of Appeals of the State of New York, *People* v. *Friedman, Brief of Amici Curiae,* American Jewish Congress et al., 16 Oct. 1950; *Religious News Service,* 17 Oct. 1950, Sunday Laws/Kosher Butchers Case, Congress files.

13. Supreme Court of the State of New York Appellate Division—First Department, *People* v. *Friedman, Brief as Amicus Curiae on Behalf of New Deal Kosher Butchers Association Inc., et al.,* 9 Feb. 1950; M. Jung to M. Kertzer, 6 Feb. 1950, Church–State/Sunday Closing Laws, Box 45, RG 347–10, AJC files.

14. *People* v. *Friedman,* 302 N.Y. 75 (1950); Pfeffer, *Church, State, and Freedom,* pp. 236–37; for developments in New York see Hyman, "Sabbatarians and the Blue Laws Controversy."

15. W. Maslow to S. Polier, 17 June 1951, Sunday Laws/Kosher Butchers Case;

L. Pfeffer to Chapter Presidents, Nov. 1953, CLSA binder, Congress files; Pfeffer, "Fading of the Blue Laws," p. 8.

16. Sol Rabkin, "The Sabbath Story," *ADL Bulletin,* 15 (Nov. 1958): 1–3, 7; *Dialogue,* 15 June 1960, CRS-L/Church–State/Sunday Closing Laws/AJC files; Detroit survey cited in JAC, A Survey of Three Areas of Church–State Relations, Spring 1958, Box 5, JAC files.

17. Richard Cohen, *Sunday in the Sixties* (New York, 1962); JAC, Survey... 1958, Box 5, Congress, Survey and Outlook for Sunday Laws, 10 Apr. 1958, Box 4, JAC files; Rabkin, "The Sabbath Story," p. 7; Paul Hartman, "Sunday Closing Laws," *ADL Bulletin,* 17 (Mar. 1960): 6, 8; R. Gordon to A. Forster, 31 Oct. 1957, to S. Rabkin, 28 Mar., 7 Aug. 1958, S. Vincent to S. Rabkin, 4 Sept. 1957, S. Rabkin to S. Sayles, 12 Feb. 1958, T. Sennett to S. Rabkin, 29 Apr. 1959, ADL files.

18. JAC, Survey... 1958, Box 5, JAC files; T. Sennett to S. Rabkin, 29 Apr. 1959, J. Belenker to S. Rabkin, 1 July 1959, ADL files; Recent Developments in Sunday Closing, Sept. 1959, CRS-L, Church–State/Sunday Closing Laws, AJC files; Eugene J. Lipman and Albert Vorspan, eds., *A Tale of Ten Cities* (New York, 1962), p. 278.

19. Notes of NCRAC executive committee meeting, 22 Apr. 1958, L. Friedberg to J. Cohen, 29 Apr. 1957, Box 4, JAC files.

20. J. Levine to J. Cohen, 19 Sept. 1955, Box 2, JAC files; L. Waldman to A. Erlen, 8 Oct. 1956, ADL files.

21. Notes of NCRAC executive committee meeting, 22 Apr. 1958, Box 4, JAC, Survey... 1958, Box 5, JAC files; Lipman and Vorspan, *Tale of Ten Cities,* p. 66.

22. Hyman, "Sabbatarians and the Sunday Blue Laws Controversy," p. 91; Leo Pfeffer, *Creeds in Competition* (Westport, Conn., 1958), pp. 63, 109–11; Congress, Survey and Outlook for Sunday Laws, 10 Apr. 1958, Box 4, JAC files.

23. Memorandum, 9 Nov. 1950, Church–State, Box 44, RG 347–10, AJC files; see David G. Singer, "One Nation Completely Under God?" *Journal of Church and State* 26 (1984): 473–90; S. Rabkin to Z. Sobel, 9 Sept. 1959, ADL files.

24. Background memorandum, 25 Mar. 1958, AJC Administrative Board Minutes, 3 June 1958, memorandum by P. Jacobson, 30 July 1958, Church–State/Sunday Closing Laws, Box 45, RG 347–10, AJC files; Engel's letter to the editor, *New York Times,* 2 July 1958; Congress, "Sunday Laws, A Violation of Religious Liberty," 1957, CLSA binder; see also references to chapter activities on Sunday legislation in 1957–59 binders, Congress files.

25. A Forster to National Civil Rights Committee, 12–13 Dec. 1957, ADL files. The ADL files reveal that at times local regions deviated from the parent organization; see, for example, B. Coopersmith to S. Rabkin, 10 Dec. 1959, on the New Jersey experience.

26. JAC, Survey... 1958, Box 5, JAC files.

27. Harold Silver, "What Is Wrong with the Sunday Blue Laws?" address delivered at Temple Emanuel, Pittsburgh, 21 and 28 Feb. 1958, Box 4, JAC files.

28. JAC, Minutes, 24 Apr. 1958, Box 1, JAC, Conference on Developments in Pennsylvania Regarding Sunday Closings, 11 Sept. 1958, Box 4, JAC files.

29. J. Cohen to JAC, 23 June 1959, JCRC of Philadelphia, memo for J. Yaffe, 24 Sept. [1959], Box 4, JAC files.

30. S. Rabkin to F. Grossman, 29 June 1959, ADL files; Moses Burak, State-

ment to the Committee on Rules, House of Representatives, Re: Senate Bill No. 405, 24 June 1959, Box 3, JAC files.

31. Murray Friedman, "Discord on Sunday," *The Progressive,* Sept. 1960, pp. 40–42, CRS-L/Pa., Church–State/Sunday Closing Laws, AJC files; J. Cohen to J. Lipsitz, 20 Oct. 1959, memos from L. Friedberg (13 Oct.) and P. Chazin (16 Oct.) on meeting with Gov. Lawrence, Box 4, J. Cohen to CRC Executives, 17 Nov. 1959, Box 3, JAC files.

32. JAC, Minutes, 22 Dec. 1958, Box 1, J. Cohen to G. Joel, 16 Sept. 1959, to G. Feldman et al., 17 Sept. 1959, Box 4, JAC files.

33. S. Rabkin to S. Kolack, 17 Nov. 1959, to J. Silverman, 26 May 1959, ADL files.

34. Memo from T. Leskes and S. Rabkin, 29 May 1959, S. Rabkin to S. Meyer, 27 Jan. 1961, ADL files; Supreme Court of the United States, October Term 1960, *Gallagher* v. *Crown Kosher Super Market, Brief of Appellees;* Robert F. Drinan, *Religion, the Courts, and Public Policy* (New York, 1963), pp. 206–7.

35. H. Ehrmann to E. Lukas, 10 Dec. 1958, CRS-L Mass./Church–State/Sunday Closing Laws/Crown Kosher, AJC files; memo by T. Leskes and S. Rabkin, 29 May 1959, ADL files; A. Lewis in *New York Times,* 22 Nov. 1959.

36. J. Silverman to S. Rabkin, 27 May, 30 June, 15, 21 July 1959, S. Kolack to S. Rabkin, 25 June 1959, S. Rabkin to S. Kolack, 26 June 1959, ADL files; *Boston Pilot,* 27 June 1959, Sunday Laws–Mass., Congress files; Robert F. Drinan, "Sunday Laws in Jeopardy," *America,* 6 June 1959, pp. 408–11. Catholic prejudice was also detected in a scholarly account of the case, where the author insisted that Crown Kosher's motives were not religious but rather commercial, that is, to secure an advantage over smaller kosher butchers. S. Rabkin to R. Ziegler, 30 July 1962 (referring to Sister Candida Lund, "The Sunday Closing Laws," *Third Branch of Government,* ed. C. Herman Pritchett and Alan Westin), ADL files.

37. S. Kolack to S. Rabkin, 8 July 1959, S. Rabkin to J. Silverman, 26 May 1959, ADL files.

38. J. Cohen to G. Feldman et al., 10 Sept. 1959, H. Roth to J. Cohen, 18 Sept. 1959, Box 4, JAC files; Friedman, "Discord on Sunday," p. 41; S. Rabkin to F. Grossman, 22 Sept. 1959, ADL files.

39. JCRC of Greater Philadelphia, memo for J. Yaffe, 24 Sept. [1959], Box 4, JAC files; S. Rabkin to F. Grossman, 21, 22 Sept. 1959, ADL files.

40. Robert T. Miller and Ronald B. Flowers, *Toward Benevolent Neutrality,* 3d ed. (Waco, Tex., 1987), pp. 290–91. *Two Guys* also included expert testimony from a Jewish professor on the origin and development of the Jewish and Christian Sabbaths. Supreme Court of the United States, *Two Guys from Harrison* v. *McGinley, Brief for Appellees,* pp. 8–9, Sunday Laws–Pa./Documents, Congress files.

41. U.S. District Court for the Eastern District of Pennsylvania, *Braunfeld* v. *Gibbons: Plaintiffs' Brief Contra Motion to Dismiss, Brief of Intervenor in Support of Motion of Defendants, Brief of the Commonwealth of Pennsylvania, Appearances,* Sunday Laws–Pa./Docs, *Brief of the Rabbinical Association of Philadelphia and Philadelphia Board of Rabbis Amici Curiae,* CLSA binder, Congress files; *Brief of JCRC of Greater Philadelphia as Amicus Curiae,* CRS-L Pa./Church–State/ Sunday Closing Laws, AJC files.

42. Supreme Court of the United States, October Term 1960, *Gallagher* v.

Crown Kosher Super Market, Brief of AJC and ADL, Amici Curiae; Gallagher v. *Crown Kosher Super Market, Braunfeld* v. *Gibbons, Brief of SCA and NCRAC, Amici Curiae.*

43. *McGowan* v. *Maryland*, 366 U.S. 420 (1961); *Two Guys from Harrison* v. *McGinley*, 366 U.S. 582 (1961); *Braunfeld* v. *Brown*, 366 U.S. 599 (1961); *Gallagher* v. *Crown Kosher Super Market*, 366 U.S. 617 (1961); CLSA *Reports*, 8 June 1961, Box 4, JAC files; on exemptions see Wilber G. Katz, *Religion and American Constitutions* (Evanston, Ill., 1964), pp. 16–19.

44. Leo Pfeffer, "The Supremacy of Free Exercise," *Georgetown Law Journal* 61 (1973): 1127; CLSA *Reports*, 8 June 1961, Box 4, JAC files.

45. Drinan, *Religion, the Courts, and Public Policy*, pp. 210–15; M. Friedman to E. Lukas, 30 Apr. 1963, CRS-L, Church–State/Sunday Closing Laws, AJC files; CLSA *Reports*, 1 Jan. 1964, Congress files; Pfeffer, "Supremacy of Free Exercise," p. 1137.

46. *AJYB* 63 (1962): 191; *Jewish Life* 30 (May–June 1963): 4; Meyer Kramer, "Is America a Christian Country?" *Tradition* 4 (Fall 1961): 5–20.

47. *Jewish Life* 28 (June 1961): 4; Marvin Schick, ed., *Government Aid to Parochial Schools—How Far?* (New York, 1967), pp. 5–6; Moshe Sherer, "Political Action: Orthodoxy's New Road," *Jewish Observer* 3 (Nov. 1966): 7.

48. Schick, *Government Aid to Parochial Schools*, pp. 8, 12–16; Sherer, "Political Action," pp. 7–9; Judah Dick, "Fighting for Shabbos on the Legal Front," *Jewish Observer* 6 (Sept. 1969): 14–17, 9 (Feb. 1973): 8–11.

49. *Sherbert* v. *Verner*, 374 U.S. 479 (1963); Pfeffer, "Supremacy of Free Exercise," p. 1139; on legal opinions, see, for example, Paul G. Kauper, "Schempp and Sherbert: Studies in Neutrality and Accommodation," *Religion and the Public Order, 1963*, ed. Donald A. Giannella (Chicago, 1964), p. 31; Nathan Lewin, "Have the Sunday Law Cases Been Overruled?" *Jewish Life* 31 (Sept.–Oct. 1963): 10–17; Winnifred F. Sullivan, "Religion and Law in the United States," *Church and State in America, A Bibliographical Guide*, ed. John F. Wilson, 2 vols. (Westport, Conn., 1986–87), 2:349.

50. Supreme Court of the United States, October Term 1962, *Sherbert* v. *Verner*, *Brief of AJC, ADL and ACLU, Amici Curiae; Brief of SCA, American Jewish Congress, Jewish Labor Committee, and Jewish War Veterans, Amici Curiae;* CLSA *Reports*, 1 Jan. 1964, Congress files; Leo Pfeffer, *God, Caesar, and the Constitution* (Boston, 1975), pp. 332–33.

51. CLSA, "Memorandum on Display of Crosses, Crucifixes, Crèches and Other Religious Symbols on Public Property," 12 Dec. 1957, p. 24, Crèches–Ossining case, Congress files; Naomi W. Cohen, "Antisemitism in the Gilded Age," *Jewish Social Studies* 41 (1979): 195.

52. Background memorandum, 21 Aug. 1957, Church–State/Public Property and Religious Symbols, Box 45, RG 347–10, AJC files; JAC, Survey . . . 1958, A. Knepler to L. Friedberg, 15 Apr. 1958, Box 5, L. Pfeffer to J. Cohen, 6 Dec. 1956, Box 2, JAC files.

53. JAC, Survey . . . 1958, Box 5, A. Soltes to E. Lipman, 27 Dec. 1957, Box 9, JAC files.

54. *AJYB* 62 (1961): 104–5; JAC, Survey . . . 1958, Box 5, JAC files.

55. JAC, Survey . . . 1958, Box 5, A. Soltes to E. Lipman, 27 Dec. 1957, J. Minsky, "The Crèche at Lake View High School, Chicago," Box 9, JAC files.

56. Memorandum on the Use of Religious Symbols on Public Property, 17 Dec. 1956, Crèches–Ossining case, Congress files.

57. Affidavit of Leo Pfeffer, *Baer* v. *Kolmorgen* (1957), CLSA binder, Congress files; *Ossining Citizen Register,* 13 Sept. 1956, Box 1, S. Estrow to L. Pfeffer, 19 Nov. 1956, Box 9, JAC files; Memorandum of Law, *Baer* v. *Kilmorgen,* 20 Dec. 1957, Crèches–Ossining case, Congress files; "Merry Christmas: A Case Study in Community Conflict," Board of Social and Economic Relations, The Methodist Church, 1959 (courtesy of Rev. Dean M. Kelley), pp. 1–3.

58. "Merry Christmas," pp. 1–4, 6; J. Cohen to JAC, 24 Sept. 1956, Box 1, S. Estrow to L. Pfeffer, 19 Nov. 1956, Box 9, JAC files; Affidavit of Leo Pfeffer, CLSA binder, Congress files.

59. Memorandum on the Use of Religious Symbols on Public Property, 17 Dec. 1956, Crèches–Ossining case, Congress files.

60. "Merry Christmas," pp. 4–7; Affidavit of Leo Pfeffer, CLSA binder, Congress files.

61. Crèche Committee Statement, 10 Dec. 1957, Crèches–Ossining case, Congress files.

62. "Merry Christmas," pp. 4, 6–15.

63. Memorandum of Law, Crèches–Ossining case, Congress files.

64. From *West Virginia State Board of Education* v. *Barnette,* 319 U.S. 624 (1943).

65. Form letter from L. Pfeffer, 23 Jan. 1958, Box 9, JAC files; Affidavits of Leo Pfeffer et al., Dec. 1957, CLSA binder, Congress files.

66. Coyne's decision quoted by Judge Gallagher, *Baer* v. *Kilmorgen,* 14 Misc.2d 1015 (N.Y. 1958); L. Pfeffer to B. Miller, 23 Jan. 1959, Crèches–Ossining case, Congress files.

67. Transcript of trial, *Baer* v. *Kilmorgen,* 25 and 26 Sept. 1958, Crèches–Ossining case, Congress files; *Baer* v. *Kilmorgen,* 14 Misc.2d 1015.

68. L. Pfeffer to B. Miller, 23 Jan. 1959, to S. Polier, 14 June 1960, Crèches-Ossining case, Congress files.

69. JAC, Minutes, 22 Dec. 1958, Box 1; form letter from L. Pfeffer, 21 Jan. 1958, Box 9, JAC files; M. Stern to author, 20 July 1990.

70. *Congress Bi-Weekly,* 5 Jan. 1959, pp. 3–4.

AFTERWORD

1. See, for example, G. Baumgarten to J. Breshin, 4 Jan. 1988, ADL files; Samuel Rabinove, "The Constitution at 200," *Reform Judaism* 15 (Spring 1987): 32; Leo Pfeffer, *Religion, State and the Burger Court* (Buffalo, N.Y., 1984), p. 124.

2. NJCRAC, *Joint Program Plan,* 1988–89, p. 50; JAC, *Safeguarding Religious Liberty* (New York, 1971).

3. JAC, *Safeguarding Religious Liberty,* pp. 9–10; see annual *Joint Program Plan* of NJCRAC.

4. On Orthodox support of aid to parochial schools see Marvin Schick, ed., *Governmental Aid to Parochial Schools—How Far?* (New York, 1967) and a paper by Schick for JAC Conference on Church and State, Oct. 1966, AJC library.

5. CLSA, The Supreme Court and the Establishment Clause, 1 Dec. 1983, Congress files.

6. S. Rabinove to S. Naturman, 2 Feb. 1983, to National Legal Committee, 17 May 1983, S. Kennedy to S. Rabinove, 27 May 1983, DAD-L 1983, *Lynch* v. *Donnelly,* AJC files; H. Hershfang to H. Squadron, 19 Jan. 1982, R. Riesman to B. Ruttenberg, 29 Jan. 1982, *Lynch* v. *Donnelly,* Congress files; *New York Times,* 6 Mar. 1984.

7. Supreme Court of the United States, October Term 1982, *Lynch* v. *Donnelly, Brief Amici Curiae of the ADL and the AJ Congress, Brief of the AJC and the National Council of Churches as Amici Curiae;* S. Rabinove to National Legal Committee, 9 Aug. 1983, DAD-L 1983, *Lynch* v. *Donnelly,* AJC files.

8. Supreme Court of the United States, October Term 1982, *Lynch* v. *Donnelly, Brief for the United States as Amicus Curiae;* Lincoln Caplan, "Annals of Law," *New Yorker,* 10 Aug. 1987; Pfeffer, *Religion, State and the Burger Court,* pp. 113–17; S. Rabinove, "The Pawtucket, Rhode Island Crèche Case," NAD-L 1984, Religious Displays on Public Property, AJC files.

9. *Lynch* v. *Donnelly,* 465 U.S. 668 (1984).

10. *Lynch* v. *Donnelly,* Congress files; *New York Times,* 7, 26 Mar. 1984.

11. M. Weinberg to NJCRAC, 6 Mar. 1984, letter from N. Redlich, 10 May 1984, CLSA Report on the Pawtucket Crèche Case, 5 Mar. 1984, Mark S. Golub in *Hartford Courant,* 7 May 1984, *New York Tribune,* 10 Mar. 1986, *Lynch* v. *Donnelly,* Congress files; J. Sinensky to ADL Regional Directors, 4 Apr. 1984, ADL files; T. Mann to N. Schlager, 24 Aug. 1984, SCA files; Pfeffer, *Religion, State and the Burger Court,* p. 120.

12. Lois C. Waldman, "After Pawtucket: Religious Symbols on Public Land," 1985, Marc D. Stern, "The Year of the Menorah," May 1987, Congress pamphlets; idem, "Crèches, Menorahs & Candy Canes," *Congress Monthly* 56 (Sept.–Oct. 1989): 5; Congress, *Annual Status Report on Religious Liberty,* 1991, pp. 5–8; NJCRAC, *Joint Program Plan,* 1989–90, pp. 61–62, 1990–91, pp. 39–40.

13. Supreme Court of the United States, October Term 1960, *Torcaso* v. *Watkins, Jurisdictional Statement,* Congress files; 367 U.S. 488(1961). On ritual slaughter, see Box 6, JAC files. On the proposed inclusion of a question on religious affiliation in the 1960 census the JAC held that the very query into an individual's religion was unconstitutional. Box 4, folders on census, JAC files.

14. See, for example, analysis by John F. Wilson, *Public Religion in American Culture* (Philadelphia, 1979).

15. The Agudah labored to obtain state protection against fraudulent ritual objects—*mezuzot* and *tefilin*—which did not conform with Jewish religious law. *Jewish Week,* 7–20 Aug. 1977. The Agudah and other Orthodox groups also litigated the right to erect an *eruv,* a cord or wire strung on public property, permitting observant Jews to carry on the Sabbath. Supreme Court of the State of New York, County of Queens, *Smith* v. *Community Board No. 14, Brief Amici Curiae of . . . Agudath Israel [et al.],* 1985. A recent flyer, *The Legal Arm of Observant Jewry* (New York, 1991), lists the multiple activities of COLPA.

16. Charles Reznikoff, ed., *Louis Marshall, Champion of Liberty,* 2 vols. (Philadelphia, 1957), 2:957–67; *Pierce* v. *Society of the Sisters,* 268 U.S. 510(1925); CCAR, *Yearbook* 49 (1939): 105.

17. Supreme Court of the United States, October Term 1971, *Wisconsin* v.

Yoder, Brief Amici Curiae of the Synagogue Council of America and Its Constituents ... and the American Jewish Congress; 406 U.S. 205(1972).

18. In *Goldman* v. *Weinberger,* 475 U.S. 503 (1986), the major Jewish organizations filed briefs on Goldman's behalf. After Goldman lost in the Supreme Court, congressional action supported by the Jews forced the military's hand. *Jewish Week,* 6 Nov. 1987, 21 Oct. 1988.

19. Ted Mann, "The Courts," *Moment* 10 (Jan.–Feb. 1985): 26–28; remarks by Norman Redlich, recipient of the Fund for Religious Liberty Award, 28 Oct. 1986, CLSA Historical Materials, Congress files.

Index

294

INDEX

Board of Delegates (1878–1925), 73, 89, 91, 99
Board of Delegates of American Israelites (BDAI), (1859–78), 52, 53, 55, 65–66, 68, 69, 70
Boston Pilot, 227
Bower, Walter, 120
Brackenridge, Henry, 42
Brandeis, Louis, 96
Braunfeld, Abraham, 228
Braunfeld v. *Brown*, 228, 229, 230
Brennan, William, 203–4, 230, 243
Brewer, David, reaction of Jews to judicial decision and book of, 100–108
Brickner, Balfour, 184
Buchanan, James, 55
Burak, Moses, 225
Burger, Warren, 242, 243
Busch, Isidor, 81

Calisch, Edward, 81, 90
Cardozo, Benjamin, 119
Case, Clarence, 190
Catholicism, 52
Catholics
    as defenders of Sunday laws and religion in schools, 129, 227
    protests of, against Protestant influence in public schools, 80, 81, 83
    reaction of, to *Engel* decision, 172–73, 175–77
    reaction of, to *McCollum* case, 145–46
    reaction of, to *Schempp-Murray* decision, 204
    as supporters of released time programs, 132
CCAR. *See* Central Conference of American Rabbis
Celler, Emanuel, 173, 207
Centennial Exposition, 75
Central Conference of American Rabbis (CCAR), 90–91, 97, 99, 102, 104, 105, 106–8, 110, 116–17, 133, 145, 152, 161, 179–81, 189, 244–45
Chamberlin, Harlow, 193, 194
Chamberlin v. *Dade County*, 194
Champaign, Ill. See *McCollum* v. *Board of Education*
Chaplaincy law, 65–66
Chicago World's Fair (1893), 90–91
China, Christians protected by American treaty with, 55
Chipkin, Israel, 121–22, 161
Christian Amendment Movement, 127
Christian Century, 127, 145, 151
Christianity. *See also* Bible reading in schools; Sunday laws
    in colonial America, 15–20

as component of state constitutions, 23–24, 40
hatred of Jews encouraged by, 4, 14
as incorporated into state law, 28–30
influence of, in public schools, 79–87
as national public religion, 3–5, 30, 48–51, 55–58, 66–67, 71–72, 87, 100, 158, 243
resurgence of, in nineteenth century, 37–43
during Revolutionary era, 20–21
Christian Statesman, 67
Christmas, Jews' acceptance of, 162, 163, 180. *See also* Religious symbolism
Church of the Holy Trinity v. *United States*, 100, 156, 169
Church-state separation. *See* Separation of church and state
Church v. *Bullock*, 156
Citizens Congressional Committee, 211
Civil War, Judaeophobia during, 65
Clark, Tom, 203
Clinton, George, 27
Coke, Sir Edward, 57
Collyer, Jesse, 234–35
COLPA. *See* Commission on Law and Public Affairs
Colquitt, Alfred, 90
Commentaries on the Constitution (Story), 57
Commission on Law and Public Affairs (COLPA), 232, 241
Commission on Law and Social Action, 124
Common law doctrine, 55–58
Commonwealth v. *Has*, 77, 78
Congress Weekly, 151
Conservative Jews, position on Sunday laws, 215
Constitution, U.S. *See also* Establishment clause; First Amendment; Free exercise clause
    Article VI, 30–31
    efforts to Christianize, 67–71
    religious amendment to, 66–67, 69–70, 127–28, 172, 174–75, 204–12
    religious freedom as promised by, 32–33, 42–43
Constitutional Convention of 1787
    appeal of Jews to, 27, 28
    religion as issue for, 30–32
Constitutions, state, and religious freedom, 23–27, 40
Continental Congress, religious freedom under, 30
Coughlin, Charles, 99
Court cases, Jews as affected by, 55–58, 100–101, 108, 111, 119, 136–38. *See also* Supreme Court